REVOLUTIONS *in* AMERICAN MUSIC

Also by Michael Broyles

Mavericks and Other Traditions in American Music

"Music of the Highest Class": Elitism and Populism in Antebellum Boston

A Yankee Musician in Europe: The 1837 Journals of Lowell Mason

Beethoven: The Emergence and Evolution of Beethoven's Heroic Style

REVOLUTIONS *in* AMERICAN MUSIC

Three Decades That Changed a Country and Its Sounds

MICHAEL BROYLES

W. W. NORTON & COMPANY
Independent Publishers Since 1923

Printed in the United States of America
First Edition

For information about special discounts for bulk purchases, please contact W. W. Norton Special Sales at specialsales@wwnorton.com or 800-233-4830

Manufacturing by Lakeside Book Company
Book design by Lisa Buckley
Production manager: Anna Oler

ISBN 978-0-393-63420-4

W. W. Norton & Company, Inc., 500 Fifth Avenue, New York, N.Y. 10110
www.wwnorton.com

W. W. Norton & Company Ltd., 15 Carlisle Street, London W1D 3BS

1 2 3 4 5 6 7 8 9 0

To Denise

CONTENTS

The 1950s

INTRODUCTION
A Personal Statement

This book began with an observation drawn from many years of studying American music, that three decades, the 1840s, the 1920s, and the 1950s, stand apart as pivotal. Each witnessed a radical shift, or revolution, in music making at all levels, from the most humble expressions of a folk or popular style, to the most elaborate creations for connoisseurs or, more often, would-be connoisseurs. Intertwined with these musical developments were two forces that have dominated American society and culture for centuries: technology and race. I knew they were important aspects of these times as they have been throughout American history, but only after digging deeply into these decades did it become clear just how foundational they were to musical and cultural developments. It also became clear how race and technology as manifested in the music of these three decades have vexed American society. Along with the idea of revolution itself, these two forces have been, for better or worse, at the core of the American experience. Consequently, while this book focuses on music, it is really about defining forces in the shaping of a nation.

This book does not pretend to be a comprehensive musical history of these three decades. Much that could be said has been left out, as the music of each decade itself could fill several volumes. I hope that others continue to expand upon and clarify the picture I paint here.

I have approached each decade attempting to understand not just what occurred but how and why people saw their world the way they did. We try to understand, not necessarily to condone, but also to confront. Consequently I have included many statements, pieces, and images that today would be considered offensive. The thinking of the time needs to be seen directly and fully, in its raw and unvarnished form. With one exception I have left quotations as they were, with all the odiousness that some embody. The one exception is the N word, which has been indicated with N****r. Only by engaging those quotations in their entirety can one go beyond them to challenge the forces that elicited them, and only then can one grasp the fullness of their impact on our world today.

As a historian, I believe we must confront the past to make sense of the present. We must seek to enter the worldview of those who lived then, in order to grasp the assumptions and societal pressures that affected everyone. The historian Robert Darnton warned that in studying the past, "other people are other," and Bernard Bailyn spoke of the need to encounter the past, recognizing its strangeness: "The establishment, in some significant degree, of a realistic understanding of the past, free of myths, wish fulfillments and partisan delusions, is essential for social sanity." In advertising their book *The 1619 Project*, Random House succinctly stated the need for engaging the past: "To understand the present, we must clearly see the past."

We know that we can never write pure objective history; I cannot speak other than from my own position in today's society. As a writer on sensitive topics in American history I believe it important to be transparent about who I am and where I come from. I am a cis-hetero, white, Anglo-Saxon male. I am not a member of the one percent, but I grew up with all the privilege accorded mainstream white ethnicity in the United States. The historical journey necessary to write this book has also been a journey inward, transforming my own self-knowledge. My hope is to present a story that helps further an understanding of the depth and breadth of some of our country's most intractable problems.

It has become even more critical, in our complex, connected world, to fathom a worldview separate from our own—in time, in geography, in culture or ethnicity. It might even help explain something of where the turbulence, partisanship, and polarization of these times come from. Studying the music of these three decades will not solve today's problems, but as an exploration of how interwoven that music is with our country's culture and history, it may move us a little closer to that end. This book was written in the spirit of that goal.

REVOLUTIONS *in* AMERICAN MUSIC

CHAPTER 1

Three Pillars and the Nature of Revolution

Each of three decades, 1840s, 1920s, and 1950s, saw what can aptly be called a revolution in music, and in each of those decades the most important driving forces behind the revolution were race and technology. Revolution, race, and technology form the three pillars upon which an understanding of these times is built. These three ideas were not only the defining issues for those decades, but I believe essential constructs without which American history cannot be understood. Their applicability to these decades in music demonstrates how central they have been to the entire American experience.

The notion of revolution has been embedded in the American psyche since the founding fathers succeeded in creating the United States. Over the years it has taken on many meanings, a protean term to be used and misused, sometimes for those with a specific agenda, sometimes loosely and casually, taken as a premise, almost a birthright. Understanding the nature of revolution and its place in American thought is critical, especially for a book that features it as a principal metaphor and in its title. To do so we can begin at a seemingly innocuous place, a summer afternoon at Jones Beach, New York, where Denise and her sisters have decided to build a sandpile. Like sandpiles everywhere, it is a gradually emerging conical, symmetrical shape, and for the moment it is stable. Then the challenge begins—"how much sand can we pile on before it collapses?" Slowly and carefully, not to strike the sand with any sudden force, they work. The sides become steeper, but the cone remains. More sand is added, "slowly, carefully, we don't want to disturb anything."

Inevitably the sandpile collapses.

While this game is repeated on beaches all over the world, Danish theoretical physicist Per Bak and two postdoctoral fellows, Chao Tang and Kurt Wiesenfeld, created their own sandpile in his laboratory. This of course was no beach outing. But why would an eminent scientist spend his time in a lab building sandpiles, and what does this have to do with revolutions in American thought?

From Bak's sandpiles came two important concepts: self-organized criticality and, particularly important for the historian, punctuated equilibrium. History does not unfold in a continuous, uninterrupted process. Change more often happens in fits and starts. For many reasons the present becomes unstable, and suddenly new actions unleash new forces or disrupt old ones, and new patterns emerge.

Bak's sandpiles stand as metaphors for ways that scientists, social scientists, and historians understand change in a complex, fluid world. Important to historians are those moments when events or factors are in delicate balance between order and disorder, between stability and instability. Often after a period of stasis one more grain of sand, one publication, a new figure emerges, a new concept is introduced, or a seemingly trivial event happens, which causes the underlying structure to cascade down, necessitating that a new framework be created. This situation has been defined in various ways; it is Thomas Kuhn's paradigm shift, Malcolm Gladwell's tipping point, Wallace Stegner's angle of repose, it is that moment just before the sandpile suddenly collapses. For many Americans it signals a revolution, although not *the* revolution, a term that many reserve for describing the birth of the country itself.

In Isaac Kramnick's words, according to "the view from the academy," the term "revolution" "is a confused, complicated, and untidy set of observations." Usually it means a complete change, but of what, and how thorough must it be? Social scientists have sought not only a theory of revolution, but the very definition of revolution. This activity reached a peak in the 1960s and '70s, spurred possibly by the political unrest of the time, and the interest among intellectuals in Marxism and other radical theories. A common thread, however, runs through many of these writings: revolutions are primarily political. When scholars attempt to theorize revolution, their concern lies with the mechanics and principles by which governments or institutions are overthrown. The ultimate example is the complete overthrow of a state and the institutions that compose it. In that sense the French Revolution stands as the *ne plus ultra* revolution, followed by the twentieth-century Russian Revolution. Theory flows from the investigation of such activity.

Yet American culture has recognized many other revolutions. The Industrial Revolution and now the Digital Revolution stand out; "revolution" has become a commonly accepted and more encompassing term. Demographers speak of two demographic revolutions, statisticians speak of a statistical revolution. There have been at least three agricultural revolutions, there are social revolutions, racial revolutions, religious revolutions, revolutions in the arts. In the early twenty-first century the *New York Times* identified an "opt-out revolution," where many women, overcome by the competing forces of home and work responsibilities, exited the labor force. As of this writing, googling the phrase "housing revolution" returned tens of thousands of hits. The phrase "revolution in" yielded millions of hits.

As used in media, advertising, or popular culture, the term

"revolution" often refers to anything new, be it a new product, methodology, or sport strategy. There is a "Revolution in the Nursery," a "Mini Revolution in the Computer World," "Elizabeth David's Revolution in Bread," "Revolution in a Teepee"; "The Surrealist Revolution in France," followed by "A Bibliography of the Surrealist Revolution in France"; a "Revolution in Time: Clocks and the Making of the Modern World," and a "'Revolution' in Tin Pan Alley," where the author has cautiously put the word in quotation marks. Then there is a "Revolution in Happiness," "A Revolution in Cosmology," and "A Revolution in Tattooing." One could ask, what makes the entities under consideration revolutionary; but the more important question is, why use the term in the first place? Is its purpose hyperbolic, to suggest that the new is important? Is it a purposeful attention grabber? Or is it simply a misuse or corruption of the word itself?

The term "revolution" is so common in American discourse because the notion of revolution is so embedded in American culture. For many the idea of revolution is a badge of honor, part of a national identity that transcends political, social, cultural, and even racial divides. In the United States it has become the flag that heralds change; in common usage the term is ubiquitous. The United States itself was founded through revolution, and that concept has moved from an historical statement to a point of pride within the nation's inner being. Further, since its inception, the country has been characterized by significant and continuous change, from the expansion to the Pacific in the nineteenth century, with all its attendant strife, to the industrial and technological developments in the nineteenth, twentieth, and twenty-first centuries. Furthermore, the population itself has been in flux, with steady streams of immigrants, the emancipation of enslaved people, the spread of suffrage, and the rural-urban movement driven by industrialization.

Once the tidewater land was filled and New England and Middle Atlantic settlers spread from the earliest towns, a steady stream of pioneers pushed westward from the Atlantic Ocean, and the few natural geographic barriers—the Appalachian Mountains, the Great Plains, and the Rocky Mountains—were quickly overcome. European Americans were restless, greedy, and expansionist; so much seemingly virgin land beckoned as to render moot the arduous task of creating a stable geographically contained social order. There was always an escape clause, a safety valve just a bit further west. The land primed Americans for change, to await the new and welcome the innovative. For most of its history, the United States has seen itself as a land of new beginnings.

This story, a traditional idealistic vision told in many textbooks, has until recently mostly ignored or palliated one glaring fact, this land was not a virgin land. It was not simply waiting for the Europeans to harvest it, like fruit from a tree. It was inhabited by peoples that had been there for centuries. To make it available to Europeans, the original inhabitants had to be conquered, uprooted, or destroyed. Native Americans were viewed as just one more impediment that had to be overcome for the American dream of an expanding coast-to-coast nation to become a reality. They were displaced with impunity, and their treatment is a shameful chapter in the country's story.

Yet the plight of Native Americans is not the only blight on the record of the founding and expansion of the country. As is acutely obvious today, America's heritage of slavery and the concomitant racism that accompanied and outlived it is one of the most fraught and critical problems facing the union. In music, the role of Black performers, the obstacles they faced, the contributions they made in spite of those impediments, as well as the manner in which music has been weaponized against an entire race, are overriding issues that in one form or another dominate each of the decades discussed.

While the country's attitudes toward Blacks and Native Americans are the most obvious and widespread examples of racism today, racial prejudice and even hatred has long been rooted in American society. The Irish, who came early in the nineteenth century, the Chinese, Italians, and Jews who came later, all were subject to bigotry, discrimination, and injustice. Race itself, being a social construct, allows the racist to focus their prejudice on any number of factors: the color of one's skin, religion, language.

Yet today, even with a greater awareness of the cost to peoples that were either displaced or brought to the country's shores by force, American's enthrallment with the notion of revolution has not diminished. The dynamic nature of American society, the predilection for the new and different, and pride in the country's origins has allowed the word *revolution* to maintain its allure. It suggests the excising of the old to bring in the new. It mirrors the impatience that has driven much of the country's development.

Prior to a typical revolutionary moment, the status quo remains in place for long periods of time, masking newly emerging forces fermenting beneath the restraints imposed by the dominant culture, until the new can no longer be contained, or until the old loses its power through sheer disintegration, irrelevance, or inability to adapt. Sometimes the old simply wears out, its resources spent, only hints of its former vitality remaining. As in Bak's sandpiles, when collapse begins, change occurs rapidly.

Other metaphors than Bak's punctuated equilibrium became common in the late twentieth century, particularly around a set of interpretations that went by several names—chaos theory, complex adaptive systems, or simply, complexity. Although these terms are not identical, they all refer to the same general concept, which Neil Theise in 2023 described as "the study of how complex systems manifest in the world . . . a class of patterns of interactions: open-ended, evolving, unpredictable, yet adaptive and self-sustaining." In the ensuing discussion I will use the word "complexity" to refer to this theory. It should also be noted that complexity or chaos theory does not deal with chaos but rather the edge of chaos, when an organism, group, or society becomes unstable, balanced between moving to the new, falling back into the old, or succumbing to chaos. In other words, that moment that heralds a revolution.

Complexity in one sense reverses an approach based on reductionism, which has dominated science since the Enlightenment. According to Enlightenment thinking, in order to study an entity, break it down into its component parts and examine those in detail. Modern medicine, for example, has doctors that specialize in one specific part of the human body. Complexity suggests the opposite, "How do parts combine with each other, assemble themselves, *self-organize*, to make a whole?" Theise considers this "the beginning of a scientific revolution that continues to play out, with ever increasing profundity." Examining the three decades of this book under this lens allows a fresh and I believe more judicious understanding of how and why the changes manifest in these times occurred, and consequently how cultural revolutions happen.

The metaphors of complexity work well in history not only because they are vivid but because many are quite close to those historians already use. Much of complexity theory itself developed in biology, a field closely aligned with historical studies in two senses: complexity has been most extensively used in evolutionary biology, which is itself an historical field; and scientists themselves have compared cultural memory with genetic mapping, a principal focus in biology today. For example, culture has long been described as a landscape, with peaks, valleys, and broad plains, creativity and temporality thus being translated into spatial images. The metaphor suggests an ur-graph, although one lacking precise coordinates. The concept of cultural landscape often found in American musical historical writing, as trumpeted by two titles of the 1990s, Jean Ferris,

America's Musical Landscape, and Richard Crawford, *The American Musical Landscape.*

Biologist Stuart Kauffman, one of the pioneers of complexity, referred to the hills as fitness peaks, where some populations get stuck in the foothills, others manage to climb higher. Sometimes a status quo can extend for a long period of time, translating to a relatively flat plane. Change is seldom a steady climb or with equally spaced steps. Populations "that are too methodical and timid . . . are likely to get stuck in the foothills," but those that go too far can also fail. Kauffman also refers to small-jump and long-jump evolutionary changes, when a population has gone as far as it can go, and, to change, must leap to a new mountain range. That leap, whether a small-jump or a long-jump change, is a moment comparable to that last grain of sand or the spark that induces revolution.

While the behavior of systems on the edge of chaos is not precisely predictable, such systems do share certain features. Two of the most important are emergence and self-organization, terms that are closely related. Self-organization refers to the tendency of complex systems to organize spontaneously and out of their own inner dynamic. When a system does so, it displays properties that were not previously present or meaningful, nor explicable from an analysis of the component parts that preceded self-organization. This characteristic is called emergence. Thus hydrogen and oxygen can combine to form water, which has properties neither atoms alone exhibit. In recent years it has become one of the most important aspects of complexity.

There are many corollaries to the principles of self-organization and emergence, and they make complexity rich for cultural analysis. I will only mention a few. The first corollary is the famous butterfly effect: Complex systems are sensitive to initial conditions, and cause is not necessarily proportional to the magnitude of change, nor is cause and effect linear. Small events can produce big consequences. When Edward Lorenz attempted to predict weather patterns using computer modeling in the 1950s, he observed poetically that the flapping of a butterfly's wings in Brazil can later cause a tornado in Texas. That same butterfly could also have no effect whatsoever on the larger system.

A second corollary is bifurcation. A system pushed to the edge of chaos, particularly when it reaches a point beyond which it cannot recover, will branch, but there is no predicting which direction it will take. Most of the branching will be smooth, comparable to a traveler deciding which fork in a road to take, although occasionally the system (the traveler) will abandon the road entirely for a different one, a long-jump evolutionary change. Bifurcations are not necessarily random. Often there will be magnets pulling on the system, such as climate change affecting different species differently, or concert managers seeking to sell tickets. These magnets are referred to as attractors.

Complexity suggests a more subtle way of examining the past, one in which sudden, radical, inexplicable change can appear out of nowhere, its direction unpredictable, and most important, its magnitude not necessarily consistent with the magnitude of cause. Synthesis and continuity, felt but not always consciously acknowledged, need not be as forceful as traditional history demands. At the same time, complexity affirms a causal link in historical events, but allows that such links need not be linear or proportional. Thus, far from doing away with synthesis, complexity suggests a broader synthesis, one that encompasses the sudden bumps, the shifts to new terrain on the fitness landscape. This is particularly true when events operate at the edge of chaos, that is, when sudden, rapid change seems to prevail.

Each of the decades discussed in this book is a bifurcation point. The music of each was precipitated by a status quo that had outlived its creativity; or was held back by the dominant social order; or was characterized by new technology that opened new mountain ranges, bringing to the public a new kind of musical art whose prior existence or dissemination was either impossible or so limited as to remain hidden to the vast majority of the population.

There is no single overriding pattern for the two other pillars, race and technology. Each iteration is special, although not entirely unique. By its very nature, technology that determines change in each decade will be new. Racial issues are different: they may manifest in unique ways at different times, even though underlying attitudes that drive them continue doggedly unchanged among at least parts of the population. One can seek progress: the worst of institutionalized slavery is gone, the most heinous Jim Crow laws are off the books, Black artists can now stay in the hotels where they perform; but Blacks still encounter reminders every day that we do not live in a racist-free society. Music of the 1840s, 1920s, and 1950s evinces both the progress and the substratum of racism that continued throughout these times.

Each decade approached both race and technology differently, and in each decade these two pillars manifested differently. In some musical genres one might be predominant, although in others less visible or overt. For instance, on the surface, 1840s art music appears free of racial strife; but this is so only because it was the music of white elites and for many Blacks was an art sufficiently foreign to be unrepresentative of their life and culture. For African Americans who wished to transcend those racial boundaries, the story is quite different.

Revolutions in American music continue, such as hip-hop, globalization, and, in technology, digitalization, which has affected all aspects of life. These are beyond the scope of a single volume, but they await further historical investigations, especially ones that attempt to assess just how they have changed our musical landscape and our world.

The
1840s

CHAPTER 2

Minstrelsy: An American Musical Contribution and America's Curse

By 1840 the American experiment born of revolution was established politically. Culturally, however, the landscape had hardly changed since the eighteenth century; the United States remained a British colony. American theater managers regularly went to England to contract British theater troupes to fill the next season. What professional orchestras existed—and the term was used loosely then—consisted mostly of European immigrants. The most popular singer of the day was the British pianist and composer Henry Russell, and many popular songs had come from British theaters or were songs drawn from Thomas Moore's *Irish Melodies*. Originally published in 1807, Moore's collection was popular throughout the British Isles; pirated editions by American publishers had already appeared by 1808.

The most problematic issue that Americans faced in the 1840s was slavery. We know that slavery existed from at least 1619 in Jamestown, Virginia, roughly a decade after the colony was founded. By the middle of the seventeenth century it was an entrenched practice in colonies whose economy thrived on cotton and tobacco, namely those in the South. But slavery was not purely a Southern institution. Enslaved people worked and were bought and sold in Massachusetts, New Jersey, Rhode Island, and literally on Wall Street in New York City. New York did not officially abolish slavery until 1827.

Even before the Civil War, racial tensions had expanded beyond a Black/white color line, as thousands of Irish began to arrive on the nation's eastern shore. The Irish were the first of a number of immigrant groups that appeared throughout the nineteenth and into the twentieth century whose presence challenged the social fabric that held together the earlier settlers. During the 1820s, 54,338 Irish immigrated to the United States. That number jumped to 207,381 in the 1830s, and more than tripled again in the 1840s. Thus began the close connection between immigration, slavery, and racism, a tripartite set of associations that has plagued and continues to plague the United States.

Unlike African slaves, the Irish came willingly, seeking a new life. But unlike earlier settlers they seemed different, less in color than in attitudes and religion. Early Irish settlers were mostly from the Ulster region, in what is now Northern Ireland, and most were Protestant and well educated. By contrast, most of the Irish from the 1830s were poor, fleeing terrible conditions in Ireland. Difficulties began with the famine of 1816, the "year without a summer" created by the eruption of Mount Tambora in what is now Indonesia. This event caused massive crop failures, forcing many to flee their homeland. British policy toward the Irish and later crop failures including a potato blight only exacerbated the problem. Of great concern to many Americans, the flood of Irish arriving by the 1830s were Catholic. Many Americans considered Catholics, in their allegiance to the pope, to be beholden to a foreign power.

Their numbers created a complex ethnic situation, as hostilities ran high both between other white and Irish Americans, and between Irish and Black Americans. Economic conditions forced Irish and freed Blacks into fierce competition for jobs, at the same time often placing them in close proximity to each other. Tensions were particularly high in New York State, where the recent abolition of slavery combined with increasing Irish immigration meant many more men and women were competing for available jobs.

Young Irish men and women without means had few options for emigrating to the United States but to come as indentured servants, obligated to serve someone for a fixed number of years, often seven, in exchange for passage. The old European model of a young man apprenticing to an artisan to learn a trade hardly applied. Once arrived, many were hardly treated differently than African enslaved people, although their color protected them from some of the greatest cruelties. Some were sold on a slave market, individually or en masse. In some cases, a slave trader would buy a group of indentured servants and take them around the country, selling them off to individuals who needed workers. Consequently, many indentured servants endured conditions similar to those of enslaved Africans, often living alongside the enslaved. Some were even treated more harshly; a Black enslaved person was a valuable property, giving the owner at least a financial incentive to keep them healthy; an Irish servant had much less commercial value. There were of course at least three differences between the fate of indentured servants and that of enslaved Africans: indentured servants had agreed to their indenture, and if conditions were too harsh could more easily escape. They could readily blend into an American city, for instance. But most important, they knew their servitude was of a limited time, after which their "owner" had no legal hold on them.

The Irish found themselves looked down upon, even despised, especially by other members of the white working class. Upper-

and middle-class Americans considered the Irish below the Anglo and German working classes but slightly above Blacks on the social scale. Suffrage had expanded to white males, although not women, but by various means states denied the vote to freed Blacks and poor Irish. White Americans called the Irish "low-browed," "savage," "groveling," "bestial," "lazy," "wild," "simian," "sensual"—precisely the same insults they hurled at Blacks. Both the position of the Irish and Blacks in the social hierarchy and the complex interaction between the two groups were important factors in the creation of the most important popular music institution of the 1840s, the minstrel show.

When and where the minstrel idea originated and when and where the minstrel show began are not the same. One of the most important steps in defining minstrelsy occurred on May 21, 1830, when the white New York–born actor Thomas Dartmouth Rice appeared in Louisville, Kentucky, as a Black man, Sambo, in a play *The Kentucky Rifle, or A Prairie Narrative.* During the play Rice interpolated a song and dance, "Jump Jim Crow," which was a hit with the crowd. For dramatic purposes and possibly to establish ownership of the skit, Rice created a fiction that the character and the dance were a sudden inspiration derived from a Black stagecoach driver, or possibly a stable hand, named Cuff, who sang a song while doing an odd, disjointed, jumping dance. Mesmerized, Rice decided to reproduce onstage what he saw, including the ragged clothes which he said he took from Cuff. To complete the imitation, Rice blackened his face with burnt cork. At that moment the song "Jump Jim Crow" was born, launching the most intense musical-theatrical craze the United States had known.

The origin of the character of Jim Crow was actually more convoluted. Rice's Louisville appearance was likely not the first appearance of Jim Crow; it is only the first documented event. Rice was performing comic songs onstage as early as 1828, and some sort of incipient Jim Crow may have appeared earlier. Other performers, too, may have preceded Rice. In 1830 and possibly earlier, George Nichols, a white actor, was "doing Jim Crow" in the Midwest; and according to one source, he learned it from Picayune Butler, a Black dancer in New Orleans. At the same time, a Black New Orleans street vendor who called himself Old Corn Meal was also performing Jim Crow on his daily rounds. Rice, Nichols, Butler, and Old Corn Meal likely crossed paths in the city in 1830. Butler and Rice both appeared at the Purdy Browns Theatre and Circus in November 1830, and Rice almost certainly heard Old Corn Meal. He used words by Butler in one of his later sketches, "Jim Crow Goes to New Orleans," and when he returned to the city in 1836, he performed a skit entitled "Corn Meal."

There are also hints that as Rice traveled down the Atlantic coast as a member of the Noah Ludlow troupe he may have witnessed a song that slaves on the Georgia Sea Islands sang. The lyrics of the song were:

> Where you going, buzzard?
> Where you going, crow?
> I'm going down to new ground
> To knock Jim Crow.
> Up to my kneecap,
> Down to my toe,
> And every time I jump up,
> I knock Jim Crow
> I knock,
> I knock Jim Crow,
> *(repeated ad lib.)*

As crows and buzzards threatened the corn crops, they would often be shot. ("New ground" was an area where crops had not been planted.) One of the variants of the Jim Crow song that Rice printed in 1832 contains the following verse, which suggests at least a similarity to the Sea Island situation:

I neeld to de buzzard
An I bou'd to de Crow
An eb'ry tim in reel'd
Why I jump't Jim Crow

Whatever influences fed into Rice's skit, it probably did not fully coalesce until Rice's interactions with Nichols, Butler, and Old Corn Meal in New Orleans. Rice's song might best be called a composite, drawn from many sources and performers. I have recounted here only a few of the many that have circulated about Jim Crow. Regardless of its origins, Rice brought all the parts together into a convincing whole. His natural comedic, singing, and dancing talent allowed him to own the character. Soon Rice *was* Jim Crow; others might sing the song, but no one else achieved such a complete synthesis of all the performative aspects as Rice did. Jim Crow became Rice's alter ego as well as a force unto itself, and he performed it to wild applause throughout the country and Europe. In 1838 the *Boston Post* reported, "The two most popular characters in the world at the present are [Queen] Victoria and Jim Crow." While Rice was only briefly part of a minstrel troupe, the popularity of this act set a tone and style that did much to establish the genre. Later minstrel performers referred to him as "Daddy Rice."

With Jim Crow the minstrel idea, although not the full-blown show itself, began to crystallize, eventually setting off the first of those upheavals in American popular music that were to occur again and again into the twenty-first century. Wherever the idea came from, T. D. Rice did perform the song "Jump Jim Crow" on May 21, 1830; it became a monster hit, although not right away, and launched a new career for Rice. The historical significance if not the immediate impact of Rice's Louisville appearance can be described as that moment a revolution in American music took hold.

Although the term "Jim Crow" now has a very different

meaning from Rice's original, thanks to its identification with segregation laws in the South, its continuing presence attests to the magnitude of an institution that has plagued American culture since at least 1619. Minstrelsy was built upon slavery and racism. While the minstrel show mocked everything—the wealthy, politicians, immigrants—the defining characteristic of the minstrel show is the white performer performing in blackface and portraying an African American in crude caricature, presented as simple, ignorant, and gullible.

The original show itself consisted of a semicircle of four men in blackface, who sang, danced, played instruments, and cracked jokes, all in a rough Black dialect. The two men in the middle played banjo, which was itself of African origins, and fiddle, while the "endmen," designated Mr. Tambo and Mr. Bones, played the tambourine and bones. The endmen provided most of the comic material, although the entire group participated in heavy-handed comedy, often including satirical skits. As the minstrel show evolved, this small ensemble grew much larger.

The verses of Rice's song are quatrains of 4 + 3 + 4 + 3 feet, with lines two and four rhyming:

Come listen all you galls and boys
I's jist from Tuckehow,
I'm going to sing a little song,
My name is Jim Crow

The simple pattern allowed Rice to add hundreds of verses that could be adapted to the place and situation where he was performing. The most important part of the song, however, was the chorus, to be sung at the end of each verse:

Weel about and turn about and do jis so,
Eb'ry time I weel about and jump Jim Crow.

The structure, with short verses, each followed by a chorus, allowed Rice to interject many dance moves into his act. Rice was described as "a tall scrambling-looking man with a sepulchral falsetto voice"; his dancing was what made Jim Crow. In 1837 a critic from *The Spirit of the Times*, a New York newspaper that catered to the elite, captured the essence of Rice's success. After lamenting how low, vulgar, nauseating, and almost idiotic the act was, the unnamed critic was won over. Rice has "all the velocity of a dancing master," and "the bewitching grace of Douvernay, in partnership with the sylph-like movements of Taglioni." Most important, the critic was amazed at the creativity of Rice's dancing. In the performance he described, there were eight verses, and the song was encored six times. Each verse and each encore elicited different moves, "each bound he gives is other than the last, which proves that motion is commensurate with space, and of course illimitable." After complaining one more time about the words, which were "obscure, ridiculous, yet" (he begrudgingly admitted) "cunning," the writer concluded that Rice's moves are "inexhaustible, endless, marvellous, wonderful."

Through 1831 Rice honed his creation in the lower Midwest, in Louisville, Cincinnati, and St. Louis; by 1832 he moved to the East Coast—Philadelphia, Washington, Baltimore. With each stop his reputation grew, leading to his appearance in New York City on November 12, 1832. Dale Cockrell has described his appearance there as "tumultuous" and "the stuff of legend building."

Tumultuous it was because Rice's New York debut was not at one of the middle-class theaters, such as the Park, but rather at the Bowery Theatre in the Five Points neighborhood of Lower Manhattan. Five Points was a section bounded by Centre Street, Bowery, Canal Street, and Park Row; it received its name from the intersection of Orange (now Baxter), Cross (now Mosco), and Anthony streets. This area originally had a freshwater pond that supplied drinking water to much of the city, but in the eighteenth century industry polluted the water and the environment, causing those that could afford to do so to move out. By the nineteenth century the area had become a dirty, disease-ridden slum characterized by overcrowded tenements, violence, and crime. The Bowery Theatre catered to rowdy working-class men and, like most theaters in New York at the time, few women.

In a place like the Bowery Theatre the audience was virtually uncontrolled, to the point of throwing many types of missiles and even wandering around the stage during a performance. Dan Emmett, of the Virginia Minstrels, described the audience at the Bowery: "When their mouths were not filled with tobacco and peanuts, they were shouting to each other at the top of their voices." William T. Porter, editor of the *Spirit of the Times,* described a scene he witnessed at the Bowery Theatre in 1832. Rice was scheduled to sing *Jim Crow,* and the noted actor Edwin Booth was performing Shakespeare's *Richard III* in the featured play. "In the scene with Lady Anne . . . the spectators amused themselves by throwing pennies and silver pieces on the stage, which occasioned an immense scramble among the boys, and they frequently ran between King Richard and Lady Anne to snatch a copper." Later, in the tent scene, "several curious amateurs went up to the table, took up the crown, posed with the heavy sword, and examined all the regalia with great care, while Richard was in agony from the terrible dream." Finally, in the climactic battle scene members of the audience "raced across the stage" with the soldiers, and for the fight between Richard and Richmond they "made a circle around the combatants to see fair play."

A drawing that is now at the New York Historical Society shows just how busy the stage was when Rice performed. The scene does not exaggerate the pandemonium that ensued: "When Mr. Rice came on to sing his celebrated song of 'Jim Crow' they not only made him repeat it some twenty times, but hemmed him in so that he actually had no room to perform the little dancing or turning about appertaining to the song." In the drawing the stage is literally filled with audience members, some watching intently, some fighting, some simply strutting. Rice and his fiddler, however, are given room; the group onstage is careful to allow Rice his space. His dancing may have been restricted, but clearly Rice was well received, an honor not accorded all performers.

After the New York triumph Rice toured throughout the United States, gaining both acclaim and wealth. In 1836 he took Jim Crow to Europe for a yearlong sojourn in England, Ireland, and Scotland, with a brief trip to Paris. His reception, if anything, outdid what he enjoyed stateside. He appealed to all classes. *The New York Herald* reported, "In London, Jim Crow is even more popular than in New York, it is heard in every circle, from the soirées of the nobility, to the hovels of the street sweepers. Tis Jim Crow here—Jim Crow there—Jim Crow every where." The *Spirit of the Times*, though disdainful, could not conceal its fascination: "Nothing since the days of Garrick or Kean has equaled the popularity of the *'Virginia N****r.'* He is, by all accounts, coining money, and by no means among the loafers of the metropolis: Dukes and Duchesses, Lord Lieutenants and Field Marshals, and we shall not be surprised if the youthful Queen [Victoria] herself should send an invitation to Rice to Jump Jim Crow for her at the Palace."

Rice's income reflected his stature. In England he reportedly earned $75 a week, plus what he made in benefit concerts. In one benefit the house grossed $1,800, another $1,400, and one in Cork, Ireland, $1,900. Since the performer normally received one-third of the house, on these three evenings Rice netted approximately $1,700. This at a time when the average artisan had an annual income of $600–800. Returning to the states, Rice reportedly received $200 a night for jumping Jim Crow. He had married the daughter of a theater owner in England, and on his return was able to build a mansion on Long Island.

Fig. 7. T. D. Rice as "Jim Crow," 1833.
Courtesy of the New-York Historical Society, New York City

T. D. Rice onstage as Jim Crow

Minstrelsy was the first American musical form with no direct European precedent to successfully invade the British Isles. It was also the first popular genre that was distinctly American. Prior to minstrelsy, Americans imported the two most popular types of secular song: *bel canto* opera arias and Thomas Moore's ballads. Arias from Italian operas such as *Norma* appeared in many songbooks and instrumental collections, even though few Americans had actually witnessed the performance of an Italian opera.

T. D. Rice had created a character that had antecedents but no European counterpart. Jim Crow could have only happened in the toxic cultural cauldron of Black slavery and anti-Irish prejudice. That Jim Crow was based on a demeaning caricature, that is, a view of Blacks that was purposely derogatory and intended to mock, proved no impediment to its acceptance. In retrospect, this perverted invention of marginal Black behavior that suited whites' needs for racial superiority was more representative of American antebellum attitudes and social conditions than any other cultural product of its time. Minstrelsy for better or worse performed America.

Audiences in the 1830s believed that what minstrelsy depicted onstage was real. Rice's Jim Crow was praised for its accuracy. Noah Ludlow, the manager of the theater troupe in which Jim Crow originally appeared, commented on Rice's mimicry talents: "That talent consisted in [Rice's] great fidelity in imitating the broad and prominent peculiarities of other persons, as was evident in his close delineations of the corn-field negro, drawn from real life." "Drawn from real life": that delusion is the core of Rice's success, and that of later minstrel shows. It reinforced racialized stereotypes with audiences, opening the way for the acceptance of the multitude of later caricatures of Blacks. Whether or not Americans continue to believe in such stereotypes, they continue to permeate many aspects of American culture. Until fall 2020 anyone shopping the aisles of a supermarket could hardly miss Aunt Jemima, a Black mammy stereotype, on the Quaker Oats pancake mix of the same name.

Audiences accepted the presumed reality in part because they wanted to; in the complex ethnic and class distinctions of the time it served them well. This is particularly true of Irish Americans, who composed much of the audience in the early, formative days of minstrelsy and who later participated heavily in minstrel troupes. In Northern cities, freed indentured servants and other Irish often lived in close proximity with Blacks; economic conditions dictated it. Thus working-class Irish Americans had close personal interactions with Blacks. At the same time, Blacks competed for jobs with the Irish, who were already finding jobs scarce due to strong anti-Irish sentiment. NINA in bold capital letters appeared on many storefronts and other places of work: "No Irish Need Apply." The outlawing of slavery in New York in 1827 only exacerbated tensions between Irish and Blacks, as more Blacks were now free to enter the labor market. Fear and the need to feel superior thus combined to create an ideal audience for Jim Crow. It is not by chance that some of Rice's most important early success occurred in theaters located in Five Points, where many Irish lived.

By the late 1830s *Jim Crow* had become more a malleable form, expanded and varied as new places called for new text. Rice would adapt verses to the location: "Life in Kentucky," "Description of Baltimore," "Baltimore Railroad," "Description of Boston," "Stroll on Bunker Hill," "Jim Crow in New Orleans." Rice often played Jim Crow-like characters in full-length plays. *Oh Hush* was the first of these, an amalgamation of earlier skits that came together at the Walnut Street Theatre in Philadelphia on July 20, 1833. The Jim Crow variant there is named Cuff, which goes back to the alleged origins of Jim Crow. The last original play that Rice starred in was *Otello*, 1844, roughly based on Rossini's opera, which of course was based on Shakespeare's play. Rice's version made it into a minstrel parody. It was reduced to one act, had Otello come from the slave South, replaced Shakespeare's "muscular free verse" with rhyming couplets, and added a twist by introducing a young Otello, the son of Otello and Desdemona. By the late 1840s Rice's career was coming to an end, as an increasing paralysis began to afflict him, which affected not only his ability to dance, but his speech as well. It eventually took his life in 1860.

I have described Rice's career in some detail because he was so crucial in establishing minstrelsy. He demonstrated the immense appeal of the song, dance, and crude ethnic humor that form its basic premise, and in Jim Crow created the most durable and quintessential character of the genre. Later as the minstrel show per se gradually evolved and declined, Rice's concept of ethnic portrayal echoed through Tin Pan Alley's ethnic novelty songs in the twentieth century.

The only minstrel stage character that could compete with Jim Crow was popularized by George Washington Dixon, whose contributions further helped to define the genre. His song and skit "Coal Black Rose" had been one of the first blackface hits in the late 1820s, before Jim Crow captivated the nation. Later he introduced Zip Coon, who not only became the most important character after Jim Crow, but also in many ways was Crow's antithesis.

Like Rice, Dixon was born into a white working-class family, probably in Richmond, Virginia, in 1801. Details about his early life are scant, leading to various rumors or contrived plants, such as that he was a descendant of the King of the Congo. What we know is that he joined a circus at age fifteen, probably because of his singing voice. Circuses then featured a wide variety of entertainment, often with stage acts touring with the more acrobatic performers. While Rice was primarily an actor and dancer, Dixon achieved his success on the stage as a singer. He was described as "the celebrated Melodist" and "The American Buffo Singer," which puzzled editors occasionally morphed into "The American Buffalo Singer" (*buffo* actually refers to a comic male character in Italian opera). Later he advertised himself in Lowell, Massachusetts, as a musician, and appeared in "Grand Musical Soirées." In 1837, he presented a concert at the "Opera Saloon" in Boston, which featured several arias from *bel canto* operas.

Although Dixon did not create the song "Coal Black Rose," nor was he the first to sing it, in appearances at the Bowery and other theaters in 1829, he made it one of the first widely adopted routines in blackface. It is a narrative with two principal speakers, Coal Black Rose and Sambo, her man-friend. Rose invites

Sambo in, has a fire to warm him, and is cooking food for him, when he spots Cuffee, a rival for Rose, hiding in the room. Furious at Rose for cuckolding him, he challenges Cuffee to a duel. At the site of the duel the next morning, a white slave owner comes and asks them what they are doing. Sambo remains silent while Cuffee says he "cum to settle a bit of spute." The slave owner grabs and kicks Cuffee, who then runs away, with Sambo chasing him.

The Sambo character, another staple of minstrelsy, had a curious origin. Frederick Reynolds's British play of 1823, *Laugh When You Can*, featured a servant, Sambo. In this play Sambo has a clear moral compass and is wiser than his womanizing employer. He is the trickster who outwits his master, drawing parallels with Figaro in Mozart's opera, as well as many stock plots in eighteenth-century opera buffa. Only later did Sambo onstage devolve into a generic slow-witted, grinning, drawling, eager-to-please Black caricature without the more redeeming features of Reynolds's original. He devolved to fit right into the racist world of minstrelsy.

During a three-day run in 1829, Dixon sang "Coal Black Rose" at the Bowery, Chatham, and Park theaters in New York. The song suggests a skit, and by September Dixon had expanded it, creating *Love in a Cloud*. In this short play Cuffee hides in a barrel of flour, and he and Sambo fight right there, as flour—the cloud—flies everywhere, contributing to the chaos of the scene. That Cuffee emerges from the flour barrel all white adds another layer to the mask symbolism of minstrelsy. In some form it was later reenacted by many minstrel troupes.

In 1834 Dixon appeared as Zip Coon, painting him with the same caricatured brushstrokes Rice had used with Jim Crow. Zip Coon was the antithesis of Jim Crow, an urban dandy, a freed Black, a man of pretentiousness, pomposity, and sartorial splendor. His attempt to assume sophisticated white ways only resulted in exaggerated ostentation and malapropisms that made him into a buffoon. Whether Dixon created the Zip Coon character is disputed. Bob Farrell, a circus performer who later billed himself as Zip Coon and may have been performing it before 1834, claimed to have composed the Zip Coon song, although his claim cannot be verified. Regardless, Dixon established Zip Coon, like Rice's Jim Crow, as a central minstrel character.

The music to "Zip Coon" is one of the best-known tunes in American culture, and is often heard unconnected to the minstrel figure. It is an old fiddle tune that has been traced back to the eighteenth-century British tune "The Rose Tree." It is known today by several names, "Turkey in the Straw" being the most common, but also "Sugar in the Gourd," "Natchez under the Hill," and "The Jolly Old Miller." Many children have sung it to the words "Do Your Ears Hang Low." It was a favorite tune played by many ice cream trucks until its association with minstrelsy became well known, which prompted companies to discontinue its use.

When Dixon was making his mark in the 1820s with "Coal Black Rose," he was also singing another song, "Long Tail Blue," about a Northern urban Black dandy. "Long tail blue" refers to a dress coat men wore in the nineteenth century, of which the tuxedo with tails is a descendant. The singer, an unnamed character, is clearly proud of his dress, as he boasts:

> Some N****rs they have but one coat,
>   But you see I've got two
> I wears a jacket all the week.
>   And Sundays my long tail blue.

To music publishers, Zip Coon is Long Tail Blue given a name. Images on the sheet music covers are strikingly similar. Yet the early texts of the two songs differ noticeably in content and tone. Long Tail Blue is the urban dandy imitating elite white male behavior, and thanks to his long-tailed blue coat he impresses many women. This of course plays directly into the deepest of white racist fears, miscegenation. The original text of "Zip Coon," by contrast, places him in a rural setting, as one who plays on a banjo, "Cooney in de holler, an raccoon up a stump." He watches the "wild goose" "sailing on de ocean," and observes, "De wild goose wink an he beckon to de swaller / You hear him google, google, google, google, gollar." Like Long Tail Blue, Zip Coon has a girlfriend, Sulky, but she has "Blueskin," and feeds him "Hoe-cake and possum fat, widout any butter," hardly a meal for an urban dandy. Supporting the rural setting are further references to buffalo, owls, frogs, alligators, and snakes.

At the time the term "coon" was not a racial slur, but rather referred to a rustic, country type, or someone of the frontier. The term is probably derived from the coonskin cap many frontiersmen wore. The Whig Party, the party of Henry Clay, Daniel Webster, and, for a time, Abraham Lincoln, had adopted a coonskin as their party symbol in 1844. The term only acquired racial connotations as the Civil War approached, in part because the Zip Coon character was so prominent in minstrelsy. The original song paints Zip as a stereotypical country bumpkin, suggesting an urban dandy only when Zip claims to be a "larned scholar"; in this and other claims, he clearly is a braggard, which was a trait often associated with frontiersmen. Only the sheet music covers suggest an urban dandy. As is often the case, the picture overwhelms the words.

In the most famous cover image, Zip Coon's body shape is strikingly female, with wide, curving hips and thin waist. His stance itself is feminine: his knees are together, one leg is turned slightly back, and one hand is on his hip while the other twirls his spectacles. Long Tail Blue has a similar body shape, although his stance is different and he stares out at the viewer with a rakish expression. The artist's effeminate portrayal would have found ready acceptance among Irish workers, many of whom feared greatly the job competition from Blacks. It would also have assuaged the fears of many other whites, especially slave owners, for whom a manly Black, while desirable as a slave, nevertheless could be a danger to the Southern order.

In spite of his appearance, Zip Coon posed a greater threat to white America than Jim Crow. Jim Crow was the true "coon" in 1840s terms: backwoods, ignorant, barely articulate, rough, and ready to fight; he was in one sense a Black Davy Crockett, and as such could be tolerated as an amusing other by Northern urbanites. Zip Coon, however, particularly when he was conflated with Long Tail Blue, struck at their very core. His exaggerated finery, pretentiousness, and arrogant demeanor could be laughed at, especially when the accent and malapropisms gave him away, but the very characteristics he embodied were crude imitations of the upper classes themselves. While an outsider, he was no other; rather, he was satirizing them, while simultaneously trying to penetrate their society.

While Rice and Dixon had enormous success touring with their two minstrel creations, Jim Crow and Zip Coon, another group of actors, of whom the most important was Dan Decatur Emmett, joined together to create the basic structure that would become the minstrel show. Emmett is also at the heart of a controversy over who penned what may be the most famous song to come out of minstrelsy.

Born in 1815, Emmett grew up in Mount Vernon, Ohio, a small town northeast of Columbus. After a short career in the army, where he served as a fifer and drummer, he worked as a musician with several circuses. During this time he also learned to play the banjo, began to write blackface songs, and appeared in blackface. Emmett also met the circus singer Frank Brower. In 1842 Emmett and Brower decided to abandon the circus and seek their fortunes as entertainers in New York City. There they

"Zip Coon," created by George Washington Dixon, was the urban counterpart to the rural unschooled Jim Crow. Zip Coon is probably a derivative of the character "Long Tail Blue."

met two other entertainers, William M. Whitlock and Richard Ward Pelham.

There had been a financial panic in 1837, and theater attendance was still down, inevitably depressing the demand for actors and entertainers. Emmett, Brower, Whitlock, and Pelham decided to create their own opportunities by joining forces for an evening of entertainment. Sometime in January 1842, all four men were in Emmett's room at the North American

Hotel in the Bowery. Whitlock asked Emmett to practice some tunes with him on the fiddle and banjo, and Brower grabbed his bones and Pelham got his tambourine. They tried some songs, then decided to go across the street to the Bowery Circus, where they wore down one of the proprietors, "Uncle Ned" Howes, with their "noise," until he offered them an engagement under their adopted name Virginia Minstrels. They assumed it would be a one-time event to put some coins in their pockets, with no intention of forming a permanent troupe, and they had no inkling they were launching the second and most substantial phase of a musical revolution.

The Bowery Circus engaged the Virginia Minstrels for one week, beginning on February 6, 1843. The *New York Herald* carried the following announcement: "First Night of the novel, grotesque, original, and *surprisingly* melodious Ethiopian band, entitled the *Virginia Minstrels*, being an exclusively musical entertainment combining the banjo, violin, bone castanets, and tambourine, and entirely exempt from the vulgarities and other objectionable features which have hitherto characterized negro extravaganzas."

The success of their week at the Bowery led to engagements at the Cornucopia and the Olympic Circus at the Park Theatre. In early March they went to Boston, where a series of successful performances led to a run at the Tremont Theatre, the most prestigious house in the city. By this time they had begun to realize the magnitude of what they had created, and decided to invade the drama capital of the English-speaking world, London.

They set sail on April 21, 1843. Landing in Liverpool, they gave some concerts there and in nearby Manchester, with mostly disappointing results. Their fortunes improved in London, although they did not realize the financial success they had hoped for. Advertisements stating they were engaged for 100 pounds per week was likely a bit of public relations to interest the curious. The press also claimed they were "the only representatives of the Negro that have appeared in this country," an historical fiction.

Internal tension, whether caused by disappointing audience numbers or other reasons, soon took its toll. After a July 14 performance, Whitlock and the group's agent, George B. Wooldridge, left for the United States. The original Virginia Minstrels came to an end. Emmett, Brower, and Pelham continued to perform, until September 1844, when Emmett and Brower returned to the United States. Pelham, who married an English actress, remained in England permanently.

On his return Emmett found an entirely different minstrel landscape; minstrel troupes modeled on the Virginia Minstrels had proliferated. The Congo Minstrels, the Boston Minstrels, the Ethiopian Serenaders, the Virginia Serenaders, and the Kentucky Minstrels were only a few that Emmett would have encountered. The Virginia Minstrels continued in name throughout the 1840s, but it was a different group and had no connection to the original troupe other than appropriating the name.

Emmett continued to perform in various venues, and later joined the Bryant Minstrels. His greatest success, however, came as a songwriter. In 1859 the Bryant Minstrels asked him to write a walk-around, a song in which all the performers joined in marching around the stage and in dancing, often competitively. It frequently closed the first part of the show. In response, he allegedly wrote "Dixie's Land," known today as "Dixie." Emmett's fame is mostly based on this supposed contribution to American music. At least 37 others have laid claim to the song or had it attributed to them, but most of the other claims can be easily dismissed. For instance, friends of Harry McCarthy of Arkansas insisted he was the author, although there is virtually no supporting evidence other than their allegations that "Old Southerners . . . know well enough that Harry McCarthy, the comedian, was the author of Dixie," and their recollection that he had the words of "Dixie" on his business card. This claim was made in 1904, some thirty years after McCarthy's death in 1874.

Will Hays's claim to have written the words for the song deserves more serious consideration. A contemporary of Emmett's who lived in New Orleans, Hays left a detailed account of how he came to compose it, and claimed that D. P. Faulds published his version. Yet Faulds's copyrighted version lists words by Jerry Blossom, music by Dixie, Jr. There is no mention of Hays. Furthermore, Faulds's office is listed in Louisville, Kentucky. More recently, Howard L. Sacks and Judith Rose Sacks have presented a detailed argument that "Dixie" was composed by members of a free Black family, the Snowdens, who lived near the Emmett family in Mount Vernon, Ohio.

Whether Hays or Emmett or the Snowdens authored "Dixie" was no small matter in the nineteenth century, as the song became the South's unofficial national anthem. Emmett had stated that the phrase "I wish I was in Dixie" was common among show people as a reference to a desire to be in a warmer climate in the winter. The idea that the anthem had been written by Emmett, a Northerner who proudly identified himself as a Union man, and whose family had been involved in the Underground Railroad, and who claimed that nostalgia for the South was a climatological statement, was too much for many Southerners. That the Snowden family, freed Blacks living in Ohio, might have penned "Dixie" was an even greater affront to those Southerners who yearned for an older, racially hierarchical way of life.

The Snowdens had settled on a farm near the Emmetts. They were also musicians, and their family band became well known in the area. They frequently granted requests from white entertainers for music without insisting on copyright or other recognition. The Snowden and Emmett properties were adjacent to each other. Emmett, with his interest in music, would likely have gotten to know the Snowdens. The Sacks book raises the question, did the Snowdens compose "Dixie," and did Emmett steal or appropriate it from them? They come to no definitive answer, but several bits of circumstantial evidence hint at the possibility.

Hays claimed to have only written the words to what he said was a traditional Scottish tune. John Firth, Emmett's publisher, remembers playing the tune in a band in LaGrange, Tennessee, in 1857 or '58, two years before Emmett's publication, and he had a copy of the tune itself. Joe H. McCann, a minstrel performer, recognized it "an old n****r air they've been singing in the South to almost any words." It's thus possible that Emmett heard or learned the tune from the Snowdens, who themselves knew it from Black oral tradition. That it circulated also as a band tune suggests that it had crossed a color line and at the least was widespread before the Civil War.

Improvising on his violin, Emmett may have come up with the tune as if on his own, but actually drawing from one buried deep in his memory. Then he added words and innocently claimed the song. Or perhaps he learned the tune from the Snowdens; then, searching his fiddle for a good walk-around, he remembered the tune, and incorporated it, knowing full well that it was an old African American folk song. This scenario is plausible, as minstrels believed they were imitating Black life, in spite of being aware that they were presenting a caricature. Just as copyright was slippery in the nineteenth century, with printers often ignoring it, nonattributable borrowing was common in blackface, particularly when the tune moved from Black to white. Likely, neither Emmett, nor Hays, nor the Snowdens composed the song anew. Likely, the original words are Emmett's, and the music was in the air, being plucked by the various principals as it came past them. The intensity of the compositional question that has surrounded "Dixie" bespeaks more than a case of proper attribution, however. It demonstrates just how important this song has been and continues to be to those Americans holding onto white Southern traditions that date from the nineteenth century, and therefore, just how deeply embedded those traditions remain.

No discussion of early minstrelsy would be complete without mentioning someone who many believe to be America's greatest songwriter, Stephen Foster. Foster began as a minstrel composer, but even his minstrel songs have transcended the genre. They have over the decades become synonymous with the United States. "Oh Susannah," "Camptown Races," and "My Old Kentucky Home" have entered American folk culture, providing a soundtrack familiar to many who know nothing about their origins. They have also gone beyond the United States and the Western world. When the composer-writer William Austin visited Japan, he heard a young girl singing a Japanese rendition of "Jeanie with the Light Brown Hair." Informed about its origins, the girl could not believe it was not a Japanese folksong.

Foster never performed in a minstrel show, although he developed a close association with Edwin P. Christy, founder of Christy's Minstrels, the most important minstrel troupe of the 1840s and '50s. He is tied to minstrelsy because he tried to make a living as a song composer, an outrageous idea in antebellum America, and minstrelsy was where the market was. Many of Foster's early songs were minstrel songs, although he later wrote considerable music outside the minstrel tradition.

Auspiciously, Foster was born on July 4, 1826, amidst the fifty-year celebration of the Declaration of Independence, on the same day two founding fathers and early presidents, John Adams and Thomas Jefferson, died. With their demise, the last archetypes of the eighteenth-century colonial gentry passed, paving the way for Jacksonian democracy, which brought a complex of anti-elitism and intransigent Southern customs, exacerbating America's thorniest problem, slavery. In opening the country for westward expansion, Andrew Jackson was also

Stephen Foster late in life

responsible for the forced removal of Native Americans from east of the Mississippi to less desirable plots of land to the west.

Foster's father was a prominent entrepreneur on his way down as one venture after another failed. He was also a member of the Democratic-Republican Party, later to become the Democratic Party under Jackson. Foster thus grew up with five older siblings in a household steeped in Democratic politics and always teetering on the edge of financial insolvency. Music was ever-present, however, as his father and some of his siblings were amateur musicians.

Obsessed as he was with music, Foster originally had no intention of making it his livelihood. By 1847 he had settled into a bookkeeping position in Cincinnati, which was down the Ohio River from Pittsburgh. He wrote songs in his spare time. Then, on September 11, 1847, a "Grand Gala Concert" was held at the Eagle Saloon in Pittsburgh, to honor George M. Dallas, vice president of the United States. Included in the concert was "Susanna—A new song, never before given to the public." This song would change Foster's life.

"Oh! Susanna," as it was later known, created no major stir at its first appearance, but as it was repeated it began to catch on, prompting W. C. Peters, a Pittsburgh musician and publisher, to publish it. Foster, happy that someone he knew wanted it, asked for no compensation, but with its ever-growing popularity, and with it becoming the marching song of the California Forty-niners, Peters reportedly made $10,000 from its sales. Foster received no royalties—customarily, composers had little choice but to sell their songs outright, for whatever they would fetch. Foster was not only astounded when he received one hundred dollars from Peters for the song—"imagine my delight in receiving one hundred dollars in cash!"—but it set him on a new career: "the two fifty-dollar bills I received for it" (roughly $3,500 in 2022 dollars) "had the effect of starting me on my present vocation of song-writer."

The tune of "Oh! Susanna" has echoes of the polka as well as the minstrel stage (see Chapter 3 for a discussion of polkamania). Lyrics are firmly in the minstrel tradition, with their exaggerated quasi-Black dialect, the story told from the viewpoint of a Black person, and with mention of buckwheat cakes and the banjo. It also references industrial progress, mentioning the telegraph, a steamship that plowed the Ohio River, and puzzlingly, "the electric fluid magnified, and kill'd five hundred Nigga." Foster follows this, or maybe conflates it, with an explosion of a "bulgine." A bulgine is the steam engine on a locomotive, but similar steam engines powered riverboats, and they were prone to explosions, often resulting in many deaths. Massive deaths seem inconsistent with the jocular tone of "Oh! Susanna," but that five hundred Blacks meeting a calamitous end would be a comedic event says much about racial attitudes at that time.

Only the first verse is filled with comic contradictions. The rest is the story of a young Black man traveling south to New Orleans to find Susanna. The idea would have been pure fiction, as Blacks could not easily travel the South, because of the risk of being sold (back) into slavery. Ken Emerson sees the reference to the calamitous death of five hundred Blacks as "a recognition, which runs through the nostalgia of much minstrel music, that agrarian life and the plantation economy are threatened by progress, that slave/s and their owners alike are in danger of becoming roadkill on macadam of a rapidly industrializing America." Whether Foster had such prescience may be moot, but the song clearly resonated with many Americans in the 1840s.

Foster quickly sought to capitalize on his success as a songwriter, and in September 1849, sent an inquiry to Firth, Pond & Co, one of the largest music publishers in New York City. In it he proposed a royalty of two cents per copy of any of his songs they published. They quickly agreed, with further stipulations tying him closely to the publisher. They expected Foster to use his connections, referring explicitly to minstrel troupes and managers, to sell his songs. They also included a warning, that Foster only compose "such pieces as are likely both in sentiment & melody to take the public taste."

With this agreement Foster returned to Pittsburgh to create an entirely new career, that of professional songwriter. Prior to Foster, most of the income of American popular music composers came from performing, not publishing. Concert tickets, not royalties, kept the musicians alive. Since Foster had no desire for the concert or minstrel stage, he had to blaze a new trail. This was made all the more necessary as he now had a family. On July 22, 1850, he married Jane McDowell, and the following April 18 they had a daughter, Marion Foster. (The marriage turned out to be tumultuous, fraught with difficulties, and ended with Foster spending the last four years of his life alone.)

Foster began to succeed as a composer. In the first six months of 1850 he published eleven songs, including "Camptown Races," "Nelly Bly," and "The Voices That Are Gone." He also managed to sign a royalty agreement with F. D. Benteen, of Baltimore, in spite of his contract with Firth, Pond. As a consequence of these arrangements and Foster's industry, his earnings between 1849 and 1857 averaged over $1,400 per year from his songs. To put this into perspective, a bookbinder, compositor, or proofreader in the printing trade earned approximately $730. Further, it's reasonable to assume that Foster's income was not flat, but increased after 1850 as more songs came out, especially after the publication of "Old Folks at Home" in 1851, and "My Old Kentucky Home, Good Night" in 1853.

Foster also benefited from his connection with E. P. Christy, founder (in 1843) of Christy's Minstrels, originally known as "Christy's Original band of Virginia Minstrels." Christy attempted to soften some of the crudities of minstrelsy, add four-part harmony to the choruses, and edge more toward sentimental songs. Antislavery sentiment appears in some of Christy's shows. In one version of the song "Lucy Neal," Neal's husband only expresses his happiness with Lucy until the slave dealer comes "To tear you from my side." In the final verse he laments:

> Dis poor N****r's fate is hard,
> De white man's heart is stone,
> Dey part poor N****r from his wife,
> And brake up dar happy home.

Clearly, despite the dialect, some amount of sympathy lies with this Black enslaved person who, like many, had his family torn asunder. The character becomes real, no longer just a one-dimensional caricature. The sentiment expressed is also clearly a condemnation of the institution of slavery itself.

Christy was undoubtedly motivated by profits, for by toning down the worst offenses of the minstrel show, he could appeal to a hitherto mostly ignored group, middle-class audiences, including families. The theater itself, and the early minstrel shows in particular, were considered rough, rowdy, and unfit for persons of genteel taste, a standard to which many in the middle-class aspired. Absent old European class divisions, it was a way to separate themselves from the working class. By 1850 Christy's venture had succeeded, and his troupe was considered the preeminent minstrel group in the country. Other troupes followed, and minstrel songs began to assume the sentimental romanticism of the time. The dialect, the jokes, and demeaning caricature continued, but a new element emerged. Blacks on the minstrel stage were humanized, allowed feelings of pain and nostalgia just like whites, and slavery itself was frequently the culprit, as in "Lucy Neal." Minstrelsy thus embodied conflicting messages: The tone and the fundamental premise of the genre, to mock Blacks and make them appear as simple, slow-witted, childlike creatures, spoke to Southerners who argued that the Negro was incapable of surviving on his own and needed the paternalism of slavery, no matter how harsh its practices. Southern slave owners did their best to see enslaved people as property, not persons. The sentimental songs, on the other hand, made a gesture toward presenting the enslaved persons' humanity, undermining the slaveholder's premise. Nostalgia was often misplaced, as when a blackface singer recalled an idyllic life on the plantation in days gone by. As unreal as that scenario was, however, sentimental songs evoked emotions with which listeners could identify, not only creating sympathy for the character, but portraying him as more fully human. Many in the white audience had recently migrated from the farm to the city and could also find in the blackface presentation their own nostalgia.

Many Northerners and some Southerners had also witnessed outside the minstrel show the insidious stereotype that Black enslaved people were happy-go-lucky, childlike creatures. This came from several sources, but the most public was the coffles, the forced marches of enslaved men tied together in chains. As Southern population expanded westward beyond the Alleghenies, the need for slaves followed. Since the international import of slaves had been banned by the Constitution after 1808, a large internal slave market developed. Slave traders would gather a number of men, women, and children, and march them on foot to be auctioned off at new locations. The men would be in chains, two abreast, the women and children following but not in chains. Being sold was the greatest fear the enslaved had, as that would break up families, as well as render a future that the enslaved person had no control over. In order to distract the enslaved and to present a more positive image than the chains and armed guards indicated, the slave drivers would force them to sing and dance, creating an entirely false impression of the situation. Even Abraham Lincoln was taken in by the forced spectacle of the coffle. On board a ship in 1841 he witnessed a group of slaves being transported in chains. Although well aware of their miserable fate, Lincoln noted in a letter that with their singing and dancing "they were the most cheerful and apparently happy creatures on board." Katrina Dyonne Thompson commented that "Lincoln's conflicting opinion that slavery was atrocious but that slaves were happy was quite common among whites throughout the United States." The minstrel songs of an elder Black person longing nostalgically for the happier days on the old plantation both reflected and reinforced that notion.

Foster was not the only minstrel composer to turn to more sentimental songs, but his popularity meant his impact was considerable. Some of Foster's best-known songs were written at this time and in this vein—"Nellie Was a Lady," "Old Dog Tray," "My Old Kentucky Home," "Old Folks at Home."

Foster profited from his arrangements with E. P. Christy, who paid him to have printed on the title page "As Sung by E. P.

Christy," or some variant. That arrangement, however, went even further with "Old Folks at Home," where Foster suggested that Christy be listed as composer, although Foster continued to draw royalties. Later Foster had a change of heart and wrote Christy requesting that the agreement be canceled, which Christy refused. Importantly, Foster's letter reveals his attitude toward minstrelsy. He is concerned that being known as a minstrel composer "might injure my reputation as a writer of another style of music," but now he wanted to reinstate his name because through "my efforts I have done a great deal to build up a taste for the Ethiopian songs among refined people by making the words suitable to their taste, instead of the trashy and really offensive words which belong to some songs of that order."

This less offensive turn in minstrelsy was not to last, as tensions about slavery and its expansion escalated in the pre–Civil War decade. The Kansas-Nebraska Act of 1854 mandated that "popular sovereignty," that is, the popular vote within the state, determine whether a new state was free or slave. The law's consequences, particularly the violent conflicts that erupted in Kansas, alarmed Northerners, who feared that spreading slavery throughout the West would further strain the already fragile republic. Minstrelsy responded in a strange way: According to JoAnne O'Connell, "rather than blaming the problems on slavery, the minstrel audience put the blame on the shoulders of slavery's victim, the Black slave himself." Not wanting to aggravate the slavery debate, as the sympathetic portrayal of Blacks trapped in the evils of the system did, minstrelsy turned back to disparaging, one-dimensional depictions of Blacks. The caricaturing of Blacks as shiftless, irresponsible simpletons resumed with a vengeance. As a result, that image of minstrelsy, coupled with the "Ole Zip Coon" parody of the arrogant, self-possessed, womanizing braggart, became the cartoonish distortion of a people that continues to feed into American racism even in the twenty-first century.

Christy and Foster both responded to this development

by abandoning the genre. Christy, who was wealthy by then, retired, and Foster shifted from minstrel to sentimental parlor songs. Although he continued to compose songs that are permanently embedded in the American sound world, such as "Jeanie with the Light Brown Hair," "Hard Times Come Again No More," and "Beautiful Dreamer," he never reached the financial peak of his minstrel years. The last decade of his life was dominated by alcohol, domestic strife, and a struggle to make ends meet. He never left his wife and daughter, although Jane had to take a job as a telegraph operator, which necessitated a separation. Foster spent his last four years alone in New York City, until he was found in his room, having fainted, with a gash on his head or a cut in his throat, depending on the source. Taken to Bellevue Hospital, he died the next day. The circumstances of his death are unclear—was it a fall or suicide?—and will probably never be known. Foster was thirty-four years old.

The minstrel show itself continued and evolved. It grew from four performers to over one hundred in some instances. It became an extravaganza and later morphed into vaudeville. It began to attract Black performers. That they also had to don blackface speaks to how artificial the traditional blackface mask was, as well as what Blacks had to endure to gain the stage. Even into the twentieth century Black performers such as Bert Williams continued to wear the mask. As attitudes toward race became more enlightened in the twentieth century, the minstrel show per se began to die out. Blackface was no longer common among entertainers after the 1930s. Nevertheless, many of its stereotypes persisted—for example, in the *Amos 'n' Andy* show on radio and then television, and in later TV shows such as *Sanford and Sons* or *The Jeffersons*. Louis Armstrong's 1942 short film recording of "When It's Sleepy Time Down South" showed him on a bale of hay, with Nick Stewart performing a Stepin Fetchit routine. Minstrel stereotypes in advertising have already been mentioned.

Minstrelsy, however, had a broader and more far-reaching impact on American society than its music and staging. Matthew Morrison sees in minstrelsy what he calls "Blacksound—the sonic and embodied legacy of blackface performance—as the origin of all popular music, entertainment, and culture in the United States." Minstrelsy defined the Black American for white culture, or rather, it defined what white culture wanted to believe about Black Americans. The racial tension that the institution of slavery created was abetted by minstrelsy, which provided defenders of the institution excuses for its existence. Minstrelsy also provided white Americans a portrait of the American Black, the reach of which far outlasted the institution of slavery, as it drilled so deep into the American psyche and penetrated so many crevices of the American mind that its uprooting has defied decades of concerted effort, sometimes even to identify its presence.

America's first original contribution to the theater and to popular music was fundamentally wrapped in racial thinking and practice. The dogged endurance of minstrel characters as metaphors, the biting humor, the conventions of speech ("doodah"), the exaggerated facial expressions, demonstrate how deeply rooted prejudices remain in American society.

CHAPTER 3

Polkamania and Polk

It is hard to imagine just how different the musical culture of Federal America was from that of today. The notion that music could be art was something foreign to the American mind. Secular music was viewed purely as entertainment, to be enjoyed, danced to, sung. Concerts were rare, and where they did occur they were local events, haphazard and eclectic. Programs were potpourris: random collections of instrumental works, both orchestral and solo, glees, popular songs, and improvised variations. Orchestras were few and consisted of a few amateurs and whatever professional musicians were available. The only institutions able to provide steady employment for musicians were the church in some parts of the country, and the theater, and even then, most musicians had to scramble to find other means of support.

Opera existed, but was hardly recognizable by today's standards. Most operas were performed in theaters, rowdy places with almost entirely male patrons. The theater was not an appropriate venue for a cultivated woman. In many theaters, the third tier of boxes was used as the business address for prostitutes to ply their trade. Well-known operas were presented in highly "adapted" versions, in loose English translations, often with British ballads replacing the Italian arias. The principals were usually actors, not trained opera singers. In one production of Mozart's *Don Giovanni*, the actor taking the role of Don Giovanni could not sing, so all of his music was simply eliminated.

Sacred music still predominated in most regions, and not just inside the church. Hymns were essentially the pop songs of the day. The singing school movement of the eighteenth century, where students would meet one evening a week to learn the rudiments of musical notation and choral singing, was begun by clergy to improve music in the church service. By the end of the century, however, it had broken away from the church, and often met in a tavern. Sacred music was still taught, but the music rather than the message was the focus. In a time when interactions between the sexes were at best limited, the singing school's popularity with young people was not necessarily for religious reasons.

As popular as singing was, arguably the most ubiquitous music in the early nineteenth century was vernacular dance music, usually played on a fiddle. It was heard everywhere, in cities and small towns, in the country, in the North, South, East, and West, in homes, taverns, and ballrooms (where they existed), even in barns, as the painter William Sidney Mount documented in several canvases. It was played by a great variety of people, from European immigrants who brought the tunes with them, to tavern owners, to African American slaves, some of whom became known as the best fiddlers in their area. Many of the tunes are still in the fiddle repertoire: "Sailor's Hornpipe," "Durang's Hornpipe," "Speed the Plough," "Devil's Dream," and "Arkansas Traveler," to name a few. In fact, an old-time fiddler of today is probably the closest link that we have to the musical culture of Federal America.

While Federal-era fiddlers played many types of dance tunes, such as reels, hornpipes, and jigs, two new dances arose in the nineteenth century to revolutionize American popular music: the waltz and the polka. The waltz, in triple time, took hold first, around 1815, the polka, in duple time, later, in the 1840s. The waltz not only upended dancing styles, but challenged norms of morality. It was a couple dance, as opposed to contra dances or square dances that dominated at the time. The man put his arm around his partner's waist, which was considered outrageous. Moreover, the couple often spun themselves into a bacchanalian high as they whirled around the room, with the woman tightly pressed again the man. No dance, and few musical developments, had a greater impact on the collective consciousness of both Europe and America at the beginning of the nineteenth century than the waltz. Throughout the 1820s and '30s it reigned, the favored dance of Americans, partly because it remained risqué.

Meanwhile, an event in Bohemia (now the Czech Republic) would launch another a dance craze that had an even greater long-term impact on American vernacular music than the waltz. While the waltz challenged morals and ushered in couple dancing, the polka provided the musical template for American dance music for the next one hundred years, its rhythm and vitality not only the seed for many dances to come, but a symbol for an ebullient, ever-expanding America in the nineteenth century.

According to legend, the polka's origins can be traced back to a dance that a peasant girl named Anna Slezakova improvised to the folk song "Uncle Nimra Bought a White Horse." Sometime in the early 1830s music teacher Josef Neruda witnessed the event, noted the tune down, and began to teach others Anna's dance. It caught on, and by the mid-1830s was being danced in the ballrooms of Prague. The dance also acquired a name: polka.

Whether this account bears any truth, whether Anna was simply performing a standard folk dance, or whether she even existed, is at best debatable, although the sudden popularity of the polka in Prague ballrooms is not. Even less credible, however, is an alternate claim that the polka originated in Poland. While the name itself suggests such, and in Polish the word "polka" means Polish woman, most scholars today believe the name comes from the Czech word "pulka," which means "half," referring to the half-step found in the early version of the dance. The polka originally was a Czech dance.

Soon the polka spread to other European capitals. In 1839 the Prague Sharpshooters, a military band led by a Mr. Pergler, introduced it to Vienna, where it achieved considerable popularity. One year later a Mr. Raab, the ballet master of the Prague Theatre and dancing master of the Bohemian Estates, danced the polka in Paris at the Théâtre de l'Odéon (now Odéon-Théâtre de l'Europe) and the Theatre Ambigu. He caused a sensation. The term "polkamania" was first applied to the furor it created there. By 1844 the polka had migrated to many cities through Europe, including London, where it met with some success, if not the mania that greeted it in Paris.

On June 14, 1843, a small ad appeared in the *North American*, a Philadelphia newspaper: Augustus Fiot, "Importer of Music," listed new arrivals from Europe. Among the many waltzes and other miscellanea was *Narhalle Polka*, by J. Staab. This well may have been the first polka to appear in the United States, although the dance itself remained unknown, except to those Americans who had traveled abroad. Interest, however, was growing. In December, W. Fischer, a music dealer in Madison, Wisconsin, advertised *Favorite Polka of the Rhine* by E. Wolf, *Paris Polka* and *Rubini Polka* by P. Schubert, and *Three Favorite Polkas* by C. Labitzky.

By 1844 American newspapers and magazines were bristling with news about this new dance that was sweeping Europe: "This dance is quite the rage on the continent"; "A new dance called the *Polka*, is now all the rage at Paris"; "A very fashionable dance in Paris"; "It [polka] has created a perfect *furor* in Europe." One unnamed American, "a former Boston belle," had become the toast of Paris because of her ability to polka, something that piqued the French, and elicited national pride from one American paper: "Whooror for our side."

Soon the mania described in Europe began to build in the United States. "The Polkamania, it is said, will rage extensively this winter in New York." "The *'Polk-a'* is destined to be the *Fashionable,* as well as the *National* dance of the season." In Baltimore, "the ladies are enquiring in all directions, what kind of dance is the Polka?" They were soon to find out. According to Joseph Marks, the polka was first danced in America by the dance instructors Lawrence De Garmo Brooks and Mary Ann Gammon, on May 10, 1844, at the National Theater in New York City. A journalist for the *New York Daily Aurora* had seen it in Europe and passed the information to his editor, who in turn described it to Brooks and Gammon. Given the manner in which the dance crossed the Atlantic, the dancers having only a verbal description that had passed through several hands, and given a tendency of professional entertainers to embellish, whatever happened onstage that evening likely bore only a vague resemblance to the European dance.

On June 22, 1844, a note appeared in the Boston *Daily Atlas* that the polka, "this celebrated dance, which has created so much sensation, has been for a long time in preparation at the *Boston Museum,* and is to be danced there for the first time this evening." Word spread quickly, and on July 4, the New Orleans *Times-Picayune* reported, "They have introduced the Polka at the Boston theatres, where it has been highly successful." There is no reason to doubt that this was the European dance, if only because much had happened in the three months since the Brooks and Gammon's dance, including the arrival of professional dancers who had firsthand familiarity with it in Europe.

Thus what happened in Boston and New York was what had happened in Vienna, Paris, London and other cities: the polka was introduced from the stage. The audience witnessed professional dancers and theatrical performers dancing it for the first time. It was only natural that the steps would range from the mildly complex to the virtuosic. One critic in New Orleans complained that Mr. Wells, who performed "the real, sure enough polka," with Miss Carnahan, "attempted too many *tours de force*, and threw in a few more comic feats than the nature of the Polka demands." Yet the polka met not just with great approval but with a strong desire by many, especially young ladies and consequently young gentlemen, to learn the dance. The complexity demonstrated onstage played into the hands of those who performed it; since most were dancing masters, they immediately had enthusiastic pupils. Learning the polka at this point necessitated lessons, and as a result it began as a fashionable dance for the elite.

Unlike the early waltz, which spread quickly in part because it was simplicity itself, the early polka included not only a hop and a leap, but many combinations. It seemed almost every dancing teacher had his own repertoire, which could run into many variations. Beyond the basic "step, close, step, hop," other hops and leaps could the added. The couple could change positions, from the standard closed waltz position, to side-by-side, facing but open, circling each other, the couple turning either left or right, moving forward or backward, or sashaying as in a reel. As in many couple's dances, the man was expected to lead, and the woman's agility was tested by how well she followed even the most vigorous leaps, hops, and changes of direction.

A network of dancing schools and instruction was already in place, especially in the largest cities. Dancers and dance masters often ran in families. John Durang (1768–1822) is considered the first professional dancer in the United States; his son Charles later wrote several dance instruction books, including one of the first to describe the polka. Even more famous was the Dodworth family, who were both musicians and dancers. Thomas J. Dodworth formed the National Brass Band in 1832, and in 1842 his son Allen, who played in the band, opened Dodworth's Dancing Academy in New York City. It became the most famous dancing school in the United States, principally because of its appeal to New York Society. Allen later opened a branch in Brooklyn, managed by his son Frank, and then expanded in Manhattan with his nephew T. George. Dodworth published several books on dancing as well as an instruction manual on how to form a brass band. Always in tune with society's interests, he was also one of the early teachers of the polka in New York.

Teachers were thus available, but the spread of the polka to become a national frenzy needed a dancing master who was a powerful, dedicated advocate. That need was filled by a now almost forgotten Hungarian immigrant, Gabriel de Korponay, one of the most colorful figures of the time. Korponay arrived in New York on March 14, 1844. Stories swirled around him, many spun by Korponay himself, making him either a hero or a criminal. The *New York Herald* reported he had been involved in an altercation with a superior in the Austrian army (Hungary was part of the Austrian Empire at this time), resulting in a duel, as a consequence of which he had been forced to flee. He made his way to Belgium and finally to Liverpool, where he obtained passage on the *Sheffield*, sailing to America. At 35 he was a commanding figure, tall for his time at six feet, one inch, with a high forehead, grey eyes, and fair complexion. He was a career military officer, but he was also a dancer. He was "an elegant and accomplished man," and with his Hungarian flair, intriguing background, and mastery of many languages, he quickly made his way into New York society, and, according to the New Orleans *Times-Picayune*, "set the fashionable world agog."

Exactly when and where he first performed the polka is not known; one article claims he introduced it to New York. In 1848 the *New York Herald* stated that "the polka was first introduced into fashionable society in this country, by the celebrated Korponay, an officer in the Hungarian army of Austria." An intriguing clue lies in a short comment in the New Orleans *Times-Picayune* of June 8, 1844: "*The Polka*.—A teacher of this celebrated dance has arrived in New York. In six months time we expect our entire

Gabriel de Korponay

population will eschew other dances, and set to Polkaing like mad." The teacher was almost certainly Korponay; certainly, he did all he could to make that happen. In October 1844, *The New York Herald* prophesied that Korponay "is about to make quite a revolution in the dancing of this country." He succeeded. Later almost every article about Korponay referred to him as the man who introduced Americans to the polka.

For the next two years Korponay traveled throughout the United States teaching the polka. By July 1844, his efforts in New York City had borne fruit. The *New York Herald* reported that "under his [Korponay's] judicious management, the Polka is about to become as popular in the higher, indeed, we might add, all circles of society, as it now is in Paris and London." At this time newspapers announced that Korponay had "formed an association" with Mademoiselle Marie Desjardins, a French pianist, who had studied with Sigismund Thalberg. Together they taught polka classes and private lessons. It was more than an association: they arrived as a family, Gabriel de Korponay, Marie Korponay, and their daughter Gabriella. For the first year Marie used her maiden or professional name, but by 1845 she referred to herself as Madam Korponay, later Mary Korponay. (She may have dropped her maiden name to avoid being confused with the dancer Pauline Desjardins, who sometimes appeared on the same program as Korponay.)

Throughout 1844 and 1845 Korponay seemed everywhere, teaching the polka to America's elite. He remained in New York City until August, to migrate with the fashionable people to the summer resorts of Newport, Rhode Island, and Saratoga Springs, New York. By October he was in Boston. Staid Bostonians quickly took to the polka. He was, according to a report, "exceedingly well received," and after his departure at least three professors opened schools in Boston for teaching the polka.

He was back in New York in November; January 1845 found Korponay in Philadelphia, followed by a return to New York in

February. Late February he left for Washington, DC, staying there until April. In May he went to Baltimore, and in August ventured west to St. Louis. November he was once again in New York. By this time he was a national phenomenon, as newspapers from Boston to New Orleans tracked his movements.

The New York Herald attempted to explain his success with high society. They described him as a Hungarian nobleman, who was banished for his political offenses by the Austrian emperor himself. According to the *Herald*, he expected to be pardoned, and to return to Hungary "to enjoy his titles, wealth and honors." That of course never happened, and the story itself may have originated with Korponay. Noting his success in Boston, the paper explained, "He is not a mere dancing master; and his position in society, and gentlemanly demeanor, gained for him the most distinguished marks of respect from the *elite* of that city." This same article observed that since returning to New York his classes drew more than a hundred, and he also gave private classes, frequently to several families who would get together for them in their homes.

The size of these classes meant a substantial income. Charges varied, depending on the length of the lessons and whether they were class or private, but the average was roughly one dollar per person per lesson. Since he often taught four classes a week plus an unknown number of private lessons, he probably brought in at least $100–200 per week. This does not count his stage appearances, or his work arranging balls, or Marie's income teaching piano. At this time a cavalry private in the army earned $330 per year, including a clothing allowance, a laborer might earn $300–400 per year, an artisan, $600–800, and if a merchant earned as much as $2,000, it was a good year.

Korponay sometimes appeared onstage in not entirely flattering roles. In New York, April 1845, Niblo's Garden presented a ballet "Revolt of the Harem," with Pauline Desjardins. *The New York Herald* noted that Korponay should have been the Sultan instead of having the role of a harem eunuch, observing that "the Harem would hardly have revolted if Korponay had been Sultan." Korponay also appeared in benefits. In one for Junius Brutus Booth, the patriarch of the Booth theatrical family, he shared the stage with the Norwegian violinist Ole Bull and again with Pauline Desjardins. He sponsored or helped arrange many balls, often for charitable purposes, such as the Grand Opening Ball at the Alhambra for the benefit of deaf and blind asylums in New York City.

Korponay did not abandon his military activities. When the Mexican War broke out in 1846 he was in St. Louis, and he joined the Third Regiment of Missouri Mounted Volunteers under Colonel John Ralls as a captain. Years after his death one member of this regiment claimed he embezzled $112,500, about four million in today's dollars. No charges were filed, and Korponay's lifestyle did not suggest any sudden accretion of wealth or anything amiss; he continued both his dance and military pursuits. In 1855 he was appointed an agent for the British Recruiting Service, where he recruited soldiers in Cincinnati and Canada for the British army in the Crimean War. His whereabouts in 1856 are not known, and he may have been commissioned by the British Army to fight in Crimea. In 1857 he was back in Philadelphia, where he opened a translation business and was appointed interpreter of the United States Courts. In March 1861 he was appointed an officer in the Park Police of Philadelphia.

When the Civil War began in April 1861, Korponay joined the Twenty-Eighth Regiment of Pennsylvania Volunteers as lieutenant-colonel under the command of John W. Geary. One year later Korponay was promoted to colonel and given command of the regiment. In September 1862 he was wounded and required surgical treatment. He continued briefly with non-field assignments, at one time in command of a prisoner's camp, another presiding over court marshals. On March 26, 1863, he received an honorable discharge due to disability.

By 1865 he had recovered sufficiently to believe he would be recommissioned. That never happened. Korponay died February 14, 1866, cause unknown.

By the time Korponay made his first trip to Washington in 1845, the polka was firmly established on American soil. It appealed to all, young and old: "Youth became inspired—and age realized youth. The extraordinary result of the Polka and its music!" (Charles Durang, 1856). Inspired maybe, but several newspapers, quoting a French publication, warned, "no lady ought to dance the Polka if she have passed her thirtieth year. After thirty, the Polka only inspires ferocious ideas." While the polka originally caught on among the fashionable, that is, those able to afford lessons, as early as 1845 an unnamed dance instructor was in Lowell, Massachusetts, teaching the polka to factory girls in the mills. Soon it was simplified into a basic hop-step dance that anyone could learn, with few or no lessons.

Not everyone, however, was thrilled with the polka. Bennett of the *New York Herald* called it "disgusting and indecent." The *Barre Gazette* called it "nothing but a reel, winding up with an awful breakdown." Captain Orlando Subertash Frazer in Charleston, South Carolina, was even more disparaging. After expressing shock and umbrage at the waltz—where had he been the past twenty years?—he found the gallop and the polka even worse: "The gallop and polka step, in which gentlemen, with legs wide astride, push their fair partners along, is absolutely disgusting; and [we] will hold no mother guiltless who, after this public warning, shall allow her daughter to join in such brutal display. . . . No pretty girl—no young lady, indeed, whether pretty or not—should ever, if she values true and gallant admiration, allow herself to be associated with the recollection of any thing that is markedly ungraceful, however harmless in itself, and should never therefore dance modern waltzes, polkas, or gallopades."

George Templeton Strong, a member of New York's elite,

attended a grand ball on December 23, 1845: "'Polka' for the first time brought under my inspection. It's a kind of inane Tartar jig performed to disagreeable music of an uncivilized character." But that uncivilized music stayed with him. Throughout the night "an abominable, wooden kind of cadence upside down in one of those polka tunes haunted me like an evil spirit, and came jerking and creaking into my head whenever I began to subside into a doze." Three years later his opinion had not changed: "Wish I had the man that invented the Polka. I'd scrape him to death with oyster shell." Luckily, Korponay never met Strong.

The polka was quickly put to use in politics, thanks to the serendipitous name of the 1844 Democratic presidential nominee, James K. Polk. Jokes, cartoons, and sometimes sly, insidious allusions began with Polk's nomination and continued through much of his presidency. Before the polka even arrived in the United States the *New Hampshire Gazette* taunted, "The Polka Dance. (A very fashionable dance in Paris) The Democrats propose to make the coons" (here meaning the uncouth and uncultured) "dance this new fashioned dance from now till next November." As mentioned earlier, "coon" originally did not have a racial meaning but meant someone rough and relatively uncultured, in particular Westerners who were close to the frontier. The Whigs, realizing they needed the Western vote, took the coonskin as their symbol. After the election the *Weekly Houston Telegraph* prophesied that the outcome would favor the dance: "The Polkamania, it is said, will rage extensively this winter in New York . . . every body, they say, is running wild with a passion for the Polka—especially since the election." Given the frenzy the polka had already created, to credit it to the election seems at best hubristic.

During the 1844 campaign the Whigs charged "that the defeat of Clay and the election of Polk would ruin all business, especially that of manufacturers." The *Worcester Palladium,* reporting on the failure of that prediction in 1846, entitled the article "THE POLKA RUIN." A sandbar threatened to block Chicago's harbor, and Polk's tariff on Western industry threatened to raise expenses to dredge it, affecting Midwest farmers' transportation costs. The paper referred to the "Polk sandbar," with the fear that Chicagoans "will have to *dance the Polka* next Spring."

Songs, poems, drawings, and cartoons further infused the spirit of the polka into the campaign. An anonymous poem, "De Polka Daunce," was published in the New York *Weekly Herald*, which in its dialect attempted to imitate the minstrel voice:

Tune—"Boatman Dance."
De Coons dey are behind de day,
Wid Jim Polk we'll beat Old Clay,
Dey will but den only just diskiber
Dey are all gwine up Salt Riber.
So daunce de Polka daunce,
O, daunce de Polka daunce;
Well daunce down Clay in this new way
And set old Chapman crowing
Huzza, huzza for de Victory,
Wid our Young Hickory.

We de boys well know the way
To daunce de daunce called the Polka—
We'll daunce and sing it to dis tune,
And Larn de Polka to de Coon
So daunce de Polka daunce.
De name of Polk dey call romance—
What will dey call de Polka daunce?
It is a daunce heerd much about,
Bound to put de Clay pipe out.
So daunce de Polka daunce.
(Several more verses follow)

Edward C. Clay's cartoon "The Polka—A New National Dance Adopted by the Democratic Convention." The dancers are, from left to right, John C. Calhoun, James K. Polk, Richard Mentor Johnson, Lewis Cass, John Tyler, and George M. Dallas. The musicians are Andrew Jackson and Martin Van Buren; watching are Henry Clay and Theodore Frelinghuysen.

The poem is accompanied with a caricature of Polk and with his vice-presidential candidate, George M. Dallas, dressed in what today would be called "drag" and dancing the polka.

During the 1844 campaign Edward C. Clay, artist and arguably the best political cartoonist of his day, featured a cartoon entitled "The Polka—A New National Dance Adopted by the Democratic Convention." The democratic leaders are shown dancing the polka. At the far left of the cartoon John C. Calhoun, dancing with Polk, says, "You be damned with your Texas movement, it has made you so giddy that you carry on as if you were drunk!" The annexation of Texas was a major issue in the campaign, and Polk, who strongly favored it, replies, "How do you like this sort of thing John? This is what I call my Texas movement!" The next dancer, Richard Mentor Johnson, former vice president and rival for the 1844 nomination, comments to Lewis Cass, another rival for the nomination, "I say Cass, *we* can give them the Western touches!" Cass counters, "*You* give them the Western touches, you old fool! It takes *me* to do that!" Johnson was from Kentucky and Cass from Michigan. The final couple matches John Tyler and George M. Dallas. Tyler had a checkered political career, first as William Henry Harrison's vice president on the Whig ticket in 1840, then as president after Harrison died, only to be expelled from the Whig Party for his positions. He announced a run for president with a newly formed party in 1844, but agreed to support the Democrats after Andrew Jackson assured him that under a Democratic administration the annexation of Texas would occur. George M. Dallas became Polk's vice-presidential candidate. Tyler comments, "George I never tried this dance before but I think I can go it lik [*sic*] I don't know what!" Dallas responds, "Neither did I, but I think we can *poke* it into them famously! ha! ha! ha!" During the campaign several other bon mots in newspapers used the same poke-Polk pun.

While the dancers are showing their Polk(a) moves, Henry Clay and his running mate Theodore Frelinghuysen watch from the rear with bemusement and disdain. Frelinghuysen observes, "The first step appears to be the great difficulty, Harry!" Clay replies, "Yes Theodore and I think it will end by a general break down! ha! ha! ha!" The two musicians at the far right are former Democratic presidents. Andrew Jackson, playing the bass and looking aged, exclaims, "By the Eternal, Matty! You beat Ole Bull." Ole Bull, the Norwegian violinist, was causing a sensation touring in the United States. Martin Van Buren, Jackson's protégé and successor as president, brags, "Yes General, this is my master piece. I'll give them a touch of the double shuffle, by and by!"

Whether attributed to Matty's double-shuffle or not, the Democratic campaign was successful, and Clay was defeated in his third and final run for the presidency.

After the mania of the 1840s, the polka remained popular. *Beadle's Dime Ball-Room Companion* reported in 1868 that it was still "one of the most popular of the round dances," that is, couples dances, especially where the man put his arm around the woman. Many new dances emerged—the redowa, gallop, quick-step, two-step—but the polka remained as the standard, premier dance for the nineteenth century. It became a metaphor for round dancing in general. In a morality screed against round dancing, the polka stood for all the evils incumbent: "What father would like to catch his daughter dancing the polka in the arms of a young man when by themselves in a parlor? What father . . . would not kick the young man out of doors, and send the young woman to an asylum?" The polka symbolized other vices: in a raid on a gambling house suspected of hosting faro, a popular gambling game in the nineteenth century, the person conducting the raid said it was not faro, but "either bluff or draw polka."

No matter what new dance caught the public fancy, both the polka and the waltz persisted, even though the waltz had lost much of its cachet after the polka appeared. In 1859 dance instructor Edward Ferrero referred to the "plain Waltz, now almost excluded from our fashionable assemblies." He called it "antiquated" and considered it consigned to "some parts of the country, however, particularly in rural districts." The Boston, an offshoot of the waltz, became a fad—according to one report, "an epidemic"—in the 1870s; "at balls 'The Boston' broke out all over the room," and "young ladies rose in their sleep and danced 'The Boston.'" Yet by 1880 it had died out too, and society returned to the polka, the dance floor becoming once again to some "a large concourse of jumping jacks."

While the waltz remained, it took on a new role in later

nineteenth-century America. When Johann Strauss visited Boston and New York in 1872, he was mobbed as if a rock star. The newspapers noted the size of the crowds, especially "the ladies, several thousand of whom have already fallen in love with him, and deeply deplore the ugly fact that he is already married." His reception rested on two pillars: the popularity of the waltz, and his presence as a European. Strauss and the waltz were old Europe.

By the end of the century the waltz had become a music of nostalgia and sentimentality. Overly sentimental songs predominated, and almost all were waltzes. Loss, particularly lost love, was the most common, as in "After the Ball," which was the biggest selling (sheet music) song of the 1890s and, relative to the population of the United States then, arguably of all time. Morality tales were also common among waltz lyrics, not just about drink or similar evils, but about seemingly good choices that were deemed bad, such as "She's Only a Bird in a Gilded Cage," where a young woman marries an older man for his money, sacrificing her youth and love for material trappings.

The polka, in spite of its Eastern European origins, seemed from the first to symbolize the new country emerging on the North American continent. Already in June 1845, the *Baltimore Daily Clipper* noted that the polka reflected "the spirit of '76 . . . just as Yankee Doodle does." Its fast pace and energetic hop-skip *sans* the social graces of Europe were emblematic of the young republic. To the author and dancing master Edward Ferrero, it fit right into the "age of progress."

The polka inaugurated a large cycle of fast two-step rhythms and movements that ran through the nineteenth century, finally culminating in the dances of the 1920s Jazz Age. The popularity of the gallop, the schottisch, the two-step, and the many turn-of-the century animal dances (squirrel, chicken scratch, turkey trot) may be traced back to the polka craze. The polka was a dance of exuberance befitting an exuberant nation. Likewise, infatuation with Sousa's marches was drawn from that same spirit. For America the nineteenth century was a time of optimism, progress, and militaristic expansionism. William Lyons Hubbard expressed what many felt in the nineteenth century, that Sousa's marches "are indeed deeply imbued with the American spirit," and he further connected the marches to the birth of the two-step, which Allen Dodworth had called "the polka without the hop." The two-step connected directly to the foxtrot, and from there to a variety of dances such as the Black-influenced jitterbug and even the two-step of Texas country dancing.

That John L. O'Sullivan first used the term "manifest destiny" to describe America's right to westward expansion in 1845, at the height of polkamania, is no coincidence. They were born of a similar sentiment. Even though both the polka and the waltz originated in Europe, the waltz remained a nostalgic reminder of old Europe, but in the polka nineteenth-century America found its swagger and, it believed, its destiny.

CHAPTER 4

Classical Music Arrives

In 1842 the composer Anthony Heinrich visited President John Tyler in the White House. John Hill Hewitt, who taught piano to Tyler's daughters, arranged for Heinrich to play his "War of the Elements and the Thundering of Niagara," an elaborate programmatic composition, for the president. Tyler, relieved to discover Heinrich was not seeking a government appointment, granted him a hearing. Heinrich began to play his wild, complex piece on the piano: "his bald pate bobbed from side to side, and shone like a bubble on the surface of a calm lake . . . while the perspiration rolled in large drops down his wrinkled cheeks." Heinrich gave a running commentary as he played—this part was about "ice breaking up and rushing over the falls of Niagara," this part represented peace, these "the thunder of our naval war-dogs and the rattle of our army musketry." As the small audience, mostly ladies who were attached to or visiting the White House, sat in stunned silence, Tyler rose halfway through this energetic performance, gently put his hand on Heinrich's shoulder, and said, "That may all be very fine, sir, but can't you play us a good old Virginia reel?" Heinrich was stunned. He later told Hewitt, who sought to reproduce Heinrich's accent in his account, "Mein Got in himmel! Di peeples vot made Yohn Tyler Bresident ought to be hung. He knows no more apout music than an oyshter!"

What Heinrich did not understand was that Tyler represented Americans' view of music in the early nineteenth century. The American public did not consider music art. To the great majority of the population some music was functional, for ritual and ceremonies both sacred and secular; the rest was entertainment. Instrumentalists regularly played for dances, which often followed concerts. The concerts themselves were entertainment, a mélange of varying musical numbers played or sung by whoever was available, including both amateurs and professionals. In that context, Tyler's comment was neither impertinent nor out of place.

A series of events that began in the 1820s, took shape in the 1830s, and came to full fruition in the 1840s was to completely change those attitudes. It began in church music, where Lowell Mason advocated for a music that was proper, restrained, spiritually uplifting, and "scientific," a term that meant based on the principles of European masters. His influence was considerable because he couched his argument in terms that antebellum America understood. Mason was less interested in music as art than as a means to create the right kind of Christian worship. He went so far as to delineate a hierarchy of musical or aesthetic values, with music that was moral, that is church music, at the apex; music that was artistic occupied one rung below that. Mason himself was a product of the Great Awakening, an evangelical movement that swept the country in the early nineteenth century, and he dedicated his life to creating and promoting music in the service of the church.

Although Mason planned a career as a banker, he studied harmony with the German émigré F. W. Abel, and was active as a church music director and organist. Around 1820 he began to assemble his first tune book, which consisted of a collection of hymns and other sacred songs designed for religious gatherings.

For the most part he was not the composer but the compiler and musical arranger. He consciously set out, however, to distance himself from the creators of eighteenth-century tune books, as he considered their harmonizations crude and lacking in sophistication and decorum. In basing his settings on European models, on composers we would call classical, Mason's books contained a clear message: certain types of music are better than others and have a higher purpose. He referred to the type of music that he advocated as a "divine institution."

Mason's success came about through his connection with the Boston Handel and Haydn Society, a choral organization founded in 1815. Although its principal activity was to present large choral concerts, its original stated purpose was to improve the quality of church music in Boston. In 1822 the society decided to publish Mason's compilation, which became known as *The Boston Handel and Haydn Society Collection of Church Music*. The collection quickly became a best seller, and remained so for years. It established Mason's reputation, provided him a steady income, and allowed him to abandon his banking career to become music director in the Bowdoin Street Church and president of the Handel and Haydn Society. The publication also put the Society on a sound financial footing.

The Boston Handel and Haydn Society proved to be one of the most important musical organizations in the United States. While it continues today as a concert organization presenting both choral and instrumental music, in its early years it focused almost exclusively on choral music. That was the only musical activity that large segments of the population participated in, and consequently the oratorios of Handel and Haydn (for example, *Messiah* and *The Creation*) were quite popular. It soon expanded its repertoire to include many of the larger choral works of composers such as Bach and Beethoven. Thus, four of the most important composers in the Western canon originally became known in the United States almost exclusively from their choral music.

In 1832 Mason decided to leave the Handel and Haydn Society and help found the Boston Academy of Music. Mason had concluded that the only way to improve church music was to start with children when they were young. The Academy was a huge success, enrolling 1,500 students in 1833, its first year. The second year enrollment increased to 3,500 plus an adult choir of 500 members—this in a city whose population was about 61,000. Clearly the Academy was flourishing, and Mason could begin to realize his dream of a better and more decorous church music.

Yet in its third year, 1835, the direction of the Academy began to change, inaugurating one of the most important revolutions in American music. By 1842 choral music had been phased out completely in favor of secular instrumental music, culminating with the founding of the Boston Academy of Music symphony orchestra. Accompanied by a spirited campaign in print media, the revolutionary view that classical music, that is, music of European classical composers, was special and morally elevating, spread throughout the United States. That view continues to resonate today among many parts of the general public.

One person in particular was responsible for the change: Samuel Atkins Eliot. Eliot's impact on American music cannot be overestimated, but he has been all but ignored in American musical history, largely because he was not a musician himself. He was a most unusual figure to lead a musical revolution for other reasons as well. Eliot belonged to one of the most prominent families in Boston, and any activity beyond attending an occasional concert was beneath consideration for a member of his station.

As a youth Eliot showed no great interest in music. Even when making the *de rigueur* upper-class post-college European tour, his letters home were filled with observations about art; he said nothing about music. Upon returning, he became active in politics, eventually serving as member of the Massachusetts

House of Representatives, 1834–37; mayor of Boston, 1837–39; state senator, 1843–44; and member of Congress, 1850–51.

Yet in 1835 Eliot replaced Reverend Jacob Abbott as president of the Boston Academy of Music. How Eliot, a complete outsider, managed to get elected we do not know. Why he wanted the position is unclear, although the sudden death of his older brother William, who was interested in music, may have motivated him. Eliot wasted no time making changes. In the first year he hired J. A. Keller as instrumental professor to form an orchestra, and renovated an abandoned theater, the Odeon, to create a concert hall. In the 1835 Annual Report of the Society he sought to correct the "misapprehension" that the Academy was devoted exclusively to sacred music. In his second year he hired the German violinist Henry Schmidt as "Leader of the Orchestra."

Being an astute politician, Eliot let his revolution unfold slowly. Interest in the orchestra grew gradually as choir attendance atrophied. Mason did not object, for by 1837 his focus was elsewhere; he was lobbying to have music included as a subject in the public schools, and by 1838 he succeeded. For the first time in the United States music was officially part of a public school curriculum. For him the Academy had served its purpose, and Eliot, given his positions as mayor and chairman of the Boston School Committee, without doubt helped make Mason's goal a reality. The two apparently arrived at some sort of alliance or deal.

Eliot's plans then became clearer. In 1838 he reported that "instrumental music was gaining ground." In 1840 he attempted to unite all the professional instrumentalists in Boston into an orchestra, although he did not succeed. In 1841, however, Eliot achieved the complete transformation of the Academy. He announced that focus would be on creating "as efficient an orchestra as can be engaged," and he succeeded in securing 25 to 30 professional instrumentalists for the season. The choir was disbanded; the Academy would henceforth be a secular instrumental organization.

Eliot's efforts paralleled a broader change of mood of the Boston public. The evangelicalism of the Great Awakening had peaked by 1830–31, and the public had become more interested in secular entertainment. Eliot had in mind something more than entertainment, however, and that was the real revolution. By this time he also had a valuable ally, Theodore Hach.

Hach was a German cellist probably from Lübeck. Little is known of his background other than that he had planned to travel with Lowell Mason on Mason's German tour in 1837. Although Hach had to decline the tour, he soon arrived in Boston, possibly because of Mason. He later played in the Boston Academy of Music orchestra and other venues, but more important, he founded the *Musical Magazine* in 1839. In this journal Hach advocated an unabashedly idealistic view of music: "The art is infinite, and our conception of it will soar ever higher. . . ." That Hach used the word "art" is significant: he simply assumed music was an art, which was indicative not only of his own beliefs but of where he sensed the country was heading. In describing the role of the critic (e.g., Hach himself), he elevated music to an even higher plane: "he must have art, pure art alone in view, as the ultimate object of what falls under his notice."

Hach's journal lasted only three years. In the final issue, April 24, 1842, Hach sounded bitter: "A music periodical, however much needed for the art, it seems is not yet wanted by the people, and we submit, after three years' perseverance in the unrequited labor." He attributed America's lack of support for "serious" music to a range of factors, including the absence of European style patronage, and the pace of life in the United States. Most important, however, was the continuing association of music with "levity." Few Americans even considered music as anything other than entertainment.

Yet in spite of Hach's pessimism, new developments were

beginning to impact musical attitudes. Eliot wrote a number of anonymous articles in literary journals advocating music as art and extolling the importance of the symphony orchestra. In an 1836 article in the *North American Review* he addressed the need for a "higher" taste in music to be cultivated in the United States: "The taste of the public, too, cannot be forced; but must be carried gradually and easily along to the highest branches of the art." Eliot argued that music was "a universal language," thus accessible to everyone, and progressive, thus improving with each generation, having reached a peak in the works of Handel, Haydn, and Mozart. (Bach and Beethoven were still relative unknowns in America at this time.)

In 1841 Eliot began to speak directly of revolution. He sensed "a great revolution in the musical character of the American people has begun, and is, we trust, to go forward, like other revolutions, till its ultimate object is obtained." He saw his own organization as one of the instruments of revolution. Music also went beyond the personal; not only could it mold a person, but it could have "a permanent effect . . . upon the national character."

Eliot's belief in a new awakening in music was aided by another new force on the American musical scene, one that he could not have anticipated in 1835. European virtuosi began to arrive in great numbers beginning in 1840. European musicians had immigrated to the United States before the 1840s, but it was usually to stay. Almost all settled in one city and made their career there. These new performers came, however, not to stay, but to find new audiences, then return to Europe richer. Why the influx of European musicians at the start of the 1840s? The European scene was getting crowded, and musicians were seeking new markets. The first set of instrumentalists were not major stars, no Liszts or Paganinis or even Thalbergs. Louis Rakemann, John Nagel, and George Knoop had only modest reputations in Europe. Ever seeking new audiences, America seemed to them a wealthy virgin territory, ripe with possibilities. In 1845 the

New York correspondent to the Parisian journal *La France musicale* wrote a tongue-in-cheek description of the views of the typical virtuoso eyeing the American market: "The European artist imagines that America is a country of gold, where he will acquire a fortune in two or three months, where the president of the union will have him honored by congress; where the inhabitants of each city will give him serenades and carry him in triumph." Exaggerated certainly, but not without a kernel of truth in depicting the European virtuoso's view of the United States.

This change in motivation was undoubtedly based on a new impression of America; it was now a thriving wealthy country with a large, potentially untapped audience. But the virtuoso's interest would not have been acted on without three new inventions: the steamship, the railroad, and the telegraph. Each of these new technologies made touring possible, or at least feasible. A successful tour demanded a virtuoso give a sufficient number of concerts within a given time period. Too many days on the road cut down on the earning potential. The Atlantic crossing itself had been a deterrent, especially given the unpredictability of passage in sailing ships. Finally, the artist must also be able to make arrangements for the different cities visited, but mail then was slow, unpredictable, and expensive, often requiring the receiver to pay. Only in the 1840s were all three issues resolved, with the implementation of the railroad, the steamship, and the telegraph.

In 1830 there were 23 miles of railroad track in the United States. By 1840 the rail system had expanded to 2,800 miles, extending from Maine to New Orleans, and as far west as Kansas and Nebraska. Travel times were lowered dramatically. Prior to the railroad, travel from Baltimore to Philadelphia, a distance of 90 miles, took three days. The railroad cut that to five and one-half hours. And as virtuosi arrived throughout the decade, each year brought more tracks, until by 1850 mileage totaled over 9,000, more than tripling what it was in 1840.

While the railroad was critical to the success of European virtuosi in the United States, even enticing them to come, it goes without saying they were not the only musical beneficiaries. The railroad made feasible any type of touring musical performance, ranging from popular singers to minstrel shows to bands and orchestras and opera companies.

In the early nineteenth century a transatlantic crossing took at least five to six weeks. Arrival times could not be predicted, as the ship was fully dependent on the wind, which could disappear for days at a time, leaving it to bob helplessly until the wind came up again. While steamboats date to the late 1700s, transatlantic steam crossing did not become a regular event until the late 1830s, and almost immediately, steamship crossing averages of fifteen days became common and dependable.

A successful electric telegraph was first developed in Great Britain by William Cooke and Charles Wheatstone and patented in 1837. The American painter Samuel Morse, who was working on a similar invention, received an American patent the same year. How much he knew of Cooke and Wheatstone's solution has been in dispute. Morse's greatest challenge lay in the required stringing of wires throughout the country, and consequently it was only in the mid-1840s that the telegraph became a useful tool for traveling musicians.

Yet in spite of the technological revolutions of the 1840s, European artists still faced two large barriers to acceptance. Portions of the public remained skeptical of an all-instrumental concert. Typical concerts of the time featured overtures and symphonic movements interspersed with songs, glees, concertos, and various solos. When the Polish pianist C. Kossowsky gave an all-instrumental concert in Boston in 1839, Theodore Hach wrote, "Concerts wholly instrumental should always be short, for our public are only just beginning to appreciate them," and he further described "the arduous task of playing alone eight times, each time performing pieces every one of which would be sufficient to tire the physical or mental powers of any one in Boston except himself."

Starting in 1840, European virtuosi began to arrive in the United States in great number. The first wave of virtuoso performers included pianists Louis Rakemann and Jane Sloman, in addition to Kossowsky, who was already here; violinists Leopold Herwig, John Nagel, and William Keyser; cellist George Knoop; oboists A. L. Ribas and Giovanni Paggi; and guitarist Dolores Nevares de Gony. It is worth noting that at least two of the instrumental virtuosi were women.

Of these, Nagel and Knoop created the greatest sensation. Nagel, who advertised himself as "Composer and Violinist to the King of Sweden" and a pupil of Paganini, was hailed by New York music critic Henry C. Watson as the "greatest violinist ever to cross this side of the Atlantic," and second only to Paganini. Knoop, who went by the lengthy title "Concert Meister of the late King of England, William IV, and honorary member of the Conservatoire in Paris and the Philharmonic society in London, etc. etc.," received special accolades; according to T. B. Haywood, editor of *The Musical Cabinet*, "he stands higher than any other, of whatever description, who has visited this country; and on his particular instrument, there are very few in Europe who excel, or even equal him." Haywood also called de Gony, who had formed a musical partnership with Knoop, "an artiste of high merit." De Gony and Knoop married in 1845. Watson considered Knoop "as near perfection of his instrument as any living performer, and nearer than anyone who preceded him."

The fiddle stakes were raised significantly in late 1843 when three of the finest violinists in Europe arrived in the United States almost simultaneously: the Belgians Alexandre Artôt and Henri Vieuxtemps, and the Norwegian Ole Bull. Both Artôt and Bull crossed the Atlantic by steamer, Artôt on the *Great Western* and Bull on the *Caledonia*. Artôt and Vieuxtemps landed in New York City and Bull in Boston.

Bull soon made his way to New York, and for a period of time the city basked in having three of the world's preeminent violinists in one place—in the New World! The *Boston Evening Transcript* reported that "New York now possesses the most magnificent trinity of instrumentalists that live in the universe." The Baltimore *Sun* related how "The New York public about this time seem to be music mad—a sort of *viol-phobia [sic]* appears to pervade the whole people. . . . The concert rooms are nightly crowded with intelligent and discriminating audiences."

Arguments about who was the greatest filled the press, and each was celebrated as the next Paganini. Niccolò Paganini, now hailed as Europe's greatest nineteenth-century violinist, had died in 1840. The New York *Tribune* proclaimed Vieuxtemps "superior to any man who has ever visited this country," but then hedged its bets: "But, after all he did not move upon the hearts and the feelings of his audience as does Ole Bull." The writer further explained that Bull uses his violin "as a medium of transmitting the pent-up music within himself to his audience," while the music is within Vieuxtemps' violin, and he through his technique seeks to "extract from the instrument pleasant and beautiful sound." As a consequence "Vieux Temps pleases—Ole Bull electrifies."

Ultimately, no European musician created more of a sensation than Bull. In addition to his artistry, he was young, he was handsome, he was charismatic, and he was single. Bull's impact on the American musical scene resided partly in his playing, partly in his commanding personal presence, and partly in his love for the new country. Unlike many European virtuosi who came, did their tour, and left, Bull returned twice, eventually married an American, and divided the last ten years of his life between the United States and Norway. He considered himself an "adopted child" of America. He was an ardent Norwegian nationalist, who had announced himself as an "artiste norvégien," at the Paris Opera in 1836, an unusual move at the time. He believed strongly in democracy and fervently supported Norwegian independence from Sweden, which was eventually accomplished in 1905.

He returned to the United States in 1852 to establish a "New Norway," or "Oleana" as it was sometimes called, in central Pennsylvania. The endeavor was fraught with difficulties, and many narratives, some true, some false, and some suspect, have circulated about the problems: Hundreds of Norwegians were stranded, many dying from heat in boxcars; Bull was swindled by unscrupulous land speculators; he had to adopt American citizenship to get title to his land; and he was arrested numerous times. Even the physical size of the colony has been subject to conflicting reports, ranging from 11,000 to 200,000 acres. While the motives of the original speculators who helped finance the project remain questionable, the collapse of the colony came quickly, and it had dissolved by September 1853. In spite of all the conflicts, rumors, and charges bandied about, it failed primarily because the mountainous land was unsuitable for productive farming.

The colony is only the most extravagant example of Bull's idealism. He was a romantic visionary, using his extraordinary musical talent to support any number of plans. He built The Norwegian Theater (Det Norske Theater) in Bergen, Norway, to advance the nationalist democratic cause, and an opera house in New York City to stimulate interest in the genre.

Whatever Bull's success in various endeavors, no one could doubt his mastery of the violin, the way it did not just amaze but touched the audience in an unexpected manner. John S. Dwight—musician, writer, Transcendentalist, and founder of one of the most important musical magazines in the nineteenth century, *Dwight's Journal of Music*—was concerned, as many were, about empty virtuosity as opposed to exalted, unified, inspirational compositions such as those of the great masters, Haydn, Mozart, and Beethoven. Writing in 1845, he acknowledged Bull's violinistic talent but was disturbed by the virtuosic, improvisatory quality of his compositions. Dwight faulted his pieces for their freewheeling, changeable quality. He then assigned their reception to the "individualism of the age," which he hoped would eventually lead to a "new order of society" where individualism would be supplanted by a "Unitary Concert" and an "orchestra of genius." Dwight was also a dreamer and idealist.

Dwight's measured response and societal criticism, however, was quite different from his reaction the first time he heard Bull, which he described in a letter to the poet and abolitionist Lydia Maria Child: "The most glorious sensation I ever had was to sit in one of his audiences, and to feel that all were elevated to the same pitch with myself, that the spirit in every breast had risen to the same level. My impulse was to speak to any one and to every one as to an intimate friend. The most indifferent person was a man—a living soul—to me. The most remote and proud I did not fear nor despise. In that moment they were accessible,—nay, more, worth reaching. This certainly was the highest testimony to his great art, to his great soul." He acknowledged that except possibly some works of Mozart or Beethoven, "nothing ever filled me with such deep solemn joy," and compared to Vieuxtemps, Bull "does inspire as the other does not."

The inspirational quality of Bull's playing went far to convince a hitherto innocent American public that music had an uplifting quality, and that it deserved a place with the other arts. Bull's message was wrapped in the trappings of the nineteenth-century virtuoso, but Bull's musicality and presence went far beyond what most virtuosi in the 1840s brought. He was not just the trickster, dazzling an unsuspecting audience with feats far beyond what most could imagine, but the priest opening the doors of a temple to heights hitherto unknown. Writer and painter Christopher Pearce Cranch wrote despairingly to Dwight that New York welcomed him as a god. When Cranch met Bull personally, however, his tone changed: One week later he wrote Dwight, "The deep impression the man made upon me was hardly in harmony with the very moderate tone in which I have been speaking of his music."

With the European virtuoso making a profound impression on many Americans, with the advocacy of Eliot and Hach, Eliot was ready for his final step, the creation of the Boston Academy of Music Orchestra. It was a direct outgrowth of Eliot's beliefs, a move by a man used to implementing his ideas in the real world. It was precisely the end result of his efforts from the moment he assumed the presidency of the Academy. It was the sonic manifestation of his own beliefs about the spiritual and moral potential of music, and about what music could best achieve that potential. It was also his most powerful expression of his certitude that music was art.

The Academy Orchestra gave its first concert on November 27, 1841. On December 5, it introduced Boston to Beethoven's Fifth Symphony, an event that was to have repercussions throughout the nineteenth century. The Fifth Symphony shook the audience. It was a force of nature that could not be ignored, a whirlwind that swept up anyone within its sonic horizon. The brooding first movement leading eventually to the triumphant finale was life affirming itself. Margaret Fuller, journalist, editor, and one of the nation's first feminists, wrote of hearing the symphony: "Into his [Beethoven's] hands he drew all the forces of sound, then poured them forth in tides such as ocean knows not. . . . When I heard this symphony I said I will triumph more and more above the deepening abysses." Later she said that Beethoven, "towering far above our heads, still with colossal gesture, points above . . . Beethoven seems to have chronicled all the sobs, the hear-heavings, and godlike Promethean thefts of the Earth-spirit."

Many years later, Dwight looked back upon the early 1840s with great nostalgia: "For, be it remembered, the first great awakening of the musical instinct here was when the *C-minor*

Symphony [the Fifth] of Beethoven was played, thirty years ago or more. . . . young men and women . . . give themselves up completely to the influence of the sublime harmonies that sank into their soul, enlarging and coloring thenceforth the whole horizon of their life."

One year after the founding of the Boston Academy Orchestra, New Yorkers also had a promising new orchestra. While the Boston orchestra was an outgrowth of the Boston Academy and headed by the wealthy Samuel Atkins Eliot, the New York Philharmonic Society was in conception, organization, and governance a creation of the musicians themselves. It was a type of institution found frequently in America, a self-organizing society, a democratic group that emerged on its own volition.

If any one person is to be credited for its founding it would be Ureli Corelli Hill. An American violinist, he had studied in Europe, and on his return quickly established himself as a leading violinist, playing in theater orchestras in New York, Boston, and London, frequently as concertmaster or leader of the orchestras. And all the while he was planning his next move.

At Hill's instigation, many of the best musicians in New York met on April 4, 1842, and agreed to form an orchestral society. A constitution was drawn up, officers were elected, with Hill as president, and on April 16 the constitution was formally adopted, creating what still exists today, the New York Philharmonic.

The Philharmonic of 1842 was quite different from the current orchestra, however, mainly in governance. It remained a cooperative society until 1909, when a financial crisis forced it to reorganize. The original constitution stipulated an orchestra of at least fifty-six professional musicians ("professors of music"), a large ensemble for the time. The Boston Academy orchestra contained approximately thirty players. Most important, all the officers and members of the administrative board were musicians in the orchestra.

The New York Philharmonic presented three concerts in its inaugural season of 1842–43, on December 7, 1842, February 18, 1843, and April 22, 1843. The first concert opened with Beethoven's Fifth Symphony. The second and third concerts each also opened with a Beethoven symphony: the Third (*Eroica*) and the Second, respectively. Beyond the opening work, the programs followed the format that had been in place for decades in both the United States and Europe: a potpourri of different numbers, both instrumental and vocal, and involving various performing forces, from soloists to the full ensemble.

In spite of the traditional programming, the orchestra made a distinct impression. In reviewing the first season, *The Pathfinder*, a New York newspaper, noted, "We do not think any thing has ever been attempted in this city, that will more conduce to the advancement of musical taste, than the formation of the above society." Later it referred to the "onward march of music" and stated, "The music performed at the three Concerts given by the Society, has been of a character to elevate and improve the public taste." These are terms of nineteenth-century progress; they also indicate an awareness that music can be more than entertainment. "Taste," "onward march," "elevate" reflect a musical idealism, and a further recognition of music as an art. New York, like Boston, had through the propitious founding of a new symphony orchestra begun to establish that certain kinds of music were something more than entertainment, and that the symphony orchestra occupied a preeminent position in the emerging musical hierarchy.

The one criticism of the orchestra that *The Pathfinder* had was its sheer volume of sound, partly because no one had heard an orchestra of fifty before, and probably because many players tended to play loudly, as that was required in theater orchestras to cut through the din of unruly crowds. Ironically, the big sound could only have heightened the impact of the Beethoven symphonies, especially the Fifth, with its triumphal fortissimo beginning of the last movement. It is hard today to imagine the effect this moment would have had on virgin ears, especially those unused to such a massed orchestral sound.

Because the New York Philharmonic was a subscription society, only a small segment of the New York population could have heard these three concerts. Yet *The Pathfinder* noticed a broader change. The author was especially pleased to see "Beethoven's Symphonies arranged as duets on the Piano Fortes of young ladies, where we used to see Quicksteps and Gallops," and finally to note that "never before has there been so many concerts so well attended."

While the Boston Academy Orchestra did not last beyond the decade, giving way to a rival organization, the New York Philharmonic had some rough times but never disbanded. It is today the oldest continuing orchestra in the United States. With a total population of 312,710 in 1840 as opposed to Boston's 93,383, New York had a much larger base to draw upon. A German population of 24,000 and the absence of any Puritan hesitation about music further helped create a culture where symphonic music could survive. Like the Boston orchestra, the New York orchestra also discovered that Beethoven's symphonies resonated with the audience, performing them seventeen times in that first decade, including the first American performance of Beethoven's Ninth. Thus in the two cities that had established successful orchestras, the presence of Beethoven symphonies did as much to convince the public of the power of art music as any other activity.

One other orchestra had a major impact on musical attitudes in the 1840s, and it came from Europe. The Germania Society was an orchestra of twenty-five idealistic young men from Berlin. Many had been employed by the nobility, and they sought an environment where they could be free both artistically and politically. The society's formation was coterminous with the 1848 revolutions that swept Europe, from France to Austria and Prussia and beyond, but was not directly associated with the movement. The musicians went to the United States "in order to further in the hearts of this politically free people the love of the fine art of music through performance of masterpieces of the greatest German composers." They further stated that democracy was "the most complete principle of human society." They drew up a constitution that was based on the principle, "equal rights, equal duties, equal rewards."

They arrived in New York late September 1848, and gave their first performance on October 4. The critics were ecstatic: "Seldom have we witnessed a finer display of taste and genius . . . and as a collective band they *executed* with a masterly precision . . . The audience appeared as though awed through the whole performance." The tightness of the ensemble, which meant putting the group ahead of any one individual, was clearly something new. With a few exceptions, American ensembles were often pick-up groups, depending on who was available, had few rehearsals, and frequently encountered concert disasters including total breakdowns. This group of young, enthusiastic, dedicated men who believed in the ensemble as a statement of democracy must have seemed revelatory.

Unfortunately, top-notch musicianship did not translate to financial success, at least at first. Audiences were not large, and box-office receipts sparse—one concert in Philadelphia netted a total of $9.50. An opportunity to perform at Zachary Taylor's presidential inauguration, however, followed by a series of concerts in Baltimore, a city with a large German population, turned their fortunes around. Between 1848 and 1854 they toured extensively, traveling as far west as Cleveland, Chicago, Milwaukee, St. Louis, and Minneapolis. They also made one tour of Canada. Altogether they gave an estimated 900 concerts, some with the orchestra alone and some with touring soloists. When they first arrived in Boston, on April 14, 1849, they gave twenty-five concerts in six weeks, including at least one performance of Beethoven's Second, Third, Sixth, and Seventh Symphonies, and what became almost their theme song, Mendelssohn's *Midsummer Night's Dream Overture*, which according to H. Earle Johnson they performed thirty-nine times. The concert-to-performance ratio suggests just how popular the piece was. They made Boston their home, and Bostonians reciprocated with their allegiance.

Through 1853 their concerts drew full houses, often between 2,400 and 3,000 enthusiastic attendees. Critics wrote not only about the level of their performances but their contribution of raising audience tastes, by inculcating in listeners a love for "classical music," here the music of European masters. One writer summarized their achievement: "The 'Germania Concerts' became our standard of excellence."

In 1854 hints of a change began to occur. "C" in the *Boston Evening Transcript* observed "the rage for concerts is at last dying out," and specifically contrasted the reception of the Germania Society in 1853 with that in 1854. The writer noted that in the previous year "the Music Hall was filled to overflowing; but now many seats are empty." The writer then offered a convoluted explanation of the change, in part claiming that maybe Bostonians' taste was not as high as Bostonians claimed. He (likely a he) then attempted to explain how this has much to do with the ladies' attitudes toward concerts and rehearsals: "They go not because they understand the music, but because it is fashionable." This of course has been a reason many of both sexes have attended concerts since they existed. C goes further, however, mansplaining that even before the Germanians arrived, some women "fell in love with the beauty of the leader of the first violins" or other members of an orchestra. But "after every one of the girls had fallen in love with every member of the orchestra . . . and begun to wonder what they had seen in ———

the Germanians appeared. They had an advantage because they were "newer and handsomer and more foreign men."

C's emphasis on the musicians' appearance was not uncommon at the time. The Boston *Liberator* spoke of how the Germanians "evince[d] a manly bearing," and the Boston *Daily Evening Transcript* focused in detail on Vieuxtemps's appearance: "Vieux Temps is decidedly handsome. He is under the middle size—has a very graceful figure—a fine head—an exceedingly amiable face—and his whole air and bearing are characterized by modesty and dignity." The article continues to discuss his dress and his "finely chiseled features." H. T. Albrecht, a violist of the Germanians, recalled that "the magical effect of the sounds of the orchestra aroused not very solemn thoughts in the breasts of art-loving ladies, affections more than on the level of Platonic friendship."

A startling announcement appeared in the Philadelphia *Public Ledger* on September 24, 1854: the Germanians were disbanding. While Nancy Newman has pointed out the reasons are several, the change in the concert atmosphere in Boston probably contributed. According to the *Ledger,* however, the decision was directly related to the women alluded to by Albrecht and other writers, because "no less than fourteen of [the Germanians] . . . formed matrimonial engagements in the various cities visited during their musical tours through the country." Some of the Germanians simply wished to settle in one place, and matrimony was likely one reason; many were finding more permanent positions: Carl Lenschow had departed in 1850 to direct the Baltimore Liederkranz; Carl Bergmann went to New York to conduct the German Männergesangverein (men's choral society) Arion, and eventually became conductor of the New York Philharmonic; Carl Zerrahn remained in Boston as conductor of the Handel and Haydn Society for forty-one years, as well as several other choral groups. Most of the Germanians became American citizens, also settling in Philadelphia, Syracuse, and Chicago.

Although the Germanians existed as a group for only six years, their ensemble standards showed Americans what an orchestra could do, and their idealism, love of democracy, and youthful vigor convinced many throughout the young nation of the viability and power of music as art. Their tours took them through much of the country and to places that had never experienced a large musical ensemble before. Their final contribution was even more lasting, as most of the members continued to enrich those places in which they settled, often to become the most important musicians in their environs.

Thus by the end of the decade orchestras had been established in at least two of the most important cities, while touring ensembles introduced the orchestra to many other communities. European virtuosi flooded the country, stunning and inspiring many with their dazzling instrumental feats and a type of music whose emotional power went far beyond what most Americans had heard. The music of the "great masters," particularly the large instrumental works of Beethoven, moved many in a way that few had experienced before.

What occurred, however, was limited to a small segment of the population, particularly those of the upper classes, or at least those geographically and financially placed to seek it out. In many ways it was not music for everyone, although just what percentage of the population actually partook is difficult to determine. Yet however narrow its appeal, the arrival of classical music created another dimension to the American musical scene, as it became identified with art and all its attendant social, moral, and cultural implications. Whether one entered into the classical world or not, it created a dimension that no one could fully ignore, one that impacts the American musical world to this day. Even those most removed from the concert world have a sense that names such as Beethoven or Mozart carry some sort of cultural import.

The three years 1840–42 saw a profound change in American

music. It involved the entire class structure, from the wealthiest elites to the newest immigrant arrivals. In one sense it was two revolutions, as each confronted different attitudes and addressed different problems. Their simultaneous occurrence, however, formed a two-pronged attack on the musical status quo as each not only created new institutions, but redefined the very notion of music for the American public. It was also an American statement of cultural independence from Europe, even though in some cases European models continued to prevail. Elites established the first successful symphony orchestras and used them to convince Americans for the first time that music was an art. Irish immigrants in particular contributed to the establishment of the minstrel show, which was a direct response to the racial conditions of the United States. While the genre no longer endures, its impact resonates today in deeply embedded racial attitudes and stereotypes. It is both ironic and somehow historically fitting that America's first original contribution to the musical world would be a genre wrapped in the racial strife that has so defined and shaped the nation.

The
1920s

CHAPTER 5

The Twentieth Century: Music Technology Collapses Time and Space

At the end of the nineteenth century two inventions would change music forever: the phonograph and radio. With them, music could spread far beyond the sound wall of an actual performance and reach millions in their homes, their cars, on the beach, anywhere. Even more important, it was possible to preserve sound itself, not simply represent sound, as notation did. While many other technologies enhanced the sound produced or allowed musicians to reach more audiences, the impact of the phonograph and the radio was different. By capturing the actual sounds, these two inventions broke the strictures of both time and place. They not only allowed future generations to hear a performer, but also allowed music whose essence resisted capture in notation to spread throughout the country and the world. Popular music in particular was radically transformed, as the subtleties of different ethnic intricacies and new types of sounds could extend far beyond their original enclaves. The impact that Black artists in particular have had on twentieth- and twenty-first-century American music is a direct consequence of these two inventions.

The phonograph and radio are the most important developments for music since the invention of notation in the early Middle Ages. Western notation had allowed music to be fixed, to an extent. The sounds themselves, however, needed a performer to bring them to life, and what the performer added, how well it conformed to the composer's original vision, and what the notation could not capture, remained an uncertain, unclear, and often inexplicable puzzle. No matter how well developed a notational system, no matter how much could be passed from master to pupil, the many nuances of pitch, timbre, and temporal variations could never be fully preserved or broadly disseminated. Without the phonograph, jazz undoubtedly would have arisen but undoubtedly would not have swept the Western world with the ferocity it did in the 1920s. The rise of many new styles of popular music and their globalization today is likewise dependent on the phonograph and its descendants, tape and digital recording. Radio had a similar influence, in its effect on musical content as well as distribution.

The story of these two inventions is both complex and dramatic, involving powerful figures, rivalries, and intrigues. Because of the fundamental importance of these inventions to all subsequent music, learning how they came about, including some of the dead ends and misconceptions about their potential, is essential to understanding much of the musical world of the past hundred years.

The idea of capturing sound fascinated much of the nineteenth century, particularly three inventors who devised ways of doing so. While Thomas Edison is normally cited as the inventor of the phonograph, he should share that title with two other people, Édouard-Léon Scott de Martinville and Emile Berliner.

Although Scott was a printer, bookbinder, and bibliographer by trade, he had become fascinated with the idea of reproducing sound, and on January 26, 1857, deposited a sealed packet with the Académie des Sciences de l'Institut de France. In the accompanying letter to the president of the Académie, Scott stated that he had been working on "acoustic writing" for three years, and sought to capture sound as photography captured light, an idea the media historian Patrick Feaster later referred to as "daguerreotyping the voice." In a series of questions, Scott addressed what then must have seemed impossible:

> Can it be hoped that the day is near when the musical phrase, escaped from the singer's lips, will be written by itself and as if without the musician's knowledge on a docile paper and leave an imperishable trace of those fugitive melodies . . . ?
>
> Will one be able, between two men brought together in a silent room, to cause to intervene an automatic stenographer that preserves the discussion in its minutest details while adapting to the speed of the conversation?
>
> Will one be able to preserve for the future generation some features of the diction of one of those eminent actors, those grand artists who die without leaving behind them the faintest trace of their genius?

His answer: "I believe so."

Scott then claimed that he already had a "rudimentary apparatus" that was undergoing further refinement and construction. In the sealed document he described in detail his invention, which he called the phonautograph. The device resembles Edison's later phonograph even in many specifics.

Twenty years before Edison's phonograph, Édouard-Léon Scott de Martinville created a phonautograph that bore a striking resemblance to Edison's invention.

It consisted of a horn, or "funnel" in Scott's terminology, to collect the sound, which fed into a double membrane. A stylus was glued perpendicularly onto the membrane and was placed lightly against a cylinder onto which a paper covered in lampblack (the soot from an oil lamp) had been placed. A sound coming into the horn caused the membrane to vibrate, and when the cylinder was turned, the stylus created a groove, etching a record of the vibrations. While many improvements would be made, some by Scott himself, Scott had created the essence of the phonograph, essentially the method by which all records were made until tape in the 1940s and then digital recording in the 1970s superseded them.

What Scott did not do, however, was create a means of reproducing his recordings. Had he tried, the traces on the paper would not have withstood mechanical reproduction. Only in the twenty-first century has Feaster, through the use of sophisticated electronic technology and lasers, been able to realize the sound of some of Scott's recordings.

Scott, however, had no intention of reproducing the sounds

physically. That was not the purpose of his work. He did consider the grooves as a means of capturing the actual sound of a voice, particularly of actors, politicians, and orators as well as singers. He viewed the squiggles as written sound, just as alphabetic letters were written words. Rather than translating the grooves back into sound with a machine, he believed that one could learn to read the squiggles as one reads a book. The reader could then hear the sounds in their head. Secretaries would learn to read the grooves rather than having to use shorthand. The impossibility of his idea is easily demonstrated; look at the grooves of any 78 or LP (even magnified). Can you hear the sound? To my knowledge, no one ever developed that skill, and as far as I know no one ever tried to train secretaries to do that.

Scott conceived of his invention as a means for scientists, acousticians, and physiologists to study the voice and voice production. The few that were manufactured were marketed to those target groups. Given this limited clientele and the failure of anyone to succeed in reading Scott's grooves, he soon returned to his career as a bibliographer and bookbinder, and the phonautograph became a museum curiosity.

Some twenty years after Scott deposited his sealed envelope at the French Academy, Thomas Edison became interested in creating a machine that would record sound. According to one story, Edison had attached needles to a telephone diaphragm so he could better feel the vibrations with his finger. At one point, a needle pricked his finger. That was his eureka moment: if the vibration had that much force, surely it could be captured. Edison later joked, inventing the phonograph "cost me many sore fingers."

Edison's machine bore an eerie resemblance to Scott's. It had a mouthpiece similar to Scott's funnel, a membrane, and a stylus placed against a horizontal cylinder to which paraffin paper was attached. The cylinder was turned with a hand crank, and vibrations of the membrane were etched onto the paraffin.

Thomas Edison with his phonograph

For the next few months he worked on his sound-capturing machine, which he envisioned as a business machine, primarily for dictation.

Others, however, realized what the machine meant for posterity. Edward Johnson, "the right-hand man of Professor Edison," had been touring to display the phonograph, creating a stir wherever he went. In November 1877, Johnson wrote to *Scientific American* that a speech could be reproduced "long after the speaker was dead . . . with sufficient fidelity to make the voice easily recognizable," although he did admit that "as yet the apparatus is crude." *Scientific American* prophesied about voices from the dead, and "disseminating prerecorded musical performances." This is the first mention of the phonograph for musical reproduction, which seems not part of Edison's original concept. On December 24, he filed a patent for a "Phonograph or Speaking Machine," which was issued February 19, 1878. The patent describes the technical features of the machine, but makes no reference to its potential musical use.

Edison later claimed not to have known of Scott's work, although some historians have doubted his denial. There is no direct evidence to suggest that Edison was familiar with Scott's invention, the principal argument in favor of Scott being the similarities between the two machines. Edison did visit the Smithsonian in 1878, where he apparently saw a copy of Scott's phonautograph. That would have been after his initial patents, but before he created a marketable product. "What did he know and when did he know it" continues to be a question that at this point has no definitive answer.

By January 1878 Edison had signed a contract with a group of five investors to create the Edison Speaking Phonograph Company. They sent salesmen throughout the country, who excited crowds with their demonstrations. It was as much a show as a sales pitch, as they would reproduce any number of sounds, and would call people from the audience to speak into the machine and hear their own voices back. One salesman had a cornetist play "Yankee Doodle" and then varied the speed with the crank on playback, amazing the listeners with a set of impossible-to-play variations. In spite of Edison, music was gradually creeping into the phonograph.

From the beginning, the investors had recognized its potential for music. The memorandum of agreement called upon Edison to perfect the machine "so as to render it of great practical value for many uses, such as the reproduction of speeches and musical compositions." Edison did soon acknowledge its musical potential. He listed ten uses for the machine in the *North American Review* in 1878, of which music was number four, behind letter writing and dictation, phonographic books, and the study of elocution. He wrote, "the phonograph will undoubtedly be liberally devoted to music."

The machine needed more work, as many problems remained before it could be marketed. Edison, however, was consumed with creating the electric light bulb, and more important, the mechanisms and industrial base to supply electricity to homes so it could be used. This occupied him for the next ten years, during which time others, particularly his archrival Alexander Graham Bell, further sought to develop a sound recording device.

Bell displayed their machine, the "graphophone," in 1887, ten years after Edison's phonograph. He first sought to partner with Edison, but Edison summarily rejected the proposal. However, the encounter reinvigorated Edison's own interest in his machine. Electricity had been launched, and now he could return to the phonograph to make further improvements and prepare to market it. Edison still, though, viewed his invention primarily within the framework of a business office, and had little interest in music.

Louis T. Glass, general manager of the Pacific Phonograph Company in San Francisco, had other ideas. Using an Edison machine, he and his partner, William S. Arnold, created a device that would play an Edison cylinder if you put a nickel in a slot. The machine had four tubes with ear buds at the end, so as many as four people could listen at once. Speakers did not yet exist; they required technology not yet invented. This "nickel-in-the-slot phonograph," as they named it, was installed in the Palais Royal Saloon at 303 Sutter Street. It revolutionized the phonograph. Although it could take only one cylinder, which was changed daily, it proved so popular and profitable that Glass installed fifteen around San Francisco. He reported at the first convention of local phonograph companies of the United States that he had made over $4,000 with these machines. Soon they were being installed throughout the country. The jukebox had been invented, along with an important chapter in the music industry.

The cylinders offered more than music. As they were installed mostly in bars, it was assumed that overwhelmingly men would listen to them. The recordings included actors and in some cases amateurs with homemade cylinders reciting soliloquys, literature, poetry, and pornography, much of which was quite explicit. Like the erotic photographs of the time, these cylinders preserve the underside of Victorian sensibility in all its graphic crudity. How many nickels this actually attracted is not known, but it was enough to cause a crackdown in New York City in 1896, and stiff anti-pornographic laws in 1899.

Pornography aside, Edison, afraid that the phonograph would not be taken seriously, was unhappy with Glass's machines. In 1891 he wrote, "The 'coin-in-the-slot' device is calculated to injure the phonograph in the opinion of those seeing it only in that form, as it has the appearance of being nothing more than a mere toy, and no one would comprehend its value or appreciate its utility as an aid to businessmen and others for dictation purposes when seeing it only in that form." Possibly because of his near deafness, Edison still did not comprehend the importance of music to a society and the role the phonograph could play in that context. But events were overtaking him as the coin-in-the-slot business blossomed, and in any case, Edison could not have been too unhappy about the financial results.

Technical issues still loomed, however. One of the greatest problems was the cylinder itself. Edison only found a way to duplicate the cylinders after 1900, and even then the duplicating process would be cumbersome, the cylinders themselves limited to about two minutes, and a collection of them requiring considerable storage space. At this point in the 1890s a young German émigré, Emile Berliner, became interested in solving the cylinder problem.

Berliner had come to the United States in 1870, when he was eighteen. Educated to be a merchant, he had little formal training in science, but he became intrigued with Bell's new telephone after witnessing a demonstration. Inspired, he determined to invent a better microphone. When Bell saw what Berliner had created, he immediately hired him. Berliner worked for the company until 1884, when he decided to establish himself as an independent inventor, in the mold of Edison. A great variety of products flowed from his fertile mind: further improvements on the telephone, a parquet type of floor covering, acoustic tile, an improved loom, a prototype of a helicopter, and the rotary internal combustion engine whose design would power most aircraft in the pre-jet age. Today, however, he is best remembered for the invention he worked on beginning in the 1880s, the gramophone.

Berliner's most important step was to do away with the cylinder completely and replace it with a flat disc. The disc is so commonplace to us now that's it's hard to imagine what a new idea it was, and its success depended on solving a number of problems, most critical of which was material for the disc. After much experimentation, Berliner turned to a shellac compound. This not only withstood repeated playbacks, but could be mass-produced. Since that breakthrough, virtually all 78 rpm records used some variant of this compound until the introduction of vinyl for 45s and LPs in the late 1940s. The flat disc remained the basic storage for sound not only for records but later for CDs as well. It is hard to imagine the musical world of the United States in the twentieth century without discs.

Berliner's next improvement was the spring motor. The first

machines designed for playback were hand-cranked, which created a challenge for the listener, who was required to turn the crank steadily and at absolutely the right speed, which was 70 rpm. The spring-driven motor removed that necessity, as all the listener had to do was wind the spring and the motor would keep the disc at a constant speed. No electricity was required. Few people are around today who have wind-up phonographs, but for several decades spring-driven motors dominated the gramophone market. This was critical at a time when many homes, especially in rural areas, had no electricity.

Berliner's most pressing challenge, however, was how to market the gramophone. An unknown, he was going toe to toe with the most famous inventor-entrepreneur in the world. No cylinder machine could play discs, so the public needed to be convinced to invest in an entirely different machine, as well as an entirely different artist catalogue. Berliner first began to develop a local reputation around Washington, DC, and as word got out, by 1896 he was able to convince enough backers to form the Berliner Gramophone Company, located in Philadelphia.

Here Berliner, more inventor than entrepreneur, made several contractual mistakes. In order to avoid running afoul of antitrust laws, he partnered with Frank Seaman. Seaman recognized a loophole in Berliner's contract that allowed him to use Berliner's recordings to set up his own rival company. A series of lawsuits ensued, and although Berliner prevailed, the suits drained Berliner of his resources and forced him to pass the royalty rights of his patents to his partner, Eldridge Johnson. Berliner was never involved in the record business again. Johnson renamed the company the Consolidated Talking Machine Company, even though it was at the same address as the Gramophone Company. He then changed the name to "Manufactured by Eldridge R. Johnson," and finally in 1901 to the Victor Talking Machine Company. Thus the most important company both in the recording industry and later in broadcast radio was born.

Although broadcast radio did not begin until the 1920s, the development of radio occurred almost simultaneously with the phonograph. The path to successful radio was quite different from that of the phonograph, however; the early phonograph was purely an acoustic machine, depending only on physical properties of sound and vibration to work. Radio was all about electricity and magnetism. Both had been known for centuries, but as late as 1800 they remained invisible, mysterious, and wondrous forces. Yet by 1900 both had not only been tamed but had altered millions of people's lives, providing light, communications, and transportation.

Ancient civilizations were familiar with electricity, mainly static electricity. A device discovered in Persia (now Iraq) in 1838 and dated 200 BCE may have been the first electric battery. Its purpose is unknown, but scientists have demonstrated that it produced an electrical current and, given its composition, cannot hypothesize any other use. Greeks found that standing on an electric eel helped alleviate gout—possibly with the battery the Persians did not have to catch eels.

By the beginning of the nineteenth century scientists knew that electricity could be carried by wires and, thanks to Benjamin Franklin, that lightning was electricity. (That Franklin lived to tell the tale is itself astounding.) The first major step toward turning electricity to practical use came at the beginning of the nineteenth century, when Alessandro Volta invented a reliable battery, the voltaic pile. Soon after, the connection between electricity and magnetism was explained by Hans Christian Ørsted, André-Marie Ampère, and James Clerk Maxwell. Inventions came fast: from Michael Faraday, the electric motor in 1831; from Samuel Morse, the telegraph in 1837 (although his primacy has been challenged); from Alexander Graham Bell, the telephone in 1876; and from Thomas Edison, the electrical light bulb in 1878, to name just a few.

Radio remained an unexplored field, however, for radio waves were still a mystery. Maxwell hypothesized their existence in 1877, and suggested that they were related to light. Ten years later, Heinrich Hertz "unlocked the secret of the elusive wireless waves." He demonstrated that creating a spark on one hoop of wire caused a similar electrical current on a second unattached hoop, sometimes several hundred feet away. Not sure how this current traversed the atmosphere, he theorized the existence of another medium that permeated the universe, ether. While Hertz was wrong about ether, the term itself became part of radio lore for decades: "It's in the ether."

Hertz's experiments excited a number of scientists and inventors, who envisioned a new and miraculous means of communication without wires. It was a young Italian man, Guglielmo Marconi, who not only worked out the scientific problems but built a practical infrastructure that allowed radio to become a common communication device by the beginning of the twentieth century.

Marconi (1874–1937) was born into a wealthy family who owned a farm near Bologna. Educated by tutors, he displayed considerable interest in science, especially electricity. At the age of twenty he read about Hertz's experiments and determined to create "wireless telegraphy." Although his father considered his experiments nonsense, his Irish mother encouraged him, thus freeing the necessary funds to proceed. Through various innovations he succeeded in sending signals over a distance of a mile and beyond the sight line by 1895. Marconi then contacted the Italian Ministry of Posts and Telegraphs, but they were not interested. They considered Marconi's invention so revolutionary that when the head of the ministry read it, he scribbled on the letter, "to the Longara," a reference to the insane asylum in Rome.

Marconi next turned to Great Britain, partly because a family connection gave him access to officers in the British General Post Office. They set up a successful test between two buildings, which led to funding by the post office for further experiments. Word of his invention also drew an influx of British capital, which allowed Marconi to establish The Wireless Telegraph and Signal Company Ltd., later renamed the British Marconi Company.

Marconi and the British capitalists realized that the first important use of wireless was for those places beyond the reach of telegraph wires, such as ships at sea. Further successful experiments demonstrated its value in that regard. This got the Italian navy interested, and with their cooperation Marconi was able to extend the transmission range to twelve miles. Soon both British and Italian ships began to install Marconi's wireless devices; one was installed on the yacht of the Prince of Wales.

In 1899 Marconi visited the United States, where he sold the US Navy on his equipment and also created the Marconi Wireless Telegraph Company of America. He continued to experiment, mainly working on spanning greater and greater distances. He built a large transmitting station at Poldhu, on the coast of Cornwall, and a receiving station in St. John's, Newfoundland. To test the device, Marconi's assistant was to send the letter "s," dot-dot-dot, from Cornwall at a specific time. On December 12, 1901, Marconi, in St. John's, detected those three short bursts, which were later confirmed. Wireless communication had spanned the Atlantic Ocean.

Although Marconi attempted to create a global wireless monopoly, he could not contain the interest his success generated. Germany established the Telefunken Company to challenge Marconi. Scientists and amateurs in both the United States and Great Britain began to flood the airwaves. All of this activity created a major problem: the spark transmitters used then essentially blanketed the airwaves without respect to frequency, stomping on and interfering with each other. At its worst, this created an overwhelming sound of static, a chaotic din rendering decoding any signal impossible. A means of separating signals was necessary.

By 1899 Marconi had begun using a coil and capacitor as a method of tuning the frequency more precisely, and in 1900 John Stone patented a system in England that further focused the sound. Thus multiple radios could transmit without blocking each other as long as they chose separate frequencies, e.g., 88.9 versus 105 on the dial. This system is still in use today whenever someone turns a radio dial.

Radio was still limited to wireless telegraphy, however. The next important step was to transmit voice, something many believed to be impossible. When asked about voice transmission, Edison replied, "What do you say of man's chances of jumping over the moon? I think one is as likely as the other." Canadian inventor Reginald Fessenden was the first to realize that voice needed a different system, a continuous radio wave as opposed to discrete bursts of Marconi's system, to broadcast. He had already begun to develop continuous wave transmission for telegraphy, and demonstrated its viability in establishing the first two-way transatlantic wireless system, even though most scientists had thought his approach unworkable. With a continuous wave or carrier, Fessenden plugged in a carbon microphone, and found he could vary the signal to make the voice intelligible through amplitude modulation, that is, varying the amplitude of the continuous wave. Thus AM radio was born.

On Christmas Eve, 1906, Fessenden sent out a telegraph message to ships at sea: Be listening for something special at 6:00 P.M. Ship radio operators tuned in, expecting dots and dashes, and to their astonishment heard Fessenden's voice announcing the program for the evening, followed by a recording of the Largo from Handel's opera *Xerxes*. Fessenden then announced that his engineer, a Mr. Stein, would sing "O Holy Night" while Fessenden, an accomplished musician, accompanied him on the violin.

Unfortunately, Stein was overcome with stage fright, reducing Fessenden to a violin solo, but the first live broadcast of music ever had occurred. Fessenden's wife and his secretary, expected to read from the Bible, were also too overcome, but Fessenden then read the Christmas story from Luke, ending with "Glory to God in the highest, and on earth peace to men of good will." He signed off by wishing all listeners "A Merry Christmas."

Soon they received confirmation from ships throughout the Atlantic; they had heard it all, clearly and discernibly. Yet in spite of Fessenden's success, it would be years before commercial broadcast radio arrived.

If radio was to be successful, one further problem had to be solved: how to increase the strength of both transmitters and receivers. Early receivers and transmitters used a coherer, essentially a tube with iron filings, and later crystalline mineral, such as galena, but the coherer demanded sensitive headphones to hear the signal. At the transmitting end, radio broadcasting needed a means to amplify the signal. Bell Telephone was also interested in the problem of signal strength, as phone signals weakened in direct proportion to their length.

As often happens, several scientists independently arrived at the same solution simultaneously: the vacuum tube. The most important was John Ambrose Fleming, who in 1904 created a diode, a two-piece tube with a filament similar to that used in Edison's light bulb which emitted electric ions, and a plate that attracted them. It was a much more sensitive and, equally important, a more stable detector than crystal.

Some means of further increasing the power of the transmitter, the sensitivity of the receiver, and the volume of the resulting audio was still needed. Lee de Forest is credited with the solution to all three. De Forest received a PhD from Yale University, but for years had a checkered career, attempting to establish a radio network on Lake Michigan, being embroiled in a patent dispute with Fessenden, which he lost, and working for several companies, some involving sketchy financial moves. In 1907, when employed by AT&T, he added a third element to Fleming's diode, and discovered he could amplify signals many times. The triode, or audion as he called it, became the basis for electronic circuits for the next half-century. Until replaced by the solid-state transistor in the 1950s, the triode vacuum tube formed the core of all radio receivers and transmitters, as well as phonograph amplifiers.

Writing in 1936, Alvin F. Harlow expounded on the triode's importance:

> This may not mean much to the uninitiated, but that miniature gadget was the truest "little giant" in all history, perhaps the nearest approximation to an all-powerful genie that the brain of man ever created. It set unbelievably powerful currents in motion, magnifications of those which flicked up and down the antenna wire, and thus produced voice amplification which made radio telephony a finished product.

Harlow may have been somewhat sweeping in his claims, but without that "little gadget" there would have been no broadcast radio, no television, no long-distance telephone, no phonograph speakers, no digital computer.

At first De Forest, like everyone else, saw no commercial future in broadcast radio. Marconi's, Fessenden's, Fleming's, and De Forest's developments, however, inspired amateurs to continue to build equipment and experiment, until the United States government shut down all amateur operation during World War I. Allowed to resume in 1919, amateurs soon made the next important step in radio.

Dr. Frank Conrad, an engineer at Westinghouse in Pittsburgh, owner of amateur station 8XK—by then all amateurs transmitting had to be licensed—discovered that a number of wireless aficionados were regularly listening to him. He was building a public following. Sometime during 1920 he decided to broadcast two hours of music on Wednesday and Saturday evenings. Finding it too costly to purchase new records every week, he arranged to borrow them from a local dealer. The dealer agreed if he would mention his store. Soon the dealer was selling many more records. The first radio commercial had worked. In September, Horne's Department Store, aware of the stir Conrad was making, advertised in the newspaper radio sets for listeners to tune into his programs.

This caught the eye of Westinghouse, which manufactured electrical equipment and was in search of postwar items to replace their wartime work. They realized that a full-fledged commercial radio station would create even more demand. They subsequently obtained the first commercial license issued by the Department of Commerce, KDKA, on October 27, 1920. Conrad took charge of the equipment. They began broadcasting on November 3, by announcing the results of the Harding-Cox presidential election. An estimated 500 to 1,000 listeners followed the election returns.

The success of the election-night broadcast encouraged Westinghouse to continue. It soon became apparent that playing phonograph records was not sufficient; they moved to live music—Westinghouse had its own band; added interviews with celebrities and politicians; and began broadcasting sports events. What made the potential of radio clear to all was the heavyweight boxing match on July 2, 1921, between the American Jack Dempsey and the Frenchman Georges Carpentier. David Sarnoff, who would later become president of RCA, set up temporary station WDY in Hoboken, New Jersey, with the voice of the flamboyant Major Andrew White describing the fight. An estimated three hundred thousand people heard the broadcast, some as far away as Florida.

Through 1920 and the first half of 1921 there were few commercial broadcast stations. The great boom in radio broadcasting began in late 1921, when 31 new stations appeared from September through December. From January through May 1922, 254 new stations went on the air, covering the entire 48 states. In March 1922, *Popular Science Monthly* carried the headline "First American Radio Charts Show Nation Is Now Blanketed by Wireless News and Music." The new periodical *Radio Broadcast* reported stories of customers standing four and five deep at radio stores, only to be told "they might place an order and it would be filled when possible." The same article prophesied, correctly, "the movement is probably not even yet at its height."

For many radio stations, the license was obtained, a location was found, and expensive equipment, including large antennas, was set up, without an answer to the question, what to broadcast? For the new medium, no precedent or history to suggest what the public wanted. Further, few stations had money to pay performers. At first the sheer novelty of hearing music or a voice come into the living room was enough to fascinate listeners. The novelty quickly wore off, and the public became more discriminating—no more dull announcers or mediocre talent. For most stations, KDKA's formula continued to work: live music, vaudeville-type entertainment, news, interviews, and sports events. News itself did not have to be exciting; many stations spent hours each day reading market reports. A station was fortunate to have someone such as WDY's Major White, whose personality could light up the airwaves.

The early radio stations had a more serious problem than balancing programming, however, and that was balancing their budgets. To sustain their very existence in a capitalist economy, someone had to pay the bills. Most early stations were connected to some sort of business enterprise, the most common by far being the selling of radios, as Westinghouse did, or more general electrical supplies. Many were owned by newspapers, others by universities and churches. While businesses that owned stations used the platform to tout their own wares, the idea of selling advertising was unheard of, and many in the industry questioned whether radio could ever be commercially viable. At the time the establishment of a radio broadcast station cost at minimum about $50,000, a large sum for 1922. Clearly, many were willing to put up that kind of money, but how many had thought through the profit problem? The situation was similar to the early days of the Internet.

On May 1, 1922, American Telephone and Telegraph (AT&T) obtained a license for a new station in New York City, WBAY, which went live July 25. Many assumed that it was for scientific or experimental purposes, related to AT&T's research in electronic issues that encompassed both wired and wireless transmission. The company apparently had another plan, however. WBAY may have been the first station to realize that radio time could be sold. The application of the term "advertising" to radio was still in the future, but based on their telephone model, AT&T placed a statement offering "toll broadcasting." Allowing anyone to rent broadcast time, the station, however, warned that those that bought time would be expected to "broadcast programs of merit and general interest."

Insoluble technical issues plagued WBAY, causing AT&T to concentrate on a second New York station it had obtained a license for, WEAF, and on that station the first toll broadcast occurred August 28, 1922. A real estate developer, Queensboro Corporation, presented a ten-minute program, a serious lecture extolling the novelist Nathaniel Hawthorne. Coincidentally, Queensboro was developing an apartment complex named Hawthorne Court. The excitement at WEAF is evident in the entry of the operating engineer, R. S. Fenimore:

> 5:00/5:10 Queensboro Corpn.
> "Our first customer."

Radio advertising was launched; it was no longer ballyhoo as some had claimed, and the WEAF model became the norm. Rather than the short one-minute or thirty-second plugs of later radio, most programs had a single sponsor, with which they were identified. Later log entries from WEAF indicate that by December the station was regularly selling blocks of time ranging from ten minutes to one hour. The United States from the start made broadcast radio a strictly commercial enterprise, independent of the kind of government support it had in Europe.

The final step in the development of broadcast radio in the 1920s was the establishment of national networks. Throughout 1924 and 1925 a radio group, consisting of RCA, Westinghouse, and General Electric, had fought a telephone group, which AT&T dominated, to accomplish that task. There were many technical and legal issues, involving 1920 license rights, patents, and previous agreements. Particularly in the area of patents, the telephone group had some leverage, as only it had suitable cables to connect stations in different cities, but the final result surprised everyone: AT&T suddenly decided to sell WEAF and its network to RCA and abandoned radio broadcasting entirely. What prompted AT&T's decision is not clear, but the company probably realized that broadcast radio was not its core business, and it was wise to stick to what it did best. That at least was AT&T's explanation. Six weeks later, in September 1926, the National Broadcasting Company was incorporated in Delaware as a subsidiary of RCA.

Technically, NBC had two networks: the Blue Network and the Red Network (the colors had no significance other than being the colors on a map identifying them). The Blue Network gained a reputation for high-brow programming such as the Metropolitan Opera and later, Arturo Toscanini's NBC Symphony. In practice, however, the Blue and Red networks often carried similar programs. The distinction between the networks lasted until 1941, when, under antitrust pressure from the FCC, RCA sold the Blue Network to Edward J. Noble, who would rename it the American Broadcasting Company (ABC).

Well before ABC was formed, a second radio network had emerged. Arthur Judson, impresario and manager of both the New York Philharmonic and the Philadelphia Orchestra, approached Sarnoff with a detailed plan for engaging musical artists in sponsored programs. When Judson discovered that Sarnoff accepted the plan but froze him out, Judson confronted Sarnoff, " 'Then we will organize our own chain.' With that, he [Sarnoff] leaned back in his chair and laughed heartily: "You can't do it. . . . It can't be done.' " Energized by Sarnoff's arrogance, Judson formed the Judson Radio Program Corporation in September 1926, and through his management experience, dogged persistence, and lucky breaks, was able to find a potential owner, Jerome H. Louchheim, who was willing to risk much of his fortune to weather the start-up of a new company. Earlier Judson had discovered that the Columbia Phonograph Company had the Columbia Phonograph Broadcasting System, which soon collapsed. It still existed on paper when Louchheim purchased it, and he dropped the word "Phonograph" to create the Columbia Broadcasting System (CBS).

Thus by 1929 broadcast radio blanketed the United States with two established national networks. The phonograph industry had entered the 1920s already a mature technology, only to see further improvements throughout the decade. The phonograph allowed music to be preserved and reproduced at will. The radio democratized music. It offered a universal concert hall, or dance hall, that was a shared musical experience. With the radio, thousands, even millions of people could take part in the same live musical event simultaneously, in their own homes, and later in their cars. A rural farmer in Iowa could share an experience with an urban dweller in New York City. Mass media had the potential for both good and evil, as Hitler and others realized, but through technology music could become a way to unite a multifarious, diversified country.

CHAPTER 6

The Jazz Age

The Jazz Age. Few decades in American history have been so aptly captured in one musical metaphor as the phrase F. Scott Fitzgerald popularized. Yet fitting as the term is, such a broad stroke only masks how eventful and important that time was for both creators and consumers of many types of music. At one end of the musical spectrum, new music came from a group of avant-garde composers who broke from the German hegemony that had dominated the American classical world since the 1840s. At the other end, jazz, already not a new genre in the 1920s, finally became a household soundscape, as did African American blues. Music by Blacks that originated in Black culture defined the decade. And meanwhile, another new kind of music from the white rural South spread to the North and West.

World War I did not decimate the United States like it did Western Europe, but it was still a major turning point in American society. As if suddenly throwing off the burden and the lethargy of Victorian restraint, Americans sought new thrills and new excitement. Jazz provided the soundtrack. In 1920 women won the vote, and the young woman of the twenties was determined not to be held back by the past. The automobile, now a fixture in society, confirmed that mobility equaled freedom. No more chaperones or confinement to a close geographical space; young people could travel several miles in an evening away from a small town's prying eyes. In many ways the flapper defined the age, and with it much of the music. The economy itself was in a seemingly unstoppable boom, allowing the good times to roll.

Beneath that glittery surface, however, all was not well. Millions of immigrants continued to flood Ellis Island, and a nativist backlash had begun. In both classical and popular music, hard racial lines were drawn. Conservative musicians railed against the loss of Anglo-Saxon domination. New music societies split into Jewish and non-Jewish groups. The domination of Jews in popular music appeared to some a pernicious threat. Another racial tension played out in the world of jazz, for anti-Black prejudice was at its peak, as the Ku Klux Klan spread hate and fear well beyond the South. Although the origins of jazz were unquestionably African American, white ensembles not only challenged Black ones for the jazz mantle, but had automatic advantages: better performing venues and easier acceptance with recording companies.

Writers have sought for over a century to define just what early jazz was. Musically, early jazz was a stylistic synthesis of many elements—blues, ragtime, brass bands and their marches, gospel, and a little Tin Pan Alley. Louis Armstrong is reputed to have quipped in answer to the question "What is jazz?": "If you have to ask, you ain't never gonna know." To Gershwin in 1926, "The word [jazz] has been used for so many different things that it has ceased to have any definite meaning." Sidney Bechet, one of the iconic figures of early jazz, saw jazz for what it expressed: it was the music of emancipation, of freedom. It was also a musical amalgam: "That music, it wasn't spirituals or ragtime, but everything all at once, each one putting something over on the other."

Where history lacks evidence, myths propagate. The traditional jazz story holds that jazz originated in the brothels of New Orleans; made its way up the Mississippi to Chicago, with a side trip, metaphorically if not geographically, to Kansas City; then somehow got to New York. At the same time jazz remained unheard and unknown to most Americans until the Original Dixieland Jazz Band stunned the world with the first jazz recording in April 1917.

There is some truth to this myth, some oversimplification, and some misrepresentation. New Orleans does hold a place of primacy in the jazz narrative, although its exclusivity as a jazz birthing ground was early on exaggerated. Storyville, the red light district of New Orleans in the early twentieth century, figured prominently in jazz histories because many musicians worked there. To be sure, an incipient jazz was not limited to this sixteen-block area, as marches, private parties, and street life throughout New Orleans fostered a variety of instrumental ensembles. New Orleans alderman Sidney Story, a prominent citizen, proposed the law creating Storyville in 1897 and, probably to his chagrin, became immortalized by its name. According to the city fathers, geographic confinement of prostitution made it easier to monitor and control not just that profession but auxiliary vices, such as drugs and gambling. Storyville existed until 1917, when the Department of the Navy forced its closure out of concern for the health of the sailors stationed in New Orleans.

Some of Storyville's brothels, or "sporting clubs" as they were called, were quite lavish, and correspondingly expensive. Lulu White's Mahogany Hall was the most opulent. Built at a cost of $40,000 (the equivalent of over one million in today's dollars), it employed forty prostitutes and had four floors, five parlors, and fifteen bedrooms, and was decorated with huge chandeliers, Tiffany stained glass windows, and expensive oil paintings. Other clubs catering to high-end clients aspired to the same upscale interior appointments. Most of these larger houses had either a pianist or a small musical ensemble to entertain the "guests." In addition, Storyville had many saloons and dance clubs, all of which needed musicians. As the clientele tended not to be too critical, or rather too focused on what was played, musicians could experiment. Improvisation was the norm, and the conditions allowed a relatively free and open situation for performers to try new licks.

In this freewheeling atmosphere, several ethnicities competed: whites, Blacks, and Creoles. The distinction between Blacks and Creoles is more an ethnic and cultural than a racial one. New Orleans had two Black communities: those descended from Anglo-American slaveholders who entered Louisiana after 1803, and Creoles of color, those descended from slaves who were brought in during French sovereignty in the eighteenth century. The former concentrated in uptown and the latter in downtown New Orleans. Anglo-American Creoles were often the offspring (or descendants) of a white slave owner and a Black female slave. The city's Black Code of 1724 allowed such slaves and their children to be freed, and many slave owners who had fathered them gifted them generously. They came to represent a wealthy class in New Orleans. Racial mixing occurred in both communities, and consequently Creoles have been characterized as possessing a lighter skin, even though some do not. A traditional but erroneous jazz narrative holds that draconian segregation laws passed in the 1890s redefined Creoles as Black, dramatically changing their status. While the laws did hurt Creoles, it was not because of a change in racial identity; they had always been considered legally to be Black. But while Creoles and Blacks were seen as racially similar in the eyes of the New Orleans power structure, their cultural backgrounds were different.

Several early jazz figures, including Jelly Roll Morton, Sidney Bechet, and Edward "Kid" Ory, were Creoles. Both Creole and Black musicians primarily found employment in Storyville, partly because the Jim Crow laws adopted in the late nineteenth century limited their opportunities, both musical and otherwise. While many of the Storyville bands were segregated, musicians of different ethnicities did sometimes play together.

The early rumblings of this new music, of a new feeling, which gradually emerged as jazz, were not, however, confined to New Orleans. By the late nineteenth century, a new style of entertainment called vaudeville blanketed the United States. Vaudeville troupes were a mixture of singers, dancers, comedians, and anyone else who could hold an audience. After the Civil War, many African Americans formed minstrel troupes, which included blackening their faces, a mask within a mask, Blacks portraying the white imitation of Blacks. In part because actual African Americans were onstage, minstrelsy itself was changing, expanding its content and loosening its format. Minstrel shows gradually became variety shows, although many retained the minstrel title. In 1895 Edward Albee (grandfather by adoption of the famous playwright) introduced the French name, vaudeville, for variety shows, thinking it gave the entertainment a more sophisticated, European aura.

Many musicians who were creating the new art form, jazz, toured with vaudeville or circuses. These included Jelly Roll Morton, William "King" Phillips, Buster Bailey, and Wilbur Sweatman. Circuses at the time included variety shows, often in sideshows. Many band members were New Orleans players, frequently because a circus or variety show that had traveled through the town would need an extra musician and send for one of the local players. New Orleans guitarist Danny Barker remembered the New Orleans music scene: "You would see a cat disappear, you would wonder where he was, and finally somebody would say he'd left for one of the shows, that they had sent for him."

Through vaudeville and circuses, an incipient jazz began to spread throughout the country. In 1938 clarinetist Buster Bailey described King Phillips, who regularly toured the vaudeville circuit, as "one of the first jazz clarinet players I ever heard." In 1925 Bandleader Dave Payton wrote of Wilbur Sweatman's playing in 1906, "Little did we think that Mr. Sweatman's original style of playing would be adopted by the greatest jazz artists of today; but it is and Mr. Sweatman can claim the honour of being the first to establish it." Sweatman toured with P. G. Lowery's circus from 1902 until 1908, when he formed a band in Chicago. Sweatman's 1902 schedule has survived, and it shows just how widely these groups traveled. Staggering as it was, the schedule was by no means unusual. Between April 2 and November 19, they covered 25 states and two Canadian provinces, in 237 days playing 217 shows in 168 different cities. And we don't know how many performances occurred on each day or how many acts the band had to accompany.

While musicians like Sweatman were touring, another event occurred in 1917 that was to be a critical moment for the new type of music. There was already a booming phonograph industry, yet no one was producing jazz records, until suddenly, in 1917, almost all major labels awakened to the existence of an untapped market. Wilbur Sweatman has a bona fide claim for making the first commercially available jazz recording, "Down Home Rag," in 1916. Whether "Down Home Rag" is jazz, however, is a matter of dispute. Sweatman, a close friend of Scott Joplin, was known primarily as a ragtime and vaudeville performer, and had composed several ragtime numbers, including "Down Home Rag" in 1911. He recorded that piece in December 1916, at the studios of Emerson Records in Manhattan. Emerson was a small outfit that specialized in five- and seven-inch discs, as opposed to the standard ten-inch, or the extended twelve-inch. A seven-inch version of "Down Home Rag" has survived, which explains why the piece is only 1:40 long, and partially why it is not well known. Lagging sales, listeners' preference for longer records, inadequate financing, and poor business decisions forced Emerson into receivership in 1921.

"Down Home Rag" features Sweatman on clarinet and a small group of studio musicians on piano, saxophone, and violin. The piece itself clearly is ragtime, in typical AABA song form, and

Malvin Maurice Franklin, who was a noted ragtime pianist, lays down a strong ragtime beat. Later, while the saxophone plays the melody, Sweatman improvises a counterpoint on top. The clarinet's wails and embellishments are typical early jazz.

Does this, however, make it a jazz recording? If nothing else, it illustrates how close ragtime and jazz were in the 1910s and '20s. Sweatman was not leading a band, and there is no mention of the word "jazz" on the label. (Jazz had several spellings at this time—Jass, Jas, Jasz, Jazz.) More important, early jazz usually involved some sort of contrapuntal improvisation by the entire ensemble, and here jazz improvisation seems limited to Sweatman's solo late in the recording.

Given the fluidity of the terms "jazz" and "ragtime" in the 1910s, the Internet site *Red Hot Jazz Archives* decided upon a linguistic criterion to determine the first jazz record: whether the word "jazz" was on the label. Regardless of the validity of this approach, that is, whether or not the music fits a twenty-first-century definition of jazz, use of the word at least indicates that the record company believed the term would resonate with the public. Recording activity in early 1917 demonstrates that many record companies simultaneously came to the conclusion that jazz was a hot item and they'd better get their licks in quick. The term suddenly was bandied about, even though some of the music did not warrant it.

Arthur Collins and Byron G. Harlan's "That Funny Jas Band from Dixieland" was released on an Edison cylinder in March 1917. Sources claim the recording was made December 1, 1916. It is a comic vocal duet by two white performers, but the instrumental breaks have a jazz quality. It did not sell well because Edison cylinders greatly limited mass reproduction. Collins and Harlan re-recorded it for RCA in January 1917, and it was released in April. George H. O'Connor cut "Ephraham's Jazbo Band" on February 10 for Columbia. Four days later, Borbee's Jass Orchestra recorded two numbers for Columbia, which were not released until July. Only the word "Jass" in the band's name has anything to do with jazz, however. Columbia originally intended the record to be released under the name Borbee's Tango Orchestra, which is more in keeping with the music. In early 1917 Sweatman had formed a jazz band, and in April they recorded seven instrumental pieces on the Pathé-Frères label under the name Wilbur Sweatman and His Jass Band. Several other musicians, including Arthur Fields, Charles Prince, and the Frisco Jass Band added to the list of jazz records. Altogether, twenty-eight songs or pieces that used some variant of the word "jazz" in either the title or the group's name were recorded by the end of May 1917. Except for Sweatman and band, all the musicians mentioned above were white.

By far the most influential jazz event in 1917 was the Original Dixieland Jass Band's recording of "Dixie Jass Band One-Step" and "Livery Stable Blues," for RCA Victor. It may not have been the first jazz recording, as has been claimed, but its success and impact eclipsed all others. Some estimates have the ODJB topping one million in sales, a staggering number for 1917.

The ODJB consisted of five white men originally from New Orleans: Nick LaRocca, trumpet, Larry Shields, clarinet, Eddie Edwards, trombone, Henry Ragas, piano, and Tony Sbarbaro, drums. The group began in New Orleans as a band led by drummer Johnny Stein, LaRocca later joining to replace the original cornetist Frank Christian. A visiting Chicago café owner, Harry James (not the later trumpet player), heard them and contracted them to appear in Chicago. They created a sensation. According to legend, their music was described as "jass" for the first time when a somewhat inebriated customer stood on the table and yelled, "Jass it up, boys." James quickly realized the potential of that evening. He promised the inebriate all the free liquor he wanted if he would repeat the stunt regularly, and the next day the marquee read "Stein's Dixie Jass Band."

Within three months, the four players left Stein over a salary dispute, sent for Sbarbaro to replace Stein as drummer, and formed the ODJB. They soon got their big break. Al Jolson was in town, heard them, and recommended them to his agent Max Hart, who signed them to the Reisenweber Restaurant in New York City.

They were originally billed simply as "The Jasz Band," but by February 1917 they were advertised as the "Original Dixieland Jazz Band." In the meantime, they had a chance to record. They first went to Columbia Recording Co., which turned them down partly because the limits of the acoustic recording process could not capture the loud, raucous music successfully. On February 26, 1917, Columbia's archrival RCA Victor decided to try. After much testing, the sound engineers solved the technical problems and recorded them. The cover of the Victor catalogue for March 17, 1917, featured a photograph of "The Original Dixieland Jass Band," with the explanation "Spell it Jass, Jas, Jaz or Jazz—nothing can spoil a Jass band," and a curious bit of history: "Some say the Jass band originated in Chicago. Chicago says it comes from San Francisco—San Francisco being way across the continent."

San Francisco?! Probably the writer had in mind Bert Kelly, a white banjo-player-band-leader-speakeasy-owner from Seattle who began his career in San Francisco, then moved to Chicago in 1914. He claimed to have first used the word in 1915 to advertise his band, "Bert Kelly's Jazz Band." One night the band was booked for a party for several motion picture stars. Richard Travers, a well-known silent-film actor, filmed the band and added a caption reading "The Originators of Jazz." Even though the band could only be seen and not heard, and even though the film's impact remains unknown, Walter J. Kingsley, in the *New York Sun* in 1919, wrote, "that party really started the country-wide vogue for jazz music." Kingsley's article also quotes Kelly attesting that the success of his band at one of Harry James's clubs convinced James to seek a New Orleans jazz band. How much these unverified claims stemmed from the fact that both bands and bandleaders were white is an unknown, as is the extent the ODJB's recording was hailed as groundbreaking for the same reason. Given the time, however, it is hard to imagine that the racial element was not a factor.

For anyone in the record business, *The Talking Machine World* was the industry standard trade journal. It kept anyone making or selling records or equipment informed of the latest news and information: new machines, recent patents (of which there were many), and soon to be released recordings. The magazine came out the fifteenth of each month, with a lengthy, detailed list of new recordings. Since 1905, when the magazine began, opera excerpts, popular tunes, Hawaiian songs, Broadway numbers, symphonies, rags had all been present. Jazz was largely absent—until April 15, 1917. In that issue, the ODJB's first recording, as well as recordings by Sweatman and His Jass Band, Collins and Harlan, Fields, and O'Connor, were all listed.

What happened to suddenly ignite record companies to pay such attention to a type of music that they had hitherto ignored? It's implausible that all the jazz activity was a reaction to Victor's sound engineers, and there were no major new technological developments; they still used the same methods that had developed in the 1890s. The United States entered World War I on April 17, 1917, two days after the April issue of the journal, and there seems to be no connection. Probably the best answer is a simple one: jazz had invaded New York, and that was where the recording studios were.

The first attempt to record New Orleans–style jazz in New York occurred when the Original Creole Orchestra, sometime called the Creole Ragtime Band, appeared in 1915. The band was led by bassist Bill Johnson, but cornetist Freddie Keppard was considered the musical powerhouse driving the ensemble. RCA Victor wanted to record them, but no recordings emerged. Several stories why have circulated: Keppard did not want anyone to steal his licks, or financial terms could not be agreed upon. Purportedly, Keppard was offered twenty-five dollars and responded, "Twenty-five dollars? I drink that much gin in a day!" Or Keppard insisted that he be paid what Enrico Caruso, RCA's biggest star, received. Another rumor holds that they actually did record, but RCA considered the band too "hot" for their catalogue.

Whatever happened, the Original Creole Orchestra left New York to continue touring the vaudeville circuit, and Keppard was not captured on record until the mid-1920s. Like Keppard, Wilbur Sweatman had made New York his home base, but he too continued on the vaudeville circuit. Considered a clarinetist without peer, in 1911 he decided to move from the vaudeville pit to the vaudeville stage. For a Black man at the time this was a bold move. For a Black man to think he could win a vaudeville audience as a solo act with just his clarinet seemed preposterous. For a Black man to refuse to blacken his face or dress like he belonged on a plantation, this was a guarantee of failure. Sweatman appeared onstage as himself in formal clothes. His mastery of many musical styles from the hottest rags to the slowest soulful songs, his ability to switch to the bass clarinet, and finally to climax his act by playing Ethelbert Nevin's song "The Rosary" on two, then three clarinets simultaneously, made him a highly successful vaudeville performer. In December 1914 the *New York Age* reviewed his appearance on a bill at the Lafayette Theater in Harlem: "Wilbur Sweatman, clarionetist, . . . is in a class by himself and has one of the best singles in vaudeville." The strength of Sweatman's virtuosic fame on the vaudeville circuit had led the Emerson Phonograph Company to invite him to record in December 1916.

The arrival of the ODJB in New York on January 15, 1917, did much to ignite white interest in jazz, as the Reisenweber's 400 Room catered to the upper classes, thus placing jazz in front of elite New York society. At first the elites were bewildered;

this was not a smooth orchestra of violins playing sedate dance music, nor the twang of Hawaiian music, which was popular at the time. It seemed a full frontal assault on their aesthetic senses. Most listeners were frozen, as if in shock; one customer started a chant, "Send those farmers back to the country." The manager then announced, "This music is for dancing," and a few brave souls took to the floor; gradually more and more as the rhythm took hold, creating an intoxicating excitement they had not known before. Within a few weeks Reisenweber's was so popular that the club raised the band's salary to $1,000 a week, an unprecedented amount for the time.

Record companies quickly realized the bonanza that jazz records brought, and many recordings followed. These recordings in the late teens did more to justify F. Scott Fitzgerald's characterization of 1920s as "the Jazz Age" than any number of live performances. Jazz itself was a product of technology; it was the first music to achieve widespread popularity that depended on the phonograph for its spread and preservation. No sheet music could adequately capture what happened on those records.

Yet in spite of New York's recording scene and its impact, Chicago remained the hotbed of live jazz throughout much of the '20s. Around 1917 many jazz musicians began to migrate there from New Orleans. The 1917 crackdown on Storyville was only one of the reasons. After World War I the Great Migration of African Americans from the South to Northern cities escalated, as they sought to escape the more rampant institutionalized racism and limited opportunities of the South. For in spite of its unique international flavor, New Orleans was still part of the South. Clarinetist Buster Bailey, who went to Chicago from Memphis, recalled, "At that time, everybody from New Orleans and many people east of the Mississippi and as far west as Arkansas were migrating North. The word was there was lots of money in Chicago." When he arrived, Bailey observed, "There were many of the New Orleans groups in Chicago then—King Oliver, Freddie

Keppard, Sidney Bechet, Preston Jackson, Jimmie Noone, Manuel Perez, et cetera—twenty or thirty of them."

For New Orleans musicians, Chicago was a logical destination. Prohibition following the ratification of the Eighteenth Amendment in 1919 gave rise to speakeasies and other illegal venues around the country. The Chicago crime syndicate of Johnny Torrio and his heir Al Capone saw to it that both speakeasies and brothels were available to the town's citizens. Earlier, many ragtime players had settled in Chicago, and a vibrant Black community had led to the creation of many cabarets and theaters run by Black managers for Black patrons. The African American population had grown from 14,271 in 1890 to 109,458 in 1920. In a city of 2,701,705, that still represented a small minority of the population, but as segregation was still the norm in the North, it was sufficient to allow African Americans to create, in essence, a city within a city.

The Black population of Chicago was centered in an area several blocks wide in the South Side, running from Twenty-Second Street to Fifty-First Street. For the community, South State Street was Broadway, Lenox Avenue, and Main Street combined. Around 1920 the musical and entertainment center occupied a strip between 3000 and 3600 South State Street. This area became known as the Stroll. Among the most important venues was the Elite No. 1 Club, soon to be followed by the Elite No. 2, both owned by the Black entrepreneur Henry "Teenan" Jones, who was considered the leader of the cabaret scene on South Side. Another was Dreamland, originally opened in 1914, later reopened in 1917. There was also the Pekin Inn, the Deluxe Café, and the Café di Champion, founded by the heavyweight boxing champion Jack Johnson.

In these cabarets Black and Creole musicians found regular work. Most arrived with the great migration after 1917, but Jelly Roll Morton and some others were there as early as 1914. The Chicago *Defender*, a Black newspaper, described pianist

W. Benton Overstreet's music as "jass" on September 30, 1916. Overstreet was performing with Estella Harris, who had been labeled as a "Coon Shouter" and a "Rag Shouter," typical terms used for Black female singers at the time.

The large number of young, single Black men and women who migrated to Chicago created a strong demand for places of interaction and entertainment. Since African Americans were shut out of the larger ballrooms and other white establishments on the North Side, or at the least discouraged by the proprietors, the clubs and cabarets along the Stroll had a built-in clientele. This promised steady work and decent pay for Black musicians. The racial makeup of the audiences varied. Although no formal racial prohibition existed, some clubs were de facto strictly for African Americans; in all, most customers were Black, although as word spread of this new, exciting music on the Stroll, more and more whites ventured to the South Side to hear it. There were no clubs such as the later Cotton Club in New York that featured Black performers but catered strictly to white audiences, at least through the 1920s. The Chicago musicians were happy to see whites in the club, as that usually meant larger tips.

As prohibition took hold in the United States, Torrio and Capone saw to it that Chicago was well supplied with alcohol. By 1924 they and other members of the underworld had fifteen breweries operating, and as many as 20,000 saloons stretched across the city. William Hale "Big Bill" Thompson, who was elected mayor in 1919, turned a blind eye to establishments serving alcohol as long as they were not too flagrant in their disregard of the law. The term "speakeasy," as the clubs were called, had originated in dry states in the 1880s; it meant "speak softly when ordering." By the 1920s its meaning perfectly fit the Chicago scene.

The Great Migration, prohibition, and the tacit understanding between the gangsters and the mayor created an ideal situation for the South Side clubs to flourish. The northern migration made the many clubs and cabarets possible, the gangsters made alcohol available, and prohibition combined with the strict geographical segregation of the city made visiting the South Side clubs just dangerous enough for whites to find it appealing. Thus, by the early twenties jazz was no longer an ethnic niche, as word of it had begun to spread throughout the city.

The most important South Side club was the Dreamland Café. It was purchased in 1917 by William Bottoms, an African American entrepreneur who also had part ownership in the Deluxe Café and the Royal Gardens Café. Bottoms converted it into a café and cabaret, refurbished it at considerable expense, and began to bring in top-line vaudeville acts.

For residents of the South Side, having a Black owner such as Bottoms was important. Blacks were fully aware of "the rotten and immoral conditions right under their nose" that existed in some of the white-owned clubs, where, according to the weekly Chicago *Broad Ax*, "shooting affairs and the ending of men's lives are as common as drinking down a big glass of old Kentucky redeye." They also resented white owners getting rich from "relieving or robbing them" of money needed to support their families. Bottoms guaranteed that his place would not allow rowdiness and generally unsavory conduct. "Dreamland is one place that will demand a grade of behavior by all which will make it a safe place to bring wife, mother, sister or daughter."

In addition to providing an elegant, indeed opulent well-run club, with such features as a glass dance floor illuminated by 3,000 watts of electric bulbs beneath it, Bottoms was recognized as having the best jazz bands in Chicago. In September 1918 the *Broad Ax* referred to the musicians as "the best rag time band in Chicago." The band was led by clarinetist Lawrence Duhé, although its personnel changed several times, as was common for club bands then.

In 1917–18 Duhé added a teenage piano phenomenon, Lil Hardin, who has become well known, as she later married Louis

Armstrong. She was an outstanding jazz pianist, and not only played in several bands, but later in the twenties led her own band. She was not the only Black woman, however, to succeed as a jazz instrumentalist in the 1920s. While most bandleaders and members were male, and most women held the more traditional role of singer, several women carved successful instrumental careers. The most important were Cora "Lovie" Austin and Mary Lou Williams. Austin was a pianist, composer, arranger, and leader of her own band, the Blues Serenaders, which at times included Kid Ory, trombone, and Johnny Dodds, clarinet. She also led the house band for Paramount Records and recorded as pianist with many blues singers, including Ma Rainey, Alberta Hunter, and Ethel Waters. Among her compositions was "Down Hearted Blues," one of Bessie Smith's hits.

Mary Lou Williams had the longest, most successful career of all female jazz musicians to emerge in the 1920s, although her most important work occurred after that decade. A child piano phenomenon in Pittsburgh, she had paying gigs for dances and other occasions, including an undertaker's parlor while still a preteen. In 1922, when she was twelve years old, she had the opportunity to tour briefly with the vaudeville show *Hits and Bits*. Two years later she returned to the group until it suddenly disbanded. By then she had partnered with saxophonist John Williams (whom she later married), and then toured with other vaudeville groups, taking them to Chicago and Harlem, where she heard and was heard by many of the most important figures in jazz, including Armstrong, Ellington, and Morton. By 1930 Williams was composing, arranging, and recording, both for Andy Kirk's band, which included John Williams, and as a solo pianist. She was twenty years old.

Other Black women of 1920s jazz include Sweet Emma Barrett and Billie Pierce on piano and Dolly Jones on trumpet. Barrett's career unfolded in New Orleans, where she played with Oscar Celestin's Original Tuxedo Jazz Orchestra and from 1928 with Bebe Ridgeley's Tuxedo Jazz Orchestra. She later became well known as one of the original members of the Preservation Hall Jazz Band. Billie Pierce, née Wilhelmina Madison Goodson, accompanied several blues singers, including Ida Cox and, briefly, Bessie Smith as early as 1922, when she was fifteen. By 1930 she was leading a small band in New Orleans, and her work continued there into the 1970s. Dolly Jones, whose mother Diyaw was also a trumpet player, was part of the family band that performed with Josephine Baker in 1919. After forming the trio Three Classy Misses in Kansas City, she toured with Ma Rainey, Ida Cox, and later in Lil Hardin Armstrong's Harlem Harlicans. She is considered the first female trumpet player to record, with Albert Wynn's Gut Bucket Five in 1926.

Duhé had added several important male musicians to his band, including Sidney Bechet, considered one of the great clarinet and soprano sax players of early jazz, and trumpet player Joseph (King) Oliver, who had been in Kid Ory's band in New Orleans. By October 4, 1919, Oliver had taken over the band; the *Chicago Whip* referred to Duhé's band as "the New Orleans jazz band led by Mr. Joseph Oliver." In 1921, when they were in San Francisco, the band became King Oliver's Creole Band. They returned to Chicago in 1922, where Oliver asked a hot young cornetist in New Orleans, Louis Armstrong, to join him. It was an unusual move, as New Orleans jazz bands seldom had two cornetists. Most likely Oliver was already experiencing pyorrhea, a periodontal disease that in a few years would end his career completely, and he needed help carrying the cornet part.

The addition of Armstrong to Oliver's band brought the most important jazz musician of the 1920s to Chicago. Armstrong was thrilled. He had grown close to Oliver in New Orleans and looked upon him as a father figure, even referring to him as "Papa Joe." When Armstrong's friends urged him to stay in New Orleans, Armstrong responded, "Joe Oliver is my idol; I have loved him all my life."

All was not smooth, however. It was Oliver's band, and Oliver did not like to be upstaged. Armstrong had a sound so large that when acoustic recordings were made, he had to stand some fifteen feet behind the band to balance the recording. His improvisational ability was also maturing. He was by all accounts the better cornet player, and Oliver almost certainly knew it. He told Lil Hardin so. He also told her, "As long as I keep him with me, he won't be able to get ahead of me." He made sure that Armstrong knew he was second cornet, and limited Armstrong's solos.

After Armstrong had won a couple of "cutting contests," Oliver began to give him more improvisatory freedom. Cutting contests were common in jazz then. Two soloists would square off against one another, alternately playing solos in front of a crowd. One day in the fall of 1922, Johnny Dunn, a trumpet player with a considerable reputation, came into Lincoln Gardens, walked up to Armstrong, and said, "Boy! Give me that horn. You don't know how to do." Oliver, visibly angry, told Armstrong, "Go get him." Clarinetist Barney Biggard recalled, "Louis blew like the devil. Blew him out of that place." Literally! After Armstrong's solo, Dunn was nowhere to be found. Shortly after that, Freddie Keppard came in to the Lincoln Club without his instrument and stood beside the bandstand, listening. Finally, he went to Armstrong, and said, "Boy, let me have your trumpet." Lil Hardin then describes what happened: "Freddie, he blew—oh, he blew and he blew and he blew and then the people gave him a nice hand. Then he handed the trumpet back to Louis. And I said, 'Now get him, get him!' Oh, never in my life have I heard such trumpet playing! . . . Boy, he blew and people started standing on top of tables and chairs screaming. He [Freddie] eased out real slowly."

In 1923 the group, which now included Johnny Dodds on clarinet, made some important jazz recordings for several different labels. Except for an earlier recording made by Kid Ory's band in Los Angeles in 1921, these were the first records cut by a Black New Orleans band. Because Ory's recordings were made on an obscure California label named Nordskog Records and distributed only by Ory at his live dates, few have survived. Instead, Oliver's recordings have come to define the early New Orleans jazz sound.

The first recordings were by a rather minor label, Gennett, in Richmond, Indiana, which had an unusual history. In 1915 Henry Gennett, owner of the Starr Piano Company, expanded to manufacturing phonographs. To entice customers into his stores, he started Gennett Records and sought to record any act that had wide appeal. A jazz ensemble such as King Oliver's clearly had the draw, but it's hard to imagine that the band would have been willing to make the five-hour train ride from Chicago to Richmond, Indiana, had they known that Gennett was also the unofficial recording company for the Indiana Ku Klux Klan, and that many employees were active members of the Klan. At the time, Indiana was reputed to have more Klan members than any other state.

Klan literature was typically in public view at the studio, but whether it was present when the Oliver band arrived is not reported. It was another complex racial situation Black musicians had to negotiate—having traveled five hours to get there, wanting to be paid, wanting to make a recording, should they stay? Did they go knowing the Klan connection? They did have allies at the studio: Henry Gennett himself was not a member of the Klan, although clearly he did not disapprove of the Klan itself; the chief recording engineer, Ezra Wickemeyer, had refused to record Klan material. In spite of this situation, Gennett managed to record many of the best-known Black musicians of the time, as well as many white jazz players. Nevertheless, Richmond, Indiana was not a welcoming place for African Americans, and to travel there had to be a calculated risk.

Oliver decided to take the risk, and posterity has benefited.

With an all-star cast and a style defined by improvised polyphony, the band is remarkably tight in these recordings. "Dippermouth Blues" is typical of the style. The title itself a reference to Louis Armstrong, who early in his career was nicknamed "Dippermouth." On this recording, however, Oliver takes the cornet solo with his wa-wa mute. In fast blues time, the piece begins with a homophonic introduction, then a New Orleans–style polyphonic, improvisatory tutti section in a twelve-bar blues pattern, followed by a clarinet solo by Johnny Dodds over a stop-time 1 2 3—| 1 2 3—| pattern. Dodds stands out on this recording. Another full ensemble chorus, Oliver's solo, and a final tutti follow, with an abrupt ending, something common on recordings at the time. The rhythm throughout features four equal beats to the measure, characteristic of New Orleans jazz, except for the stop time, more typical of Chicago. The drummer is heard mostly on woodblocks, probably a concession to the difficulty of picking up drums, especially the bass drum, with acoustic recording techniques.

The band's success with the Gennett discs and at the Lincoln Gardens, and an opportunity to play a set at the Music Trades Convention at the most prestigious hotel in Chicago, the Drake, led to further recordings on some of the largest labels, including OKeh, Paramount, and Columbia, as well as a return session at Gennett. The *Chicago Defender* bragged, "Why they are the ones that put jazz on the map."

Throughout the recording sessions and subsequent live performances, more and more attention was focused upon the second trumpet player, even though the time constraints of 78 rpm records had truncated his solos. Armstrong was developing his own following, and Lil was taking notice. Their relationship had already blossomed into a romance, and Lil, though not yet Louis, believed it was time for him to go out on his own.

Having grown up in extreme poverty in a rough section of New Orleans, Armstrong was unsure of himself. He was born to Mary (Mayann) Albert Armstrong, a fifteen-year-old Black woman, whose husband deserted her soon after she gave birth. When Louis was about seven years old he got a job helping Morris and Alex Karnoffsky, peddlers who pushed a junk wagon around town. The brothers were Lithuanian Jews who, though impoverished, impressed Armstrong with their industriousness and determination, in spite of racial prejudice directed against them.

Part of the job was delivering coal in Storyville, where Black kids were strictly forbidden. Policemen were known to be rough on Blacks, but they left him alone because he was with the Karnoffskys. That was a lesson Armstrong held the rest of his life, and it speaks to one strategy many Blacks, especially in the South, had to deploy at the time. Later when he was about to head to Chicago, Slippers, a bouncer at a club in which Armstrong performed, summarized it: "When you go up North be sure and get yourself a white man that will put his hand on your shoulder and say, 'This is my n****r.'" Armstrong later explained, "If you didn't have a white captain to back you in the old days . . . you was just a damn sad n****r." To paraphrase his further explanation, if, for instance, you got in jail and a white man vouched for you, you would be released; if not, "yonder comes the chain gang." Armstrong experienced that directly when still a teenager in New Orleans. The police raided Henry Matranga's honky-tonk, looking for a Black robber. Seeing Armstrong, who played there, they took him to the Orleans Parish Prison—any Black man would do. After several days in the foul, dangerous conditions, Armstrong was suddenly released. Matranga, part of one of the largest Mafia families in New Orleans, had used his influence to secure his freedom. This pattern in the South is of course just one step above slavery, a clear continuation of the paternalism that pervaded the institution of slavery, and a sharp defining point between the races that slavery had not ended. Armstrong, for all his accomplishments and success, never fully divested himself of this mindset, even though Lil Hardin worked hard to counter it.

Working for the Karnoffskys gave Armstrong arguably the most important opportunity in his life. They wanted him to do something to attract attention, and he decided to buy a tin horn to blow. Even though it was just a dime-store novelty item, costing literally ten cents, he soon discovered he could make music with it, playing popular tunes, attracting amazed crowds to the delight of his employers. The Karnoffskys were sufficiently impressed that when Armstrong saw a cornet in a pawn shop, they helped him acquire it.

With no instruction, Armstrong could soon play many popular tunes, but his life took another downward turn. A New Orleans custom had been for adults to fire rifles and pistols into the air on New Year's Eve. Armstrong surreptitiously borrowed his stepfather's .38 revolver and walked along Rampart Street firing it. He was soon arrested for firing a gun in a public place and sentenced to the Colored Waifs Reform School. Although the school was strict, even harsh, Armstrong received his first systematic instruction on the cornet, eventually becoming the student leader of the brass band. He remained there for three years.

After his release, Armstrong began to find work in clubs and honky-tonks, and to attract the attention of other musicians. Joe Oliver heard him and became a mentor; he also met Kid Ory, who invited Armstrong to join his band when Oliver left for Chicago. When Oliver invited Armstrong to come to Chicago, he was hesitant to leave, but he couldn't resist Oliver's call. Armstrong also had another reason to leave: he was in a disastrous marriage with Daisy Parker, one of the prostitutes of Storyville, who was known to wield a knife or a razor, not uncommon accoutrements among Storyville women. Louis and Daisy fought constantly, and she frequently threatened him with the razor. He was never certain she would not use it. A job in Chicago might be a means to get away from her. Only after he had been in Chicago more than a year did he file for divorce, in Illinois. There is no record of Daisy contesting it.

Armstrong stayed with Oliver until June 1924, when Lil finally convinced him to turn in his notice. Soon he received an offer from Fletcher Henderson in New York. Henderson's band could not have been more different from Oliver's. Although Henderson and his musicians were Black, the band catered to white society. It was not a hot band, but one that played arranged music which, if perhaps tamer, was more tightly organized, and on the surface more sophisticated. The band performed in venues such as the Club Alabam and the Roseland Ballroom in midtown Manhattan—that is, in white venues. The Roseland advertised itself as "The Home of Refined Dancing," and the manager of the Roseland was well aware of the difference between a dance orchestra and a jazz band. When he advertised for the job that Henderson got, he stated that he wanted "two high-grade Dance Orchestras . . . Jazz bands will not be considered."

Henderson was from Cuthbert, Georgia, from an established Black middle-class family. He graduated from Atlanta University in 1920 with a degree in chemistry, and migrated to New York, intending to study chemistry. He quickly realized that racial prejudice would make a science career difficult, and turned to song plugging for the Pace and Handy Music Company. This led to occasional gigs with orchestras, and when in 1920 Harry Pace formed Black Swan Records, the first Black-owned recording company, Henderson became the musical director and the in-house pianist for recordings of many blues singers. The Fletcher Henderson Orchestra emerged from his role organizing ensembles for recordings.

Henderson was able to attract some of the best sidemen in New York, in particular musicians who could both read and improvise. When his band performed in midtown, he was insistent that its members were clean-shaven and wore tuxedos, with shoes shined. The appearance of the band, their demeanor, and the very sight of music stands sent an explicit message that this band was closer to Paul Whiteman's orchestra than Joe Oliver's or Clarence Williams's Jazz Kings. In 1942 Hugues Panassié dubbed Henderson's band the "Paul Whiteman of the race."

Paul Whiteman was one of many white musicians who adopted jazz for their own purposes. Born in 1890, he grew up in Denver, Colorado, studying classical violin and viola. By 1907 he was playing viola in the Denver Symphony, and by 1915 he had moved to San Francisco and secured a seat in the San Francisco Symphony Orchestra. In San Francisco he also heard jazz for the first time, commenting, "It hit me hard." On his first experience, "My whole body began to sit up and take notice. It was like coming out of blackness into bright light." After a stint leading a Navy band during World War I, he formed a dance band playing in San Francisco, and then Los Angeles. His exposure there led to a contract at the Ambassador Hotel in Atlantic City, New Jersey. Atlantic City was booming, and the Ambassador was its largest and most prestigious hotel. An RCA Victor recording executive heard the band in June 1920 and offered a recording contract. The first record, "Whispering," with "Mr. Sandman" on the reverse, became an instant hit. The many hit records that followed did more to solidify and expand Whiteman's reputation than any local appearances.

Whiteman was never a virtuoso jazz player, but he excelled at organization. He hired excellent sidemen and treated them well. He often had multiple bands up and down the East Coast. In that sense he might be called the first band franchiser, although the different ensembles were careful to claim a close connection with Whiteman. Whiteman was also a showman on the podium and, especially, a master at publicity.

Whiteman expanded the typical dance orchestra of trumpet, clarinet, trombone, and rhythm section by adding saxophones and strings. Instrumentation varied depending on the gig, but photographs from the early 1920s show as many as six saxophones and eight violins, in addition to trumpets, trombone, French horns, a harp, and the rhythm section. Mario Perry, one of the violinists, also played accordion and was sometimes featured on the instrument. At first Whiteman advertised his ensemble as a dance orchestra, not a jazz band, and his early recorded numbers were labeled "fox-trots." A fox-trot was not one of the turn-of-the-century animal dances such as the turkey trot, but rather a moderate-tempo two-step invented by Harry Fox in 1914. The name of the dance became almost a generic designation for dance records, excepting those featuring the triple-meter waltz, for the next thirty years.

Whiteman's vision represented one of the two extremes of jazz, symphonic jazz. French composer Darius Milhaud's 1922 work *La création du monde* did something similar. But Milhaud was clearly borrowing a culture foreign to him in the same manner that many nineteenth-century composers had used folk and exotic elements, while Whiteman considered his bands to be in the mainstream of American jazz. Whiteman was criticized for "trying to make a lady out of jazz."

At the other extreme was Joe Oliver's band, with its polyphonic, improvisational hot sound. For many throughout the country, that sound was exemplified by the Original Dixieland Jazz Band, with their blockbuster 1917 hits. Although white, the ODJB was from New Orleans, and they were playing what to them was their natural style. Even Armstrong was impressed with them. Inflections born of Black speech and African roots were heard or imagined to be heard in their music, but they had not absorbed them from the cradle; such inflections were but some of many musical influences they had experienced. Doors and opportunities were open to them that were not available to Blacks, and they had taken advantage of the privileged position their race provided to play in many parts of New Orleans.

Clearly, African Americans had an irrefutable claim to jazz; it was primarily the Black American experience that gave birth to jazz. Yet in the convoluted cultural definitions of race, and in 1920s attitudes toward race, many questions swirl: Who owned jazz; who had a right to play jazz; who produced the "real" jazz; and what was "false jazz," if it existed? I will not attempt a definitive answer to those questions, if any is even possible, but the early 1920s provide a telling if temporally limited set of circumstances to at least address these issues. In 1924, in a remarkable convergence, three seemingly disparate cultural and racial lines came together to form the sides of an unlikely triangle: Fletcher Henderson, with his African American orchestra playing so-called commercial jazz; Paul Whiteman, with his white orchestra playing symphonic jazz; and Louis Armstrong, when he joined Fletcher Henderson's orchestra in October 1924. Each connected to the others metaphorically if not physically at the angles. The hottest trumpeter in the world was now ensconced in an ensemble believed to be a dance orchestra, not a jazz band. A Black band was likened to a white band whose jazz credentials have been debated. Finally, all of the three principals, each coming from a different social stratum, at one time or another had been dubbed the "King of Jazz."

In a country still rigidly segregated as the United States was in the 1920s, in which the Ku Klux Klan was at its height, where Jim Crow laws were rigidly enforced—*de jure* in some parts of the country, *de facto* in others—racial tensions, stereotyping, and conflicts were omnipresent. A band such as Fletcher Henderson's occupied an ambivalent place. Just like Armstrong, Oliver, and Ory, the musicians were interested in earning a living, but clearly the music they played mattered to them. Yet how different were they from Bach or Haydn in providing what their patrons wanted to hear? Until he became a star, Armstrong was constantly calculating how best to maximize his income. Even though he was a hot player, even though his reading skills were limited, Armstrong readily accepted the job with Henderson. There were factors other than money influencing his decision. The Black bandleader Sam Wooding was supposedly willing to offer Armstrong $100 a week, compared to Henderson's $55, although whether the offer was actually made is questionable; but $100 was still far below what the best white players earned. Whiteman paid a minimum of $175 per week, plus $50 per side for each recording. Armstrong, or Lil Hardin at least, was likely thinking long term and about issues other than salary. For Hardin, the job with Henderson distanced Armstrong from Oliver; for Armstrong, Henderson offered a chance to break into the New York market and the opportunity to play in the most prestigious Black band in the country.

Henderson's middle-class background permeated his musical activities. When at Black Swan Records he preferred concert musicians. He refused to sign Bessie Smith when she auditioned because her style was too coarse. Fully aligned with the aesthetic and political beliefs of Harry Pace, the founder of the company, who believed in the power of "music of the better sort," Henderson sought and recorded several African American artists, including Revella Hughes, a soprano who appeared on Broadway; C. Carroll Clark, baritone, who recorded art songs, and Antoinette Garnes, soprano, who recorded Verdi arias and later taught voice at Wilberforce University and Hampton Institute. These and other singers also recorded spirituals, a genre favored by W. E. B. Du Bois, who included snippets of them in musical notation at the beginning of each chapter of his book *The Souls of Black Folk.* To Du Bois, the spiritual, or "sorrow song," "stands . . . as the most beautiful expression of human experience born this side the seas," and "remains as the singular spiritual heritage of the nation and the greatest gift of the Negro people."

Henderson was caught in the middle. He sought refinement and uplift but was defined by his skin. He was the living embodiment of Du Bois's mantra: Blacks should build their own independent economic foundation. This frequently translated to create their own business, and at the same time demonstrate they were "thinkers, strivers, doers, and were cultivated." In doing so, they could achieve assimilation, one of Du Bois's goals. At Pace and Handy and at Black Swan, Henderson was directly influenced by Du Bois, who personally supported the record label, as he considered it an exemplar of his philosophy.

Whatever Henderson's band's style, it was readily accepted in the Black community. Armstrong joined in part because he knew it was prestigious. Duke Ellington referred to it as "the greatest dance band anyone ever heard," and modeled his band on Henderson's.

That Henderson could compete successfully with Whiteman, at least break into midtown venues, was a point of pride for Harlem, and apparently for Armstrong as well. Henderson knew his audience and provided what they wanted. He never turned his back on jazz, however; otherwise Armstrong would not have been in his orchestra. While Armstrong returned to Chicago in less than a year, the list of other top jazz players who were in Henderson's band supports the assertion that Henderson's gigs were "the elite level of jobs for Black musicians." In addition to Armstrong, the band included Coleman Hawkins, Buster Bailey, and Don Redman. Henderson was doing exactly what he had done all his life: living on the edge of two worlds, the place where many middle-class African Americans found themselves in the early twentieth century. His band was that blend.

Hindsight has claimed Henderson's band as the future of jazz. The combination of a large ensemble—relative to New Orleans–style groups—playing written arrangements with specified moments of improvised solos defines 1930s big band swing. It also defines both Henderson's and Whiteman's bands, although their emphasis was different. Henderson's band was closer to hot jazz than Whiteman's, as Henderson sought players like Armstrong and Coleman Hawkins. It also became the model for swing ensembles.

Benny Goodman's band is generally considered the most important hot big band of the 1930s, in no small part because of Fletcher Henderson's arrangements. Because of the Depression and Henderson's own style of leadership and financial management, he could not keep his band together in the early 1930s. Instead, through a fortuitous turn of events, he shifted his attention to arranging. Goodman asked him to arrange for a new radio show, *Let's Dance.* Soon Henderson became Goodman's preferred arranger. The combination of Goodman and Henderson is culturally telling: in part because of Henderson, the white bandleader Goodman made millions. Precisely what Henderson was paid throughout their years working together is not clear, but for Goodman and the *Let's Dance* show, the radio contract called for $37.50 per arrangement. While Henderson was able to revive his own band in 1936, he later observed about those years, "It was good money." Still, it was clearly not Benny Goodman–level money.

Whiteman had different aspirations. He had known the symphonic world from the inside, and after his band's success often kept a box at Carnegie Hall. As a member of white society, Whiteman understood how many looked down on jazz. He wanted to do more than "make a lady out of jazz." He wanted jazz to acquire some of the prestige of classical music. A few Black classical musicians such as Florence Price, William Grant Still, and Antoinette Garnes sought to make inroads into the classical world. For Black jazz players, however, even some who had classical training, classical music represented what was essentially a foreign culture. Their goals were more direct and more pragmatic: play what most deeply expressed their world and at the same time create an exciting type of music that the public would want.

To meet his goals, Whiteman began to refer to his music as

symphonic jazz. He was not the first to do use that expression. On December 23, 1920, the San Jose *Evening News* advertised a performance of the musical comedy *Marrying Mary*, with "Paul Ash, the Creator of The Symphonic Jazz." Leo Flanders's "Symphonic Jazz Orchestra" toured the West Coast with Kolb and Dill's comedy, *The High Cost of Living*. On February 8, 1923, the *Los Angeles Times* advertised "A complete concert of Symphonic Jazz" (unfortunately with no further information other than the location). Caroline E. MacGill, in the *North American Review*, November 1922, referred to the "latest revues, post-futurist art, [and] symphonic jazz." By 1924, the terms "symphonic" and "symphony" were commonly used in reference to large jazz ensembles, by Frank Silver, "McVickers Symphony Orchestra," Roy Ingraham, Erskine Tate, Vincent Lopez, and others. Most of the 1920s symphonic jazz orchestras were no closer to a standard symphony than the 157 "opera houses" in Iowa in 1888 were to opera ("opera house" in the nineteenth century being used to refer to any building that could provide a venue for some sort of stage entertainment). Rather, most were jazz bands, often enhanced with a few extra musicians to form a slightly larger ensemble. A common thread had most, but not all, associated with a theatrical or vaudevillian venue.

Whiteman, however, had a more expansive view of symphonic jazz. He viewed jazz through the nineteenth-century notion of progress, which allowed him to claim his jazz as superior to hot jazz. He wrote in 1926, "The soft jazz rhythms of the present day represent great progress from the crudities of ten years ago." One can hardly miss the racial implications of this statement. This is also a nineteenth-century classical music attitude, one that assumes a hierarchy of musical values. For over a century the symphony stood at the apex of a musical pyramid. Associating jazz with the symphony thus sent a musical as well as a racial message that was barely coded.

Whiteman's claim to the term rests mainly on one concert,

which has become historic. On February 12, 1924, he presented "An Experiment in Modern Music," at Aeolian Concert Hall, in New York City. The venue itself was a statement, as Aeolian Hall primarily hosted classical music, with many of the most important classical musicians of the day performing there. The concert was then repeated several times in New York, culminating in a Carnegie Hall concert on April 21, followed by a national tour.

The concert is now famous for the premier of George Gershwin's *Rhapsody in Blue* with Gershwin at the piano. Although the original poster advertising the event did not mention jazz, the program was, in essence, a history of the evolution of jazz, interspersed with other genres, such as Zez Confrey's "Three Little Oddities: Romanza, Impromptu, Novelette, or Ferde Grofé's "Russian Rose. It began with "1. True Form of Jazz," and featured the ODJB piece "Livery Stable Blues," the evolutionary story continuing with "3. "Contrast—Legitimate Scoring vs. Jazzing" and "7. Semi-symphonic Arrangement of Popular Melodies," eventually culminating in "10. George Gershwin." It closed with Elgar's *Pomp and Circumstance March*. The success of *Rhapsody in Blue* would lead Whiteman to adopt it as his theme song, performing it whenever possible. For him, it epitomized symphonic jazz.

Whiteman's concert created a challenge for the music critics. They were not used to writing about a jazz concert, and most had only their classical background as their frame of reference. For the first time, jazz was compared directly with classical music; given the writers, jazz fared better than expected. Lawrence Gilman, of the *Tribune*, had mixed feelings: "It seems to us that this music is only half alive. Its gorgeous vitality of rhythm and instrumental color is impaired by melodic and harmonic anemia of the most pernicious kind." He also considered Whiteman's orchestra "the conservative, reactionary elements in the music of today."

W. J. Henderson, writing in the *Herald*, held a much more

positive view. The concert eclipsed totally "all of the other kind of moderns—all save one." Henderson then envisioned Stravinsky shaking hands with Irving Berlin, Gershwin, and Whiteman, and shouting "(in Russian of course), 'Great is Rhythm! Great is dance! Great are wind instruments!' "

Olin Downes, music critic of the *New York Times*, was thoroughly impressed. He even delighted in "Livery Stable Blues," calling it "a gorgeous piece of impudence better in its unbuttoned jocosity and Rabelaisian laughter than other and more polite compositions that came later [in the program]." Downes concluded, "there was realization of the irresistible vitality and genuineness of much of the music heard on this occasion, as opposed to the pitiful sterility of the average composer."

From at least 1923, Whiteman had expanded his orchestra to approach symphonic proportions. In 1926, his "Concert Orchestra" had 27 players, including four violins, three violas, two cellos, a bassoon, and timpani, in addition to the usual winds. White critics began to extoll his accomplishments, in some cases precisely because he was white. Cultural critic Gilbert Seldes saw in Whiteman a hope for jazz; he contrasted the Negro's "desirable indifference to our set of conventions about emotional decency" with "civilization," and claimed that while many Black bands were good, none were as good as Whiteman's. Henry O. Osgood's book *So This Is Jazz*, ostensibly the first history of jazz, is more than anything a paean to Paul Whiteman. His photograph is on the frontispiece, and much of the book is either about Whiteman, musicians such as Whiteman's arranger and pianist, Ferde Grofé, or George Gershwin. Reading it, one comes away believing that jazz was a white invention. Missing is any reference to Louis Armstrong, Joe Oliver, Kid Ory, Johnny Dodds, Fletcher Henderson, Wilbur Sweatman—the list could go on. There is a chapter about "the concert repertoire of jazz," discussing classical composers such as Emerson Whithorne, John Alden Carpenter, and Leo Sowerby, but the reference to African

Americans in any context is limited. Vaudeville singers such as Bert Williams and Will Marion Cook and a few other Black performers are mentioned briefly. W. C. Handy is the notable Black exception, featured in the chapter "The Blooey Blues." Handy is also the lone African American accorded a photograph among the eleven white musicians.

While Whiteman was establishing his credentials, Louis Armstrong had returned to Chicago in late 1924. Hardin had formed her own band and found a home for it at the Dreamland Café. She wanted Armstrong to be part of it. She had seen to it that his contract with William Bottoms, the owner, assured him top billing, as well as more money. No longer would he sit as second or third trumpet, constrained by his position and the leaders of the orchestra. Here he could play unfettered. By now he had an established reputation that continued to grow, especially given the prestige of the Dreamland venue and his place in the band. Hardin did all she could to make a star out of him, including billing him as "The World's Greatest Trumpet Player," a title he was not yet comfortable with.

Even more important to his reputation and to the history of jazz was the opportunity to record with OKeh. They wanted to record a small New Orleans–style combo, and Armstrong put together a group from various musicians working at different clubs, naming them Louis Armstrong and His Hot Five. Armstrong was on trumpet, Hardin on piano, Johnny Dodds on Clarinet, Kid Ory on trombone, and Louis St. Cyr on banjo. It was strictly an ensemble for recording; they never performed regularly as a band. Brian Harker has spoken of these recordings as "redefining jazz and placing it on a new course, one more revolutionary and far-reaching than any subsequent upheavals in the music's history."

The Hot Five soon became the Hot Seven with the addition

of Pete Briggs on tuba and Johnny Dodds's younger brother "Baby" Dodds on drums. Dodds had been the drummer in Joe Oliver's band with Armstrong. The change in the band's percussion was driven partly by technology, as OKeh's switch to electronic recordings in 1926 allowed the company to capture a greater range in both dynamics and pitch; the deep slaps of the bass drum as well as the paradiddles and rim shots of the snare drum could now be heard.

In December 1925, Erskine Tate offered Armstrong a job playing in the Erskine Tate Little Symphony at the Vendome Theatre. In a later interview, Armstrong recalled, "I became so popular at the Dreamland that Erskine Tate came to hire me to join his symphony Orchestra. I like to have fainted." Erskine Tate's Little Symphony was a group of twelve to sixteen players—the typical 1920s jazz band supplemented by added saxophones and violins and cello. The Vendome was a movie theater, and the orchestra provided music for the silent films and performed between shows, playing some classics arranged for a jazz orchestra, as well as some hot jazz. When it wasn't performing in the movie pit, it was known as Erskine Tate's Jazz Syncopaters.

The Vendome Theatre, at 31st and State Streets, had all the sumptuousness and splendor of the largest movie palaces for white urban Americans. Seating 1,500, it had a domed thirty-foot ceiling, gilded plasterwork, crystal chandeliers, a large stage, and a mammoth organ. It opened in 1919 and quickly became a premier entertainment spot for Blacks. With their intermission features, the orchestra was as much a draw as the films. Armstrong was clearly a star attraction. At some point he would rise from the orchestra pit and climb onto the stage, where he had free rein to improvise on his trumpet, sing, and even indulge in comedy. Armstrong the musician, singer, and showman all emerge at the Vendome. His tenure in the orchestra notably contributed to Tate's success as well as his own reputation, for a movie house would draw many patrons that might not frequent clubs.

With Armstrong's work at the Vendome, the triangle of Armstrong, Henderson, and Whiteman became complete. Armstrong, the quintessence of hot jazz, was now playing in the jazz version of a symphony orchestra. Whiteman, meanwhile, had found his hot trumpet player in Bix Beiderbecke, who, while white, was the only musician in the late 1920s who could compete with Armstrong as the outstanding jazz trumpeter of the time. Their styles were quite different, however: Armstrong was noted for his powerful delivery, especially in the high range, and would create solos that grew organically, from the first motives. Beiderbecke, who had studied classical piano as well as trumpet and who listened to modern classical composers such as Stravinsky, Ravel, and Debussy, incorporated some of their innovations such as the whole-tone scale into his jazz. Although he had good tone, he did not have the power of Armstrong; he seldom ventured into the extreme high register, and in his solos, he added classical allusions to his jazz licks.

The musicologist Thomas Brothers hears in Armstrong what he terms the "fixed and variable model," which he traces back to sub-Saharan Africa. One instrument or group of instruments plays a steady repeating pattern. Other instruments ride on top of the steady rhythm, weaving in and out, creating patterns that at times coincide, at times clash with the fixed pattern. Such a situation is ideally suited to improvisation, that is, to jazz itself. Harmony and melody, particularly the tonal inflexions of blues, are part of this mix, but rhythm is especially important. According to Brothers, the fixed and variable model points to Armstrong's African roots, with one significant difference: rhythmic patterns in African drumming are quite complex, but burdened under the yoke of slavery, the model became simplified, down to the basic two- and four-beat patterns of early jazz. Under such circumstances, peeling off musical layers to determine how much jazz was African and how much was Western is not always possible. Yet even given the cauldron of acculturation, stylistic differences between Armstrong and Beiderbecke reveal their disparate racial and social backgrounds. Beiderbecke toys with the fixed rhythm by laying subtle passages around it, as if seeking to compromise it. His rhythm is Stravinsky turning beyond the strictures of Western's regular meter. Armstrong attacks the fixed rhythm head on; in doing so he acknowledges it, but his clashes are more driving and outspoken, as if seeking to break free of its restraints. His is the fire and fury of the oppressed, the slave seeking a new direction but not forgetting his past.

Meanwhile, Henderson continued to maintain a middle ground through the twenties, preparing for the flowering of swing in the 1930s, in which he would play such a large part. He was the base of the triangle, holding together the Armstrong and Whiteman-Beiderbecke sides.

Armstrong's gig at the Vendome ended in 1927, after which he, Earl Hines, and the drummer Zutty Singleton attempted to found their own club. With their lack of business experience, the venture was a financial disaster, and soon Armstrong was back with Clarence Dickerson's band at the Chicago Savoy.

By the mid-twenties, a complex of factors initiated a decline in club life and hence the music scene in South Side Chicago. Chicago's mayor, Big Bill Thompson, had been lenient with the clubs, giving them room to operate. In 1923, a prohibitionist Democrat, William Dever, defeated Thompson and began to close clubs. Most were able to adjust and reopen, even though the climate was not as favorable. More than the actual raids and closings, however, Dever's crusade had a dampening effect on patrons, especially white patrons who would visit the Stroll. In addition, several of the clubs got a reputation as being especially rough and dangerous, further keeping away North Side clientele.

Thompson was re-elected in 1927, but the decline in club revenues, and hence Chicago jazz, continued. Federal agents, whom Thompson could not control, had stepped up enforcement efforts, and federal judge Adam C. Cliffe had issued the "hip-flask" ruling, which held the club responsible even for liquor brought in by the customer. In addition, Vitaphone and Movietone, which supplied recorded sound for movie theaters, began to arrive in 1927, eventually throwing hundreds of musicians out of their jobs. Further, the mob began to acquire many of the clubs, creating an atmosphere of violent competition, which led to brawls and bombings. Radio, especially the emerging national and regional programs of the networks, often featured jazz or comparable musical entertainment. This further drained customers away from the clubs. All of this was well before the stock market crash eviscerated the club scene as well as the financial world.

As jazz musicians saw their income dwindle, Armstrong and others began to look elsewhere. New York especially was inviting. It was the largest city in the country, a thriving Black culture existed in Harlem, and most of both the radio and recording industries were headquartered there. The New York of the late teens and twenties was a somewhat stodgy town, led by Mayor John F. Hylan, a bland teetotaler and a product of Tammany Hall. Jimmy Walker, a flamboyant lover of nightlife, was elected mayor in 1926, and promptly ushered in a new era for the club scene. He was opposed to prohibition and did all he could to discourage enforcement of the Eighteenth Amendment. Speakeasies flourished, and as both recordings and radio became deeply embedded in American culture, New York was the place to be.

In 1929, Armstrong left for New York City for the second time. Now a star, he began to tailor his performances more to white audiences, including movie roles. Paul Whiteman's popularity peaked with the release of the 1930 film *King of Jazz*, only to decline throughout the 1930s, even though he remained active on radio. The jazz that Fletcher Henderson and Duke Ellington pioneered—a larger, tighter ensemble, consisting of group riffs or written arrangements with improvised solos interspersed—became the model for the 1930s. Ellington's and Henderson's careers, would, however, diverge. Henderson became most widely known as Benny Goodman's arranger, while Ellington's fame as an innovative orchestra leader, arranger, and composer was just beginning. With the Depression and the ending of prohibition in 1932, both the club scene and record sales were devastated. Radio remained, and primarily through it, the small improvisational ensembles of 1920s jazz gave way to 1930s big band swing.

CHAPTER 7

Blues, Hillbilly, and Crooners

Perry Bradford was a pianist, composer, vaudevillian, and producer from Atlanta, Georgia. He began working in minstrel shows throughout the country in 1906 when he was thirteen, and like many musicians he eventually gravitated to New York. Yet while other Black musicians were turning to jazz after World War I, Bradford was interested in blues. He would hang around the Colored Vaudeville Benevolent Association clubrooms on Lenox Avenue playing blues for hours, to the consternation and displeasure of fellow members, who saw no future in that music. It was too close to the rural South they had left behind. Yet he persisted.

In 1918 Bradford wrote and produced a revue, *The Maid of Harlem*, starring an established Black vaudevillian singer, Mamie Smith. The revue was one of the few in New York to feature blues. Smith, from Cincinnati, had begun as a dancer at age ten in a touring group, The Four Dancing Mitchells. After several years performing in other ensembles, she chose to remain in New York as a cabaret singer, where Bradford first heard her.

Taken by her voice, Bradford became convinced that she should be recorded. He went from record company to record company, trying to sell Mamie Smith and the blues. He persuaded Wilbur Sweatman to help; Sweatman went to Columbia, but was told, no thanks. Bradford went to Victor; they recorded her, but chose not to release. He returned to record producers, day after day. He argued strenuously: this was an untapped market, there were thousands of record buyers waiting to hear what she had to offer. No wonder Bradford's contemporaries at the Colored Vaudeville Benevolent Association had nicknamed him "the mule."

Bradford firmly believed that a strong Black market for blues existed. His persistence finally paid off with a new, independent label, OKeh. It was founded in 1918 by the German émigré Otto K. E. Heinemann (hence the company's name), who had been the American manager for the German Odeon Records. Heinemann, looking for a niche in a competitive field, had begun to make ethnic records for various European-American communities—German, Swedish, Czech, Yiddish, Polish. Possibly for that reason, Bradford was able to persuade Frederick W. Hager, the company's musical director, to try another ethnic market.

On February 14, 1920, Mamie Smith went into the OKeh recording studio to record "That Thing Called Love" and "You Can't Keep a Good Man Down," both written by Bradford. Backed up by the Regee Dance Orchestra, Smith's rendition is as much vaudeville as it is blues. The orchestral arrangement is full and lush, without any of the growls heard in instrumental blues, and Smith sings straight, with little melodic inflection. The song does not lend itself to the call and response type of 1920s blues number. Perhaps Hager, Smith, and Bradford were all hedging their bets, but it didn't matter. Even before the record was released in July 1920, the *Chicago Defender* heralded the upcoming event: "Now we have the pleasure of being able to say that they [the record industry] have recognized the fact that we are here for their service; the OKeh Phonograph Company has initiated the idea by engaging the handsome, popular and capable vocalist, Mamie Gardener Smith of 40 W. 135th Street, N.Y.C, and she has her first record, . . . apparently destined to be one of that great company's big hits."

The Black community responded, and sales far exceeded Hager's and Heinemann's expectations. As a consequence, Smith was back in the recording studio within a month. This time she recorded "Crazy Blues," in which she allows a blues inflection to emerge much more fully. She also had a Black band backing her, reflected in the record label's "Mamie Smith and Her Jazz Hounds." Later, personnel changes were made in the band, specifically putting Johnny Dunn on cornet and Bradford on piano. "Crazy Blues," also written by Bradford, was a reworking of his "Harlem Blues," which Smith had sung in *The Maid of Harlem*. The tune itself had been circulating in Black culture for years, originally "'an old bawdy song played in the sporting houses' titled 'Baby, Get That Towel Wet.'" The recording established female blues as an important genre of American popular music and created a rush by nearly every record company to release blues songs.

Original sales stunned even the OKeh executives. Within four weeks an employee noticed that 75,000 recordings had been shipped to Harlem. Heinemann and Hager assumed there was an error in the books. Their shipping director told them this was no mistake. Still dubious, they sent a salesman to Harlem, who reported back that yes, thousands were being sold in just that one part of New York. They then knew that the recording needle was doing more than cutting lateral grooves; it was shaking the ground of the industry, and it was also upending American culture. A new art form, which had lain in the shadows in Black life, had suddenly burst onto the wide plain of American popular music.

The industry's original reluctance to record Smith cannot be explained purely on the grounds of race, for the recording world had not ignored Black singers. In fact, the first major star of the burgeoning recording industry was Black. George W. Johnson recorded the song "The Coon Whistler" in mid-1890. Johnson, born in northern Virginia in 1846 probably as a slave, had migrated to New York, where Victor Emerson heard him singing and whistling on the streets. Emerson worked for the New Jersey Phonograph Company, and had persuaded its reluctant owners that the foundering company could be saved through coin-in-the-slot machines. He agreed to pay Johnson twenty cents for each song performance, or "round." Emerson suggested "The Coon Whistler," an old minstrel tune, even though it had racist lyrics. On that point, musicologist Tim Brooks has tried to explain, "When you were hungry and needed money to eat you sang what they wanted you to."

Because cylinders were not duplicable at the time, Johnson was put in the center of about six machines all with their horns pointed toward him. He sang his song; they changed cylinders and he sang it again. This went on all afternoon, and by the end he had earned four or five dollars for singing the same song over and over. This was good money for a street musician's afternoon work. Later he cut "The Laughing Song," which includes Johnson's hearty laugh aligned precisely to the harmony and rhythm of the music.

Johnson continued to record for Emerson, and was also recruited to sing both songs for the New York Phonograph Company. The New Jersey Phonograph Company did not object, possibly because each had its own territory. These two songs became so popular that they were put into the Broadway play *The Inspector,* with Johnson singing them. Johnson was also asked to record for Edison's North American Phonograph Company in 1891. We don't know what other songs Johnson recorded, but by the mid-1890s the *Edison Phonograph News* proclaimed that "the 'Laughing Song' by Geo. W. Johnson has had the largest sale of any phonograph record made, and next 'The Whistling Coon' by the same individual—and a colored individual too."

By 1897 Johnson was known coast to coast, thanks to the many exhibitors of the phonograph. Soon, however, his life supposedly took a dramatic turn, which also illustrates how historical misrepresentation can occur. According to Fred Gaisberg, the author of the 1942 book *The Music Goes Round*, Johnson became famous and very wealthy, only to have it all end in 1899. Gaisberg reported that he was tried for murdering his mistress by throwing her out the window of his apartment, and then hanged.

In his 2004 book *Blacks and the Birth of the Recording Industry*, Brooks unearthed the truth: Johnson did become well known but he was never rich, and he was tried, acquitted, and lived another fifteen years. The absurdity of the charge about his mistress is apparent if for no other reason than Johnson lived in a basement apartment. He did continue to record after the trial, but technology and competition made it increasingly difficult for him to earn a living.

Many other singers imitated him, and new recording methods allowed masters to be duplicated so that continual recording sessions were not necessary. He was never paid any royalties, only a small flat fee for his time in the studio, which became less and less. Johnson had been so thoroughly associated with "The Whistling Coon" and "The Laughing Song" that record companies showed little interest in broadening his repertoire. Soon his name disappeared from the catalogues, and in his last years he was all but forgotten. He died penniless in Harlem in 1914.

Other Black singers or groups recorded in the first twenty years of the industry, including the Fisk Jubilee Singers, the Kentucky Jubilee Singers, several male quartets, and entertainers including Bert Williams and George Walker, among many others. The "jubilee singers" recorded spirituals; most of the other performers were associated with the theater, some in minstrel shows. Once jazz caught on in 1917, a number of Black jazz musicians were recorded.

There was a large white market for Black spirituals and theatrical, vaudevillian, and especially minstrel-type songs. The record companies, however, considered women blues singers to have less racial crossover appeal. To record executives, blues seemed a genre specifically for Blacks, and they assumed that Blacks could not afford phonographs. This attitude was so prevalent that in 1916 the *Chicago Defender*, a Black newspaper with a national circulation, launched a campaign to persuade record companies to record more Black artists. They asked each family with a phonograph to send their name and address to the newspaper's office. The idea apparently came to naught, however, as there was no further mention of it in the newspaper.

Mamie Smith's "Crazy Blues" had an immense impact on both sides of the 1920s Black-white divide. Sales figures themselves suggested that the popularity of the blues went beyond an ethnic niche. Clearly, it wasn't just the Black community buying these records. To the historian, this speaks of a white America quickly taking to the genre. To the industry, it didn't matter, it meant sales.

Smith's success itself was a mark of pride for the Black world. One of their own was not only providing music for their culture, but placing into the mainstream a sound that came directly from Black experience and feelings. She was idolized: the "Queen of Syncopation and Jazz," "one of the outstanding sensations of the race," "The World's Sensation"; "the greatest jazz attraction that has ever been sent on tour"; "she has done more than any other record star, white or Black, to popularize the 'blues.'" She broke attendance records wherever she appeared. Smith herself stressed the ethnic source of the blues and its place in American music: "The typical blues song comes from the very heart of the colored race. . . . It is the foundation of American folk music more so than Indian or the plantation melodies."

OKeh's next step was to keep her busy recording as many songs as possible. Between August 1920 and December 1922 she cut at least fifty sides, counting only those that were released. In the meantime she became a superstar, drawing royalties estimated at over $100,000 and commanding up to $1,500 a week for appearances.

Smith lived a lavish life style as the first blues queen, setting a standard for the many later claimants to the throne. She appeared onstage in elaborate dress, bedecked in diamonds, sometimes in a gown of gold cloth, with a cape of ostrich plumes, which reportedly cost $3,000. Most blues singers emulated her, and as the many newspaper reports stressed, the sartorial splendor blues women displayed was an essential part of their appeal.

Although Smith dominated the blues market for the next two years, competition arose quickly. Through 1921 many blues singers were recorded, and while some such as Ethel Waters, Lucille Hegamin, and Alberta Hunter are still well known, many others have fallen into relative obscurity. But there were two singers in particular who rose to challenge Mamie Smith for her position as the crowned head of blues royalty: "Ma" Rainey and Bessie Smith.

"Ma" Rainey was the first. Born in Columbus, Georgia, as Gertrude Pridgett in 1882, she begin singing blues early in the new century. In 1904 she married a Black minstrel entertainer, William Rainey, who had performed under the moniker "Pa" Rainey. Soon they had a dual act, "Ma" and "Pa" Rainey. How she came to incorporate the blues of the Mississippi Delta into her act is not clear. In later years she claimed that in 1902 she heard a young girl singing a "strange and poignant" song different from anything the troupe had heard before. Taken with it, she incorporated the song into her act, and hence her blues performances began. Given the prevalence of blues in the rural South and her affinity with it, one can surmise she had heard something similar before, although to be sure, she did not live in the Mississippi Delta. In any event, she made blues her own, and may have been the first singer to incorporate blues into a minstrel show.

The Raineys worked with several of the top minstrel shows over the next decade, including the Rabbit Foot Minstrels and Tolliver's Circus and Musical Extravaganza. Before long her work eclipsed that of her partner, and she began to be the main draw not only for the team but for the troupe itself. She was soon billed as "Mother of the Blues" and acquired the title "Madame." One Paramount ad observed, "She is the first Blues singer ever elevated to the heights of 'Madame.'"

Information on Rainey for the period from 1917 to 1923 is sketchy. We know that William died on June 28, 1919, and that they had separated, probably around 1916. She formed her own band, was billed as Madam Gertrude Ma Rainey and Her Georgia Band, continued to perform, and apparently remarried, to someone not in show business. There is some mention of her in different southern cities but little else of her whereabouts. One account holds she spent some time in Mexico in 1921.

In some ways this silence on Rainey is not surprising; marginalized people, especially Black women, often disappear into an historical void, even when a certain degree of fame has been attained. That Rainey's work at the time was almost completely confined to the South and away from the large urban centers of the North, where most mainstream newspapers and magazines were located, further undercut her chances of public notice. Her apparent departure from Tolliver's troupe would have driven her even deeper into the historical abyss, as Tolliver had a formidable publicity machine that kept his organization constantly in the Black press. Further, touring in the South often meant tent shows. The Rabbit Foot Minstrels, for instance, toured by railroad car with an 80-by-110-foot tent and a stage consisting of wooden boards on a frame, which could be easily erected and folded for the next show. Sometimes minstrel groups followed the fall harvest throughout different parts of the South, drawing a distinctly rural African American audience. That kind of event would hardly make mainstream newspapers. Given the deadness of a tent on outdoor ground, and without electric amplification, a performer had to have a strong voice, and that of course suited Rainey well.

The veil of uncertainly about Rainey's activities ended in December 1923, when Paramount Records brought her in for a recording session. She cut eight songs that day, and Paramount chose "Moonshine Blues" to release and publicize. From the start, Paramount sensed they had a special voice in Rainey. They put a half-page ad in the *Chicago Defender*, touting her as "Madam 'Ma' Rainey, the wonderful gold-neck woman who starred for five years in three theaters in Pensacola, Atlanta, and Jacksonville!" The "gold neck" refers to her signature piece of jewelry, a necklace made up of five-, ten-, and twenty-dollar gold coins. The ad goes on, "If it's blues you want, here they are. 'Ma' sings 'Moonshine Blues' like she meant 'em."

Rainey's style was distinct from Mamie Smith's or Alberta Hunter's, women who had honed their acts on the Northern vaudeville stage. She not only had the rough edges of the rural South in her sound but a deep, husky voice that literally moaned the blues, when she didn't cut loose with a massive sound that could fill any tent. Her moaning, especially during instrumental sections, was almost a trademark, as was her authenticity, which Paramount advertised as her "low-sobbing voice," singing "mean, low-down blues that's really 'too bad.'" Her colleagues talked about how she could hold an audience by her earthy delivery as well as her presence onstage, something that recordings could never fully capture. Her niece Ruby described her appearance: "With her thick straightened hair sticking out in all directions, gold caps on her huge teeth, a fan of ostrich plumes in her hand, and a long triple necklace of shiny gold coins reflecting the blue spotlight that danced on her sequined Black dress, Ma was a sight to behold."

Rainey soon joined the Theater Owners Booking Association circuit as a headliner closing the show. The TOBA was a vaudeville agency for Black entertainers. It was owned by whites, and while stars were treated well, it became known among aspiring Black performers as "Tough on Black Asses." By 1926 Rainey had her own company, "Ma Rainey's Flapper Girls." "She packs 'em in" was a standard refrain, and sold-out shows were common. As one reviewer in Louisville, Kentucky, observed, it was not only "one of the hottest shows" played there, but hers was the first that ever necessitated the S.R.O. sign outside.

While Rainey assumed the appellation Madame and many other blues singers were identified as Queen, if only in the announcer's pitch, Bessie Smith went one better: soon after her first recordings she was hailed "Empress of the blues." Smith had grown up in Chattanooga, Tennessee, in extreme poverty, especially after she became an orphan; both parents had died by the time she was nine years old. To supplement the family income Bessie began to perform on the streets of Chattanooga sometime between the ages of ten and twelve, accompanied by her elder brother Andrew, who served as both guitar player and protector.

Around 1908 or 1909, when she was fifteen, Smith began to appear in professional revues or minstrel shows. Precisely how her professional career began is not known; the oft-repeated story that Ma Rainey heard her and kidnapped her to join Rainey's troupe is urban legend. Smith was in Atlanta in 1909, maybe earlier, as a member of the chorus at either the Arcade or Eighty-One Theater. For the next two years she traveled throughout much of the South with various troupes. She first met Ma Rainey in 1910 when both were performing at Eighty-One Theater, and then continued briefly with Rainey's troupe, as a member of the chorus. In 1912 her brother Clarence, who had been on the vaudeville circuit for some time, persuaded her to audition for the Stokes troupe, of which he was a member and which also included Ma Rainey. A few months later Rainey and Bessie were together again, with another troupe.

Precisely what interactions occurred between Rainey and Smith is not known, but Smith had plenty of opportunity to observe Rainey onstage and undoubtedly benefited from watching the established performer. Whether Rainey actually taught Smith anything about the blues or singing beyond giving her general show business advice is unknown, although Rainey was known for being helpful to young aspiring show persons. Smith was absorbing show business knowledge, learning her craft, and Rainey, already a seasoned veteran, at the very least provided a model.

In 1911 Smith met tap dancer–vaudevillian Wayne Burton, and by 1912 they had formed the duo Burton and Smith. Smith's partnership with Burton allowed her to step out of the chorus line, and because of Burton's dancing abilities, Smith concentrated on singing. Their bill identified him as "The Boy with the Insane Feet," and her as "The Girl with the Ragtime Voice." (No blues is mentioned at this point.) The partnership did not last long, however, as Burton soon replaced Smith with Ebbie Forceman, whom he married. Wayne Burton and Bessie Smith did occasionally continue to appear on the same bill, and he was still part of Smith's company as late as 1925.

Smith always had a big voice, and was first billed as a "coon shouter," a common term then for Black female singers. By this time the term "coon" was being used to refer to Blacks, and its association with minstrelsy added to its derogatory connotation. The "shouter" part of the label came from Black females' need to make a large sound to claim the stage. In that context, she stood out: in 1912 "Miss Smith is undoubtedly the best coon shouter ever seen in this house." She gradually refined her blues style, although she was always a rough, Southern country blues singer like Ma Rainey. She could also communicate something more than the sound of the best voice in vaudeville: she "knows how to put her songs over the floodlights in a way that makes her audience scream with delight." By 1918 critics sought to understand what distinguished her, even hinting she might be able to succeed in opera; one Black reporter who heard her, Billy E. Lewis, claimed, "Her voice is profoundly affecting, and which if employed in the higher realms of music, owing to its soulfulness, she would be a leading contralto or baritone singer of the day regardless of race." Of course her race would not have been disregarded in the 1920s; besides, Smith sang what was inside herself and her culture. The same reporter described another Smith performance: "Not only is Miss Smith's voice big, it is musical. Added to this is that peculiar strain and quality only known to our people, and which makes for what is now called blues singing. . . . you must have the feeling, and Bessie has got it."

In 1917 Smith joined Toliver's Circus, which also included Ma Rainey. They had not performed together for five years. These two women were clearly the central acts of the troupe, both huge draws by this time, and newspapers hint that Smith may have outshone Rainey: "Gertrude (Ma) Rainey was given a tremendous ovation. . . . The votes for favors goes to Bessie Smith. She found it decidedly easy to corner the popular honors." The competition did not last long, however; for whatever reasons, both singers soon left Tolliver's show.

Accounts of Smith's whereabouts between 1918 and 1923 recordings are sporadic, if sufficient to indicate that she continued to perform mostly in the South, but at least as far as Chicago once, where she appeared briefly with Burton.

Mamie Smith's success had convinced Columbia Records to initiate a new department, "Race Records," with Frank Walker, a white man, in charge of it. After an unsuccessful attempt to lure Alberta Hunter from Paramount, he turned to Bessie Smith, who had not yet recorded. On February 15, 1923, Smith was in the studio. By the end of the second day they had two songs, "Down Hearted Blues," and "Gulf Coast Blues," which were announced in May and released in June. Curiously, on the label they listed Smith not as singer or vocalist, but as "comedienne."

"Down Hearted Blues" sold 780,000 copies in six months, immediately establishing Smith as a new force in the blues world. Walker in particular was surprised; Alberta Hunter had already had a hit with her recording the year before, followed by other singers. Smith, however, had interjected something new into it, not the least being the way she threw herself into a song. There was that voice, but there was more. Even Hunter, with whom Smith had at least one serious row, called Smith "the greatest of them all. . . . Nobody, least of all today, could ever match Bessie Smith." Hunter identified what made her unique beyond her voice: "She had a sort of tear—no not a tear, but there was a *misery* in what she did. It was as though there was something she just had to get out."

Her stage presence only enhanced what listeners heard on the recordings, as her charisma was visual as well as aural. Like other blues queens, she wore elaborate dresses, jewelry, and headpieces which altogether weighed as much as fifty pounds. As with other great artists, there was an indefinable quality about her ability to hold an audience. Guitarist Danny Barker gave a vivid account of Smith onstage: "She dominated a stage. You didn't turn your head when she went on. You just watched Bessie. You didn't read any newspapers in a night club when she went on. She just upset you. . . . She could bring about mass hypnotism. When she was performing, you could hear a pin drop."

Soon Smith was billed, accurately, as "The Greatest and Highest Salaried Race Star in the World." By February 1924, she was "Queen of the Blues, and more," and by May she had gained the new title "Empress of the Blues." Who crowned her? All we know is that the *Chicago Defender* used the term "empress" for the first time in print on May 3, 1924, calling her "Empress of Blues Singers." Two weeks later the same newspaper referred to her as "Blues Empress." The title has stuck, even to this day.

Smith's reign continued for most of the twenties, as her reputation grew. Smith's touring also confirmed what blues singers' record sales had already suggested, that blues women's appeal crossed racial boundaries. The South of course remained segregated, but in it she gave special performances for whites only. The first on record was in Atlanta in 1923. She repeated this in 1925, and mainstream newspapers took pride in reporting on her success. Tim Owslay headlined his article "Bessie Pleases Ofays" (a derogatory term used in Black culture for whites) and reported she "scored a complete knockout." The *Preston News* reported that in Atlanta her performance sold out days ahead, and that "few white homes here are without her records." A white record dealer claimed that her records "out-sell everything else in the catalogue." When she gave a whites-only performance in Nashville, she "knocked all the tin off the roof of the theater," and the audience refused to leave, wanting more.

As the 1920s neared an end, changes in technology and audience tastes hit all the blues singers hard, although Bessie continued to draw large crowds. However, 1928 saw a change in approach, as much of show business was impacted by Jerome Kern and Oscar Hammerstein's 1927 hit musical *Showboat*. Smith and others sought to create more integrated revues, specifically referring to them as "musical comedy." Smith's first, *Mississippi Days*, opened on April 9, 1928. It was more an extravaganza than a play in the sense of *Showboat*. On October 22, another extravaganza opened, *Steamboat Days*, a clear offshoot of *Showboat*, at least in title. Some references to "good-sized crowds" suggest Smith was no longer the draw she once was, but other reports suggested otherwise. W. R. Arnold, writing in the *Pittsburgh Courier*, noted that the show was playing to "turn-away business." He also believed that *Steamboat Days* had found the right formula: "The public seems to want this sort of entertainment. The theatergoers are apparently sick of the old stuff."

In early 1929 Maceo Pinkard approached Bessie about starring in a Broadway show, *Pansy*. It appealed to her and she accepted. What she didn't know was that the show was already in production, its prospects were not bright, and Bessie was signed on in the hopes of saving it. But the production was so bad that not even Bessie Smith could rescue it. According to one review, "*Pansy* is . . . the sort of thing that children of five might put on in somebody's barn with costumes borrowed from their elders"; another reviewer called it "the worst show of all time." The critics were unaware that six of the principal characters had just walked out, not wanting to be associated with the impending, inevitable disaster.

Bessie had one more opportunity to try another venue that year, with the emergence of talking pictures on the horizon. W. C. Handy and Kenneth W. Adams suggested a short (sixteen-minute) film based on Handy's "St. Louis Blues," recorded with the new RCA Phototone process, technology that allowed sound to be imprinted onto film. The film met with little success, but it was a portent for Bessie. After records and radio had done their damage, talking pictures were the final technological nail in the vaudeville coffin. Unlike the two earlier technologies, however, sound films embraced the entire spectrum of vaudeville and eventually smothered it. The Depression dealt the coup de grâce as recording sales plummeted, and the large tent shows and extravaganzas were no longer financially viable.

Both Rainey and Smith continued to perform into the 1930s, but more sporadically and in smaller venues. In 1935 Rainey retired to Rome, Georgia, where she owned two theaters, the Lyric Theater and the Airdome. She managed them until her death in 1939. Smith continued to sing wherever she could, with her life ending suddenly in an automobile crash April 15, 1937.

Other changes were also taking place in the late 1920s as the popularity of women blues singers began to wane. Advances in recording methods opened up entirely new vocal genres, and country blues sung by Black men with a single guitar became the latest blues fascination. The first of the Black male singers to record was Blind Lemon Jefferson. He was born in 1893 in Wortham, Texas, about seventy-five miles south of Dallas, and by most accounts was born blind. Given a guitar at an early age, he quickly mastered it. In the early 1920s he began singing in Dallas, where he eked out a living performing in clubs, bars, and on the street. He also worked with Huddie Ledbetter, better known as Lead Belly. Alerted by a local record store owner, Art Laibly of Paramount Records heard him and quickly arranged a trip to Chicago for Jefferson to record.

Either December 1925, or January 1926 Jefferson cut his first recordings. They were two religious numbers, "I Want to Be Like Jesus in My Heart," and "All I Want Is That Pure Religion," which Paramount issued under the pseudonym Deacon E. J. Bates. The two hymns convinced Paramount of his potential, and they brought him back to the studio in March 1926, where he recorded his first blues, "Booster Blues" and "Dry Southern Blues," this time under his own name.

Paramount stressed Jefferson's roots and his authenticity: "Here's a real, old-fashioned Blues by a real, old-fashioned Blues singer. . . . With his singing, he strums his guitar in real southern style—makes it talk, in fact." This was no vaudeville act, and there was no jazz band backing him, it was "Blind Lemon Jefferson and His Guitar." With this recording Paramount had reoriented the market and begun to redefine the blues genre itself for the 1920s public.

Jefferson was extremely successful. Altogether he recorded 92 numbers for Paramount, and both OKeh and Columbia tried to lure him away. He went to OKeh briefly but soon returned to Paramount. He earned enough to have a car with a chauffeur, and was given a small share of the royalties. Like many Black musicians, however, he never earned what he should have; Mayo

Williams, the producer at Paramount who wrote the recording contracts, made sure of that.

Jefferson's career ended abruptly in 1929 one wintry night in Chicago. Accounts diverge about what happened, and even when it happened. Jefferson was on his way somewhere, it was bitterly cold, and snowing. He was later found dead on the street. One account had him leaving a recording session and heading to a house party. Another had him waiting for his driver, who never showed up. A third had him suffering a heart attack. Even the date is unknown—there is no death record. It was probably December, as his body arrived back in Wortham on Christmas Eve.

After Jefferson, a number of other blind male blues singers appeared in the late 1920s and early 1930s. They included Arthur Blake (1896–1934), Reverend Gary Davis (1896–1972), Willie McTell (1898–1959), Joe Reynolds (1900–1968), Willie Johnson (1902–1950), Willie Dunn (1902–1933), and Allen Fuller (né Fulton, 1907–1941). All used the moniker "blind" before their name. Of these the most well-known was Blind Blake.

Details of Blake's life are at best elusive. He has been connected to Jacksonville, Florida, where he was purported to have been born, although his death certificate states Newport News, Virginia. His birth date is uncertain, probably sometime between 1893 and 1896. Most of what is known of his whereabouts between his birth and the beginning of his recording career is based on rumors or inferred from his songs. In 2011 Alex van der Tuuk and others discovered his death certificate, which showed that he died from a pulmonary hemorrhage in Milwaukee, Wisconsin, on December 1, 1934. He had chosen to live near the Paramount Records studio, although Paramount had officially folded by December 1933, and had not made any recordings there since April 1932.

Among blues singers Blake was unequaled as a guitarist. He had a smooth rhythmic sound, and interspersed his breaks with rapid passages, which contrasted with the more emphatic but less fluent high-register dyads in Lemon Jefferson's recordings. His playing essentially imitated a piano, something not uncommon for Delta blues singers, but he added more figurations, often syncopating with his right thumb in his fast passages. Blind Gary Davis remembered, "He was very, very rhythmic and incredibly fast—I don't know anyone who can get to that speed."

Around 1926 one of Paramount's dealer-talent scouts noticed Blake, and soon Paramount had him in their studio. He was first used as a solo guitarist for Leola B. Wilson. Within a month Blake was back as singer and guitarist, recording "Early Morning Blues" and "West Coast Blues." "West Coast Blues" is less a blues than a ragtime guitar instrumental with Blake talking as if to an audience as he plays. It is clearly a vehicle for his virtuosity. From that first solo session to Paramount's closing in 1932 Blake recorded almost as many sides as Jefferson, altogether at least 90.

The popularity of Jefferson, Blake, and the many subsequent blues singers who attached the "blind" moniker to their name raises the question how blindness functions in the selling of a singer. According to Joseph Witek, it acts as a sign of otherness. The audiences have an underlying assumption that blues singers have suffered and are expressing their inner suffering in music; thus, to be believable they must have suffered, and congenital blindness can only enhance their authenticity. Add being born blind to being Black, poor, and from the rural South, and it's hard to find a more powerful mix of hardship and otherness. There is also a long history of the blind musician in many oral-narrative societies going back to ancient Babylonia and including the Greek poet Homer, the medieval Italian musician Francesco Landini, and the seventeenth-eighteenth-century Celtic harper Turlough O'Carolan. That makes the blind blues singer even more real: he is part of an historical community with a long and impressive legacy. Well into the late twentieth century Black musicians who were blind such as Ray Charles, Stevie Wonder, and the gospel group The Blind Boys of Alabama have had a major impact on American culture, although their individual styles differed considerably.

All of the recordings of female blues singers in the early twentieth century as well as Blake's and Jefferson's first recordings were done acoustically. The voices of the women singers, large and piercing, were ideal for acoustic technology, as it could catch the full range of their art. Most male blues voices could also match the limitations of the acoustic needle, but the guitar accompaniment was more difficult to capture. Acoustic technology itself constantly evolved, with new patents issued every month, as the popular trade journal *Talking Machine World* (1905–28) reported. Then in 1926 electric recording became common.

Electric recording borrowed from radio and telephone by adding a microphone and amplification to drive the stylus. The microphone pickup revolutionized the industry as it could capture sounds not easily caught acoustically, and with greater clarity and tonal range. Blues singers no longer had to possess the power of a Bessie Smith or the "elastic, thin-veneered whine" of Lemon Jefferson. Blake, for instance, had a lower voice, sang in a deeper register, and without the vocal intensity of a Smith or Jefferson, and sounds more laid back on recording, balanced by his instrumental virtuosity to create an overall propulsive quality. Blues was only one of many genres Blake recorded.

Another genre to benefit from electric recording was white country music, or hillbilly as it was then called, although it was well established by the time electric recording became a reality. As a white Southern folk tradition, hillbilly music had for many decades run parallel to the geographically overlapping Black folk tradition. Although the power structure mandated segregation through both legal and illegal measures, the two musical streams hardly ran separately, and recordings provide a documented means to peel down to the concrete underside of racial interactions in the early twentieth-century South, to uncover relations in a social stratum that public records often miss.

1920s country music began with fiddling, an activity going back to the British Isles, which on the surface seems far removed from Black music making. Much of 1920s hillbilly music did rely on its European roots, but much of the music reveals a more complex picture of Southern culture than the nasty politics and vigilantism of the time suggest. In the nineteenth century white dancers in the South needed fiddlers, most of whom were Black. Plantation culture had encouraged this situation, as few upper-class men took up music, and women were expected to play the piano. Having an enslaved person able to play the fiddle meant someone was readily available to play for balls and other occasions, and being the preferred fiddler beat dying in the cotton fields. Consequently, many slaves took up fiddling, and along with it the European repertoire, that is, what white dancers wanted. Even after emancipation, the best fiddler in a region would often be Black.

Fiddling was nevertheless popular among white Southerners, particularly in modest rural homes where servants were nonexistent and farm life engendered a degree of physical isolation from neighbors. Families often entertained themselves with singing and whatever instrumental activity members could provide, especially during the winter. In the nineteenth century, the fiddle was gendered male, and the ability as well as the instruments themselves often passed down from father to son. Some families with enough people and musical talent formed small string bands.

On June 29, 1922, John Alexander "Eck" Robertson and Henry Gilliland walked in the Victor Talking Machine studios in New York City, wanting to record. One can only imagine the reaction of the Victor people when they saw this unusual pair. Robertson, from Amarillo, Texas, was dressed in full cowboy uniform, and Gilliland, from Altus, Texas, who was older and a Confederate veteran, was wearing his Confederate regalia.

Both came with many years of experience in the fiddling and entertainment business. Each had won numerous fiddle contests throughout the South and Southwest, and Robertson had traveled with a medicine show for several years. By 1922 both had settled down to pursue other careers, Robertson as a piano tuner in Amarillo and Gilliland as justice of the peace in Altus. When they met, they found their playing complementary, and began to make occasional appearances together.

Victor had to that point shown no interest in fiddle music or white country music of any sort. According to Robertson, the Victor manager "come out with a long piece of paper with names on it. He done that on purpose, you see, thought he'd get rid of me just like he had all the rest of them." The manager insisted he play something right then and there. "Well, I didn't get to play half of 'Sallie Gooden'; he just throwed up his hands and stopped me. Said, 'By Ned, that's fine!,'" and they were given the go-ahead to record the next morning.

They recorded "Arkansas Traveler" and "Turkey in the Straw" together, and the next day Victor recorded Robertson alone, playing "Sallie Gooden," "Ragtime Annie," and at least two other tunes that were not released. Victor's first recording, with Robertson's "Sallie Gooden" on one side and the Robertson-Gilliland duo's "Arkansas Traveler" on the other, had a limited release in September 1922, but was advertised more fully in March 1923. It was the first commercial recording of white country music. At first Victor was not sure how to classify it. In the March ad it was placed under "Dance Music" along with several fox-trots and waltzes by Paul Whiteman and others. By November Victor seems to have become aware of the potential of the genre: they released a second record, "Turkey in the Straw," with both fiddlers, and "Ragtime Annie," with Robertson. This time the record was classified as "Melodious Instrument," with the comment, "Two old-fashioned dance numbers by genuine cowboy fiddlers. Theirs is genuine American, not hybrid, music. You will find such musicians, today, only in out-of-the-way places."

However Victor felt about this music, Robertson did not record again until 1929, and Gilliland died April 24, 1924. Yet between April and November 1923, other companies had begun to record fiddlers, and the public had responded enthusiastically. Interest in white country fiddlers was sparked especially by the other new technology of the time, radio.

Country fiddling first went over the airwaves on September 9, 1922, when Fiddlin' John Carson appeared on WSB in Atlanta, one of the first broadcast radio stations in the South. WSB had been on the air only six months, having begun March 15. Carson, an indefatigable promoter as well as a well-known fiddler who frequently appeared in northern Georgia, proved an instant success: "Telephone calls, telegrams, and letters poured in for weeks afterward." WSB began to feature Carson regularly, and his music could be heard throughout the 1920s, as well as other hillbilly music, mostly fiddlers and string bands. Even though WGM, which began operating in Atlanta on March 17, 1922, was assigned the same frequency, tense time-sharing of the airwaves between the two stations allowed WBS to be heard at night as far as the Rocky Mountains and Canada. Carson became a national figure.

Further West, WBAP began broadcasting in Fort Worth, Texas on May 2, 1922. Like most stations, its musical fare consisted principally of popular styles, including jazz and Hawaiian music. Moses J. Bonner, another fiddle champion and Confederate veteran who used the title Captain M. J. Bonner, convinced WBAP to put him on the air. Backed by a string band used to playing Hawaiian music, Bonner regaled the audience for over an hour with his fiddle, his banter, and square-dance calling. His performance provoked the greatest response the station had ever received, and demonstrated that here was an untapped audience most stations did not know existed. Soon WBAP inaugurated a regular "barn dance" show featuring various hillbilly performers, well before the famous *National Barn Dance* of WLS in Chicago, or the *Grand Ole Opry* of WSM in Nashville.

WLS began its National Barn Dance show one week after it began broadcasting on April 12, 1924. As it was owned by Sears & Roebuck, then primarily a catalogue company that catered to rural customers, the station sought entertainment for that clientele. In response, Edgar L. Bill, the station's director, conceived a program that combined fiddling, square-dance calling, and old-fashioned heart songs. Gradually the show evolved into predominantly country, or hillbilly, music. It aired until 1968.

WSM in Nashville, Tennessee, first aired on October 5, 1925. On November 9 they hired George B. Hay as their "radio director." Hay, who went by the nickname "the solemn old judge," was already known as the announcer of the WLS *National Barn Dance*. He was determined to replicate the program on WSM, although he met with opposition from both Nashville citizens and WSM executives. Nashville society prided itself on its sophistication, which had earned the city the nickname "Athens of the South," and did not want to be identified with rural, hillbilly music. However, the National Life and Insurance Company, which owned WSM, had an interest in selling policies to rural and working-class people, and consequently gave Hay the go-ahead with his experiment. On November 28, 1925, Hay launched the WSM Barn Dance, which featured a fiddler, Uncle Jimmy Thompson, accompanied by his niece Eva Thompson Jones on piano. Like earlier stations that aired fiddlers, WSM was inundated with positive responses, and the WSM Barn Dance became a fixture, in spite of the societal opposition. Soon many musicians from the area, mostly fiddlers and string bands, came to WSM, and Hay allowed many to appear on the show. In 1927, when the show that preceded it on the air, the "NBC Music Appreciation Hour," hosted by Walter Damrosch, ended,

Hay announced, "For the past hour we have been listening to music taken from grand opera, but from now on we will present the *Grand Ole Opry.*" Thus the longest running program in radio history got its name. As of this writing it is still on the air.

The first major star of the *Grand Ole Opry* was Uncle Dave Macon, an experienced vaudevillian, virtuoso banjoist, comedian, and colorful character. An outsized, outgoing man with a boisterous, exuberant style, Macon captivated audiences. Whether picking his banjo, singing, telling jokes, engaging in repartee, or even twirling his banjo and dancing, he was all entertainment. Opry star David Akeman, known professionally as "Stringbean," summed him up, "He's not the best player, and he's not the best singer, but he is the best something."

Next to Macon, the most popular performer in the early years of the *Grand Ole Opry* was DeFord Bailey, a Black harmonica player, who also toured with Macon and later Roy Acuff and Bill Monroe. How Bailey as an African American managed to get on the Opry and remain a star for fifteen years is one of the more unusual stories in country music. Bailey was born in rural Tennessee in 1899, the son of a sharecropper and the grandson of a slave. His family was known locally for their musical abilities, especially his grandfather Lewis, who was considered "the best fiddle player in Smith County." Lewis's repertoire of white British-American fiddle music, what DeFord would call "Black hillbilly music," harkens back to his slave heritage, when he would be called to play such music for white dances.

When DeFord was three years old he was stricken with polio, and was given a harmonica to amuse himself as he was bedridden for a year. Soon his talent became clear, as he could not only pick up tunes, but imitate many of the sounds of his rural surroundings. The harp, as he called it, became his obsession.

After the death of his mother he was raised by his older sister, Barbara Lou. When she married and moved to Nashville with her husband, DeFord followed, and soon was working as a houseboy for the weathy Nashvillians Mr. and Mrs. J. C. Bradford. When they heard what he could do with the harp, he became their in-house musician, playing quietly in the corner for the many dinner parties they held. Word soon spread among the Nashville elite of his amazing talent. The death of Mrs. Bradford in 1923 ended that job, and for a while Bailey returned to whatever odd jobs he could find.

In the meantime L. N. Smith had started a radio supply store, Dads, for the many young men enthralled with building their own radios. His manager, Fred "Pop" Exum, convinced him to start his own radio station. On September 3, 1925, WDAD went on the air, the first radio station in Nashville, beating WSM by thirty-two days. Exum had heard Bailey and invited him to appear on the station.

Another regular performer on WDAD was Dr. Humphrey Bate, a physician who led his own string band. Soon Hay lured Bate to the WSM Barn Dance, making his "string orchestra" the house band on the program and renaming the band The Possum Hunters. For a time Bate continued on both stations. A harmonica player himself, Bate invited Bailey to appear on the Barn Dance. At first Bailey resisted: "I was ashamed with my little cheap harp and them with all them fine, expensive fiddles, guitars, and banjoes up there." Finally Bailey agreed, but on arrival they ran into Hay, who insisted no one go on the show without an audition. After Bate said he would stake his reputation on Bailey, Hay relented, and Bailey became the first person to appear on Barn Dance without an audition. Playing his harp solo, he immediately impressed Hay, and from then on was a regular.

In April 1927, Hay arranged for Bailey to record in a Brunswick label series "Music from Dixie." He recorded eight tunes, of which "Pan American Blues" and "Fox Chase" were the most popular. Both are mimetic. "Pan American Blues," a reference to a passenger train that ran between Cincinnati and New Orleans, was a realistic imitation of a steam locomotive, and "Fox Chase" was a harmonica rendition of a traditional fox hunt, including the sound of the hunting horns. Although sales figures no longer exist, and although these were not the first harmonica recordings made, they had a major impact on later harmonica players and did much to bolster Bailey's reputation as a harp virtuoso. He was also the only Black musician to record for this series.

Bailey continued to appear regularly on the *Grand Ole Opry*, until 1941, when Hay fired him. Hay and Bailey gave conflicting accounts of what happened. According to Hay, he wanted Bailey to learn new tunes, gave him a year to do so, and Bailey failed to heed him. Bailey denied that Hay ever told him that, and pointed out that many other Opry stars, such as Roy Acuff, would sing the same songs year after year. Bailey also said he had learned new tunes over the years, but had been told to stick to his old repertoire. The issue may have been related to a fight going on between the two royalty collecting agencies, ASCAP and BMI. ASCAP had raised their fees for broacast performances significantly, which had forced the radio industry to form BMI, the Broadcast Music Association. ASCAP then imposed a boycott of their songs on the radio. Many of Bailey's songs, even traditional ones, had been copyrighted by ASCAP, so Hay could not allow Bailey to continue to play them.

According to Hay the parting was friendly. Bailey, however, did not see it that way. He returned to the shoe shine stand he had in his earlier days and remained hurt and bitter for years. Many journalists and scholars tried to ask him about his years at the Opry, but he did not want to talk about it. His time as the only Black man at the Opry, his musical career, and his leaving raise several issues. Why was he accepted by white audiences? How did other Opry musicians view him? What did he have to endure when traveling? At the same time that jazz and swing bands remained strictly segregated, when Benny Goodman later integrated his trio and quartet but feared integrating his big band, some of the most rural Southern white performers playing for some of the most rural audiences welcomed Bailey. Did white performers view him through a minstrel lens, as the do-da Black stereotype, or did they accept him as a performing artist in his own right?

When it came to the musicians and managers of the *Grand Ole Opry*, Bailey found himself in the mesh of the friendly paternalism that still characterizes many racial interactions in the South. He was admired and respected for his musicianship, and when he was on tour many of the musicians went out of their way to make things better for him. This was the Jim Crow South, however, and while Bailey could appear onstage, he could not eat or sleep where the other musicans stayed. Some of the white musicians fought for him. They would try to slip him by hotel managers as part of the group. Macon would claim Bailey was his valet and needed to stay in the hotel with him. Sometimes one or two of the musicians would accompany him, at two or three in the morning, helping him find a place to sleep. Acccording to Bailey, the Delmore Brothers, two white guitar players from Alabama, frequently told restaurant managers, " 'If you can't feed little DeFord, we can't eat here either.' "

Even when allowed into the restaurant, Bailey was often forced to eat in the kitchen. Other times he would stay in the car while the white performers brought him a sandwich. Opry musicians often traveled five or six to a car at that time, sometimes taking turns sleeping while traveling overnight to the next date. DeFord described traveling with Roy Acuff: "I slept on his shoulder and he slept on mine." Unfortunately, sometimes Bailey had to sleep alone in the car, while all the white musicians were allowed into the hotel.

Bailey was accepted and supported by white musicians in part because the Black-white Maginot Line had long been breached in the musical South. The interaction between Black and working-class and rural white musicians is apparent in the music itself. Many white country musicians readily acknowledged the importance of a Black performer as either a mentor or major influence. A. P. Carter, Jimmie Rodgers, Bill Monroe, Hank Williams, Jerry Lee Lewis, Tom T. Hall, and many others had close contacts with Black musicians, learned from them, and, in spite of the never-forgotten color barrier, respected them. One can ask, however, did white musicians advance their careers by appropriating from Black musicians, and was the interchange ever a two-way street? Yes, white musicians did appropriate, and most of the time it was not reciprocal. Although many white musicians in the rural South personally looked up to Black musicians, at least musically, whether it benefited Black musicians is another story. This issue would come to a head in the 1950s.

Notwithstanding his success at the Opry, Bailey could never forget who he was and what the racial situation was. He would sit alone backstage until other performers came over to him. He did not want to seem pushy. "I stayed in my place. I didn't push myself forward." On tour when the other musicians would go out between performances Bailey remained, to either sleep backstage or play his harp. Years later he described his situation: "This is a great big world, but, you know, I ain't never been free. Even now, I can't go in a restaurant without worrying about whether I should go in or not. I been to places with Honey Wilds [a white comedian] where they would not sell him a sandwich for me. I didn't suffer, but I was handicapped. I been penned up all my life. You got to know how to take it and go on."

Bailey's relation with George Hay exemplifies the narrow path Bailey had to trod. Their relationship went beyond the employee-boss connection at the Opry. Hay was effusive in his praise of Bailey and supported and defended him. Hay watched out for theater managers that tried to take advantage of an illiterate Black man. Bailey considered Hay his friend. In 1927 Hay arranged to have three of his acts including Bailey recorded by Columbia. After recording the other two acts, there was little time left; Bailey was allowed only two songs. Hay, angry at how Bailey was treated, canceled the contract and immediately set out to arrange Bailey's Brunswick recordings.

Yet Hay could be quite paternalistic in his approach to Bailey. He had him working as a houseboy in his home—imagine Dave Macon or Roy Acuff pressured to work as a houseboy. The job did help Bailey, as he needed extra money. That need, however, was in part because Hay was taking advantage of Bailey's relative ignorance and innocence about contracts and pay. Hay took 25 percent of Bailey's recording income "for arranging the session," and doled out the rest of the Brunswick fee in installments, letting Bailey believe it was for his WSM appearances. Only after Bailey briefly defected to WNOX in Knoxville was he able to demand Hay raise his WSM fee from seven to twenty dollars per appearance.

Bailey was much like Louis Armstrong in his views about his fate as a Black man. He mostly accepted the status quo. He understood the need to have a white man such as Hay look after him, even though Hay's actions often benefited Hay. Bailey would quote his grandfather: "Figgers are figgers, oughts are oughts, all for the white man, none for the n****rs." Another reason Bailey was able to swim in the shark-infested sea of white hillbillies was his physical appearance. Because of his childhood bout with polio, he was diminutive, four-foot-eleven, and walked with a limp. He was not threatening to white Southern males. This combined with his good-natured temperament and the apparent absence of a rebellious streak made him seem benign to white Southerners. Or to put it another way, from the standpoint of white Southerners, he knew his place. He tolerated the nickname that the *Grand Ole Opry* gave him, "Our little mascot," a phrase that encapsulates Southern racial attitudes of the early twentieth century.

As early as 1923 Ralph Peer, the A&R (artist and repertoire) director for OKeh records, began to take his equipment beyond the studio to seek talent, both Black and white, in the South. In June he set up a portable recording station in Atlanta mainly to discover Black talent. Polk Brockman, whose furniture store in Atlanta was the largest distributor of OKeh records in the country, was able to persuade Peer to record Fiddlin' John Carson. Carson's first efforts yielded "The Little Old Log Cabin in the Lane" and "The Old Hen Cackled and the Rooster's Going to Crow." Bill Malone described Peer's reaction: "He responded with disbelief; he thought the singing was awful and insisted that only Carson's fiddle tunes be recorded." Brockman, familiar with the Atlanta market, demanded that the record be pressed and that he would buy 500 copies. When Brockman ordered a second batch within a few weeks, Peer realized what radio audiences already knew: there was a ready market for this music. OKeh released thirty other Carson recordings in the 1920s, some with his daughter Rosie Lee, who used the stage name Moonshine Kate. He cut as many as 88 sides between 1924 and 1927, and his recording career continued into the 1930s, altogether with an estimated 165 songs.

In 1927 Peer took his recording apparatus to Bristol, Tennessee, for a recording session that has been mythologized in country music. Nolan Porterfield called it "The Big Bang of Country Music . . . the place where it all started." Johnny Cash referred to it as "the single most important event in the history of country music." It clearly was not the beginning of country music. By 1927 WLS's *National Barn Dance* and WSM's *Grand Ole Opry* were firmly established, and recordings by Fiddlin' John Carson, Uncle Dave Macon, Vernon Dalhart, and others had sold in the thousands. It was also by no means Peer's first portable rodeo. In addition to his 1923 trip he returned to Atlanta and to Asheville in 1925, and he held a session in Memphis before going to Bristol.

Bristol has been accorded special status for two reasons: the Carter Family, and Jimmie Rodgers. Both made the trip to Bristol to audition for Peer, and from there they became the most popular, influential, and enduring acts in country music. They were quite different. The Carter Family, consisting of A.P., his wife Sara, and his sister-in-law Maybelle, played old-fashioned Appalachian music, sang in tight harmony, and was grounded by the innovative guitar playing of Maybelle. A.P. and Sara divorced in 1936 but continued to sing together, and brought in the next generation, especially Maybelle's three daughters, Anita, June, and Helen. This group often performed as Mother Maybelle and the Carter Sisters. Later, June married Johnny Cash to establish another generation of country royalty. Today their son John Carter, and Roseanne, Cash's daughter from his first wife, continue their legacy. This lineage as much as the sound and innovations of the original Carter trio account for the veneration accorded the family.

The most direct and specific musical offshoot of the Carter Family was bluegrass. With its fast picking, high straight-whistle-tone vocal sound, and tight harmony, it is the white folk music of the Appalachian hills. Missing from the Carter sound are only the other instruments that have gone on to define bluegrass: fiddle, mandolin, and later, banjo. They represent the later evolution of the Carter sound.

Jimmie Rodgers represents a different style and a different influence. His is the second stream of country music. He was a solo singer, often recording with only his guitar, and he mined many different types of music, from blues to Tin Pan Alley to hillbilly. Yet he put his distinctive stamp on each, making him by far the most popular country singer of his day, and one of the most successful singers of any category. Between 1927 and his death 1933 he sold an estimated twelve million records, although the exact number is not known, and some have speculated as high as 75 million. Bill Malone, whose book *Country*

Music USA is considered the definitive study of country music, called Rodgers "the most famous hillbilly star in history," and further commented, "one would be hard pressed to find a performer in the whole broad field of pop music—whether it be Al Jolson, Bing Crosby, or Frank Sinatra—who has exerted a more profound and recognizable influence on later generations of entertainers."

Rodgers was born in Pine Springs, Mississippi in 1897, the sixth of seven children. His father was a foreman of a railroad repair gang, and his mother died when he was five or six. His father's job necessitated extensive traveling to places where rails needed repair, and Rodgers traveled with him. When he became a little older his father got him a job as a water boy for the rail gang. Most of the workers were Black, and were known at the time as "gandy dancers" for the work songs they sang. Rodgers thus heard a lot of Black music; he also probably learned to play the guitar from the workers.

Rodgers's obsession was to be an entertainer, but he also worked off and on at various railroad jobs, as brakeman or flagman. This gave him his later nickname, "The Singing Brakeman," which he exploited in publicity photos with railroad dress and hat.

In 1925 Rodgers was diagnosed with tuberculosis, which at the time was tantamount to a death sentence. He continued, determined to succeed in show business, and had some minor success. By 1927 he was in Asheville, North Carolina, appearing occasionally on WWNC. He had also joined a group, the Tenneva Ramblers, and persuaded them to rename themselves the Jimmie Rodgers Entertainment. At that point they heard about Peer's visit to Bristol.

The Tenneva group decided to audition separately, which left Rodgers alone with his guitar when he appeared. He sang two songs, "The Soldier's Sweetheart" and "Sleep Baby Sleep." Peer chose to release them, and they sold modestly at best. However,

Peer recognized Rodgers's potential and brought him into the studio a second time, in New Jersey. There he sang "Blue Yodel," also known as "T for Texas." With the success of this recording Rodgers became a major star, eventually recording 111 songs in the six years left of his life. His biographer Nolan Porterfield estimated that Rodgers accounted for 10 percent of all Victor sales at that time.

In spite of his disease, or maybe because of it, Rodgers led a busy, almost hectic, performing life. He and his family moved to Kerrville, in the Hill Country of central Texas, to take advantage of the dry climate, but that was his only concession to his infirmity. He traveled with several vaudeville organizations and various tent shows, in addition to performances in auditoriums, schools, lodges, and frequently on radio.

Almost all of Rodgers's touring was in the South and Southwest, and in his last years tuberculous had so weakened him that he confined his performances to Texas and nearby places. Had he slowed down as doctors insisted, he may have lived longer, but that was not in his nature. He lived for each moment, savoring it as long as he could.

His last recording session, for Victor on May 24, 1933, has become an integral part of the Rodgers legend. He had come to New York and recorded six songs on May 17–18, including his final "Blue Yodel, no. 12" ("Barefoot Blues"), and then gone to Cape Cod to rest. On his May 24 return, Victor set up a cot for him in a rehearsal room. He recorded two songs, then lay down to recover. He recorded another number, then returned to the cot until he had regained enough strength to sing another song. After the third song, the accompanying musicians had been released, and Rodgers returned to make his final recording, alone with his guitar. Porterfield pointed out that it was not "Old Love Letters," one of his best, as legend holds, but rather "Years Ago." The song itself is not particularly memorable, but Rodgers's voice, and his yodel especially, are strong, giving no sense of his desperate health. After the session Rodgers spent one day on the beach at Coney Island, and on Friday, May 26, less than forty-eight hours after the recording session, he died in a hotel room in New York City.

As much as any country singer, Rodgers reflects the complex racial interactions of the South. The most obvious example is his famous "blue yodel," which became his identifying mark. Rodgers absorbed the blues, or a quasi blues, to the extent that his first hit named "Blue Yodel," was followed later by "Blue Yodels" numbered through 12. Among other features, these incorporate a traditional twelve-bar blues structure. Here two musical streams that seem far apart, Alpine yodeling and Black blues, come together. The term "blue yodel" itself may seem an oxymoron. Yet the streams overlap in both white and Black culture. The appropriation of blues by white singers has a long history in American music. Sophie Tucker was one of the earliest and most prominent white entertainers to do so. Al Bernard, minstrel performer, made over a dozen blues records between 1919 and 1930, his most successful being his rendition of W. C. Handy's "St. Louis Blues." Marion Harris was one of the first white woman to sing blues onstage in the 1910s and recorded several blues songs for RCA Victor beginning in 1916. W. C. Handy commented about her: "She sang blues so well that people hearing her records sometimes thought that the singer was colored."

While western movies of the thirties and forties established the yodel as a product of white singer cowboys, they created a fiction on at least two fronts. First, a large percentage of the cowboys in the West were persons of color—Latinos, Native Americans, and Blacks. Second, the yodel has appeared in cultures throughout the world, especially in Africa. It was used by the Pygmies of the Central-West African rainforest, the Bushmen of the Kalahari Desert, and the Bantus, spread over much of south-central Africa. Elizabeth Ofosuah Johnson has posited that the Portuguese brought Bantu slaves to Europe beginning in 1414, and later offered slaves as gifts to rulers in other parts of Europe. Since the first account of Alpine yodeling does not appear until 1545, it may have been derived from Bantu communication techniques, which is what Bantus used yodeling for. Johnson also has noted that the first slaves brought to America in 1619 were Bantus, and yodeling was observed in America in the seventeenth century.

W. R. Boyd remembered slaves singing "a peculiar singing call, something between a yodel and a chant." In 1856 Frederick Law Olmsted described what he called "Negro jodling" as "a long, loud, musical shout, rising and falling, and breaking into falsetto." He transcribed the sound as "eeoho-eeoho-weeioho-i."

The most well-known Black yodeler in the 1920s was Charles Anderson. He had a natural high voice that included the alto range, and the yodel came naturally to him. In his case the falsetto break or leap, a defining trait of the yodel, was hardly a break at all. Born in Alabama, probably in the 1880s, Anderson worked in vaudeville from at least 1909. By 1913 he had developed his yodeling and bird-like falsetto imitations, earning him the moniker "The Male Mockingbird." He would at times appear in female dress and sing such songs as "Crow Jane," a spoof on "Jim Crow." He recorded eight songs for OKeh, of which five included the yodel. His most famous song, "Laughing Yodel," is reminiscent of George W. Johnson's 1890 recording "The Laughing Song," only Anderson, after imitating Johnson's laugh on tonic and dominant harmonies, then breaks into full yodel, over a similar piano accompaniment.

Earlier Black yodelers included Monroe Tabor, Hayward Wooten, Professor T. H. Price, John Churchill, Coleman Minor, and Beulah Henderson. Wooten, considered Anderson's mentor, performed in the Silver-toned Quartette and the Dixie Rangers, two Black male quartets in the late nineteenth and early twentieth centuries. T. H. Price was called "The Black Emmett," in reference to J. D. Emmett, the vaudeville comedian and singer noted for his portrayal of the character "Fritz, our Cousin-German." Little is known of John Churchill other than that he cut two records for Paramount in 1923, and was part of the Rabbit Foot Minstrel show in the mid-1920s. Even less is known about Coleman Minor except that he sang at the Crown Garden in Indianapolis in 1915, and he published a letter in the *Freeman,* November 18, 1916, accusing Anderson of stealing some of his music.

Beulah Henderson, née Washington, pioneered both blues and yodeling in vaudeville. She was from New Orleans, and is first mentioned in 1905 in a troupe headed by Billy Henderson. They soon formed a team, Henderson and Washington, and married thereafter. Beulah was first praised as an outstanding coon shouter, but by 1911 she was identified for her yodeling. In October 1911, Tim Owsley, manager of the New Crown Garden Theater, Indianapolis, commented: "In fact she is one of the first lady yodelers that we have had the pleasure of hearing." By 1913 the couple billed themselves as "The Class Colored Comedy Pair The Jolly Hendersons featuring Beulah Henderson, America's only Colored Lady 'Yodler.'" A month later she was billed as "America's Greatest Yodler." Unfortunately she never recorded, and nothing is known of her after some appearances in New Orleans in 1915.

Even Bessie Smith made some attempt at yodeling. She recorded the Clarence Williams song "Yodeling Blues," with the refrain, repeated several times, "I'm gonna yodel my blues away." Near the end she moves into the high register twice, with at least the yodel break, although not quite a full-fledged yodel. Smith's voice and her style of blues and the deep recesses from which her sounds and emotions emanated were too heavy to be compatible with a style dependent on flexible and fast head-tone breaks.

The direct lines from Black yodelers to Rodgers's "Blue Yodel" can be traced through two of Rodgers's recordings, "Sleep, Baby, Sleep," and "In the Jailhouse Now." "Sleep, Baby, Sleep" was the first song Rodgers chose to record. It had a long history in both white and Black yodeling, having been previously sung by Beulah Henderson, Hayward Wooten, Monroe Tabor, John Churchill, and Charles Anderson. Anderson and Churchill had both recorded it. The white yodeler George P. Watson recorded it first in 1901, followed by other white singers, Frank Wilson, Ward Barton, Matt Keefe, and Riley Puckett. The song had clearly crossed racial boundaries, and the various performances are quite similar, in singing style and yodeling. No one version can be singled out as the direct predecessor of Rodgers's version, but rather the song's sheer ubiquity demonstrates its staying power across racial divisions.

A more specific lineage from Black singer to Rodgers can be traced in Rodgers' "In the Jailhouse Now," recorded February 15, 1928. Like "Sleep, Baby, Sleep," the song had been sung by a number of performers, mostly Black, and recorded by several. The Black blackface team of Toots Davis and Ed Stafford copyrighted it in 1915 and made it their calling card, claiming it "Their Original Song Hit." Two other Black groups recorded the song, Whistler and His Jug Band in 1924, and Earl MacDonald's Original Louisville Jug Band in 1927. White hillbilly singer Riley Puckett recorded it in 1927, and blues singer Jim Jackson recorded it in January 1928.

The most specific link to Rodgers's recording, however, was Blind Blake's, which he cut in November 1927. Rodgers did rewrite some of the lyrics, but Blake's and Rodgers's vocal inflections are remarkably similar, as if Rodgers was trying to cover Blake. Whether he consciously was or not, Rodgers has thoroughly internalized Blake's interpretation. The principal differences are in the blues breaks, the second part of each phrase. Blake fills in his phrase with his masterly guitar playing—it becomes a second voice. Rodgers's guitar playing was more limited; his yodel replaced Blake's guitar, becoming the responding voice in the blues phrase.

The knotty history of the blues, as well as of yodeling and

pop music in general, only confirms just how complex ethnic interaction in the United States, and especially the South, was at that time. The most rigid segregation, accompanied by the most repressive and vehement vigilante enforcement, could not stop or even mask the cultural interchange that led to new musical forms of the twenties, an interchange that not only shaped the sound of many genres, but also brought Black artistic achievements to the forefront of mainstream America for the first time. And this thanks to the development of the phonograph and radio.

The second half of the 1920s saw the rise of another type of singer who was totally embedded in white culture, specifically Tin Pan Alley, and totally dependent on technological advancements: the crooner. The soft, laid-back, sentimental, intimate approach of the crooner could only be fully captured on record after electric recording came into its own. While the voices of some earlier singers were barely sufficient for acoustic recordings, the crooner not only needed the carbon microphone to be heard satisfactorily, but his—the crooners were predominantly male—entire style depended on the amplification the microphone allowed.

The two most prominent crooners in the late twenties were Rudy Vallée and Bing Crosby, although Ted Lewis had adumbrated the crooner in the combination of his hot jazz clarinet with his own band and a sentimental vaudeville style when singing and dancing. Always sporting a top hat, he sang songs such as "Is Everybody Happy?," "Me and My Shadow," and "King for a Day." His was not the later personal address of Vallée and Crosby but rather a sentimental philosophical uplift message, which was prevalent when a national obsession was multiple repetitions of Émile Coué's phrase "Every day, in every way, I am getting better and better."

More than anyone, Rudy Vallée popularized the modern crooner style. Born Herbert Prior Vallee in Vermont, he grew up in Maine, studied clarinet, and switched to saxophone upon hearing recordings of saxophonist Rudy Wiedoeft. Wiedoeft so influenced Vallée that he changed his name to Rudy. He attended the University of Maine for one year, then switched to Yale, graduating with a degree in philosophy in 1927.

After graduation Vallée put together a band, first named the Yale Collegians, later the Connecticut Yankees. On January 28, 1928, they landed a job at the posh Heigh-Ho Club in Manhattan. Soon WABC began broadcasting from the club, with Vallée serving as bandleader, saxophonist, announcer, and singer. His voice, which most considered too soft for a singer, found its medium in radio, where the microphone was already an essential, and he quickly attracted a national following.

Vallée's first recordings were for the Harmony, Diva, and Velvet Tone labels, which were all subsidiaries of Columbia; often identical material would appear on more than one. His first two records featured upbeat numbers that required fast, rhythmic singing. In them Vallée's voice comes across as just another instrumental break with lyrics. The singing style that made him a 1920s heartthrob emerged in full bloom on his second recording on the Velvet Tone label, "Bye and Bye, Sweetheart," cut October 10, 1928.

In the Velvet Tone recording, which is in a smooth waltz time, Vallée croons into the recording horn. Here he is relaxed and makes full use of the quasi-falsetto sound of his voice. More important, his voice is close and intimate; one can hear the smooth imploring, as if Vallée is there talking directly to the single listener with no mechanical devices in between. He sounds sincere and real. This is what later gained him so many fans, especially female fans.

Surprisingly, Velvet Tone and Harmony still used acoustic recordings. According to reports, however, Columbia, taking advantage of many improvements in acoustic technology, had redesigned their entire apparatus just before electric recording came in, including patented laminated shellac pressings. They then split their equipment, electric for the Columbia label, the new acoustic for the subsidiaries. That the acoustic improvements could capture many of the subtleties of Vallée's voice suggests why they did not want to abandon the new-old technology entirely. Only when he switched to Victor on February 6, 1929, however, did all the nuances of his singing match what thousands of fans heard on radio.

Rudy Vallée's singing style, his youthful good looks with his wavy hair, his suave demeanor, and his Yale—that is, Joe College—imprimatur elevated him to become more than just another popular singer, rather the first of a line of media heartthrobs that went through Frank Sinatra, Johnnie Ray, Elvis Presley, and the Beatles. These were sexy young men who elicited a visceral, almost orgiastic, emotional response from young women throughout the country. In December 1929, *Radio Revue* tried to understand Vallée's success. They described described him as "a national figure and, in some respects, almost a national problem—the joy of the wife, the despair of the husband, the idol of the flapper, and the envy of the young man." One story circulated of a Midwestern woman who was listening to Vallée's program when her husband came in and demanded, "Why don't you get something worth listening to?" She turned and shot him dead.

Many contemporary writers commented on his popularity with females. "Feminine Hearts Caught in His Magic Net of Song and Music," a *Philadelphia Inquirer* sub-headline read. When he made his first movie, *The Vagabond Lover,* based on the title of his hit song, the *Chicago Daily Tribune* described him as "the crooning blonde whose hypnotizing vocalizing over the radio caused him to be swept to Hollywood on a wave of feminine adulation." On leaving the theater, the same writer noticed "a goodly number of determined looking men there, you could see, hell bent on wresting from the charmer the secret of his hold on women."

Richard Watts Jr. of the *New York Herald-Tribune* sought to understand the Vallée phenomenon. He noted that Vallée was "wistful rather than wisecracking" and his crooning makes "each woman in the audience think he is singing directly to her." Still, Watts was puzzled: a commonplace-looking young man, with a commonplace voice, and a second-rate orchestra, he still managed to be the matinée idol of his day. Watts then categorizes what women had written to the paper about Vallée. In order, "(1) He is a gentleman; (2) he is modest; (3) he is adorable; (4) he croons nice sentimental melodies; he is . . . anything but a hardened Broadway showman type, and therefore a refreshing change."

Like other men of the time, Watts had trouble understanding why these qualities led to such success. To Watts, "these suddenly admired qualities . . . are so negative and, hitherto, so completely neglected." Modesty, reserve, a quiet manner, these are not paths to popularity, "and the news that being modest and a gentleman aid in Broadway success, is just a bit overwhelming." Watts finally concedes that Vallée's succeeding through an absence of aggressiveness and blatancy may have been a sign of genius, as if Vallée calculated it as such. In spite of it all Watts still could not understand why these traits "should cause the emotional hysteria among the girls that Rudy Vallée has aroused."

Watts seemed to still be living in Victorian times, when separate spheres predominated, and men were expected to go out into the world and be aggressive, hardened, and not vulnerable, while women were to find a husband with those qualities, so they could remain at home, shielded from the harshness of society, while inculcating in their children the values of a proper lady or gentleman. The twenties had smashed that mold, and many young women of the time, whether flappers or not, wanted something different, and in essence, something more.

They had gained the vote, finally, and wanted to extend that freedom and to have more a partner than a provider. The combative hero of the nineteenth century no longer fit the times; equality and sensitivity mattered.

Following Vallée another popular crooner, Bing Crosby, emerged, although his fame as a solo singer did not come until the 1930s. During the '20s Crosby was a member of a trio, The Rhythm Boys, under Paul Whiteman's band. The group (although not the name) began as a duo with Al Rinker in Spokane, Washington. Crosby, who was born in Tacoma but grew up in Spokane, was in his third year at Gonzaga College, studying law. He had become fascinated with show business and decided to become a drummer. Rinker, five years younger than Crosby, had formed a band and needed a drummer. Even though the rest of the band was composed of high-school students, Crosby was happy to join. But by 1925 the high-school members of the band were graduating, and the ensemble dissolved.

Rinker and Crosby stayed on—Crosby by that time had abandoned the notion of being a lawyer—and they landed a job at the Clemmer Theater, a large movie house that, like many, used vaudeville acts between screenings. At first Crosby sang and Rinker played piano in the pit. Then they began to work as a singing duo. Soon they sought to escape what Crosby considered "the smothering provincialism of the 'cornfeds.'" They headed to Los Angeles and worked several revues, starting with *The Syncopation Idea*. After about a year Paul Whiteman became interested and hired them as something different for his band. Whiteman added a piano-singer Harry Barris, to complete the trio, and named them "The Rhythm Boys."

Soon Whiteman was using Crosby as a solo singer. His first hit was "Ol' Man River," in a fast fox-trot version, where Crosby as band singer simply has one chorus. He sings with a rhythmic vitality and syncopation, including quarter-note triplets on "rollin' along," and ends on an octave-higher tonic. The later Crosby style can be heard, but it is confined by the pace and instrumental arrangement.

The Rhythm Boys left Whiteman in 1929 to join Gus Arnheim and His Cocoanut Grove Orchestra, and there Crosby's crooning began. Arnheim's orchestra was predominantly a sweet band, and Crosby's style began to evolve, as the audience wanted to hear more of his solo singing. Rinker and Barris became essentially backup musicians. Soon Crosby left for a solo career and the group dissolved.

"I Surrender, Dear," recorded in 1931, is considered Crosby's first solo hit. Yet he is still framed within the jazz band of the time. Here he is still part of Gus Arnheim's orchestra, and appears in the middle, after several instrumental choruses that vary from Arnheim's sweet sound to double-time solo improvisations. Curiously, there is a hint of Al Jolson in Crosby's voice in this number. Crosby does break the band singer mold at the very end when he returns for a final climactic tag.

While Crosby is considered the heir to Vallée, there are noticeable differences in their styles. Vallée sang in a high breathy voice, whereas Crosby had a much fuller, richer baritone sound. Vallée was the handsome, dashing college boy who could make the girls swoon. Crosby had neither Vallée's good looks nor his collegiate bearing, but his nonchalant, relaxed appearance made him appealing if not sensually scorching. In that sense Crosby was a singer for the 1930s. With the coming of the Depression, people needed to be soothed more than stimulated, and the jazz-age flapper was now facing the more serious problem of pure survival in a difficult world. The hot jazz of the 1920s never completely disappeared, as it evolved into swing, but a sweeter sound emerged, whether that of Crosby, Guy Lombardo, or later, Glenn Miller. The recording industry was devastated, as the public turned to radio, which provided free entertainment, or the movies, which, by then with sound, provided escape. The never-ending good times of the 1920s had ended, and the mood of the public had changed. The music industry had no choice but to adapt.

Yet the 1920s left a permanent imprint on American culture. Recordings, that is, the actual sound of the performer, replaced sheet music as the norm for public consumption. Radio demonstrated that performance had no geographical limits, eventually leading to the Internet and streaming of today. And finally, in jazz and blues, the color line was cracked if not broken, at least in the public consumption of music. While many racial barriers still existed, while many theaters continued segregated, while radio stations remained predominantly white, the 78 rpm record was out there, to be purchased by anyone, the only criterion being, "I like the music."

CHAPTER 8

The Ultramodern Revolution and Music Appreciation

On December 29, 1915, composer, conductor, and musical radical Edgard Varèse arrived in New York from Paris. Surveying the musical scene, he was "amazed that nobody knew anything about modern music." Four years later, after a less than successful career as a conductor, he leveled his frustration at the current musical establishment: "Too many musical organizations are Bourbons who learn nothing and forget nothing. They are mausoleums—mortuaries for musical reminiscences."

Varèse's criticism bore some truth. In classical musical circles, it could as well have been the 1890s. Many organizations, orchestras especially, were playing the same programs as they had in the late nineteenth century. Richard Strauss was still considered the height of radicalism, even though his most performed tone poems, *Don Juan, Death and Transfiguration, Till Eulenspiegel's Merry Pranks, Also sprach Zarathustra, Don Quixote,* and *Ein Heldenleben,* were all written before 1900, several before 1890. To Frederick Martens, American writer and biographer, modern music in 1918 meant César Franck's Sonata for Violin and Piano, a thoroughly Romantic composition written in 1886. Franck had died in 1890. Sergei Diaghilev toured the United States with his Ballets Russes in 1916 but surprisingly did not program Stravinsky's *Rite of Spring*, which had become world-famous due to its riotous premier in 1913. America was not ready for the *Rite*, which was not heard on its shores until 1924.

What Varèse, Diaghilev, and much of the concert-going public did not fully recognize was that there was already an incipient modernist movement in the United States, and it involved music. The central figure in establishing modernism in America was Alfred Stieglitz, photographer, gallery owner, and disputant extraordinaire. Through his own work, his support of others, and his outspoken ideas, he gathered around him a coterie of like-minded radicals who would challenge the status quo in many arts.

Stieglitz, who came from an upper-middle-class family in New York City, enrolled in the Technische Hochschule in Berlin in 1882, where he studied chemistry with Hermann Wilhelm Vogel, who had done pioneering work in photographic processing. Stieglitz became hooked on photography and from then on made it his life's work. At the time photography was useful for documentaries and family mementos but was considered no more an art than music had been in Federal America. Some photographers were trying to create artistic photographs, but their approach was to imitate painting, producing hazy, gauzy images of Romantic appeal. Stieglitz returned to New York in 1890 determined to change that.

His first goal was to establish photography as an art in its own right, not as a pale imitation of painting. In New York he saw a new subject matter for photography, the gritty, bustling, industrial city, the metaphor for the modern age. Photography was to be an art for the twentieth century. To Stieglitz, photography and modernism were one. Two of his most iconic photographs produced at that time, *The Terminal* (1892) and *Winter* (1893), reflect

Alfred Stieglitz's photograph *The Hand of Man* depicts an industrial twentieth century, showing both its successes and its environmental despoliation.

that new direction. Then in 1902 he produced his strongest industrial statement, *The Hand of Man*, a work that resonates today.

The glistening light of the crossing railroad tracks snakes toward the reader while a locomotive bellowing black smoke dominates the center-right of the image. To the left can be seen telephone/telegraph/power wires, and in the distance, large smokestacks. To the right are two small buildings, with larger industrial edifices just beyond them. The entire scene has a dark, grey, gritty tone, with steam merging into clouds, and nowhere is a person or any unspoiled nature to be seen. An early twentieth-century observer would see the arrival of the industrial age; a twenty-first-century one would likely see the hand of environmental degradation.

Stieglitz knew he must go beyond the creation of photographs to advocate for photography's place in the art world. When he first returned from Europe he consolidated two earlier organizations to create the Camera Club, along with its magazine *Camera Notes.* In 1903 he created *Camera Work*, the first magazine to include quality images. In 1901 he gathered a group of photographers to create the Photo-Secession, whose mission statement began, "We are searching for the ultimate truth." In 1905 he opened the Little Galleries of the Photo-Secession, which later became Gallery 291.

Soon both *Camera Work* and Gallery 291 began to include art other than photography. Painters such as Henri Matisse, Pablo Picasso, John Marin, John McNeill Whistler, Marsden Hartley, and Georgia O'Keeffe appeared either on 291's walls or in *Camera Work* or both. Equally important, Gallery 291 became the gathering place for avant-garde artists of all stripes, including poets and writers. New, exciting ideas were hotly debated, although Stieglitz's own personality impeded as well as stimulated discussion; his strong opinions were often voiced in lengthy monologues, and he did not encourage disagreement. Nevertheless, the intellectual spark coming from the gallery did much to kindle an intense modernist flame that would spread throughout all American arts.

Almost all the arts! Music, it seemed, lay outside the Stieglitz orbit, even though Stieglitz himself was a serious amateur pianist. Musical modernism existed in the United States, only hidden, particularly in an insurance agency in New York City, run by Charles Ives and Julian Myrick. Ives had come from one of the most prominent families in Danbury, Connecticut. His ancestors were bankers, abolitionists, and leading citizens of the town. His father, however, was the black sheep in the family; he decided on a career in music. That was not an acceptable profession for an upper-class man in nineteenth-century New England. Yet even though the Ives clan had misgivings, they closed ranks and continued to support him. While George Ives performed the role of bandmaster and provider of music for many occasions, he also had an experimental streak. His son Charles, obsessed with music, absorbed—inherited—George's free thinking and took it even further. Developing a formidable piano technique, Charles originally considered a career in music, but soon realized that his unorthodox sounds were not compatible with earning a good living: "If he [the composer] has a nice wife and some nice children, how can he let the children starve on his dissonances." Ives's music was not only highly dissonant, but tonally complex, rhythmically uneven, and melodically fragmented, often drawing on vernacular sources—popular songs and hymns—that would often appear in isolated or sometimes overlapping motives.

Thanks to support from his uncle, Lyman Bristow, Ives graduated from Yale in 1898 and moved to New York City to establish a career. He found a position with Mutual of New York, in what was then a new field, life insurance. Soon he and his partner, Myrick, were running the largest agency in New York. Ives was the creative force in the partnership, establishing many concepts and approaches that remain in use today. He is still remembered within the industry.

Meanwhile Ives married, and he and his wife, Harmony—yes, that was her real name—built a home on 18.5 acres in Redding, Connecticut. Ives would spend as much time there as possible, usually in a room upstairs composing—songs, piano pieces, chamber music, symphonies, and more. For the most part he kept this activity secret, although he made a few efforts to have his music known. Most of these came to naught, however, and until 1919 Ives did not pursue this tack with any diligence. Then in 1921 he had his huge *Piano Sonata No. 2, Concord, Mass., 1840–60,* printed, followed by a group of *114 Songs* the next year. He sent these, free, unannounced, and un-copyrighted, to as many musicians as he could find addresses for. Results were to some extent predictable: "It is incomprehensible to me"; "I frankly do not like this manner of sound association"; "Some of the songs are most startling to a man educated by the harmonic methods of our forefathers."

Yet Ives struck a more harmonious chord with a few musicians, particularly T. Carl Whitmer, Henry Bellamann, and Clifton Furness. These young men started to promote Ives's music, until by the end of the decade it had been taken up by other performers and conductors, with premiers in both the United States and Paris.

In spite of its resuscitation, Ives's compositional career was mostly finished by the time he sent the two volumes out. In 1919, when Ives was fifty-five years old, he suffered what was apparently a heart attack. He also developed diabetes and after 1919 was never in good health. Yet to many in the 1920s he became something of a father figure, the original pioneer of the ultramoderns, a position helped in no small way by Ives's generous financial support of modern music. Ives had made a fortune in the insurance business, and he was glad to spend some of it on a cause he held dear.

One other event in the 1910s presaged the ultramodern musical explosion of the 1920s. At the Bandbox Theater, January–March 1915, Leo Ornstein shattered the New York musical world with a series of four concerts. Ornstein, a piano virtuoso, had arrived in New York from the Ukraine in 1906, when he was twelve years old. He had studied at the St. Petersburg Conservatory from the time he was 10. He spent the next several years preparing for a career as a concert pianist, but then in 1913, he began hearing strange, highly dissonant musical sounds in his head. Next thing, complete pieces came tumbling out. Years later Ornstein described the experience:

> I still wonder at the age of eighty, why should I have thought of that? A boy that had been sitting at the piano

> practicing the *Twelfth Rhapsody* [of Liszt] to try to astonish the ladies with the speed and accuracy of the passages, and blind the audience with the terrific glissandos and what not. Why suddenly that thing came into my head—I'll be blessed if I know. And as a matter of fact, I really doubted my sanity at first. I simply said, what is that? It was so completely removed from any experience I had ever had.

Ornstein played the piece, probably "Danse Sauvage," for his teacher Bertha Feiring Tapper, who also doubted his sanity, or at best thought it a practical joke. After Ornstein repeated it three times, however, she realized that he might be onto something. Following a brief European tour, in which he created a sensation in London, Ornstein returned to present his Bandbox concerts, which launched him as a concert artist and stamped him as a revolutionary or, according to some newspapers, a "musical anarchist." His program consisted mostly of new European music that had not been heard in the United States—Ravel, Schoenberg, Isaac Albéniz, Vítězslav Novák, Cyrill Scott, Launy Grøndahl, and of course Ornstein himself.

Paul Rosenfeld hailed Ornstein as "the *diabolus in musica.*" He was compared favorably to Schoenberg, Stravinsky, and Scriabin: Frederick Martens, Ornstein's first biographer, quoted an anonymous London critic who dubbed Ornstein "the sum of Schoenberg and Scriabine squared"; Waldo Frank prophesized that of Stravinsky, Schoenberg, and Ornstein, "Ornstein, the youngest of these, gives promise to be the greatest." Yet to much of the public he seemed either a madman, or a lone wolf, disassociated from the American concert mainstream. He did not create a school, and few other pianists played his radical pieces, possibly because few dared.

Ornstein was not alone in his artistic quest, however. He became very much a part of the Stieglitz circle. He developed close relationships with the writers Waldo Frank and Paul Rosenfeld and the painters John Marin, William and Marguerite Zorach, and Georgia O'Keefe, who later became Stieglitz's wife. Rosenfeld and Frank especially saw Ornstein as the means to round out the modernist agenda by introducing new music to the public, and conversely, Ornstein served to bring modernist music into the wider Stieglitz circle.

Yet Ornstein's impact was limited, partly his own doing. After he had composed his most radical piece in 1915, the atonal Violin Sonata, Op. 31, he thought, "I would say that Op. 31 had brought music just to the very edge. . . . I just simply drew back and said, 'beyond that lies complete chaos.'" He then turned to a more conservative, in his words, "expressive" style. Rosenfeld, his most ardent and influential champion, all but abandoned him. Ornstein left the concert stage in the early 1920s, for reasons not entirely clear, and virtually disappeared from public view.

Musical ultramodernism thus had to wait until the 1920s, and the burden shifted back to Varèse. In 1921 he struck at the heart of the dilemma of musical modernism, its inability to convince the impresarios, agents, and managers to support the movement. For them, whose first responsibility was to the box office, the fear of empty seats exceeded any artistic or aesthetic considerations. Varèse was determined to eliminate that roadblock; he would bypass the musical establishment. In 1921 along with his wife Louise and the Spanish harpist and composer Carlos Salzedo, he formed the International Composers' Guild, an organization of musicians that would sponsor their own concerts, using venues not normally associated with classical music. Varèse was clear in the intent: "The International Composers' Guild . . . is an attempt to eliminate the commercial manager and give the composers a wider opportunity for having their works produced without the thought of whether they will please the public." Ever the European radical, he issued a leaflet with the word MANIFESTO typed in large print at the top. He promised the ICG would fight "for the right of each individual to secure 'fair and free presentation of his work,'" and ended defiantly, "The present day composers refuse to die."

The first concert of the ICG occurred on February 19, 1922, at the Greenwich Village Theatre. The theater had been built in 1917 in the heart of Greenwich Village, which had already gained a reputation for bohemianism, radicalism, and nonconformist lifestyles. The entire program consisted of complex modern works. The concert and the two following, in March and April, proved so successful that Clare Reis, who had assumed the position of executive secretary of the ICG, leased the Klaw Theatre for the second season.

The Klaw, seating 805, was a larger venue than the Greenwich Village Theatre, which seated 500. Clearly Varèse and the modernists had found an audience. The Klaw Theatre also represented a symbolic move uptown. On West 45th Street, it was in the heart of the Broadway theater district. In artistic circles, "downtown" usually meant the bohemian enclave around Greenwich Village; "uptown" was establishment, closer to Central Park and Carnegie Hall, later to Lincoln Center. This distinction held throughout the twentieth century, resurfacing especially after World War II. With Reis's move the 1920s modernists were no longer bohemian outcasts, but were invading proper uptown New York.

Critics also began to notice the ICG. The first concert at the Klaw, December 17, 1922, was described in detail in the *New York Times*, which also noted a "distinguished audience present." The anonymous critic could not, however, help lampooning the pieces while praising the performance: "These modern musical explorations, cubist contraptions of tone and tempo, fit for ears to which harmony is a lost illusion and melody a lost art, were handsomely presented by skilled interpreters and in three instances by the composers themselves."

By 1924 the ICG was a part of mainstream musical New York. To be sure, many skeptics remained. Richard Aldrich, for instance, described the much anticipated 1923 ICG American premier of Arnold Schoenberg's *Pierrot lunaire* as a "succession of disagreeable and unmusical noises," its overall impression being "simply null or more or less wearisomely repugnant." Reis, however, was ready to take the modernist revolution into the heart of uptown, at Aeolian Hall, an 1,100-seat auditorium that saw performances of many of the leading concert stars of the day. Lawrence Gilman, music critic for the *New York Herald Tribune,* acknowledged changes in the New York music scene: "It is no longer possible to doubt that there is a public—large, alert, inquisitive—for the significant new music of our time."

All was not tranquil in the modernist world, however. Within a year a group of composers, including six of the eight members of the executive council, had broken from the ICG and formed a rival organization, the League of Composers. Varèse considered the ICG his organization, and the dissenters could not abide his high-handed ways. Reis, who left to assume a position with the League, later referred to Varèse as a "dictator." There were disputes over programming, the ostensible cause for the split. When the ICG gave the American premier of Schoenberg's *Pierrot lunaire,* many members wanted a second performance. Varèse refused, on the premise that ICG practice was to premier new works, not condone repeat performances. His intransigence made many members realize the truth of co-founder Carlo Salzedo's statement: "This is Varèse's society; it must belong to him."

There was an even deeper current stirring between the ICG and the League, as the 1920s witnessed a peak of anti-Semitism in the United States. Millions of immigrants, most of them Jews, had arrived in the country in the early twentieth century, and the 1920s witnessed a backlash. Books such as Lothrap Stoddard's *The Rising Tide of Color against White World-Supremacy* carried a blatantly racist message in an apocalyptic tone. Henry Ford, arguably the most powerful industrialist at the time, brought anti-Semitism fully out in the open with his anti-Semitic crusade; he believed that the Jews formed the greatest threat to American culture. Through the *Dearborn Independent,* a small newspaper he bought, and later in books, he resurrected the myth of the Protocols of the Elders of Zion, supposedly a secret plan by Jewish leaders to gain world domination through financial manipulation, control of media, and fostering of religious discord. By 1921 the Protocols had been exposed as a complete fabrication, a plagiarism taken mainly from a book by David Joly, *Dialogue aux enfers entre Machiavel et Montesquieu* (*Dialogue in Hell between Machiavelli and Montesquieu*), written in 1864. Joly was satirizing the French reign of Napoleon III, which had nothing to do with Jews. Later in the 1920s Ford was pressured to recant, probably because of the damage that his campaign was doing to automobile sales, but that did not undo the damage of his publications.

Varèse, along with Carl Ruggles and possibly Carlos Salzedo, key members of the ICG, harbored anti-Semitic sentiments. He saw jazz, which many composers such as Aaron Copland were incorporating, as a kind of Jewish scheme: "Jazz is not America, it's a Negro plot, exploited by the Jews. All of its composers from here are Jews." In the 1930s his anti-Semitism became sharper: in a letter to composer André Jolivet he suggested that Hitler might be right, and in a letter to artist Will Shuster, he added at the bottom, "Heil to Hitler." Ruggles was constantly outspoken about Jews; in 1933 he wrote to Henry Cowell, "I agree with Adolph [Weiss] and Salzedo that it is a great mistake to have that filthy bunch of Juilliard Jews in the Pan American [a new musical organization]. They are cheap, without dignity, and with little, or no talent. . . . They will double cross you, Henry, I'm sure, in every possible way. My advice is to promptly kick them out, before it's too late. Carl."

When the issue of *Pierrot lunaire* was discussed by the ICG board, the meeting became so acrimonious that three members walked out. They formed the core group advocating a new society, and they were all Jewish. The executive board of the newly founded League consisted of Louis Gruenberg, Lazare Saminsky, Alma Morgenthau Wertheim, Arthur Bliss, Leo Ornstein, and Emerson Whithorne, soon to be joined by Aaron Copland. Except for Bliss and Whithorne, all were Jewish, and Bliss, an English composer temporarily residing in the United States, was essentially an honorary member.

From the start the League professed a more open approach to programming, announcing that it would present new music of all styles, including "the safe middle-road," and promising that the five composers on the board would not use their position to fill the programs with their own works. Both points were aimed directly at Varèse. In practice, however, programming of the two societies did not vary significantly in content, although enmity remained sufficient that a composer played on one organization's program could count on being excluded from the other's.

Several other new music societies followed, but these two dominated the New York scene throughout the 1920s, until in 1927 when Varèse suddenly announced that he was disbanding the ICG. To this day it is not clear what prompted that move, although he did form a second organization almost immediately, the Pan American Association, which brought in composers from Latin America. The League continued until 1954, when it became the United States Chapter of the International Society of Contemporary Music. It is still active in that form in 2023.

By the mid-1920s musical modernism had spread beyond New York, especially to two other cultural centers, San Francisco and Chicago. In San Francisco Henry Cowell, one of the most original figures in American music, founded the New Music Society in 1925.

Cowell is one of several artists from the western United States of a strongly independent and anti-traditional streak, whose training and career broke norms and who followed a highly individualist, even eccentric path. His parents were San Francisco bohemians, and his mother Clarissa considered herself an anarchist. When Henry was six his parents divorced, and after Clarissa's failed attempt to establish herself as a writer in New York, she and Henry lived just outside of San Francisco in extreme poverty that was exacerbated by Clarissa's health issues. Henry was almost completely home-schooled, in Clarissa's haphazard way. Yet he showed a remarkable if uneven intelligence. Louis Terman, a psychology professor at Stanford who was developing the IQ test, became interested in Henry because of his unusual educational background. He described Henry at the age of twelve: "Henry's appearance was odd. . . . His speech was quaint, and rather drawled and stilted; his face was childish, but he looked at you with eyes that seemed utterly void of self-consciousness."

Thanks to Cowell's precociousness and his family's connections to the San Francisco bohemian world, he attracted friends and supporters. Ellen Veblen, wife of the economist Thorstein Veblen, bought him a piano and arranged for lessons; the poet John Varian treated him as an adopted son and took him to Halcyon, a Theosophist center near Santa Barbara, California. He was also able to study composition at the University of California, Berkeley with the new head of the Music Department, Charles Seeger, another ultramodernist who would become an important figure in 1920s New York. Seeger commented on those lessons, "I discovered very quickly that he was an autodidact and the best way to handle autodidacts was to let them didact and work around from the outside, as it were."

After his mother's death in 1916 Cowell went to New York and began what Joel Sachs called his "bi-coastal life," his time divided between New York and California. Seeing the ICG and the League inspired Cowell to spread the musical revolution to the West Coast. He formed the New Music Society, which he considered a West Coast branch of the ICG. He originally based it in Los Angeles, possibly because of the presence there of Dane Rudhyar, a composer, Theosophist, and astrologer he had known both at Halcyon and in New York. Finding Los Angelenos mostly cool to modern experimental music, though, he moved the society to the more receptive San Francisco, where the society presented concerts from 1927 to 1936. At first the critics were puzzled by what they heard. They were pleased, however, that the latest, most avant-garde sounds had reached the West Coast, although to them the sounds ranged from the unpleasant to the unfathomable. Redfern Mason, critic for the *San Francisco Examiner,* commented, "like olives, ultra modern music is an acquired taste."

In 1927 Cowell launched another vehicle, the magazine *New Music Quarterly.* As Stieglitz had demonstrated with *Camera Work,* as Samuel Atkins Eliot had demonstrated in his many anonymous articles selling the very idea of art music in the 1830s and '40s, artistic revolutions require more than the art itself: a case must be made for it and a means to propagate it beyond its premiers or first showings must be found. *New Music Quarterly* served the latter purpose; it was a magazine of scores. When major music publishers considered ultramodern scores toxic or at least unsalable, the presence of Cowell's magazine allowed musicians outside the immediate circle of ultramoderns to study, understand, and in some cases perform the strange new sounds. *New Music Quarterly* continued to publish until 1957, when the Theodore Presser Company bought the entire catalogue, which by then had become substantial.

Prior to computer music typesetting programs, publishing music was an expensive process, necessitating hand engraving of what in the case of ultramodern scores seemed to engravers bewildering. Charles Ives at one time had to write to his copyist, "Mr. Price, do not correct any of the wrong notes. The wrong notes are right."

NMQ was able to succeed thanks to Ives. When Cowell first

announced the magazine, he was surprised to have over 600 subscribers, far exceeding the 200–300 he expected. To Cowell this meant success, "if I can keep them." Alas, that did not happen: after they saw the first volume consisting of Carl Ruggles, *Men and Mountains,* about half of the subscribers withdrew.

At that point Charles Ives came to the rescue. He originally ordered fifty subscriptions, but gradually began to supply much more money anonymously, allowing the journal to continue. At the time Ives was mostly unknown, at least to the general public, although his music had begun to be programmed. He did benefit by having several of his compositions published in *NMQ,* but only after the journal ended did Cowell reveal the extent of Ives's generosity.

NMQ served an important function in making the music of the ultramoderns more widely available. Missing still was a vehicle that allowed composers to discuss and refine ideas, to explain their approaches, and in general, to argue their cause. For that purpose Minna Lederman launched another magazine, *Modern Music Quarterly,* in 1925. Lederman and Reis were of a generation of women who served an important but highly restricted role in American musical history. They were extremely involved in music, and were talented performers, but they were born into an upper class that disdained women in public professional roles in music, especially as performers. So they served in a way that their class and culture sanctioned: they assumed executive positions within the ultramodern community. As mentioned earlier, Reis became executive director of the ICG and then the League of Composers; Lederman founded the principal advocacy magazine for modern music, and served as its editor until it ceased publication in 1946.

Modern Music was both a propagandist tool for the ultramoderns and a platform that allowed practitioners to debate aesthetic as well as practical issues. Lederman made it clear that this was a magazine by composers for composers, although scholars and critics often appeared. The magazine welcomed analytical articles discussing technical issues, but few were submitted. Typical was Virgil Thomson's 1932 article discussing Aaron Copland, who by then had become the most successful and widely known of the ultramoderns. The article has curious twists, typical Thomson asperity, and more than a hint of jealousy. For Thomson, Judaism explained Copland: "He is a prophet calling out her sins to Israel." He then discusses two early Copland pieces, the *Symphony for Organ and Orchestra* and the *Piano Concerto*. Thomson dismissed the *Symphony for Organ:* "That has been his one wild oat. It was not a very fertile one," not fertile because Copland "never understood that sensuality or sentiment which is the force of American popular music." Thomson then reversed his stance: "He is not banal. He has truth, force, and elegance. He has not quite style."

Copland had arrived in France to study music in 1921 and signed up for summer classes at the new Conservatory in Fountainebleau just outside of Paris. Copland's choice of France itself symbolizes a break from earlier practice where an aspiring American musician invariably chose Germany. In France he found Nadia Boulanger a rigorous and inspiring teacher and a phenomenal musician, familiar with a wide range of music from Renaissance polyphony to the latest works of Stravinsky and Ravel. Soon many of the most important twentieth-century American composers honed their craft under Boulanger. She counted among her pupils Walter Piston, George Antheil, Roger Sessions, Louise Talma, David Diamond, Roy Harris, Elliott Carter, Philip Glass, Burt Bacharach, and many more. Throughout the years Copland, however, remained her favorite.

Upon his return to the United States in 1924 Copland quickly established himself as an important young composer. He was, however, far from the American icon he later became, with the performance of his ballets, *Rodeo, Billy the Kid,* and *Appalachian Spring*. Those works, in their employment of folk elements and Copland's sparse, open, but spiky harmonies, were easily approachable and spoke directly of great American myths and spacious landscapes. In 1925 his compositions breathed European modernism tinted with 1920s jazz. His first major work to be performed was the *Organ Symphony,* premiered by the New York Philharmonic under Walter Damrosch, followed by a Boston Symphony Orchestra performance under Serge Koussevitzky. Boulanger played the organ part for both. That same year Koussevitzky premiered Copland's *Music for the Theater.* In part thanks to Boulanger, who introduced Koussevitzky to Copland, Copland was able to break out almost immediately from the tight circle of ultramodern societies even though his music aligned well with the League of Composers, which he had joined.

Yet Paul Rosenfeld, like Thomson, thought Copland to be still a work in progress. In 1927 he wrote: "His gift is decidedly proficient but small, as yet so immature that it makes the impression not so much of something human, as of something coltlike: all legs, head, and frisking hide; cantering past on long uncertain stilts. . . . With all his grandiosity and *élan,* Copland has not yet found a largely symbolic and inclusive form for his gift." Copland of course soon would find an idiom ideally suited to his gifts and aesthetic sensibilities.

The ultramoderns succeeded through the use of a principle as old as the universe itself: the idea of self-organization. It was hardly new with American culture, or even human society. As demonstrated by work in chaos theory in the 1970s and '80s, or, as it came to be called, complex adaptive systems, self-organization is endemic to the nature of the universe, a way that matter from the atomic level to the cosmos acts. Self-organization is apparent in vortices of water just before it boils—usually noticed by bubbles—the spin of a hurricane, the rotation of galaxies, or sometimes human interactions in social systems. Its mathematical principles have become staples of sociological, economic, and business analysis.

Self-organized systems usually begin with a bifurcation point, a destabilizing event or factor that causes a new or different organization to arise. This establishes a feedback loop as new organizing principles redirect the future of the system. Further, as the principles affect the environment in which they arose, the changes in the environment affect the principles.

Self-organization united with revolutionary ideals has defined much of American history. Historians may argue about the cause of the American Revolution, that is, the precise bifurcation event, but the result was the founding of a self-organizing society, the Continental Congress, and eventually the drafting of the Declaration of Independence, leading to the Revolutionary War and the creation of the new nation. The success of the war eventually led to the rise of another self-organizing entity, the Constitutional Convention, whose document established the federal government as it stands today. Much feedback for more than two centuries has necessitated modifications in the government the founders created, but its own flexibility has allowed it to remain.

Self-organization was particularly important to the arts after the American Revolution. Unlike in Europe, there was no aristocracy to organize and direct the course of musical events or to dictate artistic tastes, no one to put a Haydn in a servant's uniform and demand new symphonies. When various electronic means of dissemination appeared in the twentieth century, there was no state media as in Europe, no state-controlled radio and television to support cutting-edge works and performances. Concert impresarios in the United States were obligated neither to further society or the arts, nor to inculcate in the public higher moral or spiritual values, but rather to listen to the box office. This guaranteed conservatism.

The ultramoderns were faced with a force too strong to allow them to climb beyond the foothills of the landscape they were on. Several factors collaborated against their success. Composers first had to persuade their agents about the value of their work, who then had to convince impresarios to contract a performer to program their compositions, which must meet audience approval. There are thus five entities involved, composer, performer, agent, impresario, and audience. Any one of the four beyond the composer theoretically could consign the piece to oblivion, although the further up the line, that is, the closer the impediment was to the composer, the more likely the composition would meet a quick, untimely death.

Sometimes the composer is a performer, as was the case with Ornstein. Yet Ornstein succeeded in part because audiences flocked in disbelief to see what he would do onstage. Only because of his virtuosity did he remain successful on the concert stage, and many viewed him as some sort of diabolic phenomenon, to watch in bewilderment, astonishment, and, in some cases, bemusement as he seemingly destroyed a piano. In one sense Ornstein was the pianistic bad-boy rock star of the 1910s.

By 1922 Varèse and others saw no solution to their problems but to leap to a new mountain range. That move in fitness landscape terms as described in the first chapter is the heart of revolution and can be found repeatedly in American society. Clearly, the metaphor of fitness landscapes and the reality of the physical American landscape have much in common. Geography determined that America would be a society on the move. "Go West, young man" was more than a metaphor in the nineteenth century. Even after the frontier closed in 1892, large movements of populations continued throughout much of the twentieth century: the influx of immigrants from Eastern Europe in the early part of the century; the waves of Midwesterners going to California during the Dust Bowl; the Great Migrations of African Americans from the South to the industrial North particularly after World War I.

Invariably a society on the move reinvents itself in many ways, and whether each sweeping wave of people represents a revolution is another question; but not only these large migrations but many smaller and less geographically based changes speak at the very least to transitions. Such transitions are almost always prompted by a bifurcation point, and the strategy of the 1920s ultramodern musicians forms a classic example. They were boxed in and left with little choice if they were to succeed.

The core of the ultramoderns' revolution was to eliminate three, sometimes four, of the five operators that constituted the classical musical world. The ICG and the League, in sponsoring their own concerts, did away with agents and impresarios. Sometimes the composer acted as their own performer. About the audience the ultramoderns were ambivalent. To Varèse, the audience was the bourgeois and the bourgeois were hopeless. He had indicated from the beginning that whether he pleased the public was irrelevant. When the ICG considered touring, Varèse was concerned about "the stupidity of the provincial audiences." Ruggles was equally disdainful: once incensed by a full house, he commented, "I would prefer to see only six people at our concerts! If you had a full house last Sunday it only goes to show you've descended to catering to the public." Yet reality dictated they needed and expected an audience, and the early reports of the two societies suggest they succeeded.

The ultramoderns guaranteed that classical music would never be the same. New sounds, techniques, and approaches once introduced could not be recalled, and while there was a retrenchment in the 1930s as modernists sought an idiom that would be more appealing to a broader public, nevertheless the residue of the 1920s remained. The ultramoderns had familiarized the unfamiliar, making it more palpable to American audiences, and a legitimate tool for composers of all persuasions.

While the ultramoderns were upsetting the musical world of the 1920s with their noisy revolution, other composers and performers continued as they always had, creating music of a more conservative bent, which satisfied a wider audience. Still others were working to spread the broader gospel of classical music itself. This took the form of the music appreciation movement, which began as an outgrowth of the nineteenth-century belief in the moral effect of "good" music but later became a vehicle for other causes, including an advocacy for pure music, which in this context meant formalism, an approach that ironically supported the modernist cause. Indirectly it would eventually provide a theoretical basis for post–World War II revolutionary composers.

The music appreciation movement began in England in 1893 when composer Charles William Pearce read a paper to the Royal Music Association. He was motivated by the desire of John Stainer, president of the association, for "intelligent hearers." Stainer compared the listener who may be moved by a symphony but cannot follow its intricacies, to a child who delights in looking through a kaleidoscope: "Both are on the same low level." Pearce outlined a formidable set of requirements for the intelligent listener: they need to know the exact period of musical history in which the composer lived and worked, "whether the composer had any definite aim or program when designing his work . . . an intimate acquaintance with the laws of harmonic progression, contrapuntal fluency, methods of modulation, and the usual orchestral 'idioms' . . . experienced knowledge of the particular formal design in which each movement is cast."

Stainer's and Pearce's aims found a broader audience in 1907 when Thomas Whitney Surette and Daniel Gregory Mason published the first music appreciation textbook in the United States. It is essentially a study of forms, beginning with basic motives, then moving from the combining of phrases to sonata form and the organization of other large music structures. The concept of unity is stressed, and elaborate charts that guide the listener through compositions by focusing on structural elements appear throughout the book. Yet only on the very last page do the authors admit to "an ulterior aim": "The great object of musical analysis must always be to concentrate the attention of the music-lover, to focus his mind as well as his ears on the melodies, and their developments, which he hears, . . . and to help him to substitute for that 'drowsy reverie, relieved by nervous thrills,' an active, joyful, vigorous co-operation with composers, through which alone he can truly appreciate their art." These goals are very close to Pearce's, although there is no evidence of a direct connection.

Many music appreciation books followed, soon to be augmented by radio programs in the 1920s. While the pure music or anti-programmatic goal of these endeavors was usually implied, Aaron Copland stated the prevailing twentieth-century attitude overtly in his 1939 book, *What to Listen for in Music,* and at the same time clarified what concerned Surette and Mason. He divided different musical responses into "three planes": the sensuous, the expressive, and the musical.

The sensuous plane is to Copland almost non-listening, a "brainless" activity in which the listener is engaged in some other activity or may "use music as a consolation or escape." Regarding the expressive plane, those listeners who add mental images or a narrative to a composition are "simple-minded souls," whose activity "should be discouraged wherever and whenever it is met." The purely musical plane is that of "the intelligent music lover," who may find in music general emotions but who is also aware of the notes themselves and how they combine. He must hear the melodies, the rhythms, the harmonies, the tone colors "in a more conscious fashion," and he must understand musical form. The intelligent listener must be aware of the way in which the composer manipulates the musical material. That is a reward in itself, and a goal toward which the "ideal listener" should strive.

For many listeners, music alone stimulates the visual imagination, which was precisely what concerned Surette, Mason, and Copland. But in spite of their best attempts to deprogram listeners, the effort was doomed to failure, a point acknowledged by music critics and scholars beginning roughly in the 1990s. The application of metaphorical associations is no longer outside the scholarly mainstream, the question of meaning has reentered musical dialogue, and most writers have abandoned "the precepts of Copland's typology." Yet twentieth-century musical modernism, indeed the position in classical music throughout much of the twentieth century, was beholden to Copland's perspective.

In the 1920s radio stations had to consider what music should be played. Profits and prestige clashed, and given the newness of the medium, there was no model to guide them; there were no precedents, polls, or focus groups. At first radio stations broadcast a combination of popular and classical music. A log of the first day that station WBAY was on the air, July 25, 1922, indicates what may have been typical programming:

[4:30 P.M. sign-on]
4:32 1. Polonaise
4:40 2. Ave Maria
4:44 3. On Wings of Song
4:49 4. Meditation de Thaïs
4:52 5. Love Scene—Strauss
4:58 6. Marseillaise
5:02 7. Choc de Boc
5:07 8. Carry me Back to Old Virginny
5:12 9. Rhapsody
5:21 10. Melody F—violin
5:25 11. March, National Emblem
5:28 Signing off.

Stations gradually began to expand their classical music offerings. The first opera broadcast occurred on March 15, 1922, when

WJZ broadcast Mozart's comic opera, *Der Schauspieldirektor* (*The Impresario*). It was not a stage production but a studio broadcast, where many of the bewildered singers were introduced to the intricacies of radio for the first time—absolute quiet, no moving while performing, singing directly into the carbon microphone (called the "tomato can" for its looks), and sticking strictly to the script and timing. That winter another Westinghouse station, KYW in Chicago, put much of the season of the Chicago Opera Company on the air, this time directly from the opera stage. The popularity of the performances did much to sustain the newly established station as well as bring opera to many homes whose inhabitants had never attended a live performance. By 1926 WEAF, now connected to several affiliate stations, had its own "Radio Opera Company," and WJZ and its affiliates had a regular Saturday night series of performances by the most important symphony orchestras in New York and Boston.

In 1924 General James G. Harbord, president of the Radio Corporation of America, spoke of the importance of classical broadcasts to American society: "Such concerts have captured the attention of millions of people who are now thinking and talking in praise of good music and the great artists." The music appreciation boom was about to be in full swing, and radio become an important tool in its dissemination. Doing so increased radio's prestige as an important cultural force as well as a commercial enterprise. This was not a trivial issue when the need for regulation of this new industry was seen as both necessary and acute.

No one did more to promote music appreciation on the air than Walter Damrosch, conductor of the New York Symphony and a member of the most powerful musical family in New York. On October 29, 1923, he gave a lecture recital on Beethoven on WEAF. Its success led to several other appearances on the radio by Damrosch, as pianist in collaboration with other performers, as conductor, or as lecturer. By 1927 Damrosch had retired as conductor of the New York Orchestra and devoted himself almost exclusively to radio, logging 23 hours on the air in the 1926–27 season. The culmination of his radio activities was a series of music appreciation courses that ran from 1928 to 1942. Originally conceived as part of a "University of the Air," Damrosch created three program types: for schoolchildren, for high-school age youth, and for adults. Each type aired at a different time to reach the intended audience, with accompanying text material available. It was first titled the *RCA Educational Hour,* then the *Music Appreciation Hour.*

Yet in spite of the advocacy for art music, stations feared that a steady diet of opera and classical concerts would limit audience numbers. *Radio Broadcast* was quick to point that out. Torn between the idea of the "moral value" of good music and the need to please an audience, the journal advised: "The radio audience is heterogeneous. To send out nothing but highbrow music would be to discourage many listeners. But nothing amateurish is permitted. Jazz is mixed with the classic, but it must be accomplished jazz and there must not be too much of it." The dilemma of jazz—its popularity and for some its moral questionability—is clearly on display here, as is the coded racial message in the phrase "accomplished jazz."

With the coming of the Depression of the 1930s and the resulting collapse of record sales, radio became even more important in providing musical entertainment. The preferences of much of the American population and the recognition by radio stations that these larger audiences meant greater profits pushed classical music further into the background, although it always remained. The ultramodern revolution itself did not fare as well; it had lost its force by 1930. The ICG was gone; the League continued, but its impact diminished. Cowell continued the New Music Society's concerts on the West Coast until 1936, even though he had turned from ultramodern to Asian-inspired compositions.

Several composers all but went silent. Ruggles stopped composing and turned to painting. Dane Rudhyar, an important member of the ICG, abandoned composition in favor of astrology, where he became a leading writer. Varèse's output slowed to a trickle. After *Ionisation,* in 1929–30, he completed only two pieces between 1931 and 1946, *Ecuatorial,* a twelve-minute work for bass voice and small instrumental ensemble, and *Density 21.5,* a four-minute work for solo flute. Ruth Crawford Seeger, whose string quartet was arguably the most enduring composition to come out of 1920s ultramodernism, limited her creative output to folk-song arrangements.

Other composers adopted left-wing political views and changed their style. After his *Piano Variations* of 1930, Copland turned to ballets based on folk themes and film scores. Roy Harris, one of the new voices of the 1930s, attempted to capture the spirit of the American West in grandiose but conservative symphonies. Virgil Thomson, among others, followed in the same vein. The Depression changed art music along with the rest of the country.

The modernist revolution may have ended, but its effects continued. The broad plain of romanticism had given way to a new landscape, more varied and more rugged, opening up new possibilities for American musicians. German music continued to be heard, but the German hegemony was broken, and American musicians could stand as equals to their German, indeed European, counterparts. The new landscape provided many peaks, valleys, and crevasses for composers, freeing them to explore a vast range of possibilities that would only widen in the coming decades. The Depression of the 1930s and the world war of the 1940s, however, put radical developments on hold, as most composers reverted to a more accessible idiom. At the same time, jazz continued to evolve, as swing gripped the country with exciting new sounds, creating a frenetic escape from the somber times and giving its name to the decade itself.

The 1950s

CHAPTER 9

After the War

By 1945 many of the big bands had disbanded or were on life support, suffering from multiple blows caused by World War II. Gasoline rationing and a shortage of rubber made travel nearly impossible for an ensemble of twenty-plus musicians. Even staffing a band was difficult, with many musicians in the armed forces. Then in July 1942 James C. Petrillo, head of the American Federation of Musicians, called a strike against the recording industry, forbidding any union musician to record. The strike hit the bands hard. As it dragged on until November 1944 and the record companies depleted their backlog of unreleased recordings, the bands lost another important source of revenue.

Those bands that somehow survived the war faced a new reality. The mood of the country had changed. The public no longer favored the jitterbugging, toe-tapping hot sound of Benny Goodman, but the fuller, heavier, sweet sound of Guy Lombardo or Freddy Martin, who boldly plundered the classics, including one top-ten recording entitled *Symphony*. The public wanted to be soothed, and the big-three record companies, Columbia, RCA, and Decca, obliged. Sentimental Tin Pan Alley songs prevailed, sung by velvety singers with lush instrumental backing.

Most young men who came home from the war in 1945 were no longer youth raring to jive in the ballrooms but adults ready to settle down to a quieter life. Their initiation into adulthood had been abrupt, protracted, and sobering. Many young volunteers or draftees had a senior party consisting of four years of hell, witnessing death and destruction, scraping to do their job and to just stay alive. Those that survived were exhausted. Some had married, hurriedly, before going off to war. Returning home, many found welcome surprises. Corporal Howard Taubman arrived in Chicago March 1945 delighted to find the Christmas tree still waiting for him. His mother was determined the tree would stay up and decorated until he returned, "even if it took until mid-summer." Staff Sgt. Gene Birdwell found a more complex situation. Shot down over Borneo, Birdwell was in a Japanese prison camp for over a year. His wife had assumed he was dead and married his uncle. Fortunately, Sgt. Birdwell's story had a happy ending: when she heard he was alive, she quickly had the marriage annulled and met him at his returning ship. What the family dynamics were after that is not clear.

Picking up where old relationships left off was not always easy. One unnamed girl wrote to columnist Sheila John Daly, fearful that her boyfriend had seen and done so much, "he will think I'm too young and inexperienced for him." Davis advised her that "he may seem like a stranger . . . for the first ten minutes anyway. He may have changed, but will remember you as you were when he left, and that's the way he wants to find you when he comes back."

What Daly didn't say was that many women had also changed. They had served the country in a variety of ways, some in the armed forces, some in auxiliary brigades, and some in the workforce, assuming essential jobs that men previously held. Like the men who left, many women looked forward to raising a family and a return to normalcy. But after their own war experiences, what was normalcy? For many middle-class women, the new reality meant a home in the suburbs, children, and a single breadwinner, *The Man in the Gray Flannel Suit*. The relief of war's end masked the frustration that a taste of freedom, independence, and opportunity had provided. Advertisers bombarded women with messages: "A woman's place is in the home," "Women do not make important decisions or do important things," "Women are dependent and need men's protection." If ever there was a recipe for a bomb waiting to explode, this was it, but it would be another decade before the frustrations of such a limited role would erupt in the second-wave feminist movement.

In the meantime, smooth, sentimental romantic songs and their singers dominated the charts, as sadness and loss lingered for many, and for others, seeking a partner took a more subdued and serious turn. Two songs in particular capture the mood of the postwar years: "Sentimental Journey," the number one hit from 1945, and "To Each His Own," the biggest hit of 1946. Each song reflected the postwar changes in taste. While songs by and large continued to be recorded by bands with their vocalists, it was the singer who got top billing and whom people remembered. "Sentimental Journey" was recorded by Les Brown and his orchestra, but was famous for the debut of a new vocalist with the orchestra, Doris Day. It became her song.

"Sentimental Journey" speaks of nostalgia, of returning home after a long absence. It is about a metaphorical, but for many a very real, trip back home. In 1945 many soldiers had not been home for three or four years. VE and VJ day ignited immediate spontaneous celebrations, with wild exuberance flooding the streets. Washington, DC saw "the greatest celebration the nation has ever known"; in Chicago "a million people danced in the streets"; in Seattle "it was wine, women and song, mostly song, as servicemen and civilians threw dignity aside"; Times Square in New York saw two million people "scream their elation for twenty-four hours" as the newscaster exclaimed, "never before or since has there been a celebration like this."

With the long trek back to the United States and then to home, however, sobriety returned, as well as a longing that had been building throughout the war. The GIs were inevitably changed, and it was time for a new life. Once the transports landed, the GIs piled on the railroad; affordable domestic air travel was still years off, and no one who had been overseas for years had a car waiting for him on the docks. As "Sentimental Journey" stated, "Long to hear that 'All Aboard.'" The song's only reference to the war is oblique and ironic; the third verse asks, "Why did I decide to roam?," a rhetorical question that in 1945 needed no answer.

The tune itself is an entrancing mid-tempo ballad with a catchy melody and a small range of a fourth within the refrain, something that everyone could sing. As if launched by the restraint of the four notes, the melody expands in the bridge just beyond the upper tonic, while keeping a dotted rhythmic pattern in the refrain. There's just enough chromaticism at the end of the main phrases and major-minor twists when the principal motive returns to intensify the longing and nostalgia the text evokes.

While "Sentimental Journey" got the soldiers home, "To Each His Own" spoke to desires many men and women felt in 1946, for a sustained love that grows over time. Its metaphors are temporal, about devotion, growth, and dreams for the future, about a mature love. It is not about wanting "Five Minutes More," or being consumed by a "Kiss of Fire," as later songs described, but rather a lifelong commitment. As years of desire had built up, the young men who had gone to war and the young women who had helped sustain the war effort or been wartime bobby-soxers had grown up and were ready for the next phase of their life. "To Each His Own" resonated with that important postwar moment.

A carefully constructed melody contributes much of the song's appeal. A repeated four-note pentatonic motive launches the main phrase into a soaring upward line which has just enough chromaticism to wring every last ounce of emotion from the text. As if having accomplished its task, the line then settles back to close on the title words. The arch of the melody meshes perfectly with the text. The harmony is early-mid-twentieth-century Tin Pan Alley—full, lush chords, with many sevenths, a distillation of late-Romantic sound.

Another sign of the changing culture of the war and postwar years can be seen in the career of Frank Sinatra. During the war he was more than the hottest and most controversial vocalist in the United States; he was an unprecedented phenomenon. He had started as a lead singer for the Harry James and then Tommy Dorsey bands, and he left Dorsey in 1942 to establish himself as an independent vocalist, following the model of Bing Crosby.

On December 30, 1942, Frank Sinatra appeared at the Paramount Theater in New York along with Benny Goodman's orchestra. Goodman and Jack Benny were the headliners of the show, but what happened stunned everyone. Thousands of teenage girls showed up, "bobby-soxers," so named for the short, thick, rolled white socks they wore. Screaming and swooning, it was an orgiastic affair. Benny Goodman later commented, "I thought the goddamned building was going to cave in. I never heard such a commotion. . . . All this for a fellow I never heard of." Goodman clearly knew of Sinatra, but the audience response was completely unexpected by both the media and the musical world. According to Bob Weitman, manager of the Paramount, "All 5000 [fans] were of one voice, F-R-A-N-K-I-E-E-E-E-E! . . . One of the managers came over to me and said, 'the balcony is rocking—what do we do?' We struck up the National Anthem."

For a time the same mania followed Sinatra everywhere he went. It reached its peak when he returned to the Paramount on October 12, 1944. Lines started forming the night before for the first of five shows at 11:00 A.M. While the Paramount Theater held 3,600, those that got seats refused to leave for the next show. By custom, someone could occupy their seat as long as they stayed in it. After one show, only 250 people left. The 25,000 (police estimate) girls outside went berserk, clogging midtown traffic and reportedly smashing windows. Some 200 police were called to the scene; afterward, the event became known as the Columbus Day Riot.

Sinatramania, as it was called, was a harbinger of similar events in the 1950s and '60s. At the time it was a new phenomenon, although anticipated by the Rudy Vallée craze in the 1920s. Many asked the question, why, and why Sinatra? Inez Robb of *The Atlanta Constitution* was flummoxed: "If this undersized, pleasantly homely kid is the reincarnation of Rudolph Valentino, Rudy Vallee, Bing Crosby and Charles Boyer, then I am Lana Turner in a bathing suit! What Frankie has got that the rest of you boys haven't got is beyond me."

In one sense Sinatra tapped into the same swing market of the 1930s, where young people followed the big bands with fervor hitherto unknown. The swing era bands, however, appealed to young people of both sexes and to young adults. The bands were enjoyed as part of a larger social activity, especially as an opportunity to dance. The bobby-sox phenomenon represented a different and specific demographic, adolescent girls, and their relationship to Sinatra was personal and internal. Former bobby-soxer Janice Booker recounted, "The screaming and moaning was a legitimate, socially acceptable catharsis for budding sexual longings, at a time when emotion was more internalized, . . . when sexuality for young teenagers was not expressed as blatantly as it is now." It was also a bonding experience for adolescent girls, as they and only they understood each other.

Yet this does not explain why Sinatra. He was a skinny pleasant young man who did not have the raw sexuality of an Elvis Presley or the boyish appeal of the Beatles. He sang the same Tin Pan Alley ballads many other singers sang. Sinatra's appeal was to the loneliness and anxiety the war engendered. Sinatramania filled a specific wartime condition. Sinatra recognized the situation: "It was the war years. There was a great loneliness. I was the boy in every corner drugstore, the boy who had gone to war."

Sinatra did look younger than the 29-year-old that he was in 1944. The boy at the corner drugstore was now on some island in the Pacific or crawling across Western Europe under gunfire. For World War II girls, from 13 to 21 years old, lonely and fearful and seeing their safe world asunder, Sinatra was everyman, or every young man, the one for whom they longed. His voice, rich and nuanced, was like his songs, both soothing and heartfelt. He conveyed the loneliness and the desire, the hurt and the anxiety. Journalist and friend Pete Hamill spoke of the sounds of anguish, loss, and loneliness evident in Sinatra's voice, and added, "Sinatra had only one basic subject, loneliness." It is thus not surprising that with the end of the war his career plummeted. He reminded too many people of what they'd just as soon forget.

In 1947 CBS canceled Sinatra's weekly radio program, and his record sales at Columbia began to drop. In 1948 he slipped to fourth in the *Down Beat* poll of best male vocalists, and in 1949 he did not even make the list. The bobby-soxers of the war years were no longer teenagers in need of emotional release. His most loyal fans had not forgotten him but saw him in a different light. To Betsey Weer, president of the Sinatra Fan Club, the swoons, screams, tearing of hair were considered "such childish pastimes." Sinatra was now "a father, a brother and a friend." Betsey had been one of the youngest bobby-soxers and in 1946 at 16 was still in the throes of all of the angst that comes with being a teenager.

The large majority of Sinatra's fans were past teenage infatuation. They were moving on to college, jobs, marriage, in essence establishing their place in an expanding, thriving America. The United States had emerged from the war victorious, and it was the only major industrial country whose infrastructure remained intact. Europe and Asia clamored for its products. In the optimism and prosperity of the postwar boom and America's now dominant position in the world, reality beckoned more strongly than fantasy.

Ballads and low-key love songs interspersed with overt novelty numbers dominated the charts of the second half of the forties. The soothing voices of Perry Como and Bing Crosby held more sway than the electrifying appeal that Frank Sinatra had commanded. Nostalgia remained, but after the huge 1945 Andrews Sisters hit, "Rum and Coca-Cola," the war was seldom mentioned.

While America seemed to promise unlimited possibilities after World War II, that held only if you were white and middle-class. For others, the future was not as rosy. Blacks had served valiantly in the armed forces during the war, but in segregated units. They returned home to find discrimination and, in the South, the continuation of Jim Crow laws. Harry Truman attempted to rectify some of the most blatant inequities but met with stiff resistance, which made it impossible to implement many of his proposed solutions.

Blacks were increasingly unwilling to live under the status quo, and began to challenge discriminatory practices. Irene Morgan had already committed an act of civil disobedience in 1944 when she refused to relinquish her seat on a bus traveling from Virginia to Maryland. The resulting Supreme Court decision against the Virginia law banned discrimination on interstate buses, a ruling that was mostly ignored in the South. To test it, a group of eight Black and eight white men took a Journey of Reconciliation bus trip through the upper South in 1947. They encountered hatred, threats, some violence, and either ignorance or willful disregard of the Supreme Court decision by bus drivers and policemen alike. Some were arrested, and in Chapel Hill,

North Carolina, two Black riders, Bayard Rustin and Andrew Johnson, were sentenced to thirty days on a chain gang. Judge Henry Whitfield was even harsher on Igal Roodenko, one of the two white men arrested. He did not hide his racism: After asking Roodenko if he was Jewish, he said, "It's about time you Jews from New York learned that you can't come down here bringing your N*****s with you to upset the customs of the South. Just to teach you a lesson, I gave your Black boys thirty days, and I give you ninety." The other white man, Felmet, who was not Jewish and was from North Carolina, received thirty days. The trip did not change sentiment or practices in the South, but it served as model and inspiration for later freedom riders.

In spite of ongoing discrimination, many African Americans saw their economic situation improve. This was the time of a third Great Migration, when millions of Blacks left the South for work in the industrial North. Thanks to unions and the need for labor in booming industries such as automobiles, many were able to escape the worst of the poverty and the most blatant racism in which they had been enmeshed.

With increasing affluence came a demand for music, radios and phonographs in particular. The music industry was happy to oblige, but like much of 1940s America they viewed the Black market as separate. Of the three major labels, Columbia, RCA Victor, and Decca, only Decca released recordings strictly for the Black market under their own name. Columbia later reserved a subsidiary label, OKeh, but most blues or R&B recordings were released by independent labels, such as Atlantic, Apollo, Chess, and Queen, the R&B department of King. Radio was just as compartmentalized, as stations specialized in different formats. Virtually every large metropolitan area had at least one radio station aimed specifically at Black audiences, and few other stations played such music.

Billboard magazine clearly recognized the racial dimension of the music industry. In 1942 it began to chart music for African

Americans separately under the rubric "Harlem Hit Parade." In 1945 it retitled the list "Race Records." At the time "race" was a positive term in Black culture for someone who proudly embraced his or her heritage. It was, however, a term to be used strictly by Blacks. It did not translate to the general public as a signifier, probably because it was too close to "racist." In 1949 Jerry Wexler, then a journalist for *Billboard*, suggested a new term, "Rhythm and Blues." It stuck and became a household phrase for an important strain of Black music. Sixty-plus years later it is still used.

Some Black musicians broke through the color barrier in the 1940s by adopting a laid-back, emotionally restrained style and demeanor—in other words giving the white audience what it expected of white singers, with the added burden of appearing amenable and nonthreatening to a public still harboring many racial prejudices. The most successful Black musicians were the Mills Brothers, the Ink Spots, and Nat King Cole.

The Mills Brothers, who were actually brothers, John Jr., Herbert, Harry, and Donald, were transitional. They first rose to mainstream popularity in the early 1930s with their tight harmonies and jazz sounds. Their father owned a barbershop in Piqua, Ohio, and had also founded a barbershop quartet, The Four Kings of Harmony. Between the sound of the quartet and the choir at the Cyrene African Methodist Episcopal Church, they absorbed vocal harmony as naturally as the average person learns to speak.

When the oldest brother, John Jr., was 16 and the youngest, Donald, was 12, they began to perform at Mays Opera House. Because Harry forgot his kazoo one time, they began to imitate musical instruments with their voices. Soon the sounds of the trumpet, tuba, trombone, and saxophone became part of their act. They were so successful that their early records carried the disclaimer, "No musical instruments or mechanical devices used on this recording other than one guitar."

They began to appear regularly on WLW, Cincinnati, and soon CBS signed them to a contract in 1930. They were the first Blacks to have a regular network radio show. A recording contract soon followed. Their first recording, "Tiger Rag," rocketed to number one, followed by a string of hits throughout the 1930s. Harry's "trumpet" was often featured in jazz solos. His was the most realistic imitation of an instrument; the "saxophone" is more easily heard as a scat vocal, and the "tuba" is the thumping vocal bass sound that later became the staple of many doo-wop groups.

The hits continued well into the 1950s, but the prestige of the Mills Brothers declined around 1940. Their fortunes revived considerably in 1942 with the biggest hit of their career, "Paper Doll," which became *the* Mill Brothers song.

"Paper Doll" demonstrates how they straddled two decades. The Mills Brothers' version begins as a crooning Tin Pan Alley ballad, in a slow, flexible tempo featuring Donald as lead singer. The tempo and rhythmic vitality picks up in the second half as Harry takes the lead. The arrangement then assumes the style and rhythm of big band swing, minus, of course, the big band. The first half is 1940s, the second half 1930s.

This same decadal dichotomy can be found in the career of Nat King Cole. Cole, originally Nathaniel Coles, was primarily a jazz pianist. In 1937 or 1938 he formed a trio consisting of piano, bass, and guitar; it was an unusual sound in the big band era, no drums or wind instruments. Cole preferred playing the piano but would occasionally sing at the request of club patrons. After attaining moderate success, the trio recorded a song that Cole had written, "Straighten Up and Fly Right." The recording is anchored primarily by the strong pulse and improvisation of Cole's piano. Cole's voice swings as much as his piano, and the other members of the trio, Johnny Miller on bass and Oscar Moore on guitar, join in vocally on the chorus. A hint of the Mills Brothers 1930s style can be heard in the jazz vocal timbre and the tight harmony of the three members. The song stayed at number one for twelve weeks on Billboard's Harlem Hit Parade, and reached number nine on the pop charts. The recording was also an important milestone for Capitol Records, a fledgling company that had been formed only the year before.

For the next three years Cole continued his jazz work with his trio. In late 1946 Mel Tormé and Bob Wells persuaded Cole to record a song they had composed, "The Christmas Song (Chestnuts Roasting on an Open Fire)." More important, Capitol persuaded him to add strings, although Cole's piano can still be heard. The song marks a turning point in Cole's career. The change of style in the arrangement, the composition itself, and Cole's own voice are pure 1946: a smooth, soft, laid-back sound, with a jazz inflection. Although Cole would keep his trio active, his greatest success would be with his romantic ballads: "Nature Boy," "Unforgettable," and "Mona Lisa."

If the 1930s belonged to the Mills Brothers, the 1940s belonged to the Ink Spots. Like the Mills Brothers, the Ink Spots began in the Midwest, specifically Indianapolis, in the late 1920s, and were soon appearing on local radio stations. Unlike the Mills Brothers, they were not brothers; the original quartet consisted of Orville "Hoppy" Jones, Ivory "Deek" Watson, Jerry Daniels, and Charlie Fuqua. The lineup only coalesced after taking a circuitous route, as various members went in and out of an ever-changing array of vocal groups.

Their repertoire at the time consisted mostly of swing and jazz numbers, similar to those of the Mills Brothers. Unlike the Mills Brothers, however, they featured real instruments in their early recordings. Jerry Daniels played lead guitar, Deek Watson and Charlie Fuqua, backup guitar, and Hoppy Jones, cello, which he used like an upright bass on stork legs. By 1936 the Ink Spots had a network radio show and were purportedly earning $5,000 per week. Jerry Daniels, fed up that he was receiving only $200 of that, decided to leave the group. Their manager

Moe Gale then brought in a young tenor from Baltimore, Bill Kenney. It did not go well at first, for Kenney's forte was romantic ballads, and he could not play an instrument. The early Ink Spots never had the smooth blend of the Mills Brothers, but they made up for it with their drive and energy, their "hotcha" sound, as reviewers called it.

When Daniels left, the main force behind their hotcha groove was gone, and for the next two years the Ink Spots worked to fit Kenney into their sound, not always successfully. Their fortunes changed dramatically on January 12, 1939. They were scheduled to record an up-tempo number for Decca, "Knock Kneed Sal." For the B side they were given a Jack Lawrence song, "If I Didn't Care," which they did not particularly care for. After a couple of quick run-throughs they decided to contrast Kenney's high tenor with Jones's talking bass, something they had experimented with but never set on wax. Adding to the effectiveness of Jones's bass was the hesitancy in his voice—according to one source, this occurred because Jones was not entirely familiar with the lyrics, and Deek whispered them to him as he spoke.

This song created the formula that made the Ink Spots: The song began with a soft rocking boom-ba-da-da guitar introduction, followed by two choruses sung by Kenney, with Jones speaking the second bridge in his deep mellifluous voice while Kenney added a soprano counterpoint. Kenney then completed the song, ending on a high falsetto. To this they also added a piano accompaniment. The high-low concept on romantic ballads became their trademark, and for a time made them the most important vocal group of the 1940s.

It is of course not coincidental that this style spoke to the postwar mood. Because of the smooth, easy-going style and the Ink Spots' care in their stage appearance and demeanor, white audiences embraced them despite the still racially tense time.

As the 1950s economic boom continued, new technologies directly affected both the production and consumption of music.

Some, such as the phonograph, were evolutionary, building on inventions and practices from earlier in the century. Until 1948 virtually all recordings beyond Edison's cylinders were done on 78 rpm shellac-resin records. While several sizes existed—7, 10, 12, even 14-inch—all were heavy, breakable, and limited to about three to five minutes per side. The first recording of an opera, Giuseppe Verdi's *Ernani* in 1903, consisted of 40 single-side records; double-sided discs, invented in 1902, were not yet common. Although the weight of 78s varied, due to different thicknesses, early 12-inch 78s weighed at least 10 ounces. Thus the opera was captured on at minimum twenty-five pounds of shellac. One can only imagine the weight of an opera like Wagner's five-hour *Parsifal*.

After World War II, record companies turned more to vinyl, which was lighter, less brittle, and allowed smaller grooves and slower turntable speeds. Much more content could be pressed onto one side. The new technology created for a brief time the "war of the record speeds." In May 1948, Columbia announced the vinyl 33-1/3 rpm record. RCA, whose experiment with the 33 1/3 speed in 1931 had proved disastrous, countered with a 45 rpm vinyl in December. Decca stated it would continue to produce 78s. Eventually, the demands of the market won, as each speed had certain advantages over the other: the 12-inch 33 was clearly better for classical music, due to the longer content of each side; the 7-inch 45 appealed to youth, particularly for popular music, as it was casual and easily carried from place to place; the 78 continued simply because many people still had only 78 players in their house. By mid-1950 all three record companies began to release recordings using all three speeds.

While two other inventions, television and the tape recorder, were not new, only in the 1950s did they become the most powerful and essential tools to revolutionize both classical and popular music. Broadcast television flourished only after the war, when industry had sufficient resources to blanket it throughout the country, and the tape recorder in its viable form was unknown to the Western allies until the war ended. The musical revolution of the 1950s would not have happened as it did without these two technological innovations.

Stimulated by the amazing potential of radio in the early twentieth century, scientists, writers, and industry leaders began to envision a world where moving images could be sent through both wires and the ether. In the December 1909 issue of *Modern Electrics* Herbert Gernsbach described a television system built around a selenium cell and a spinning disc. With enough cells, "a good picture could be projected upon a screen—in theory." In theory! Gernsbach's system was never practical, but enough interest had been generated by the promise of television that *Modern Electrics* devoted 685 pages to the topic, before it merged in 1914 to eventually become *Popular Science*.

Scientists and industry groups began to pursue the real possibility of moving picture transmission over the airwaves after World War I, but virtually all solutions involved some combination of electronic and mechanical systems, such as spinning discs, which required an unrealistic synchronization between the discs at the transmitting and the receiving end. Needed was a purely electronic system. That came from a most unusual place, a farm in Idaho, and an unusual person, a teenager, Philo T. Farnsworth.

The story of Philo T. Farnsworth is the American Horatio Alger myth encapsulated in one person and one groundbreaking invention. By the late nineteenth century American innovation had moved to large industrial complexes, with massive resources thrown at a particular problem. Even Thomas Edison, the quintessential American inventor, had ten to twenty teams of researchers working for him simultaneously. When we include the manufacturing element his enterprise numbered 5,000 employees. Farnsworth, born in 1906, harkened back to the notion of the solitary American figure, somehow creating *sui generis* and then conquering forces much larger and more powerful than himself. In his case Farnsworth came against David Sarnoff, the driving, robber-baron-oriented head of Radio Corporation of America. It is the twentieth-century David and Goliath story, the pioneer, the Lone Ranger, the Marlboro Man of advertising fame, all of whom embody the American myth: at the heart of American culture we envision ourselves as an individualistic society, even in the digital age, where our massively intertwined world suggests such a stance is no longer viable.

But this is a myth; America never was a truly individualistic society. Acting as a collective allowed the Puritans to establish a foothold and a town; the southern plantation was not only rigidly hierarchical, but who can call an operation with hundreds of enslaved people individualistic? From nineteenth-century utopian societies to 1960s hippie communes to mega-corporations, collectivity and communalism have reigned. Even the cowboy, the ultimate myth of American individualism, did not live a solitary life. Cowboy life was some of the most controlled in the American workplace. Cowboys were young men for whom even marriage was proscribed. They were expected to live in bunkhouses; they ate together, slept together, and worked together. Their entire life was tightly regulated by the owners and managers of the ranch. Unlike the mythic cowboys that Hollywood and early western writers portrayed, they were not the big-ego Anglos; a large percentage were Latinos, African Americans, and Native Americans.

In 1918 Farnsworth's family moved onto a farm with a main house that was electrically powered by a Delco generator. Philo became fascinated with electricity and convinced all at the farm of his uniqueness when the generator soon broke. Many service calls were draining the family's budget, and his cousins laughed derisively when Philo announced he could repair it. Their tone changed when it was soon up and running.

When Farnsworth entered Rigby High School, chemistry

teacher Justin Tolman found him far above any high-school level in science. Tolman gave him complete access to the lab and all of his own scientific books. One day in 1922 Tolman came into his classroom to find an elaborate drawing Farnsworth had made on the blackboard. Farnsworth explained that he had just invented television. Farnsworth explained this totally electronic process to him—nothing mechanical, no spinning discs. He elicited a response from the startled Tolman, "This just might work." Farnsworth then drew a simplified model in his notebook and gave it to Tolman. The blackboard got erased but the drawing remained, to become an important exhibit in a critical patent suit years later.

After graduation Farnsworth considered publishing his television ideas, when he met Leslie Gorrell and George Everson, who agreed to finance his idea. After the first experiments ended in "Bang! Pop! Sizzle!" as Farnsworth's wife Pen described them, further financing, a move to Los Angeles, and a patent application on September 7, 1927, Farnsworth was able to transmit a simple image. At first it was only a single line, followed by symbols such as a triangle and a dollar sign. But it was an image projected purely electronically. By July 1928 photographs were transmitted, the first a picture of his wife, and motion was achieved, a moving image of cigarette smoke in the laboratory.

Soon Farnsworth had a working television set of 250 lines per inch, which began to attract visitors: Guglielmo Marconi, the inventor of radio, Lee de Forest, the inventor of the vacuum tube, President Herbert Hoover's son Herbert Jr., and the most famous couple in Hollywood, Douglas Fairbanks Sr. and his wife Mary Pickford.

Yet no visit had more repercussions than that of a young Russian émigré, Vladimir Zworykin. Zworykin had grown up in a wealthy family in Russia, and attended the St. Petersburg Institute of Technology, where his professor Boris Rosing invited him to work on a new project, called electrical telescopy. This was 1907, two years before the word "television" was ever used. The device Rosing had built proved too unwieldy, volatile, and explosive to ever achieve any consistent success, but there were flickering moments of transmission. Most important, the heart of the system was a cathode-ray tube, the same device that Farnsworth would build his system on.

The Bolshevik Revolution of 1917 forced Zworykin's family to flee to the United States. He eventually ended up at Westinghouse, and continued to experiment with cathode-ray tubes. In 1923 he filed a patent for an all-electronic television system. He never could get the system to work successfully, however, and by 1929 he had returned to mechanical devices, this time vibrating mirrors.

When Zworykin arrived at Farnsworth's lab in August 1930, he was well known in the electronics world. Farnsworth was delighted to have a colleague with whom he could converse at the highest technical level, and demonstrated to him all his equipment. What Farnsworth didn't know was that this was a case of industrial espionage. Farnsworth had been set up by the most powerful man in radio at the time, David Sarnoff.

Sarnoff had arrived in the United States in 1900, one of the flood of Russian Jewish immigrants. In 1906, at age fifteen, he began working as an office boy at the Marconi Wireless Telegraph Company of America, and quickly rose through the ranks. By 1930 Sarnoff had become president of RCA and had begun to consolidate the entire industry under him. He expanded into the record business, acquiring the Victrola Corporation to create RCA Victor, founded the National Broadcasting Company, and managed to bring all radio-television research that had been at the sister corporations, GE, AT&T, Westinghouse, and RCA, into RCA's laboratories. He had also secretly hired Zworykin to head a television initiative.

Zworykin may have had an early patent, but he had no working system. Thanks to Sarnoff, he had a very deep pocket to continue his research. Soon, however, Zworykin and Sarnoff discovered a roadblock: this Western upstart Farnsworth held some of the key patents.

Sarnoff bluffed, visiting Farnsworth's lab and noting Farnsworth had nothing they needed. He put out public statements that Zworykin's system was independent of Farnsworth's. He then tried to buy out Farnsworth, who turned him down. Finally Sarnoff began to challenge Farnsworth's patents, knowing that Farnsworth's lab was constantly strapped for money and Sarnoff had virtually unlimited legal resources behind him.

One patent in particular was critical, Farnsworth's original patent for his TV camera, or "image dissector." It had been written so broadly as to cover any purely electronic work in that area. Sarnoff's argument was that Farnsworth's 1927 patent infringed on Zworykin's original 1923 patent. The dispute hinged on "priority of invention," which revolved around three issues: "the conception of the idea, the disclosure of the idea to an outside party, and its eventual reduction to practice."

Farnsworth was safe on the third point; on the second he had disclosed his system to patent attorneys in 1926, but that was after Zworykin's patent. His claim that he conceived the idea in 1921, when he was a fifteen-year-old freshman in high school, was going to be a hard sell, made even harder by the phalanx of RCA attorneys. Clearly, Farnsworth's claim needed substantiation or the case was lost. That was when Farnsworth remembered his chemistry teacher, Justin Tolman. Somehow Farnsworth's lawyers were able to track down the now-retired Tolman, and depose him; but more important, Tolman was able to find the sketch that Farnsworth had made. Did the case turn on that drawing? We don't know for sure, but the case, which seemed lost, was resolved fully in Farnsworth's favor. In essence he owned television.

However, Sarnoff was not done. He kept the case alive for years on appeal, draining further Farnsworth's resources while proceeding with his own development. He never won, but knew that he was hamstringing Farnsworth from capitalizing on his invention, and that by 1941 the patent would run out. In the meantime there were plenty of profits to be made in radio. Farnsworth struggled to create his own television station, but the strain of financial issues and his rapidly deteriorating health crippled his success. Thus when the 1939 World's Fair opened in New York, Sarnoff was there with his new medium and all of RCA's publicity muscle behind it. Farnsworth, who planned on showing his accomplishments, was careening toward a nervous breakdown and was so lost in drink that he missed the fair entirely.

Farnsworth had one final triumph, however. Sarnoff knew that to capitalize on the excitement of the Fair, he had to come to terms with Farnsworth. While Farnsworth was recovering in Maine, the two adversaries' people reached an agreement; Sarnoff, who had adamantly refused to pay royalties to anyone, finally agreed to pay a large cash sum plus royalties to Farnsworth.

The first television broadcast began in 1939; by 1941 NBC and CBS were broadcasting regularly, but only for brief periods during the day and only to the New York City area. America's entry into World War II brought an end to commercial broadcasting as well as all production of television sets. Only after the war did the TV industry blossom, with exponential growth. In 1947 there were approximately 44,000 TV sets in the United States; by 1951 there were 13,000,000. By the end of the decade, an estimated 42 million households had TV sets, some with more than one.

Shows hosted by the likes of Milton Berle, Ed Sullivan, Steve Allen, and Jack Benny featured up-and-coming musicians, or the latest hot talent, and did much to spark the rock 'n' roll revolution. Elvis Presley's appearance on the Ed Sullivan show was an iconic event in both the history of music and of television. It was only one of many such episodes. In 1951, *Billboard* commented: "The companies, the publishers and the talent agencies have learned by experience that appearances on TV programs can do more toward putting over the disk, artist and tune on a national basis than anything since the days of pre-war radio."

While television did much to propagate new types of music, the tape recorder did even more to shape musical production. Although the original idea went back to the nineteenth century, only Germany continued to develop it in the twentieth, and only at the end of World War II did surprised American army officers discover it.

The tape recorder as a concept began in 1878, when the American engineer Oberlin Smith conceived the idea of recording telephone conversations onto a steel wire. As Smith apparently made no attempt to realize his concept, the Danish inventor Valdemar Poulsen created and patented the first magnetic wire recorder, which he called the telegraphone. Many improvements were to follow, but Smith's and Poulsen's work formed the basis for all magnetic material recording to the present day.

Poulsen was acclaimed the "Danish Edison." To many the machine appeared miraculous because the sound was clean and undistorted, without the scratchy background noise that plagued early phonograph recordings. A group of American investors purchased the rights to the machine and created the American Telegraphone Company (ATC). Their purpose was to market it as a dictating and telephone answering machine, which conformed with Poulsen's original intention. Unfortunately, the company's mismanagement, along with strong opposition from the American Telephone and Telegraph Company (AT&T), which controlled 80 percent of the phones in the United States, soon forced them into receivership. American Telegraphone Company folded in 1920. Due to the ATC fiasco and the dominating presence of AT&T, American businesses lost interest in magnetic recording, and little further development happened in the United States.

In Europe, a robust interest in the telegraphone remained, and soon two drawbacks were overcome: first, a way to reproduce sound electronically, which necessitated its amplification, and second, finding suitable storage material. One early technology, the drum method, allowed only short recordings, and starting and stopping was problematic, something critical for a dictating machine. Another technology, the spool type, required a heavy steel wire, more like that of large tape measures, that remain stiff when used. This much mass not only necessitated a large, heavy machine but created the same problem of efficiently starting and stopping it.

Steel tapes not only were massive but were difficult to manufacture and often had uneven magnetic qualities. In 1932 the German company Allgemeine Elektricitäts-Gesellschaft (AEG) purchased the patents of a Dresden inventor, Fritz Pfleumer, who had glued steel filings onto a strip of paper. After further experimentation, AEG created the Magnetophon, an instrument that used oxidized magnetic tape quite similar to that of later tape recorders.

Germany found the Magnetophon particularly useful for propaganda purposes. Hitler's speeches, for instance, could be recorded and played later on radio stations without his presence and without the telltale sign of the phonograph's limited reproduction quality. Hitler thus seemed to be everywhere. Many Magnetophons were manufactured for the armed forces, but they were also used in civilian radio stations. Pre-war German improvements created a machine with the tone quality of later high-fidelity equipment, including the ability to record in stereo.

In Great Britain during World War II, a young American officer, Jack Mullin, loved to tune into German radio to hear classical music. Mullin, who had been trained as an electrical engineer, was amazed by the clarity of the German broadcasts; it was as if he was listening to live concerts. After D-Day Mullin was in Paris and heard from a British officer of some advanced recording machines in Frankfurt. Returning from a mission with his unit, Mullin had a choice: "I could turn right and drive straight back to Paris or turn left to Frankfurt. I chose to turn left. It was the greatest decision of my life." He found the radio station just outside Frankfurt and there discovered two Magnetophons. Upon hearing a demonstration, he knew that was what he had heard in Great Britain. Mullin later commented, "The reason we didn't know about the Magnetophon was that the Germans never bothered to classify it as top-secret."

Mullin eventually received permission to ship two machines back to his home in San Francisco under the War Souvenirs Act. On May 16, 1946, he demonstrated them at a meeting of the Institute of Radio Engineers (now the Institute of Electrical and Electronics Engineers, IEEE). In the audience were several engineers from a fledgling company, looking for potential postwar products. They were interested, but not entirely sold. In the meantime, Bing Crosby, the hottest name in radio, had tired of having to do two live shows a night, one for the East Coast, one for the West Coast. When he heard of Mullin, he hired him to tape the shows. The Magnetophon proved so successful that the fledgling company with only six employees, Ampex, knew it had found its product. It delivered their first two Model 200a machines to Mullin in April 1948.

Ampex eventually became a multibillion-dollar company, as the tape machine revolutionized all aspects of the American music industry. Soon every recording studio, whether popular, country, or classical, recorded on tape. The most important recording innovations, such as Sam Phillips's at Sun Records in the 1950s, would have been impossible without it. Its sound quality, the ability to record multiple tracks, and the potential for many types of editing all set it apart from cutting a master disc. Only when digital recording arrived in the 1970s did tape begin to fade in the recording studio.

With the tape recorder for production and television and new record formats for distribution, technology was again to reshape the American musical world. With the major record labels still riding the postwar formula of lush, smooth, white sounds, with Black groups still confined to an ether ghetto on predominantly segregated radio stations, and with a generation too young to have fully experienced the impact of the war, a cultural clash was inevitable. The result was the emergence of an entirely new strain of popular music in the 1950s. A bifurcation point had been reached, and another musical revolution was soon to occur.

CHAPTER 10

Johnnie Ray and the Rise of Rock 'n' Roll

As the 1950s arrived, the euphoria Americans felt with the end of World War II had begun to fade. New tensions and anxieties emerged, by far the most overarching, impactful, and darkest being the incipient cold war, with the threat of the atomic bomb. As early as February 1946, George F. Kennan, deputy chief of the US mission in Moscow, had warned of Stalinist expansionist desires. In his "long telegram" he argued for the need for containment. One month later Churchill gave his famous "Iron Curtain" speech, warning the West, "From Stettin in the Baltic, to Trieste in the Adriatic, an iron curtain has descended across the continent." In spite of these warnings, the Truman administration did not fear the Soviet Union, believing it was too weak militarily to be a threat. One year earlier John M. Hancock, former delegate to the UN Atomic Energy Commission, had stated that the Soviet Union was about twenty years away from building a bomb. That position imploded on August 29, 1949, when the Soviet Union exploded its first atomic weapon, and the Cold War began in earnest.

Other bombs followed, including the hydrogen bomb, many times more powerful than the original plutonium version. For the next forty years the specter of nuclear annihilation hung over everyone's heads. Youth were especially affected, as atomic raid drills became commonplace in schools, and children were taught what to do if they saw a giant fireball in the sky. Many families created bomb shelters in their basements or backyards, and many more stocked up with water and canned goods—just in case. This activity could not help but affect impressionable young minds.

Yet in spite of an omnipresent nuclear fear, technology and economic good times redefined the very role of youth, as the term "teenager" assumed more than a numeric meaning. The general affluence of the country meant disposable income for young people, whether from a weekly allowance or a part-time job, of which there were plenty. Automobile production was booming, and every middle-class family owned at least one car. When a youth reached the age sixteen, the acquisition of a driver's license became a rite of passage. For privileged, mainly white teenagers, car culture had arrived. Whether the young man had his own car or had access to the family car, the automobile meant freedom, for both him and his friends, especially girlfriends. Teenage girls drove also, but '50s mores dictated that boys supply the automobile in mixed company.

Technology meant new freedom for youths to discover new music, and in that regard the most important piece of technology was the car radio. Prior to World War II car radios formed a significant technological challenge. The electricity from a six-volt battery had to be converted to alternating current, not an easy trick, and the vacuum tubes that were required for radio were large, heat-generating, and fragile. The first commercial car radios, which appeared around 1930, were 26-pound black boxes that had to be mounted on the floor, with a speaker just as large, and extra batteries the size of a car battery under the seat. They were also prohibitively expensive, in some cases costing a fourth the price of the car. By 1940 miniature vacuum tubes and other electronic advances made in-dash radios practical and more reliable. By the 1950s car radios were common, and one can assume few teenagers' cars were without one.

The automobile meant teenagers could find radio stations that would not normally be heard at home. In the car, Father no longer controlled the dial. I can personally attest that in the 1950s many white teenagers in Houston, Texas, had one radio button set on the Black station KYOK.

Mainly through teenagers' car radios, the sounds of Black music began to seep into mainstream white America. Rhythm and blues quartets, later labeled doo-wop groups, were some of the first to achieve national recognition. The Mills Brothers and the Ink Spots had prepared the way; the Ink Spots in particular influenced some of the early groups, including the Ravens and the Orioles. The Ravens modeled their quartet on the Ink Spots, although they were sometimes referred to as the anti–Ink Spots because Jimmy Ricks, who often took the lead, was a deep bass, thus inverting the Ink Spot sound, which featured Bill Kenney's high tenor voice. The Ravens never had the mainstream popularity of the Ink Spots, but were quite successful on the R&B charts and in personal appearances.

The Orioles, an R&B group from Baltimore, were founded in 1948 and were the first to perpetuate the bird names the Ravens had started, a trend that would continue with the Penguins, the Larks, the Flamingos, the Cardinals, and others. The Orioles were built almost completely around Sonny Til, their lead singer, with the others functioning more as backup vocalists. Like the early Ink Spots, they used only a single guitar and bass as accompaniment. Their first recording, "It's Too Soon to Know," hit number one on the Billboard R&B charts and crossed over to the pop charts, topping at number thirteen. The recording greatly resembles the Ink Spots, but without the talking bass. In this smooth ballad with an easygoing rhythm, Til sings in a tenor voice with only a slight Black accent.

While these doo-wop groups achieved a foothold in white America, they represented evolution, not revolution. The Ink Spots themselves were in decline by 1950. Through a series of personnel changes and internal lawsuits, Kenney came to control the content of their releases. As mid-century approached, however, their formula began to wear with the public. Their output became predictable, an assembly line with interchangeable parts. Reviewers wearied: regarding "I'll Make Up for Everything," released in 1948, *Billboard* stated, "The old inflexible Ink Spots style. Will attract their fans but few added starters"; regarding "The Best Things in Life Are Free," "Typical Ink Spots treatment. 'Nuff said." They remained in demand for shows well into the 1950s, but their slip in record sales is apparent from 1947. "To Each His Own" was their last number one hit, and only a few of their later songs charted. They were not even included in the list of thirty-four artists in *Billboard*'s "Top Record Artists" poll in 1950.

The Ink Spots' declining popularity exemplifies the situation in the music industry near the end of the forties. The industry had become complacent. It had discovered a workable formula in the slow sentimental ballad, interspersed with novelty numbers or out-and-out parody pieces, such as those of Spike Jones. Instead of changing the formula, they doubled down. The accompaniments became lusher, with large orchestras and thick arrangements, something already apparent in Nat King Cole's recordings. The sumptuous orchestral sounds of Hugo Winterhalter, Nelson Riddle, and Ray Conniff could be heard on many songs of the time. Unlike the Ink Spots, however, the industry could bring in new talent with fresh voices and styling, even though the production formula might remain the same.

By the 1950s tensions in American culture were leading to a breaking point: a music industry stuck in its ways, exciting new technology, a new generation of youth that had only distant childhood memories of World War II, the bomb, the heating-up

Cold War, teenage affluence, car culture, angst, racial isolation and strife—as with many revolutions, multiple strands came together to form a critical mass poised to explode. All that was needed was someone to light the fuse. That someone was Johnnie Ray.

In 1951 OKeh was the R&B subsidiary of Columbia, a label that catered specifically to Black audiences. No one expected that one of their releases in October would upend the music industry. Johnnie Ray, who was white, recorded "Cry," with "The Little White Cloud That Cried" on the flipside, October 15, 1951, and the recording was released to retailers November 15. By December 29 it had reached number one on the Billboard popular music charts, followed quickly by the same spot on the R&B charts. A white singer in both number one slots! Later, other artists such as Elvis Presley would duplicate Ray's Billboard feat, but at the time this was unprecedented. "Cry" remained number one on the pop charts for eleven weeks, and by January 11 had sold over one million copies. By April it reached two million. At the same time, "Little White Cloud" charted as high as number two, kept from the number one spot only by its flipside.

Even more sensational were Ray's personal appearances. The crowds were not just large but filled with screaming teenage girls whose unchecked enthusiasm rivaled what later greeted Elvis or the Beatles. Headlines and leads tell the story: "Johnnie Ray has smashed box-office records so far in practically every town he's played"; "Johnnie Ray Proves Sensation at Shrine (Los Angeles)"; "Johnnie Ray Woos Atlanta Bobby Soxers"; "Johnnie Ray, armed with his own brand of melodic tear gas, came to Atlanta Friday night amid one of the wildest bobby-soxer demonstrations ever witnessed here"; "$hrieks $upport Johnnie Ray": "When Ray came on the stage at the end of a series of song and dance acts, the shrieks, whistles and applause threatened to lift the star-studded roof of the theater."

His background is as surprising as his sudden success. Ray was born in Dallas, Oregon, a small farming community. His father Elmer was a welder and his mother Hazel, a devoted Christian and very proper citizen of a conservative small town. The family was always close. Because the defense industry needed welders when World War II broke out, the family moved to Portland. Johnnie always seemed a bit eccentric, but nothing too strange; he grew up playing the piano and singing whenever he had a chance.

When he was twelve years old, he was playing a game at a Boy Scout jamboree, in which they tossed each other into the air with a tent. Ray fell from a toss when one boy let go of a corner, landing in some straw and puncturing his left eardrum. He could never hear properly after that, although it was some time before his hearing disability was discovered. As a result he became withdrawn, lonely, and shy. Only after a few years was he was fitted with a hearing aid. Hearing aids in the 1940s and '50s were large, bulky affairs, often needing a separate battery strapped to the torso. Later the obvious hearing aid that he wore became almost a trademark when he performed, although even with it he never again had normal hearing.

Sometime after high school graduation Ray headed to Hollywood to fulfill his dream of becoming an actor. He failed utterly, but kept himself alive by playing piano and singing in various bars and dives around LA. Finally admitting defeat, he returned to Portland, and for a time knocked about the Portland area, finding whatever club work he could, while writing songs. Then a vaudeville-type team he had met in Los Angeles, Jan Grayton and Bob Mitchell, persuaded Ray to come with them to the Midwest, where they had some jobs lined up. For a time Ray played in small towns such as Ashtabula and Cuyahoga Falls, Ohio. Other jobs included accompanying Devina, a stripper whose act consisted of stripping while submerged in a tank full of water. His first break came when Grayton and Mitchell persuaded the owner of the Flame Showbar in Detroit to let him audition. The

Flame was a black and tan club that featured black blues, jazz, and R&B performers. Even though he was white, Ray got the job.

The Flame was one of the more prestigious clubs in Detroit, and many of the most important Black singers in America had sung there, including Dinah Washington, Ruth Brown, Billie Holiday, Ivory Joe Hunter, and T-Bone Walker. Ray was the only white performer during his time at the club. Located in a Black section of the city, it was Detroit's equivalent of the Cotton Club, with one major difference: its clientele was quite diverse both racially and economically. With no cover charge, celebrities and elite white members of Detroit society mixed with working-class Blacks, many of whom had recently left the South to work in the automobile industry. Although Ray occasionally had club dates elsewhere in the Midwest, he always returned to the Flame. It became like home to him.

Meanwhile, Columbia records was aware of the new interest in rhythm and blues but was not yet ready to allow it under their imprint. They resurrected an old label, OKeh, that they had bought in 1942, and assigned a young executive, Danny Kessler, to head the subsidiary. Soon Kessler came to the Flame to hear one of the featured Black singers. He had also been told by a Detroit disc jockey, Robin Seymour, about a piano player there that no one knew about, "because as soon as the headliners finish, the place empties out." Kessler was impressed by the headliner, but "then out came a white kid wearing a hearing aid, who played the piano. There was no name introduction. I really didn't know this was the kid Robin was talking about. . . . But I was probably more overwhelmed with what I heard and saw than by anything else I had ever encountered artistically in my life." Kessler quickly arranged a recording session in Detroit, and on May 29, 1951, Ray recorded two songs that he had written, "Whiskey and Gin" and "Tell the Lady I Said Goodbye."

"Whiskey and Gin," considered the record's A side, had an

uneven success. Many disc jockeys considered its lyrics too raunchy for airplay. "I got a girl who drinks whiskey and gin," bothered no one, but "and then she turns off the light / there ain't a cloud in sight / she leads me to the river where the still waters flow" was too explicit for the time.

The record was not played in Chicago, for instance, but in Cleveland Bill Randle, a popular disc jockey, promoted it, and Ray became an instant star. Kessler sent Ray to Cleveland, and in Randle's hands Ray got his first taste of bobby-sox success. Randle took him to high schools, record stores, youth clubs, any events where teenagers might be found. Ray also appeared on some club dates at the invitation of Tony Bennett, whom Ray had met at the Yankee Inn in Akron, Ohio. Following that, Ray began to appear at larger shows. Nationally, however, he was still an unknown figure.

And then came "Cry."

Kessler played "Whiskey and Gin" and "Tell the Lady" for Columbia's new A&R director, Mitch Miller (known in the business as "The Beard"). Miller was interested enough to put together a recording date for Ray in New York. After some experimenting, Miller chose a song that had been written by a Black night watchman, Churchill Kohlman, and recorded on Cadillac by Ruth Casey. He arranged to have a new group, The Four Lads, back Ray up. At the end of the recording session The Beard asked Ray if he had any other material. Ray replied with a song that he had written, "Little White Cloud," and with a quick head arrangement that was recorded.

Comparing Ray's "Cry" with the original recording by Ruth Casey on the Cadillac label demonstrates just how radical Ray's rendition was. Casey was a twenty-two-year-old white singer from Boston in the mold of Peggy Lee, Doris Day, and Jo Stafford. Her voice on this recording is sweet, beguiling, clear but not overpowering. She was a torch singer in the best sense. She interpreted the song as a Tin Pan Alley ballad, more smooth than emotional, with no Kay Starr blasts of volume or depths of anguish. Her musicality is apparent in nuanced ornamentations as she toys with certain pitches, surrounding them with near erotic figurations. The Graham Prince Ensemble backing her resembles a big band tamed by the postwar musical ethos and fit into the fifties with the addition of strings. When the chorus is repeated instrumentally, Casey joins with her own non-texted vocalization.

Johnnie Ray, in contrast, does not sing, he erupts. Every word explodes, and when he repeats the chorus it becomes a primal cry. His entire body is a wailing, flailing, pounding organism; "Cry" becomes a single, elongated sob. Each phrase rises and falls with its own individual emotive burst. Ray doesn't ornament, he slides as he toys with the end of a phrase, almost with each syllable. Here he is more a Black blues singer than a white crooner. In the repeat, each beat itself is an accent. The background has left the big band world. Prominent is the vocal quartet that Miller favored and that became so important in rock 'n' roll. The orchestral accompaniment features a glockenspiel, with cadence breaks filled in with electric guitar. With a simple song, the postwar years are left behind.

Sam Phillips, owner of Sun Records, allegedly said, "If I could find a white man who had the Negro sound and the Negro feel, I could make a billion dollars." Had he only met Johnnie Ray. The Black inflections in Johnnie Ray's voice accounted for much of his success. Kessler noticed them when he first signed Ray for OKeh; Miller noticed them when he chose to release "Cry" on OKeh rather than Columbia. For Johnnie Ray, that sound came naturally. Growing up, he was drawn to Bessie Smith and Billie Holiday recordings. His time at the Flame was crucial. "Negroes Taught Me How to Sing," Ray trumpeted in the headline of an article he wrote for *Ebony* magazine. Maurice King, the Black leader of the Flame band that backed him, befriended him, acted as a father figure, gave him show business advice, and encouraged him to let loose with his voice, in essence to sing in the same way that got him fired at several white clubs. Ruth Brown, who also sang at the Flame, recounted, "We used to laugh all the time and say, are you sure that you're not a brother, are you not a brother. We said it."

Ray often spoke in particular of Black female singers who influenced him. At one time he claimed Maude Thomas as having the greatest influence. Thomas was a Black blues singer from Baltimore who made no records and about whom little is known except that she performed in the Midwest. Ray explained that he heard her in Akron, Ohio, before he went to Detroit. Later he said that two singers he heard in Detroit were especially important to him, Little Miss Sharecropper and Little Miss Cornshucks. Asked about Dinah Washington, Ray dismissed her: "I never heard Dinah Washington in person, but I bought all her records and I don't dig her." However, he acknowledged, "I don't deny I've been influenced by her." Ultimately Ray was adamant that the strongest single influence on his singing was Little Miss Cornshucks.

Little Miss Cornshucks, Mildred Jorman, née Mildred Cummings, never became well known to the general public, but those in musical circles greatly admired her. Ahmet Ertegun, founder of Atlantic Records, said "she could sing the blues better than anybody I have ever heard, to this day." According to Ertegun, hearing her perform in Washington, DC inspired him to go into the record business. Ruth Brown commented, "Little Miss Cornshucks was the most important voice that I'd heard, and I'm proud to say, she was a big influence on me. There was something really deep in her meaning."

Miss Cornshucks developed her act gradually in Ohio, her home state, trying different types of costumes; she discovered that Black audiences, mainly from the rural South, responded best when she adopted a country look. At first it was a plaid shirt, but gradually it became an entire specially made outfit. By

Johnnie Ray called the blues singer Mildred Jorman, whose stage name was "Little Miss Cornshucks," the most important influence on him.

1943 she was traveling the country, playing in small Black clubs, where Ertegun heard her. At some point she married Cornelius Jorman, who became her manager. By the late '40s she was in demand at the more prestigious Black clubs such as the Club DeLisa in Chicago, where she performed off and on for several years.

Jorman's country act set her up well. Barry Mazor described it: "She'd arrive on stage barefoot, her close-cropped but pig-tailed wig topped by a little-girl ribbon or a frayed, wide-brimmed Huck Finn straw hat and wearing that ragged, country girl's make-do dress," usually with bloomers. She would place a straw basket at the front of the stage for tips. There would be a certain amount of clowning around, more coyly acting country and naïve than telling jokes. The audience wasn't sure what was to come. "But from that distracted, unkempt little girl would come this no-joke woman's voice."

Jorman gradually faded from the scene in the 1950s and '60s. Her marriage fell apart, she had some health issues, her drinking became heavy, and she would often be unreachable, her whereabouts unknown. To many blues aficionados and musicians, she never had the career she deserved.

Little Miss Sharecropper, LaVern Baker, did have a major career. Her Sharecropper act was in direct imitation of Cornshucks's, created by a manager at the Club DeLisa in Chicago. While never particularly happy with the act, she continued it until 1951, singing for some time at the Flame in Detroit. She may have been brought there because Cornshucks was appearing at the competing Apollo. While at the Flame she and Johnnie Ray became close friends, often socializing and visiting after-hours nightspots together. Baker, who was even less well known than Jorman at the time, went on to record R&B hits in the 1950s, including two that crossed over into the pop charts, "Tweedlee Dee" and "Jim Dandy."

Whatever Ray learned from Bessie Smith, Billie Holiday,

Dinah Washington, or LaVern Baker, Jorman's vocal style supports his comment about the depth of her influence. It is fully on display in her rendition of "Try a Little Tenderness," originally a crooner's song recorded by Bing Crosby in 1933 and later by Frank Sinatra. Jorman showed that it could be a blues song. With her the music does not flow in the long line, continuous sound of LaVern Baker or Ruth Brown, but rather spills out in a series of seemingly disconnected outbursts. She sings with great rhythmic freedom, almost as if she is toying with each syllable, yet one cannot help but be carried by a rhythmic groove that seems to occur in spite of her delivery. And it is Jorman that creates the groove, not her backup band, which provides a steady backdrop for her aural flights.

Her voice is a full-throated cry capable of great dynamic range. The sharp, nasal quality of the blues singer is always there, but her voice modulates with colors from a deep, rich resonance to a soft murmur. Each phrase is an entity in itself, rising and falling in fits and starts. The result is a dramatic performance of great emotional power. You feel the song, the content, the emotional message. When she sings it, it is personal and intimate.

This could easily be a description of Johnnie Ray, except that if anything Ray was even more emotional than Jorman, particularly in the way he threw his whole body into the song. The piano became a prop, to be banged on as well as played. Presaging Jerry Lee Lewis, the piano bench would go flying, he would play standing up, even jumping on the piano itself. He would rip off his coat, arms and legs would flail, fists would clench, with his long fingers possessing their own involuntary choreography.

The bobby-sox response to Johnnie Ray was reminiscent of the response to Sinatra. Both Ray and Sinatra were thin, with boyish faces that made them look younger than their mid-twenties age. Each appeared vulnerable, drawing on their own deep wells of loneliness; and their careers emerged at a time of upheaval and uncertainty. Yet there were significant differences both in the times and in the needs each singer filled. Sinatra's appeal was to the loneliness and anxiety that World War II engendered. When that ended, his career plummeted. Ray responded to a complex of factors of which the Korean conflict and the Cold War were only two. Affluence had allowed young people to self-identify as a group, and what they found was a society unable to recognize the many inner tensions they felt. This was coupled with a different worldview from their parents, whose outlook had been etched by war and the Depression. The society's deep repression of sexuality and the expected role of women troubled them, although that would not result in overt protest until the 1960s. Johnnie Ray provided an outlet for all of these feelings, but more than anything he was a catalyst for what came later, specifically the full burgeoning of rock 'n' roll.

Ray's early Black sound was no small part of the revolution he launched. Something foreign to standard pop fare was necessary to break the prevailing formula that mirrored the veneer of complacency covering much of 1950s white middle-class America. While Black voices were already making inroads through the various R&B quartets that would occasionally appear on the pop charts, given the times it is neither surprising nor ironic that it took a white singer to break open the musical establishment's view of what constituted mainstream success. The major labels' control was too great, and their formula too comfortable, for them to feel the need for change. The symbiosis between radio, television, and the recording industry allowed the major labels to continue to churn out successful Tin Pan Alley hits. The establishment simply didn't see the tsunami that was about to consume them.

Unsurprisingly, then, Mitch Miller originally assigned "Cry" to OKeh, even though he had personally supervised the session, had a white group back up Ray, and knew full well that Ray was white. Only after it became apparent that "Cry" was indeed selling in the white market did Miller agree to move it to the Columbia label.

The year 1952 proved a whirlwind for Ray. In addition to his many concerts filled with bobby-soxers, Ray had the opportunity to appear at the Copacabana, the most sophisticated nightspot in New York City. This was an entirely different audience, including many New York celebrities; it was a test of whether Ray's appeal went past age seventeen. Critic Earl Wilson summarized his success there: "He pulled off one of the greatest stunts in show business history."

Signs of an impending downfall, however, were already present for Ray in 1952. In April he married Marilyn Morrison, daughter of the owner of the Mocamba, a nightclub in Los Angeles. The marriage was over in seven months, and in April 1953, *Confidential* magazine detailed his arrest for having solicited a male police officer in a men's room in 1951. Ray had pleaded guilty and paid a small fine, thinking it would create no stir because he was just a seventy-five-dollar-a-week pianist at a predominantly Black club. Fifties bobby-soxers then realized they were swooning over a man who not only was partially deaf but who had married and divorced within one year and was a homosexual. This, sixteen years before Stonewall, did not fit 1950s attitudes and mores.

Ray always had a serious alcohol problem, and it was getting worse, compounded by speed pills he had started taking. Several displays of public drunkenness and erratic and wild antics led to multiple arrests. Although such behavior for a pop musician may have just made him ahead of his time, a second arrest for soliciting in 1959 further damaged his image.

Possibly even more important than his personal antics, his musical style was changing, as Mitch Miller sought to fit Ray into the mold of a Columbia-label crooner. Miller worked to squeeze the Black sound out of Ray's voice, and Ray, who was a trusting naïf, did not fight back. Miller admitted, "I didn't want Johnnie to be noted just for his Black-inspired singing." Consequently, on many of his later records he sounds more like a white crooner with a high voice than the blues singer of his earlier recordings. After 1955 his records still sold, but he had only one major hit, in 1956, "Just Walking in the Rain," a song he originally called "this piece of crap."

Ray stayed in the news, thanks in part to a steamy affair with columnist and TV personality Dorothy Kilgallen, but his hearing continued to deteriorate. In January 1958, he underwent surgery to recover some of what he had lost, but it proved disastrous. Two operations later he was without any hearing in his left ear and possibly 35 percent in his right. With absolute pitch and the help of Herman Kapp, a drummer whose pounding Ray always placed close to him, he continued to perform, but never with the same abandon and confidence that had characterized his style. His American career never recovered, although he remained popular in Great Britain and Australia.

In the standard histories of rock 'n' roll, Ray is either ignored or barely mentioned as a transitional figure. With a few exceptions, the standard narrative points to R&B groups such as the Ravens, Orioles, and Clovers, who had some early success on the pop charts, then pivots to Bill Haley and the Comets. His contemporaries and followers, some of whom became rock icons themselves, however, saw things quite differently.

In a 1992 interview Tony Bennett recalled first working with Ray before "Cry," even before Ray went to the Flame. "Johnnie did something that was completely different. Music, in those day, was still a kind of sweet, long line of singers like Dick Haymes, Bob Eberly, and of course Frank Sinatra, who sang very sentimental, lovely, well-written songs, done very sweetly. But Johnnie became a visual performer. He was the first to charge an audience. He had to rip the curtain down, bang away on the piano, or jump on the piano. . . . And I really consider Johnnie Ray to be, in that sense, the father of rock and roll."

In describing "Whiskey and Gin," Mitch Miller later said, "I look back now, and say that it was probably the very first rock and roll record." John S. Wilson, New York editor for *Down Beat* magazine, later the first *New York Times* music critic to cover popular music, observed, "it was his rhythm and blues style of singing that help lay the groundwork for the rock-and-roll that turned Mr. Ray's entertainment world around."

Ringo Starr stated that in their early days the Beatles listened to three singers in particular: Little Richard, Chuck Berry, and Johnnie Ray. Ringo, who saw Ray at the Palladium, "called him his hero, saying Johnnie Ray inspired him to be a performer." Pete Shotton remembers John Lennon playing harmonica to "Little White Cloud."

Rosemary Clooney considered Ray's stage gyrations "the kinds of antics rock stars would pick up later." Bob Dylan was effusive in his praise of Ray: he "was the first singer whose voice and style I totally fell in love with"; "Johnny [*sic*] Ray knocked me out, Johnny Ray was the first person to actually really knock me out."

Elvis Presley acknowledged Ray's influence on him. Bill Franklin, one of Ray's later managers, paraphrased an announcement Presley made when he saw Ray in the audience, "There's a man in the audience tonight who, when I was in high school, had the top three [actually two] records in the whole world all at once. He was a great influence on me—he made me believe in myself, made me go ahead and become what I am." In 1956 Ray and Presley were both playing the Vegas Strip; Franklin stated that Presley came over to the Desert Inn to watch Ray's act numerous times. Jonny Whiteside believed Presley was studying Ray's performing style. Ray and Presley became friends.

Had Ray continued in the style of his two OKeh recordings, his historical place might be different. But Ray's later years as a crooner were the way most people remember him. Even for those who recall his early emotionalism, which never left, memory may have dimmed just how Black he originally sounded and, as a consequence, how well he was received by the R&B audience.

Possibly Ray just didn't fit the post–World War II wholesome American narrative. In another decade, issues of sexual orientation would have presented fewer problems in the rock world, as David Bowie, Elton John, Pete Townshend, Prince, and others demonstrated, but 1950s rock 'n' roll could not admit of homosexuality, particularly when it was tied to two vice arrests in men's bathrooms. Rock 'n' roll was a masculine, indeed a macho genre. In spite of the bobby-sox frenzy Ray generated, he was just a fresh-faced skinny kid who did not ooze raw sex. Once other singers such as Elvis Presley and Jerry Lee Lewis adopted his supercharged emotional intensity, he could not compete.

Ray's masculine image was further undermined by the field day the press had with his hit song. He became the "Cry Guy," the "Prince of Wails," the "Nabob of Sob." Headline writers could not help themselves: "Johnnie Ray to Weep Self into Town Friday," "Johnnie Ray, Their Darling Cry Baby," "None Other Than a Bawling Ray." The cry metaphor haunts their copy: "The Johnnie Ray Story is a tear jerking tale. If you aim to read further, get out your crying towel."

Ray was not a rock 'n' roll singer per se. Missing in his early recordings is the strong dance beat that was central to so much later rock 'n' roll—the boogie piano of Fats Domino, Jerry Lee Lewis, or Little Richard, the power chords of Chuck Berry's or Buddy Holly's electric guitar, the wailing saxophone of Domino's or Bill Haley's bands. Is Ray, however, the butterfly whose wings flapping in Brazil can set off a hurricane in North America? It might be too much to trace the entire rock 'n' roll movement to Johnnie Ray, but according to complexity theory's butterfly effect, one singer can at least foment a revolution. Ray placed a Black sound in front of white audiences, when most Black sounds were still ghettoized by the media industry. He further annihilated the smooth, laid-back sameness that the industry, with its iron grip, continued to feed the public. Johnnie Ray broke several barriers, and in doing so opened the door for an emotional, hypercharged, melodically inflected Black sound to penetrate the living rooms of white middle-class America. Like so many cultural changes, youth first gravitated toward this sound, as the older generation resisted, but also like many cultural changes, resistance ultimately was futile.

Had Ray more discipline and insight into the nature of his artistic gifts, he might have survived the scandals and the press. But his own naivety and willingness to trust others with his career coupled with his increasing deafness and his own self-destructive tendencies, especially his alcoholism, were too great for him to overcome. Yet in spite of his tragic demise, he remains an epiphanic figure in the history of rock 'n' roll. His presence wrecked the complacency that pervaded the music establishment, no small feat in itself, and pointed the way for later stars to complete the revolution he did much to launch. In that sense he was more than a transition figure, he was a model for future artists and an agent provocateur, shattering the sonic status quo. Would it be too much to state that the rock 'n' roll revolution needed a Johnnie Ray to explode the thick, lush sounds and saccharine atmosphere of the postwar music industry?

CHAPTER 11

The Summer of '55: Rock 'n' Roll's Turning Point

As "Cry" faded, the establishment settled back into its well-groomed post–World War II mellow, sentimental mode. Ray, however, had tapped into ur-forces that could no longer be contained. A primarily white youth market had asserted itself and had no intention of retreating to the old standards. Perry Como, Doris Day, even Frank Sinatra—this was not their music. With the freedom of affluence, automobiles, and portable electronic devices, white teenagers sought a sound that was raw, stimulating, danceable, and, above all, not of their parents. For three years their voice and desires mounted, growing in volume and intensity, until 1955, when it reached a crescendo that radically changed the American musical landscape.

Ray had opened up the pop market to a super-emotionalism and a vocal timbre many perceived as Black, things that many adults feared. He also set loose a frenzy of sexual excitement among teenage girls, when stiff mores allowed few outlets. What he did not provide was music to dance to. Since the early nineteenth century generations had sought that rhythmic drive, that heady experience when music and moves combined to create an exhilaration masquerading, if not openly acting, as a thin cover for sexuality. The waltz, the polka, the many animal dances, ragtime, jazz, swing had all served that purpose. Now that the sobering effects of World War II were receding, a new generation too young to fully understand what had happened just a decade earlier needed something more dynamic than the low-key sentimentalism that pervaded the airwaves and record stores. They needed to move. Swing was gone, remembered only in a few nostalgic biopics. Besides, that was their parents' music. Tin Pan Alley, which had soothed the '40s generation and still considered its market to be adults that had come home from war, was hopeless. Bill Haley had begun to catch on to the need for something more rhythmically dynamic, but he did not have the personal or musical gifts to fully satisfy it. Young people instead found it in rhythm and blues. R&B had the added benefit that to young whites it seemed forbidden, it demanded defiance of adult mores, including racial prejudices. It was edgy and implied a hint of danger. Thus it appealed to teenagers.

As R&B began to seep into the white teenage market, Cleveland became the epicenter for a burgeoning rock 'n' roll movement. It had two white disc jockeys who were willing to feature R&B on their shows: Bill Randle at WERE and Alan Freed at WJW. Freed was a rock 'n' roll P. T. Barnum, a fast-talking blur of energy and hutzpah, equal parts record-spinner and promoter of blockbuster shows, whose riots and near riots only enhanced his image. His ego and ambition seemed limitless, until his deal making caught up with him. He became the central focus in the payola scandal that rocked (no pun intended) the music industry later in the decade, garnering even more headlines. To some he epitomized all that was wrong with popular music, to others he was a tragic figure, brought down by his own ambition. That, however, is getting ahead of the story.

Randle was in some ways similar to Freed: he was also a fast-talking disc jockey and radio personality with plenty of ego, as well as a producer of shows that featured Black performers. In other ways, however, he was different. Tall, studious, with thick horned-rim glasses, Randle looked more like a professor, which he later became. Intellectually restless, he abandoned the radio business several times for other pursuits and knowledge. Beginning in the 1960s he earned graduate degrees in sociology, communications, and education, as well as a law degree and a PhD in American studies. He was a professor at Case Western Reserve, Kent State, and the University of Cincinnati, and in the 1990s practiced law in Lakewood, Ohio. He later commented, "Not bad for a high-school dropout."

Yet Randle always came back to radio. He had begun at age fourteen, and returned in the 1970s, and again in the 1990s. He was on the air until a few days before his death in 2004.

Randle's insistence on playing Black music on his programs got him fired numerous times; it also made him extremely popular with teenage audiences. In fact he was the most popular disc jockey in Cleveland in the late '40s and early '50s, a position that guaranteed he would always be hired back, in spite of his transgressions. That seesaw ended on Thanksgiving, 1949, when he played a gospel-blues version of "Silent Night" by Sister Rosetta Tharpe. Complaining calls caused Sidney Andorn, the station manager, to fire Randle. However, the owner of the station, Ray T. Miller, aware of Randle's many followers, almost immediately reinstated Randle and fired Anton. From then on Randle's position was secure.

Randle had been on WERE for two years and was already an established personality when Freed began his show in Cleveland on June 11, 1951. Because Randle's show was in prime time and Freed's was late night, Freed had greater flexibility in his choice of music. He adopted the moniker "Moondog," and he featured R&B almost exclusively. This gave him an enthusiastic young audience. Six months after his first broadcast Freed announced a Moondog Coronation Ball, which would feature popular R&B performers at the Cleveland Arena. By only advertising on his show Freed sold about 9,000 tickets, close to the 10,000 capacity of the arena, but a printing error apparently doubled that number. As the show got underway, thousands of teenagers remained outside, many with, some without tickets. Frustrated, they broke down four panel doors and stormed in as one giant wave. Sitting in the press box Bill Lemmon, executive vice president of WJW, described what he saw: "People without tickets broke down doors. I saw knives flashing. . . . It was madness." The *Cleveland Press* described a "crushing mob of 25,000 . . . hepcats, jamming every inch of the floor." While 25,000 is almost certainly an exaggeration, the chaos and the early ending of the show were not. The police and the fire department were called, and the fire department may have used fire hoses to control the crowd.

Many sources refer to this evening as the first rock 'n' roll show. Thirty years later, Jane Scott wrote in the *Cleveland Plain Dealer*, "If rock had any particular beginning, it was on March 21, 1952." That claim is debatable, but the show's impact on Freed was clear. From a mostly unknown late-night DJ he was suddenly notorious, and a hero to many teenagers. Equally important, the predominantly Black crowd realized for the first time that the voice they heard on the radio was white. Freed was on his way to the top.

Soon he was hired by WINS in New York City, giving Freed one of the largest microphones in the country as well as even more opportunity to produce shows. He was no longer Moondog, however, because a blind composer and street musician, Louis Thomas Hardin, known as Moondog, sued him. The court ruled in favor of Hardin. Freed's show became *The Rock & Roll Party,* which allowed him to claim that he invented the term "rock 'n' roll," although in various permutations the phrase had been in use for some time. When he attempted to enforce a copyright on the phrase, courts sided against him, on grounds the term was generic.

Meanwhile Randle remained in Cleveland except for weekends, when he flew to New York for his Saturday show on WCBS. He gained a reputation for picking hits with an almost uncanny prescience. Part of it was his ear; he could detect what would sell. Much of it, however, was hard work and research. He frequently visited schools and talked to students about their preferences, and at one point paid "the jukebox guy a buck to give me the listings for 10 or 12 jukeboxes." He also carefully tabulated responses to songs he played on the air. His success led *Time* magazine to name him the country's number one disc jockey in 1955—all of this success even though he admitted he did not like rock 'n' roll music, but preferred jazz and classical. To Randle, selling rock 'n' roll was just good business.

With Randle and Freed both playing R&B on their programs, it began to make a dent in the pop market. As the term "rock 'n' roll" began to catch on in part thanks to Freed pushing it, the question arose, what was the first rock 'n' roll record? That has been asked many times, and there have been many answers. Jim Dawson and Steve Propes devoted an entire book to it. Yet after considering in detail fifty possibilities, after devoting two hundred pages to the topic, after framing the question "On the larger scale, where does rock 'n' roll begin to appear on the long rhythm road stretching from ragtime to the present?," their answer was, "Hell we don't know."

The appearance of Johnnie Ray was one major leap in the burgeoning rock 'n' roll story. In challenging the laid-back, sentimental, Tin Pan Alley style that the major labels proffered, Ray created a new audience all but panting for rock 'n' roll, but Ray's music itself was not rock 'n' roll. In the next few years any number of artists and other figures tell part of the story, particularly a number of Black doo-wop groups, but to locate any single record as the beginning of rock 'n' roll would truly be a fool's errand.

What we can do is point to a time when rock 'n' roll became a national phenomenon, that is, when the real rock 'n' roll revolution occurred and the musical landscape changed forever.

In 1954 early rumblings of a revolution began to sound in the mainstream musical world. In April 1954 *Billboard* noticed that R&B was "no longer the stepchild of the record business," but that it had "caught the ear of the nation" and that its appeal spanned both Black and white fans. It also noted that the independent labels, the home of most R&B artists, were more than holding their own against the major labels. In other words, the power that the major labels held for so long, allowing them to dictate tastes and styles, was eroding. Teenagers were specifically credited with the rise of R&B: "Teen-agers have spearheaded the current swing to r.&b. and are largely responsible for keeping its sales mounting. The teenage tide has swept down the old barriers which kept this music restricted to a segment of the population."

In April 1954 the Crows' R&B recording of "Gee" made the popular music charts, eventually rising as high as fourteen. A new independent label, Rama, cut it on February 10, 1953; it gained popularity only slowly, but it eventually became the first million-selling doo-wop record. The Crows' success was short-lived, however. By the summer of 1954 two follow-ups had flopped, and the group disbanded.

Later in 1954 an even more important doo-wop incursion occurred, the Chords' recording of "Sh-Boom." Like many doo-wop groups, the Chords began as friends in high school (Morris High School, in the Bronx). The Tunetoppers, as they first called themselves, asked for an audition at Atlantic Records in early 1954. Aware of the growing popularity of R&B, Ahmet Artegun and Jerry Wexler signed them to a new subsidiary label, Cat, changed their name to the Chords, and recorded "Sh-Boom."

Shortly after "Sh-Boom" was released, Arnold Shaw, vice president of the music publisher Hill and Range, met with the independent record producer Marty Craft. Craft, just back from the West Coast, asked Shaw if he "could guess the No. 1 record seller" in Los Angeles. Shaw ran through the top songs on the charts, but Craft kept indicating no. Finally, "with a sly glint in his eyes," Craft asked Shaw, "Ever hear of a song called 'Sh-Boom' and a group called The Chords?" Shaw had not. Converting his surprise into business possibilities, Shaw immediately sought out the copyright holder to purchase the rights to it before whatever was happening in LA went national. He was able to obtain 50 percent rights from the equally shrewd Atlantic Record executives Wexler and Ertegun, primarily because Shaw had something Wexler and Ertegun did not: a publishing house with plenty of promotional muscle to put behind a song.

In describing the song, Shaw summarized 1950s success for the teenage market: "What I heard was an appealing dance vitality and a beguiling horniness in the lead singer," a combination many record executives sought. In this case the song punctuated romantic, lyrical lines with the more explosive "sh-booms," and a nonsense tenor phrase, "Hey nanga ding dong, alanga, langa langa, Oh oh bo bip, a dobbi doba dip," which contrasted with a verse sung by the bass, *à la* the Ink Spots. The doo-wop harmonies were backed by a jaunty shuffle, and interspersed with an R&B staple, a growling, hoarse tenor saxophone chorus.

In the meantime, unknown to Wexler and Ertegun, Bill Randle realized its pop potential. He persuaded a Canadian vocal quartet called the Candaires to change their name to the Crew-Cuts and cover "Sh-Boom." The Crew-Cuts version was, like many white covers, full of bounce and energy, but devoid of the spontaneity, vitality, and stylistic consistency of the Chords'. The backup was no longer the guitar, drums, and bass of doo-wop but rather the David Carroll Orchestra. The honking tenor sax was omitted, and the nonsense tenor line modified slightly by the Crew-Cuts, sounded out of place coming from this fresh clean-cut voice of Rudi Maurgeri.

The Chords version did well on the R&B charts, peaking at number two, but to the surprise of everyone, it entered the pop charts. Unsurprisingly, the Crew-Cuts version did better, remaining on the pop charts for twenty weeks, and in the number one spot for nine, but the Chords' recording demonstrated that a Black group could hold its own against a white cover. *Billboard* and *Cashbox* helped by combining both recordings of "Sh-Boom" on many of their charts. Although outsold, the Chords did benefit from the Crew-Cuts version; they earned royalties as the composers of the song, no matter who sang it.

By mid-1954 the music industry had awakened to "the belief that rhythm and blues material is moving strongly into the pop market," and "Sh-Boom" stood as exhibit A. Record executives as well as radio stations could no longer consider R&B a niche genre, to be played strictly on Black-oriented stations. As 1954 came to a close, anyone in the pop music world could sense that fundamental change was on the horizon. By the summer of 1955 three recordings and a movie had made it clear that change was omnipresent, that rock 'n' roll was now a major force in American culture, and the music industry, to survive, had better come to terms with it. With these four releases the rock 'n' roll revolution can be dated to the summer of 1955.

The three recordings were by Black artists—Fats Domino, Chuck Berry, and the Platters—and each was unique in style and sound. The film was *Blackboard Jungle*, which depicted life in an urban trouble-plagued high school. Glenn Ford starred as an idealistic new teacher who believes he can reach the students, one of whom was played by a new actor, Sidney Poitier. Bill Haley's "Rock around the Clock" was heard at the opening and closing credits. As such it framed the film. The movie connected the image of disruptive, rebellious youth with rock 'n' roll, a theme picked up in the film *Rebel without a Cause*, released later that year.

"Rock around the Clock" had been recorded a year earlier

by Bill Haley and his white country group–turned–rock 'n' roll cover machine. Haley began as a country singer-yodeler with several groups, the Down Homers, the Texas Range Riders, and the Four Aces of Swing. He also recorded several yodeling songs under the Cowboy Records label. In 1949 he formed the Saddlemen as a partnership with steel guitarist Billy Williamson and pianist and arranger John Grande. On June 14, 1951, Haley and the Saddlemen recorded the Jackie Brenston song "Rocket 88," their first R&B cover. In this recording Haley attempts to imitate a Black R&B accent, rather than using his own voice, which he returned to in later recordings. While "Rocket 88" did not chart, its success in the Northeast may have encouraged the Saddlemen to record a string of R&B covers, giving them greater success than they had had to that time.

On Labor Day weekend, 1952, the Saddlemen changed their name to Bill Haley and Haley's Comets, at the suggestion of Bob Johnson, the station manager of WPWA in Chester, Pennsylvania, where they had had a radio program. The following year Essex Records released "Crazy Man, Crazy," their first song to make the pop charts. "Crazy Man, Crazy" codified Haley's R&B cover style. The pseudo-Black accent was gone, and Essex session drummer Billy Gussack was added to the band. The strong backbeat, which became a trademark of Haley's recordings, is especially prominent in the chorus, "Go, go, go everybody," where Gussack follows each "go" on the downbeat with a rimshot on the upbeat. The song was not recorded live, but at the end of it Essex added an excited crowd cheering.

By far Haley's most successful song came in 1954, when he recorded "Rock around the Clock." Decca, considered one of the big-three record companies at the time, had just signed Haley, and "Rock around the Clock" was scheduled to be the B side of "Thirteen Women," a weird song about a postapocalyptic world after a nuclear holocaust where a man finds himself the only male alive in a town with thirteen women. In spite of the horror of the absurd premise, he enjoys having thirteen women fawning over him. It did not take disc jockeys long to turn the record over and discover much greater interest in the B side. "Rock around the Clock" did moderately well, but was not a major hit, appearing on the pop charts only one week at 25. It then seemed to sputter, and Haley moved on to what seemed a more promising recording, a cover of Joe Turner's "Shake, Rattle, and Roll." In the meantime the producers of *Blackboard Jungle* were seeking a song that would capture the atmosphere of the unruly youth in the urban school. Peter Ford, the son of the star of the film, suggested "Rock around the Clock." It seemed a perfect fit.

To film critics the song seemed irrelevant. In a lengthy *New York Times* review, Bosley Crowther describes the plot situation at length, but makes no mention of the song. To Crowther the song played no part in the film. To teenagers, however, the song made the film, and conversely the film made the song. Here was a song by a white singer that established a direct link between rock and rebellion, or if not rebellion, at least "hard guy" urban teenagers who seemed as tough as the brick and pavement that surrounded them. Thanks to the film, "Rock around the Clock" shot to number one on the pop charts on June 29, and became arguably the biggest hit of 1955. To many it became rock 'n' roll's anthem. Yet with it Haley peaked, never able to compete successfully with the later singers who defined the rock 'n' roll genre.

The first of the three recordings that gained popularity in the summer of 1955 was Antoine "Fats" Domino's "Ain't That a Shame." He cut it for Imperial Records on March 15, 1955, and it was released on April 14. Domino, born in 1928, was the youngest of eight children in a Creole family who lived in the Ninth Ward of New Orleans, the poorest part of town. He remained there his entire life until Hurricane Katrina forced him out in 2005. According to some reports his first language was Creole French. When he was ten years old his family acquired a piano, and his brother-in-law Harrison Verrett gave him some basic instruction. From then on Domino was obsessed with the piano, learning to play by listening to recordings on the phonograph, the radio, and jukeboxes. He was particularly drawn to the boogie-woogie music of Clarence "Pine Top" Smith and Meade Lux Lewis; from that his own boogie style developed.

Domino's shyness, which never left him, kept him from seeking new opportunities, but gradually word spread among Black New Orleans musicians of this amazing teenage pianist, and Domino had an opportunity to appear on and off with many of the top bands, such as Billy Diamond's and Paul Gayton's. After Domino had played and sung at one gig, Diamond announced to the crowd, "That's my boy, 'Fats' Domino. I call him 'Fats,' 'cause he gonna be famous someday, just like Fats Pichon and Fats Waller. And if he keeps eating, he's gonna be just as big." Domino, who was five-foot-five, did not appreciate the comment, but the name stuck. His gargantuan appetite remained with him too.

Soon Domino was asked to form his own band at a rough nightclub. Aptly named the Hideaway, it was essentially a shack hidden behind railroad tracks and overgrowth. Domino's pounding piano was balanced with two sax men who honked while running through the dance floor, squaring off as prizefighters on the bar, or playing on their backs. Domino's fame continued to spread locally, and in 1949 bandleader Dave Bartholomew took Lew Chudd, founder of Imperial Records, to the Hideaway to hear "this Fat Man" who could play a mean boogie. Chudd, a white man in a suit, was an unusual sight for the Hideaway, and people wondered why he was there. When he sent word that he wanted to hear Domino sing as well as play, Domino launched "Junker Blues," and Chudd signed him on the spot.

"Junker Blues," however, created problems; a song about heroin addiction would never get airplay. Bartholomew, who partnered with Domino throughout Domino's career, suggested the title be changed to "The Fat Man," with the necessary alterations in the lyrics. Thus in 1949 Domino's first record, a seemingly autobiographical song with a virtuosic piano part, made him an instant star in R&B. He was twenty-one years old.

"The Fat Man" never made the pop charts, but it did get as high as number two on the R&B charts. It was also the first of Domino's million-selling records—twenty-one more would follow. Bandleader, record producer, and disc jockey Johnny Otis, sometimes called "The Godfather of R&B," later put the song in perspective: "I consider ['The Fat Man'] a revolutionary record, we really perked up when we heard that shit, 'cause in those days—we didn't know it—but there was a whole new art form brewing."

Between 1949 and 1955 Domino recorded forty-seven songs for Imperial. Of those, twelve appeared on the R&B charts and two, "Goin' Home" and "Going to the River," made the Billboard Hot 100, at 30 and 24 respectively. Then came "Ain't That a Shame." The song itself had what Domino always sought, a hook at the beginning. This was one of his best, with its simple pentatonic motive and crashing syncopated stop-time chords: "you made"—[bam-bam]—"me cry"–[bam-bam]—"when you said"—[bam-bam] "good-bye"; followed by the pick-up "Ain't that a" that launches the full R&B chorus on "shame." The band's syncopated riff pushes the chorus while Domino pounds out triplets on his piano. The triplets are particularly prominent during Herbert Hardesty's tenor sax solo. By this time the honking sax, usually a tenor, had become *the* instrumental signifier for 1950s R&B, although Hardesty's choruses here and elsewhere are more lyrical than many. It is consistent with the tone of Domino's overall approach.

Domino's triplets also became an R&B standard, but they did not originate with him. Early Domino recordings featured a walking bass and occasionally a stride um-pah effect. Triplets first appeared on Domino's "Every Night about This Time," recorded October 1950, also his first song to chart since "The

Fat Man." Domino was quick to acknowledge where he got the idea: "I picked this up from an Amos Milburn recording, and from Little Willie Littlefield." He further explained, "He [Milburn] and Little Willie Littlefield, they both had the same style, but they just dropped off from it." Milburn's "Operation Blues," recorded in 1947, uses them but varies the treatment, often breaking up the chord between bass and treble to give an um-pah-pah effect. Littlefield, in "It's Midnight," recorded in 1949, pounds the entire chord incessantly. With it reaching number three on the R&B charts, Domino could hardly have missed the recording or the success Littlefield had with it.

Domino soon had competition for "Ain't That a Shame" from a squeaky-clean white singer who had grown up in the ultra-conservative Church of Christ in Nashville, Tennessee. Pat Boone began singing as a young teenager for local events such as the Lions or Kiwanis, and entered many talent contests, most of which he lost. He did win one to appear on Ted Mack's *Original Amateur Hour*, and another to appear on Arthur Godfrey's show *Talent Scouts*. By then he was married, and after he appeared on those shows he decided to move to New York. In 1955 Dot Records, a Gallatin, Tennessee, company, released a Boone recording, "Two Heart, Two Kisses," a cover of an Otis Williams and the Charms R&B recording. Boone's version did well enough that Bill Randle suggested to Dot that he cover "Ain't That a Shame." Boone, ever the proper college English major that he was, at first insisted that the title and lyrics be changed to "Isn't That a Shame," but fortunately he was overruled. The song quickly went to number one on the pop charts and established Boone as a major figure in 1950s pop music.

Pat Boone's "Ain't That a Shame" came closer to an R&B sound than many other covers did. Randy Woods, owner of Dot Records, tried to maintain the rhythmic drive in Boone's recording, although a bit of added reverberation gave it an over-processed quality compared to the cleaner and more straightforward, natural sound Domino and Bartholomew created. The sax is present in Boone's, something the Crew-Cuts avoided in "Sh-Boom." A principal difference between Domino's and Boone's recording is the use of a backup vocal group in Boone's, mostly filling in with chords, except in the sax solo, where they insert quasi-scat syllables, "bop-a-doo-wah," a curious replacement for Domino's triplets. Boone sings with emotion and some melodic inflection that imitates the R&B sound better than his later efforts. For those white teenagers who may not have experienced authentic R&B, or who may have had cultural or racial hesitations about the genre, this was close enough to allow them some sense of the visceral excitement R&B offered. As many youths were soon to discover, however, it was not R&B.

While Boone's recording was the bigger hit, a situation all but preordained in 1955 American culture, Domino's version made significant inroads in the pop market partly because of his own background and accent. His inflection was not the typical African American of Louis Jordan or Big Momma Thornton but the clipped, understated, slightly nasal sound of Creole French. Domino's own sanguine personality could not help but come through, which, coupled with his high-spirited piano and Dave Bartholomew's arrangement, creates a sound and rhythm that is vibrant, ebullient, infectious, and nonthreatening.

"Ain't That a Shame" was the first of Domino's thirty-seven singles to make the top forty, and altogether he sold 65 million recordings, second only to Elvis Presley. *Ebony* magazine called him the King of Rock 'n' Roll, a title that had been applied to Presley since at least 1956. Someone referred to Presley as the King at a press conference following his 1969 Las Vegas appearance. Presley, who had asked Domino to appear at the conference with him, said no, the title belonged to Domino. In 1988 Domino received the National Medal of the Arts.

Among rock 'n' roll figures, Domino was an anomaly. There is no flash, no dazzle, no leaping, jumping, or shouting. It's the sheer solidity, simplicity, and heartfelt authenticity that made him an international star. With his unique voice and spirit, he makes even a song such as "Ain't that a Shame," whose lyrics are a setup for a tearjerker ("You made me cry / When you said goodbye"), seem upbeat and positive. Yet if a singer's output were autobiography, we would know Domino quickly recovered, because his next hit was "Yes It's Me and I'm in Love Again."

The next moment in the rock 'n' roll revolution came on April 26, 1955, when the Platters recorded "Only You (And You Alone)," which was released the following month. It entered the R&B charts on July 9, and remained there for thirty weeks. It stood at number one for seven weeks. With no white cover to compete against, it stayed on the pop charts for twenty-two weeks and peaked at number five. No previous R&B recording had done that well.

The Platters had begun as the Flamingos in 1952 while teenagers in the volatile Los Angeles R&B scene. Personnel was never stable as different members joined other groups or just left. The most important early addition was Tony Williams, whose lead tenor would define their sound. They made their first recordings under the Federal label, and according to all reports the results were dismal. When Samuel "Buck" Ram, who would become their manager and "guiding light," first heard them, he admitted, "they were just terrible." The Federal recordings never garnered any success. Williams then auditioned for Ram as a solo act, and Ram suggested Williams find a vocal group, only to discover he was already in one. Unfortunately, it was the Platters. They had recently changed their name to the Platters because another Flamingos, from Chicago, was beginning to achieve national success.

Ram was one of those unknown giants whose multiple roles affected many aspects of 1950s rock 'n' roll, and the Platters stand as his greatest success. After receiving a law degree to satisfy his parents, Ram began to write songs and arrange for many groups in the 1930s and '40s. Soon his credits included Duke Ellington, Count Basie, Glenn Miller, Ella Fitzgerald, and the Ink Spots. He set up a talent managing agency in Los Angeles, Personality Productions, which soon expanded to offices in New York with affiliates in Argentina and Brazil. By 1956 he was managing not only the Platters but the Penguins, the Colts, the Dukes of Dixieland, Eddie Fontane, Shirley Gunter, Sam Butera, and others. He was equally successful and talented as a songwriter. By the time Ram died in 1991 he was one of BMI's top five songwriters based on airplay, which put him in the company of Paul Simon, Kris Kristofferson, Jimmy Webb, and Paul McCartney.

When Ram signed the Platters on February 14, 1954, the first thing he did was change personnel. He kept Tony Williams and Herb Reed and added David Lynch, Paul Robi, and Zoletta Lynn "Zola" Taylor to the group. R&B groups of five were not unusual, but adding a woman was. He worked with them for six months in his home, not only re-creating their sound, but improving their deportment and stage presence. Knowing that there were many Black R&B groups emerging, and that it was hard for Blacks to succeed in the pop world, Ram decided to make them different, a smooth-sounding group featuring ballads. In order to make sure they appeared "proper," he even started a rumor that Zola Taylor, who was sixteen at the time, was Paul Robi's younger sister.

"Only You" was originally written by Ram for the Ink Spots. Ironically, it had been recorded by the Platters on Federal before they met Ram, but according to Ram, "it was so bad I made them [Federal] agree not to release the record." The song itself was ideal for Tony Williams, whose sound resembles a revved-up version of the Ink Spots' Bill Kenny, a high, smooth tenor with more resonance and more punch through explosives, such as staccato uh-oh's at the beginning and end of phrases. According to Ram, the staccato sounds appeared by accident in rehearsal and Ram suggested that Williams incorporate them. Missing in the Platters' version was the high-low concept, but in its place Ram added the clink-clink-clink triplet figure, which was fast becoming ubiquitous in R&B. It was the main feature that grounded the Platters in the R&B world.

Tony Williams's tenor, Buck Ram's decision to mold the Platters into a smooth ballad-style group, Ram's previous connection to the Ink Spots, all attest to an obvious Ink Spot lineage. That the Platters chose "Only You" even before they met Ram indicates their own awareness of the connection. Drop the talking bass, add triplets, and the Platters become the 1950s R&B Ink Spots.

The third event of the summer 1955 recording trilogy occurred on May 21, when Chuck Berry recorded "Maybellene." Berry, born Charles Edward Anderson Berry in 1926, grew up in a Black middle-class neighborhood in St. Louis, Missouri. As his mother played piano, his sister Lucy studied classical voice, and the Baptist Church choir often rehearsed at his house, Berry was from birth surrounded by music, and as a teenager he gravitated to the guitar. Then in his late teens he was convicted of armed robbery and spent three years in the Intermediate Reformatory for Young Men, known as the Algoa Correctional Center. After his release he married and held various jobs, uncertain as to a career. He had considered photography, and also studied cosmetology.

Berry began playing in various St. Louis clubs to supplement his income, and by 1953 had gained enough local reputation to be asked by Johnnie Johnson to join his trio. Johnson, a pianist, was playing at the Cosmopolitan Club, one of the largest Black venues in St. Louis. With his singing, good looks, and natural showmanship, Berry became a hit and began an important long-time collaboration with Johnson. At the time Berry went under the name Berryn so as not to embarrass his Baptist deacon father.

On a hot day in May 1955, Berry made a trip to Chicago,

and there he heard Muddy Waters, his idol and greatest influence. Berry managed to get close enough to him to blurt out his admiration and ask him where he could make a record. Almost reflexively Waters answered, "See Leonard Chess."

Chess Records was established in 1950 by the brothers Leonard and Phil Chess. They specialized in blues and R&B and had already acquired a reputation with artists such as Howlin' Wolf and Bo Diddley. On Monday morning Berry was outside the Chess Studio waiting for it to open. Leonard Chess heard him out and asked for a tape. Berry hurried back to St. Louis and made one, and a few weeks later Chess set a date for him to come and record. The subsequent session yielded two songs for release, "Wee Wee Hours," and "Maybellene."

"Maybellene" is in one sense a cover, only an unusual one, by a Black man adapting a white country song. The tune was taken from a Bob Wills recording, "Ida Red." Wills and his Texas Playboys were a leading western swing band from West Texas in the 1930s and '40s. Berry was obviously familiar with country-western music, as he would occasionally throw in a country-western number when playing in Black clubs in St. Louis, much to the amusement of his Black audience. Berry had created his own lyrics to "Ida Red" and retitled the song "Ida May." He expected "Wee Wee Hours" to be the A side, but Leonard Chess, fascinated with "a hillbilly song sung by a Black man," was more interested in "Ida May." Phil Chess remembered, it was "different. Different from Bo [Diddley], different from everybody. Like nothing we'd heard before. . . . We figured if we could get that sound down on record we'd have a hit."

After much experimentation and over thirty-five takes, which included pumping up the beat and having Berry sing in the recording studio's custom echo chamber—the bathroom—the Chess brothers were satisfied they had caught on tape what was in the studio. According to Leonard Chess, "the kids wanted the big beat, cars and young love." "Ida May" had it all, except for the title, which Chess found too rural. According to Johnnie Johnson, Chess saw a Maybelline mascara box sitting in the studio and said, "Well, hell, let's name the damn thing Maybelline." To avoid legal problems, he changed the spelling to "Maybellene."

Both Berry and Leonard Chess were thinking beyond the R&B market when they recorded "Maybellene." They were after the white teenage market, and the cars in the song are only one indication. If "Maybellene" is compared to the flip-side, it's clear Berry changed his style for the white, teenage, car-struck audience. "Wee Wee Hours" is a pure blues, with a slow beat, and an inflection that surrounds each note with layers of pain. The voice and an instrument create a call-and-response effect on each phrase *à la* blues as Berry's guitar and a backup piano respond to what he just sang. "Maybellene" has the rhythmic drive of rock 'n' roll, as well as clearly enunciated lyrics, with Berry's distinctly Black inflection toned down for a white audience. Berry performed both pieces at the Cosmopolitan Club in St. Louis, and the predominantly Black audience clearly preferred "Wee Wee Hours"; it was their voice. Berry agreed: "It was 'Wee Wee Hours' that we was proud of, that was *our* music." Berry himself considered "Maybellene" a joke, but Berry and Chess knew what they were after.

"Maybellene" was recorded on May 21, but Chess Records was reluctant to release it, probably because they were doing well with Bo Diddley's "Bo Diddley." Alan Freed changed that, however. Leonard Chess asked him to play a copy on Freed's WINS show, and "by the time I got back to Chicago, Freed had called a dozen times, saying it was his biggest record ever." Immediately Chess put the presses in motion. Freed was doing no empty favor for Berry, because his name then suddenly appeared on the disc as one of the composers. This was a typical ploy for the time, a type of payola that would get Freed and other disc jockeys hauled before Congress.

From the moment of its release, "Maybellene" was a success. "Berry socks across an amusing novelty with ace showmanship and good humor," a "Review Spotlight" in *Billboard* previewed, adding, "The tune has a catchy rhythm and a solid, driving beat." Soon a great variety of covers appeared, all by white men. Within two weeks "Maybellene" had both charted and drawn the first cover, by Jim Lowe on Dot Records, which was aimed squarely at the pop market. Lowe, a mostly unknown singer and disc jockey from Missouri, would have one hit a year later, "The Green Door." One week after Lowe's recording, Mercury released Ralph Marterie's version. Marterie was a trumpeter and bandleader who recorded mostly swing but who had ventured into burgeoning rock 'n' roll in 1953 with a cover of Bill Haley's "Crazy Man, Crazy." An even less probable fit was the recording of "Maybellene" by Johnny Long's Orchestra. Long was a left-handed violinist who had several popular hits in the 1930s and '40s and who, like Marterie, was struggling against the inevitable demise of the big bands. Long's style, however, was even further from R&B than Marterie's.

By the end of August "Maybellene" had a country music cover by Marty Robbins, which is not entirely surprising given the song's origins. Robbins, like Presley, had recorded earlier R&B songs including "That's All Right," and his style was comparable to Presley's. He sang in a quasi-falsetto, with a fairly convincing R&B accent. In fact, of all the "Maybellene" covers, his came closest to the original, although the package itself was all country. Gone was the heavy electric guitar of Berry, to be replaced by country guitars, fiddles, and steel guitar. Robbins's record briefly made the country music charts, but it remained a country music curiosity. Unlike Presley, Robbins did not find R&B a natural idiom, and his greatest success came later when he returned to his roots.

One year later Berry codified the rock 'n' roll revolution with "Roll Over Beethoven." The song is both retrospective and prescient. It is first an acknowledgment of the revolution that had occurred the year before. It is also a prediction, that rock 'n' roll was more than a passing fad. In it Berry does not throw down a gauntlet to challenge the classical world or predict its demise, but rather declares that rock 'n' roll deserves a place in the musical pantheon along with the classical masters. Nearly seventy years of history have proved the accuracy of this prophecy.

"Ain't That a Shame," "Only You," and "Maybellene," the three breakthrough recordings in the summer of 1955, each contributed a different ingredient to the rock 'n' roll soup that was beginning to bubble. Domino codified the New Orleans R&B style, with a pounding piano, his own unique voice, and a honking saxophone. The Platters had a blended lineage, of the doo-wop groups, the smooth style of the Ink Spots with a high tenor, and the triplet rhythms of R&B. Chuck Berry elevated the driving guitar beat and riffs, making the guitar the principal instrument, but not the country-style guitar of an Elvis. The guitar became more than an instrument in the band. It became a symbol.

Clinking triplets, moaning sax, doo-wop blend, and electric guitar riffs were all part of 1950s rock 'n' roll, and each continued to influence later styles of rock, from Motown through the Rolling Stones and Beatles. After Jerry Lee Lewis the piano faded in favor of the electric guitar, but it remained an important component of honky-tonk and occasionally surfaced with artists such as Elton John and Billy Joel.

Styles alone, however, do not tell the most important part of the story, for by fall 1955 three Black musicians had broken the racial barrier that the musical establishment had for years imposed. Fats Domino, Chuck Berry, and the Platters all had top ten records on the pop charts. Domino made it in spite of Pat Boone's cover of "Ain't That a Shame"; Chuck Berry owned "Maybellene," in spite of the many other versions; "Only You" had covers, but they hardly made a dent in the Platters' success. Disc jockeys, always attuned to their audience base, no longer feared integrating their musical selections. The days of Bill Randle being fired for playing a Nat King Cole record had long disappeared. Buyers, mostly youth, cared not the color of the artist; what mattered was the sound, and clearly the Black inflections of Domino, the Platters, and Berry were no longer to be avoided, but were desired and accepted.

This trend followed closely on two US Supreme Court decisions. On May 14, 1954, the Court ruled on *Brown v. Board of Education* that school segregation was unconstitutional. One year later, May 31, 1955, the court followed with a second ruling instructing schools and courts to proceed "with all deliberate speed." While many parts of the country complied with the original verdict, in other parts, especially the South, racial tensions were exacerbated, leading to widespread resistance. Yet events in the pop market seemed to suggest the opposite, that musical integration at least was occurring smoothly and naturally.

The question remains, however, did the acceptance of Black musicians translate to the acceptance of Black people, did it herald the beginning of the breakdown of racial separation? For many whites, it did not. Black musicians had long been feted in the United States without undoing racial divides. They were seen as entertainers. The Cotton Club in New York featured an all-Black cast of musicians, but the audience was mostly white. Louis Armstrong, Duke Ellington, the Mills Brothers, the Ink Spots, Nat Cole, all had a huge white following, but often could not sleep in the very hotels in which they performed.

Jazz instrumentalists played their own music, and in one sense their Black individuality could be shielded by horns and pianos. But Black singers, whose presentation was more personal and direct, had to present a polish and demeanor as well as a musical style that assuaged white fears. To a varying extent they had to mask their own heritage and self-expression to conform, a situation that every African American in the United States understands.

R&B demanded no such restraints. It was raw, emotional, and powerful, originally a music by Blacks for Blacks. In one sense its move into white society mirrored what happened to jazz in the 1920s. Only there was a difference: white covers, the typical route of appropriation since the beginning of the recording industry, could no longer smother the sounds of Black musicians. The originals no longer remained in the segregated African American market. Pop music itself began to show signs of integration.

Admittedly, many Black musicians adapted their style to the pop—read white—market. Chuck Berry and the Platters consciously did. With his Creole background, Fats Domino's unique, somewhat exotic sound had its own appeal. In spite of such efforts, in these early rock 'n' roll recordings Black culture itself came closer to mainstream America than it ever had. Berry may have modified his diction for "Maybellene," but the clear Black accent remained ever-present.

In 1955 only a small minority of the population had the opportunity to see any of these performers live. The popularity of early rock 'n' roll and R&B among teenagers spread predominantly through recordings. Alan Freed's Rock 'n' Roll Dance Parties attracted thousands, only a small percentage of the 14.8 million teenagers then in the United States. Some singers appeared on TV, but programs such as Dick Clark's had not yet premiered. Rock 'n' roll movies were yet to come. Teenage infatuation in 1955 occurred mostly through the jukebox, the car radio, and the 45 rpm portable record player.

In spite of this sensory limitation, the acceptance of these stars was no small development in mid-fifties America. Whether the Black sounds intruding on the pop charts represented a greater racial acceptance or demonstrated that the major labels had miscalculated all along in their persistence with covers is not clear. What is clear is that integration occurred in the popular music field. In a January 1955 article entitled "Breaking

Down the Barriers," *Cash Box* observed how R&B was selling in markets that it never had before. Still riding the train of covers, however, the article called for more of them. By June *Cash Box* was, to use a cliché, singing a different tune. The title "American Music Becomes National Rather Than Regional" was misleading, for the emphasis was less on geographic areas than on ethnicities and subcultures. *Cash Box* noted that "rhythm and blues music no longer is limited to what used to be considered a rhythm and blues audience." The music also found a new open-mindedness in musical patrons: "People are fast recognizing that the tastes of other people in other regions are as valid as their own. And with an open mind, they are learning to appreciate qualities which they never could see before."

For *Cash Box* the implications had to do with the music business. In retrospect the implications are for the entire country: there was a new tolerance of others. Clearly that tolerance was not universal, as many events were soon to contradict this rosy conclusion. The breakthrough of Black artists into the popular mainstream, however, had its greatest positive effect on young people; rock 'n' roll was their music, and Black singers were speaking of their life, regardless of color. When Chuck Berry sang about "School Days," or the Coasters sang "Yakety Yak" with the title phrase followed by a deep bass "Don't talk back," teenagers of all colors could identify with them. Black singers themselves were clearly conscious of this racial blending, as they aimed their songs specifically at the teenage market, no longer at just the Black market.

The two years following the summer of 1955 saw rock 'n' roll reach a peak as new performers, both Black and white, appeared, and teen frenzy reached its apex. These years also saw a major backlash develop, as various social and political groups mounted an offensive against rock 'n' roll, deeming it immoral and destructive. To them the youth of America was being seriously corrupted, and in many instances the crusade against rock 'n' roll only thinly veiled an underlying racism. In some cases the racist element was blatant. Other events totally outside the backlash sidelined or ended the careers of some of the top performers, so that by 1958 the first phase of the rock scene had ended, to be succeeded by a toned-down, squeaky-clean group of young, white singers. At the end of the decade, the Bobbys had arrived.

CHAPTER 12

Rock 'n' Roll: Culmination and Collapse

"Rock and Roll has got to go, [*crash*] and go it does at KWK, we're all through playing rock 'n' roll records. This week will be record-breaking week at KWK, and after this week no more rock 'n' roll will be played on the air [*crash*]." As the KWK disc jockey announced this on the St. Louis station on January 13, 1958, he punctuated his statements by smashing 78 records from a pile on his desk. KWK thought enough of this stunt that they brought in cameras from their sister station KWK-TV to record the event. This platter-demolition scene has gone viral on YouTube, and has been included in several documentaries about rock 'n' roll.

The summer of '55 was a breakthrough, but only the beginning for rock 'n' roll. At least three major artists had emerged, but three more, including possibly the most important of all, were still mostly unknown. This chapter follows the growth of rock 'n' roll to its apex in 1956–57, with the appearance of Little Richard, Elvis Presley, Jerry Lee Lewis, and others, and then its sudden undoing in the next two years, as a series of unforeseen events combined with a religious, moral, social, and racist crusade put an end to the first flowering of the rock 'n' roll genre.

The sounds of Fats Domino, Chuck Berry, and the Platters had one thing in common: each was tuned to the white market. Domino's own voice was sufficiently unique and exotic to need no modification. Berry and the Platters were fully conscious of what they needed to do: Berry purposely stressed his enunciation; the Platters followed Buck Ram's guidance to create a smooth, mellifluous sound, stressing Tony Williams's high tenor.

The next singer to break big in the rock 'n' roll market made no such concessions. Little Richard was a high-voltage, unbuttoned whirl of energy, with a style whose singing revved up even further the emotional intensity of the black gospel church, all the while pounding the piano, dancing, jumping, and in general electrifying the stage. His biographer Charles White called him the "quasar of rock," an appellation that if anything understates the dynamism of his performances.

Born Richard Wayne Penniman, in Macon, Georgia in 1932, Little Richard was the third of 12 children. His father managed a club, the Tip In Inn, and was rumored to be a bootlegger. Richard was born with one leg shorter than the other, which gave him a walk that to other boys appeared feminine. It also gave him a fierce sense of competition: "I've always had a fierce determination to excel. . . . It was like I had to, 'cos I was in competition with my brothers, and they were all good looking." Richard was also uninhibited and always singing, as his brother, Charles Penniman, explained, "He was a showman! He wanted to be the attraction, and it didn't make any difference what he had to do to get attention."

At the core of the Penniman family was religion. Richard's father's family were members of the African Methodist Episcopal Church (AME) and his mother's family were Baptists. His paternal grandfather was a minister, as was his mother's brother. He also had a cousin who was a Pentecostal preacher. Richard was especially attracted to the Pentecostal service, "because of the music," in addition to the dancing and speaking in tongues, which he would imitate, "though we didn't know what we were saying." It was the kind of show that naturally appealed to his inner flamboyance.

As Little Richard got older he became more aware of his sexuality: "I felt like a girl." "I just felt that I wanted to be a girl more than a boy." He was harassed by boys because he acted feminine, and he first attributed it to his walk. When he got older he fell hard for the boyfriend of his (female) cousin, although nothing came of it. He said his affection "was very unnatural, but I didn't realize it then." He then began to hang out with a group of gays, which caused considerable consternation and, later, disaffection from his father.

Meanwhile he had his first professional singing experience. When Richard was fourteen he had a job selling soft drinks at the Macon City Auditorium. One day he was at the auditorium when Sister Rosetta Tharpe came in. Richard began to sing "Strange Things Happening Every Day," one of her hit songs. He sang another song, and she came over to him and asked him to appear onstage with her. After the show she gave him thirty-five dollars, more than he ever had at one time. Richard was hooked on show business, and he soon left home to join one of the traveling shows. By the time he was eighteen he had sung with Dr. Hudson's Medicine Show, Buster Brown's Orchestra, Sugarfoot Sam from Alabam, the Tidy Jolly Steppers, the King Brothers Circus, and Broadway Follies. In some shows he appeared in drag. While with the Broadway Follies he met the blues singer Billy Wright, who set him up with RCA to make his first record, "Every Hour," which met with marginal success.

Then, his father was murdered. At the Tip In Inn he had an altercation with a rowdy customer, who shot him in front of the club. Richard had to return home and take a job as a dishwasher to help support his mother's nine younger siblings, but he continued to sing with various groups when he could. He also began to change his style, toward a harder blues and R&B. Lloyd Price, who had a monster hit at the time, "Lawdy, Miss Clawdy," recommended his company Specialty Records, and nine months after Richard sent them a tape, they arranged a recording session for him. The session turned him from a small-time club singer into a megastar.

At first the session did not go well. Two days had been set aside, and by the end of the first day Robert Blackwell, Specialty's A&R man, thought there was nothing here he could use. The second day began the same, but Blackwell thought that one song by a local musician Dorothy LaBostrie, "I'm Just a Lonely Guy," might work. Blackwell knew he had to bring something back to Specialty's owner Art Rupe. During a break, however, he heard Richard messing around with a song he often performed in night clubs, "Tutti Frutti," and thought, this was it.

There was one problem with "Tutti Frutti": the lyrics. Richard had developed over time a barely disguised song about gay anal sex. The original lyrics were "A wop bop a loo mop a good goddam, Tutti Frutti, good booty, if it don't fit, don't force it, you can grease it, make it easy." At a time when NBC banned "I Can't Say No" (from *Oklahoma!*) and ABC banned "There Is Nothing Like a Dame" (from *South Pacific*) because of their sexual innuendos, no wonder everyone in the studio, including Richard, knew this song didn't have a chance. Blackwell asked LaBostrie, who was there to hear her song recorded, to write some new lyrics. When she and Richard brought in the new ones, there were only fifteen minutes of session time left, so Blackwell took a chance. Dismissing the session pianist, he had Richard both sing and play the piano. They managed two or three takes—and the record was made.

Back in Los Angeles, Rupe added some reverb. He was still

not entirely convinced, and assumed it would just be a novelty record. Richard was not too sure either: "I never thought it would be a hit, even with the lyrics cleaned up." He was back in Macon when he heard Gene Nobles on WLAC in Nashville say, "This is the hottest record in the country. This guy Little Richard is taking the record market by storm." Specialty soon called and said, "Come to Hollywood." Little Richard was on his way.

"Tutti Frutti" rose to number two on the R&B charts and seventeen on the pop charts, and soon garnered a cover by Pat Boone. Boone gave one of his most anemic performances on this recording, a far cry from his better-but-not-quite-up-to-the-original first R&B cover of "Ain't That a Shame." Richard had interjected several falsetto "whooooo's" in the original recording, a sound straight out of his black gospel background, which served to rev up the energy of the song. Boone's half-hearted attempt at that is only embarrassing. Shortly after Boone's cover, Elvis Presley recorded it, but it was somewhat lost on a four-song 45 EP (extended play) that also included "I Got a Woman" and "Blue Suede Shoes."

In its loud sound, emotional mania, rhythmic drive, and opening nonsense line, "a-wop-bom-a-loo-mop-a-lomp-bom-bom," "Tutti Frutti" set a standard for the rock 'n' roll genre. According to Richard, the opening phrase was an imitation of a drum riff. Richard also had, if not the swagger, at least the braggadocio of a rock singer: "I'm just the same as ever, loud, electrifying and full of magnetism." His hair, makeup, outlandish clothes, hyperactivity, and frenetic combination of singing, shouting, and other vocal ejaculations are in essence a preview of the history of rock for the next fifty years.

Richard followed "Tutti Frutti" with further hits the next two years. The biggest were "Long Tall Sally," which was number one on the R&B chart for nineteen weeks and reached number six on the pop charts, and "Good Golly, Miss Molly," which peaked at number four on the R&B charts and ten on the pop charts.

Along with "Tutti Frutti," these became rock 'n' roll standards, to be covered by many musicians.

When Little Richard broke into the national spotlight he was everything a pop star was not supposed to be. He was black, he was gay, he had a six-inch pompadour, a pencil-thin mustache, and constantly wore makeup. He was loud, outrageous, and boastful, with a full-throated sound that often lay somewhere between singing and screaming. Unlike previous African American entertainers, he made no attempt to bend his voice to white values or expectations. Ironically, his gay mannerisms helped him; he seemed less a sexual threat to the most fundamental white male fears at the time. Richard was aware of this: "By wearing this makeup, I could work and play white clubs, and the white people didn't mind the white girls screaming over me. I wasn't a threat when they saw the eyelashes and the makeup. They was willing to accept me 'cause they figured I wouldn't be no harm." He seemed more an exotic curiosity than a threat. Even though he privately engaged in orgies, his gay appearance seemed not to matter to the public, possibly because he had never been arrested in a men's bathroom.

His stage presence only enhanced his recordings. His contemporaries acknowledged the power of his personal appearances in the sincerest way possible: Bo Diddley, Gene Vincent, Jerry Lee Lewis, Buddy Holly, and Phil Everly all indicated that they would not want to follow him onstage. Many other singers, including James Brown, Otis Redding, Paul Simon, Elton John, and David Bowie spoke of being inspired by Little Richard. In his own modest way, Little Richard considered himself the King of Rock 'n' Roll.

Little Richard may have called himself the king of rock 'n' roll—and his influence speaks to that—but to many, that honor belongs to someone else, Elvis Presley—possibly because Elvis was white. In mid-1950s America enough racism still existed, even among teenagers, to favor a white singer as the prevailing teenage heartthrob. As Little Richard recognized, it was problematic for a Black to become a major sex symbol. Chuck Berry was soon to find out the cost of that. Elvis, however, had many bona fide claims to the royal title: he sold more records than anyone else, and for two years he dominated the popular music world like few others have. He also had an innate musical talent and a flexible singing voice that allowed him to communicate in song an excitement and expressiveness, whether in a rousing rock 'n' roll number or a tender ballad. If any one singer stands as the quintessential icon of 1950s rock 'n' roll, it is Elvis Presley.

Born January 8, 1935, Elvis was the only child of Vernon and Gladys Presley, a working-class couple in East Tupelo, Mississippi. He was a twin, but the other boy was stillborn. Possibly for that reason, Gladys lavished special care and attention on Elvis, and Elvis was particularly close to his mother. Even to people who knew them, the Presleys were like a closed circuit; they functioned well as a family but did not interact much with the world about them. Vernon, Elvis's father, later commented, "the three of us formed our own private world." Their principal social outlet was the Assembly of God Church where Gladys's uncle Gains was minister. The music in that church especially inspired Elvis.

The family also listened to the *Grand Ole Opry* every Saturday night, and Elvis learned Red Foley's song "Old Shep," a tearjerker about a boy and his dog growing up together. When Elvis was ten, his schoolteacher heard him sing it and entered him into a children's talent show at the Alabama-Mississippi Fair in Tupelo. There is no record of how well he did, and various stories told later do not agree. The most amazing part of the anecdote is that Elvis sang at all, for if any one thing characterized him when he was a child and a youth, it was his extreme shyness. Friends, teachers, and schoolmates all agreed, he was very, very shy.

Soon after Elvis's debut at the fair his mother bought him a guitar, and gradually he learned the rudiments of a few chords and other basics of the instrument. Throughout the next years the guitar was often with him. While he loved to sing, he was so shy that he preferred to perform only when it was dark.

In 1948 the Presleys moved to Memphis, Tennessee, probably hoping to find a better life. With the help of subsidized housing they made ends meet, although they never were financially comfortable. Whatever the city's effect on the family's well-being, Memphis provided Elvis with a much greater range of musical influences. In addition to the *Opry* broadcasts, there was Dewey Phillips—Daddy-O Dewey—on WHBQ. Phillips, like Bill Randle and Alan Freed, was one of the pioneering white DJs playing R&B. There was also the all-black station, WDIA, where among others B. B. King hosted his own show. Across the Mississippi River in West Memphis, Arkansas, Howlin' Wolf held forth on KWEM, which was open to local musicians of all stripes. There were many hillbilly programs, in particular Bob Neal's morning show on WMPS. Memphis radio was the melting pot of musical styles that Elvis would soon assimilate.

There was also Beale Street. A street in central Memphis running nearly two miles from the Mississippi River to East Street, today it advertises itself as "Home of the Blues." It is now a tourist attraction, with many blues clubs featuring live music. In the early 1950s, however, it was the center of Black life in highly segregated Memphis. Beginning with W. C. Handy's arrival in 1903, it grew as a center of African American musical activity, a street of clubs, restaurants, and shops strictly for the Black community.

Beale Street was still thriving as a focal point for Blacks when Elvis first saw it in the late '40s. Many white teenagers liked to walk down Beale Street then, mainly treating it as an exotic place, with all the people on the streets and the colorful stores and shops. Elvis was interested in one shop in particular, Lansky Brothers Clothing, at 126 Beale Street. By his junior year he began buying clothing there, clothing that set him apart from his fellow students. He also grew sideburns and began to experiment with his hair. In his senior year in high school he worked up the nerve to appear as an act in the Humes High School annual minstrel show (not in blackface), singing Teresa Brewer's hit "Till I Waltz Again with You." From then on Elvis sang whenever he could, to small or large gatherings. He may not have realized it at the time, but his future was taking shape. He graduated from Humes High School June 3, 1953, and began working at M. B. Parker Machinists' Shop. Then on or about June 18 Elvis walked into Sun Records at 706 Union Avenue and the Elvis myth began.

Sam Phillips opened the Memphis Recording Service at 706 Union Avenue in 1950 with the vision of recording music that other labels were ignoring, particularly local blues and country singers: "My aim was to try and record the blues and other music I liked and to prove whether I was right or wrong about this music." At first he sold the masters to other record companies. To make ends meet he also distributed cards, "We Record Anything—Anywhere—Anytime." After some success recording blues singers, including Howlin' Wolf (Chester Burnett) and B. B. King (recording his hit "Rocket 88"), Phillips opened his own record company in 1952, Sun Records.

On July 15, 1953, Elvis entered the Sun Studio. Many stories have swirled around that moment. He wanted to make a record for his mother; he just wanted to hear what he sounded like; he wanted to try out for a band. When he entered the Union Avenue studio the first person he saw was Marion Keisker. She was a well-known radio personality in Memphis when she developed a close relationship with Sam Phillips. She and Phillips created Sun Records together, although Phillips as the owner and recording engineer has gotten most of the credit. While Phillips ran the recording sessions, Keisker ran the shop.

Keisker vividly remembers the now famous conversation she had with Elvis. He asked her whether any bands needed a singer:

"What kind of singer are you?"
"I sing all kinds."
"Who do you sound like?"
"I don't sound like nobody."
[Keisker thinking: "Oh yeah, one of those. . . ."]
"What do you sing, hillbilly?"
"Well, who do you sound like in hillbilly?"
"I don't sound like nobody."

At this point, versions of the story diverge. Sam Phillips was or was not in the studio. Keisker or Phillips recorded Presley. We know he sang "My Happiness," a plaintive ballad that had been popular in 1948. There was no backing except basic chords from Elvis's own guitar. Elvis did demonstrate he could convincingly put across a slow ballad, but he was still miles away from anything resembling R&B. As far as the recording session went, Elvis received his record, but nothing more happened. In fact nothing happened for almost a year. Undeterred, Elvis went back to the recording studio several times and even cut another record, but got nothing more than a smile and some pleasantries from Keisker. He was disappointed, but years later Keisker said, "He was so ingenuous that there was no way he could go wrong."

Finally on June 26, 1955, Elvis got the call: Phillips wanted to record him. For three hours Elvis sang every song he knew, mostly ballads and gospel—nothing there that Phillips could use, but he felt certain the kid had potential. He arranged for two musicians, guitarist Scotty Moore and bassist Bill Black, to work with Elvis and come back with him for another session. The second session seemed to duplicate the first, some nice songs but nothing of commercial value. After several hours, discouraged and exhausted, they took a break. Elvis started fooling around with an old R&B song, "That's All Right Mama," and Moore and Black joined in.

Phillips, listening from the control booth, was stunned; he had no idea this kid even knew any R&B songs. He stuck his head in the recording studio: "What are you doing?"

"We don't know."

"Well back up, try to find a place to start and do it again."

After the session Phillips played the number for his friend (and nonrelative) Dewey Phillips, who aired it on his show. Dewey even interviewed Elvis, pointedly asking him what high school he attended. The answer told the listeners what he wanted them to know, that this unknown who sounded Black was white. The overwhelming response from listeners convinced both Phillipses that something important had happened in that late-night recording session. Whether Elvis realized it then or not, Sam knew the direction his career had to take.

Paired with the Bill Monroe song "Blue Moon of Kentucky," the record did not chart, but Elvis gained notice. *Billboard's* "Review Spotlight on . . . Talent" called Elvis "a potent new chanter who can sock over a tune for either the country or the r.&b, markets. . . . A strong new talent." The record's success also prompted Sam Phillips to sign Elvis to a two-year recording contract, and to issue four more Presley 45s, one in 1954 and three in 1955. Four of his Sun songs appeared on the country charts, including "I Forgot to Remember to Forget," which rose to number one. *Billboard* later reiterated his crossover appeal: "His style is both country and r. & b. and he can appeal to pop."

In spite of *Billboard*'s observation about his stylistic versatility, Elvis remained a country singer, with his market primarily in the South. He appeared on Nashville's *Grand Ole Opry* and Shreveport's *Louisiana Hayride,* and began to tour extensively, at one time with a package headed by Hank Snow. With his number one hit "I Don't Hurt Any More," Snow was arguably the hottest attraction in country music at the time. Elvis was all country except in one respect: while country singers dressed in florid outfits covered with embroidered kitsch, Elvis continued to wear his Beale Street clothes, often pink pants and a black sport coat.

At this point Bill Randle entered the picture. Tommy Edwards, who had a country-music morning show on Randle's station, WERE, introduced Elvis to Randle, who listened to Elvis's records, interviewed him, and talked at length with Bob Neal, a Memphis disc jockey who had become Elvis's manager. Randle was sold on Elvis, and invited him to appear in a documentary film, *The Pied Piper of Cleveland: A Day in the Life of a Famous DJ,* that Universal Studios was making on Randle after *Time* magazine named him DJ of the Year. The film, which was never released, showed Randle MC'ing a concert at a local high school. It featured Pat Boone, but the unexpected sensation was this new, impossible-to-pigeonhole hillbilly from Tennessee. Randle began to plug Elvis on his radio show, and according to some reports Elvis asked him to manage him. Randle turned him down, preferring to stay where he was, in Cleveland (although he also had a Saturday afternoon radio show in New York City).

Meanwhile Jack Philbin, the producer of CBS's Dorsey Brothers television program *Stage Show,* was getting desperate. Ratings were down; maybe new talent would revive the show—something different from the usual crooners like Eddie Fisher or Perry Como. Elvis was unknown, but Randle was keen on him, and Philbin was ready to take a chance. Elvis appeared on January 28, 1956. Randle had been invited to introduce him, which was unusual, since that normally fell upon one of the Dorsey Brothers. Randle's introduction compared him to Johnnie Ray, and prophesized:

> We'd like at this time to introduce to you a young fellow, who like many performers, Johnnie Ray among them,

> come out of nowhere to be overnight very big stars. This young fellow we met for the first time while making a movie short. We think tonight that he's going to make television history for you. We'd like you to meet him now—Elvis Presley. And here he is!

It was a rainy Saturday night in New York City, and the relatively small audience wasn't sure what to make of Elvis, but somehow a spark had been lit. Philbin exercised his option to invite him back five more weeks in a row. By his final appearance, on March 24, the entire country knew that rock 'n' roll had found a new star. On March 3, *Billboard* had already trumpeted in headlines: "A WINNAH! Presley Hot as a $1 Pistol on Victor."

Between Randle's first encounter with Presley and his appearances on *Stage Show*, two other important developments occurred that would decisively affect his career. First, on November 21, 1955, Elvis left Sun and signed a contract with RCA Victor. Second was a change of management. Bob Neal, who still had Elvis under contract, had begun sharing management duties with Colonel Tom Parker. With Neal's acquiescence, Parker became "sole and exclusive Advisor, Personal Representative, and Manager of Presley" two days after that final *Stage Show* performance. The two events are not unrelated, as the RCA deal was primarily the work of Parker.

Parker may best be described as a twentieth-century P. T. Barnum. He was loud, crude, flamboyant, gregarious, and shrewd, a master at sizing up a situation or a person. It turns out Thomas Andrew Parker was an alias; he was his own invention. He claimed to have been born in Huntington, West Virginia, but he was actually Andreas Cornelis van Kuijk, born in Bresda, Netherlands. Records place him in the American army as Thomas Parker in 1929–33, and he worked briefly as a field agent for the Hillsboro County Humane Society in Tampa, Florida. Most of the time he worked in carnivals, sometimes doing odd jobs, but always hustling and promoting. His schemes could be elaborate, often shady, and he felt no compunction about the victims. The title of Colonel was honorific, bestowed on him by Jimmy Davis, governor of Louisiana.

Gradually Parker worked his way into the world of music promotion, and went on to manage singer-actor Eddie Arnold and partner with Hank Snow in a venture, Jamboree Attractions. There he not only met Elvis but outmaneuvered both Snow and Bob Neal to become Elvis's exclusive manager.

Parker began by pushing for a better recording contract for Elvis. Sam Phillips was a master at putting the sounds onto acetate with just the right combination of studio backing and electronic manipulation. In some cases the limited equipment Phillips had to work with favored the raw quality of the types of music he was producing. What disturbed Parker was not the quality of the Sun product but Sun's distribution system. Sun was still a regional label, with a strong distribution system in the South but little elsewhere. Parker was already envisioning a nationwide coverage for Elvis, and for that, the marketing potential of one of the major labels was necessary.

Parker had close ties with RCA because of his connections with Eddie Arnold and Hank Snow, both RCA artists, and he assumed there would be no problem convincing Steve Sholes, head of the country division at RCA, to take Elvis. But Sam Phillips had Elvis locked into a two-year recording contract, and the only solution was to buy him out. It was not an easy sell. Phillips had developed the talent, and it was just beginning to pay off. Why should he release Elvis for someone else to profit? And how much would RCA pay for a mostly unproven singer? Finally all parties reached an agreement, and on November 21, 1955, RCA bought Elvis's contract for $35,000 plus $5,000 for back royalties owed Elvis.

While $35,000 might not sound like much in the twenty-first century, it was the most expensive artist buyout in the record industry to that time—and for someone who was still a relatively little-known regional hillbilly singer. The price was 40 percent greater than the previous record, when Columbia paid $25,000 for Frankie Laine in 1951, and Laine already had a string of hits, including two number one records.

Sam Phillips was asked many times, "Why did you sell Elvis's contract?" To many it ranked as one of the worst business deals in the recording industry. Phillips said he never regretted the deal, and explained: "I had looked at everything for how I could take a little extra money and get myself out of a real bind. I mean, I wasn't broke, but man, it was hand-to-mouth. I made an offer to Tom Parker, but the whole thing was that I made an offer I didn't think they'd even consider—$35,000, plus I owed Elvis $4000 or $5000." He didn't know that Elvis would become so big. "That was the best judgment call I could make at the time, and I still think it is. And Sun went on and did many, many things. I hoped the one thing that wouldn't happen to me was that I would be a one-artist or a one-hit label."

Elvis's first single for RCA, "Heartbreak Hotel," was released on March 3, 1956, four weeks into his *Stage Show* run. It went to number one on the pop charts and remained there for eight weeks. Steve Sholes, the RCA executive who oversaw the session, did not want to stray from the Sun sound. Scotty Moore and Bill Black were present, augmented by country-western pianist Floyd Cramer. Unlike Sun 45s, however, which read "Elvis Presley, with Scotty and Bill," they were not mentioned on the RCA 45. Within a year, they would be gone, feeling Parker was grossly underpaying them.

What Sholes and the RCA engineers did not have was Sam Phillips's recording savvy. Phillips had added a "slapback echo" to Elvis's sound by having two tape recorders next to each other and recording the sound from the first onto the second. The result was a slight delay. Both sounds would then be fed into the console, where they could be mixed together to get the echo effect. This technique later became so standard that many professional tape recorders added a third head, but at the time it was not widely known. RCA tried to imitate the effect with reverb, by placing a microphone and amplifier in a hall as far away from the studio as they could and then feeding the sound back into the studio, to be picked up by the primary tape recorder. It approximated the sound but was not the same. Sholes later tried to entice Phillips to supervise sessions as a freelance artist, but Phillips was busy with his own new projects.

Following "Heartbreak Hotel," Elvis released a string of hits in 1956–57, including eight number one records on *Billboard's* "Hot 100." Of those, five—"Don't Be Cruel," "Hound Dog," "All Shook Up," "(Let Me Be Your) Teddy Bear," and "Jailhouse Rock"—achieved the number one spot across the board, in the categories "US Hot," "US Country," and "US R&B." "Hound Dog" and "Don't Be Cruel" have been hard to place because they were both released on the same 45. Upon release, "Hound Dog" was considered the A side and it did very well, but "Don't be Cruel" gradually took off to become one of Elvis's biggest hits.

Elvis's recordings tell only part of the story. Like Sinatra and Johnnie Ray, Elvis had a sexual magnetism onstage that sent teenage girls into throes of orgasmic ecstasy. At first it was accidental, probably a surprise to Elvis himself. Scotty Moore described Elvis's first appearance before a large audience, how he would jiggle his leg, "just his way of tapping his foot," but with the loose trousers everyone wore, "it made it look like all hell was going on under there." Then during the instrumental breaks, he would back off from the mikes and be playing and shaking, and the crowd would just go wild. According to Moore, Elvis was innocent enough not to realize what was happening: "He thought they [the crowd] were actually making fun of him." Dixie Locke, his serious girlfriend from high school, confirmed, "It was his natural way of performing."

It did not take Elvis long to figure out what was really happening, and to capitalize on it. Clips from the 1950s show Elvis coming onstage, with his long hair and sideburns, sleepy eyes, and a shy look contrasting with a slight sneer curling on the left side of his lips. He would stand with legs wide apart and roll on the balls of his feet as he began to sing, only to launch into a full dance during the instrumental breaks. Both legs shimmering, hips grinding, Elvis held at least the female part of the audience in an almost hypnotic thrall. The guitar became a prop, seldom played, sometimes not even present. His guitar was not the phallic substitute of later rock singers; with Elvis's wiggling, jiggling, dancing, and pelvis rocking, he needed no further accoutrement. It is no wonder that he was nicknamed Elvis the Pelvis, and that his visual presence, whether watched or imagined, always accompanied his music. Ed Sullivan refused to show Elvis below the waist—much to the outrage of fans. It was a new step in 1950s culture; no singer before had enacted such raw sexuality on stage or television. And of course in 1950s society, it would have been the kiss of death for any Black singer to display such overt moves in a predominantly white setting.

Phillips did not lack new singers showing up at Sun Records dreaming of becoming the next Elvis. Thus in November 1956 another young man arrived who also claimed not to "sound like nobody." Phillips was out of town, but Jack Clement, his staff engineer, finally agreed to record this kid who claimed that he could play the piano like Chet Atkins played the guitar. Phillips heard the demo and told Clement, "Who is this cat? Get him in here."

On November 14, 1956, Jerry Lee Lewis sat down for his first Sun recording session. They began with "End of the Road," the song Jerry Lee had written for Clement, and "Crazy Arms," the most popular country music song of 1956 in Ray Price's recording. They tried a couple of others, but Phillips decided to release these two, with "Crazy Arms" the designated A side. The record made little splash; it would take several more tries before Jerry Lee and Phillips found the right formula for his wild talent.

The session did, however, provide further work for Jerry Lee, as Phillips realized he had found a session pianist. In later recording sessions with Carl Perkins, Billy Lee Riley, and Johnny Cash, Lewis's piano can be heard. Phillips also signed him for three more of his own recording dates. Even though "Crazy Arms" did little in the market, it demonstrated Lewis's ability to take a song and make it his own. Price sang "Crazy Arms" straight, with a full, mellifluous voice, smooth phrasing, and only a slight country accent. Lewis added his own unique inflections, ornaments, and improvisations, both vocal and instrumental. His pounding boogie piano set the overall tone, and his voice, with all its hiccups and rising and falling, captured the sense of the lyrics. Lewis's style is fully formed in this first recording, and it varied little throughout his career except possibly when he let loose more on some of his later rock 'n' roll numbers. He always considered himself more of a stylist than a composer: "There's only been four of us, Al Jolson, Jimmie Rodgers, Hank Williams, and Jerry Lee Lewis. That's your only four fuckin' stylists that ever lived."

Lewis went through a variety of songs on his next recording dates, but none yielded anything Sam Phillips saw fit to release. Toward the end of the second session Lewis suggested they try a Big Maybelle number, "Whole Lotta Shaking Going On," but he had not worked out his own part, and it had not yet jelled with his new trio, James Van Eaton on drums and his cousin J. W. Brown on bass. After a few weeks of live performances they were ready to record. In that session Phillips knew he had a hit, although he also feared that it was too risqué.

While Jerry Lee had no claim on the creation of the song, he clearly made it his own. Like Elvis with "Hound Dog," Jerry Lee sped up the tempo, and he gave it his signature boogie beat. He also improvised the famous breakdown near the end where he tells the intended, "Easy now, shake. Awww, shake it baby . . . Now let's get real low one time now . . . All you got do, honey, is stand in one spot, wiggle around just a little bit, that's what you got, yeah!" In his biography of Lewis, Jimmy Guterman called this passage "the most frankly lecherous breakdown in fifties rock and roll."

Jerry Lee's background resembled Elvis's in many ways. Both came from poor Southern families. Jerry Lee was born in Ferriday, Louisiana, a small town on the west bank of the Mississippi River. Elvis had a stillborn twin; Jerry Lee had a brother five years older, Elmo Jr., who was killed by a drunk driver when Jerry Lee was three. His mother, like Elvis's, doted on him, and his father, like Elvis's, struggled, not always successfully, to provide for his family. Elmo Lewis, Jerry Lee's father, had a small farm that never yielded enough, and supplemented his income in various ways, including bootlegging, which resulted in two prison terms.

The Lewises were closely intertwined in complex family relationships with the Gilleys, the Swaggarts, and the Calhouns. Intermarriages, something not uncommon in the rural South, resulted in what Jerry Lee referred to as "double-kins." Jerry Lee was especially close to Jimmy Swaggart, who went on to become one of the most popular television evangelists in the 1970s and '80s. Mickey Gilley had a successful career in country music.

Two activities predominated in the extended clan, the American Pentecostal Church and music. Many members played the guitar and fiddle, and some played piano. Singing, especially hymns, were common, as was listening to records on a windup Victrola—at first Elmo Lewis's house had no electricity. According to Jerry Lee, his musical epiphany came when he was four or five. His parents were visiting Lee and Stella Calhoun's house; Lee Calhoun was the one relatively wealthy member of this family. Jerry Lee came upon Aunt Stella's piano. He touched one note, then another, and soon had picked out "Silent Night." "I don't know what happened. Somethin' strange. I felt it in my whole body. I *felt it*. It was deliverance." Elmo and Mamie, Jerry Lee's parents, were convinced they had a prodigy, and mortgaged their home to buy a piano. Jerry Lee simply knew what he wanted to do: play the piano.

Mamie dreamed of Jerry Lee becoming a church singer and piano player, for her world centered on the church, and other music was sinful. The Pentecostal faith stressed the avoidance of worldly pleasures, an emphasis on the afterlife, and a rousing service, with singing, dancing, shouting, and speaking in tongues. The church made a deep impression on Jerry Lee, and throughout the rest of his life he struggled with his devil, which in the Pentecostal world was very real.

He could not resist the devil's music. As a child he would steal across the river to Haney's Big House, a famous juke joint that brought in some of the best Black musicians in the country, including B. B. King, T-Bone Walker, and a young Fats Domino. It was strictly segregated, for Blacks only. Jerry Lee snuck in frequently and frequently was caught, but he kept coming back. Here for the first time he heard what he later said was rock 'n' roll.

While still a teenager, Jerry Lee began playing the devil's music in clubs around Ferriday and Natchez, Mississippi, some twelve miles away. He tried to compensate by promising to become a preacher and enrolling in the Southwest Bible Institute, a Pentecostal school in Waxahachie, Texas. He lasted until he boogied the hymn "My God Is Real" during a talent show. He later tried his hand in Nashville, but was supposedly told to put away the piano and take up guitar. That was when he decided to go to Sun Records.

Jerry Lee's struggle with the devil can be heard in the session in which he recorded "Great Balls of Fire," a song he was conflicted about. The studio was set up, the session musicians were in place, and the tape was running. Jerry Lee suddenly balked, spelling emphatically H-E-L-L as he realized what in his mind the "great balls of fire" meant. He and Sam Phillips then began a heated discussion, of which the following is only a brief excerpt:

> "Jerry, Jerry, if you think that you can't do good and be a rock-and-roll exponent . . ."
>
> "You can do good Mr. Phillips. Don't get me wrong."
>
> "Wait a minute, wait a minute, listen. I mean, I say, Do good . . ."
>
> "You can have a *kind heart.*"
>
> "I don't mean, I don't mean just . . ."
>
> "You can help people."
>
> "You can save souls!"
>
> "No! No! No! No! How can—how can the devil save souls? What are you talkin' about? Man, I got the *devil* in me. If I didn't have, I'd be a Christian."

Phillips, also a Southerner, knew his Bible, but he was also interested in getting the recording made, as were the session musicians, who interjected "pluck it out," "let's cut it man," and one sarcastic "Hallelujah." Jerry Lee of course settled down, and the recording as well as history was made.

Flannery O'Connor once commented, "While the South is hardly Christ-centered, it is most certainly Christ-haunted." Jerry Lee may not have been Christ-centered, but he was haunted. The specter of the devil never left him. In 1957, before the Colonel draped Elvis in gold lamé and before Elvis surrounded himself with his bought hangers-on, Jerry Lee and Elvis got close and would meet at Graceland, singing and playing songs and hymns into the night, two young men remembering their common Pentecostal past and a less complicated youth. In one of those evenings Jerry Lee asked Elvis:

> "Can you play rock music . . . and still go to heaven? If you died, do you think you'd go to heaven or hell?"
>
> [Elvis's face turned blood-red]
>
> "Jerry, don't you never ask me that. Don't you *never* ask me that again."

Jerry Lee never escaped his devils. In an otherwise typical *People* magazine interview when he was 43, he got thoughtful for a moment, and whispered: "Salvation bears down on me. I don't wanna die and go to Hell. But I don't think I'm headin' in the right direction. I been lustin' a bit lately. I'm lost and undone, without God or son. I should've been a Christian, but I was too weak for the Gospel. I'm a rock'n'roll cat." Even when he was eighty years old he remained troubled: "I was always worried whether I was going to heaven or hell. I still am. I worry about it before I go to bed; it's a very serious situation. I mean you worry, when you breathe your last breath, where are you going to go?" Jerry Lee never left the stage, but also never escaped his own inner hell.

After "Great Balls of Fire" hit the charts, Jerry Lee was challenging Elvis for the rock 'n' roll mantle. Then suddenly it all came apart. In May 1958 Jerry Lee headed to England for a six-week tour, encompassing some thirty-six shows. Trouble began as soon as he landed. The press crowded around, and one spotted a very young teenage girl in the entourage. Asked who she was, Myra calmly replied, "I'm his wife." Jerry Lee confirmed that yes she was, and lied that she was fifteen years old. To the British that was scandal itself, but when they found out that she was actually thirteen, that she was his first cousin once removed, and that Jerry Lee had been married twice before, had two sons, and had married Myra before divorcing his second wife, whom he had married before divorcing his first wife, that story overshadowed anything else about the trip. The British tabloids screamed "BABY SNATCHER! 'GO HOME' CROWD

SHOUTS AT SINGER"; "Lewis: Bigamist." His London hotel told them to leave.

The London trip was canceled after two concerts, and when the entourage returned home, the fallout was less shrill, but scarcely less consequential. Dick Clark, who by then had the highly successful teenage TV show *American Bandstand*, wanted nothing to do with him; disc jockeys stopped playing his records and his records stopped selling. The shows dried up. He could still occasionally get a big venue, but mostly it was small bars, nightclubs, any place that would take him. It was joints like he once played before Sam Phillips. "I never shunned a show. If I had to cut my price down to nearly nothin', I'd take it. To keep workin'." "Had to keep on goin', 'cause if you quit, you die, and I wasn't raised to quit." This continued until 1968, when Jerry Lee resurrected his career as a country singer.

Jerry Lee's British disaster and the subsequent reaction back home was one manifestation of trouble that had been brewing in the musical world since 1954. Sexual mores, racial prejudices, and an internecine war between two major royalty-collection organizations, ASCAP and BMI, exploded in 1957 with echoes that reverberated all the way to the halls of Congress and threatened the future of the genre itself. Sexual and racial issues in particular were so intertwined as to be virtually immune to disentangling.

The content of lyrics—or, as *Variety* called them in 1955, "leer-ics"—had been a problem since at least 1951, when disc jockeys in several cities, including Chicago, refused to play Johnnie Ray's "Whiskey and Gin." Lyrics with double entendre had been a staple of music for the predominantly Black market since the 1920s. In 1929 Bessie Smith recorded "You Got to Give Me Some." Wynonie Harris, whom some say Elvis imitated, recorded "I Like My Baby's Pudding," "Sitting on It All the

Time" and others. According to Harris's record producer, "When you saw Elvis, you saw a mild version of Wynonie." R&B groups regularly recorded risqué songs, such as the Swallows' "It Ain't the Meat, It's the Motion," or the Toppers' "Baby Let Me Bang Your Box." As long as the records remained strictly in the African American market, there was no outcry against the innuendoes of these songs.

In 1951, however, the Dominoes' "Sixty Minute Man," a smash hit in the R&B market, made a dent in the pop field. The lyrics could hardly be misunderstood: what the singer could accomplish in bed in one hour was broken into specific fifteen-minute activities. Not surprisingly, many white radio stations banned the song, yet it rose to seventeen on the Billboard pop charts.

In 1991 writer John Jackson tried to explain how it escaped 1950s *de facto* censorship. He argued that it survived partly because of racial attitudes in segregated America: "It reinforced the white stereotype of a slow-witted, sexually obsessed black man." The song featured bass Bill Brown, not the group's tenor Clyde McPhatter, and to some Brown's lumbering delivery sounded like "sexual braggadocio blatantly overstated"; hence it was not a threat to the white America that feared the (imagined) sexual prowess of the black man. It was a novelty song, not to be taken seriously.

In 1954, *Billboard*, alarmed that local law enforcement was confiscating jukeboxes, fining operators, and local newspapers were pressuring radio stations to ban records, warned that the music industry itself must clean up their offerings before those outside the industry did. This was aimed specifically at the R&B market and the entire distribution chain: record producers, manufacturers, radio stations, disc jockeys, station librarians, and management. *Billboard* noted that it was only a minority of records that created this problem, but feared that censorious groups and state legislatures might step in, and stations could even lose their franchise.

Had R&B only minimally expanded from the Black market, the outcry would have been minimal, but as R&B began to seep further into the "wholesome" white world of the 1950s, the uproar about "leer-ics" became more intense. Not coincidentally, this happened in 1955, just as Black singers began making significant inroads into the pop field. The *Variety* article that coined the term "leer-ics" issued a stern warning about "a total breakdown about sex," while also echoing racial attitudes prevalent in the '50s: "In the past such material was common enough but restricted to special places and out-and-out barrelhouses." To *Variety* it was the (white) youth who were being corrupted by these unacceptable leer-ics: "Our teenagers are already setting something of a record in delinquency without this raw musical idiom to smell up the environment still more."

By 1955 *Billboard*'s worst fears were starting to be realized. The Boston Catholic Youth Organization policed teenage record hops, pressuring the DJs not to play suggestive records. The Chicago Inter-Student Catholic Activists established a "Crusade for Decent Disks." The Juvenile Delinquency and Crime Commission in Houston circulated a list of records that radio stations should ban, threatening to file formal complaints with the FCC for stations that did not comply. The San Antonio Commission, which included members of the police and the judiciary, circulated a similar list and claimed cooperation from all stations.

Feeling the pressure, many radio stations and disc jockeys throughout the country voluntarily screened records for their content. The networks took the problem to almost absurd lengths, going after many Tin Pan Alley and Broadway standards as well as R&B. NBC banned "I Can't Say No" from *Oklahoma!*; CBS, "Soliloquy" from *Carousel*; ABC, "There Is Nothing Like a Dame" from *South Pacific*. Two networks banned Cole Porter's "I Get a Kick Out of You," while the third changed the lyrics. Other songs either had their lyrics changed or were banned outright, including "Rum and Coca-Cola," which became "Lime and

Coca-Cola," "Doing What Comes Naturally," "Frankie and Johnnie," "Slipping Around," and "Pistol Packin' Mama." Ironically, Richard's "Long Tall Sally" managed to get past the NBC censor because after listening to it several times he confessed to a producer, "How can I restrict it when I can't even understand it?"

According to critics, rock 'n' roll not only broke down sexual morals but unleashed unbridled emotions that led to juvenile delinquency. In their assessment, it made hoodlums out of otherwise upstanding teenagers. Moondog's Coronation Ball was only one of several riots that occurred at rock 'n' roll concerts, providing for many conclusive evidence of the genre's destructive influence. Another example occurred on March 10, 1956, when Bill Marlowe, a popular Boston DJ, organized a rock 'n' roll concert at MIT. The concert was in the field house, and the performers were on a temporary stage in the center. The field house was packed, and the crowd began pushing toward the stage, causing some to fall down. Fights erupted, the performers were surrounded, the stage collapsed. Marlowe was able to work his way out along with the other performers, including Miss Massachusetts, who had arrived with Marlowe and was physically accosted by some of the crowd. CBS referred to the incident as a race riot because of the mixed crowd, white and Black teenagers as well as MIT students. How much was race, how much rock 'n' roll, how much overcrowding, how much bad planning? It was not a race riot, but it was a riot, and its publicity only further stigmatized the genre.

Some of the backlash against rock 'n' roll was without question purely racist. White supremacist Asa Carter was so extreme he was fired from station WILD in Birmingham for his racist remarks. He founded the North Alabama Citizens Council and a renegade KKK paramilitary group, the Original Ku Klux Klan of the Confederacy. He called rock 'n' roll "the basic, heavy-beat music of Negroes. It appeals to the base in man, brings out animalism and vulgarity." He further believed that rock 'n' roll was some sort of nefarious plot: "The obscenity and vulgarity of rock 'n' roll music is obviously a means by which the white man and his children will be driven to the level of the N****r."

While other critics were less virulent in their racism, it was nevertheless present, barely camouflaged. In his Lenten pastoral letter Samuel Stritch, cardinal of the Chicago Diocese, wanted to ban rock 'n' roll in Catholic schools because of the music's "tribal rhythms." A pamphlet that circulated in New Orleans under the heading "Help Save the Youth of America" referred to "the screaming, idiotic words and savage music" of rock 'n' roll. The Reverend John Carroll of the Archdiocese of Boston said in a speech, "Rock and roll enflames and excites youth like jungle tom-toms." Many references to jungle music, jungle rhythms, or some other jungle variant were heard at this time.

Beyond the moralistic and racist cries about rock 'n' roll, another anti-rock argument began to gain force by 1956: that it was, simply, bad music. Mel Tormé called it "rubbish"; to Broadway composer Meredith Willson it was "utter garbage," and "should not be confused with anything related to music or verse." These criticisms were often translated to mean, it was not adult music. Addressing the annual Disk Jockey Convention, Mitch Miller ripped the attendees for playing too much rock 'n' roll. Although he never used the word, everyone knew the referent: "juvenile stuff," with a "paralyzing monotony," that "hardly qualifies as music." "It is not the creation of musicians and—most damning of all—it has no entertainment value for anyone over fourteen." Frank Sinatra was not to be outdone by Miller: "[Rock 'n' roll] is the most brutal, ugly, desperate, vicious form of expression it has been my misfortune to hear"; "It is sung and played by the most part by cretinous goons," and is "the martial music of every sideburned delinquent on the face of the earth."

Sinatra's thoughts exemplify a larger struggle occurring at the highest levels of the music business. The American Society of Composers, Authors and Publishers (ASCAP) was founded in

1914 to protect the rights of those in the music profession, and specifically to see that they received proper compensation for their work. As it matured it developed strict standards for admission. It was a creation of Tin Pan Alley and favored such music. It expanded to include classical musicians as well as jazz and swing, but it drew the line at R&B and rock 'n' roll. R&B musicians turned to Broadcast Music, Inc. (BMI), originally founded by the National Association of Broadcasters in 1939 in response to ASCAP's demand for a substantial increase in royalty fees. BMI sought artists ignored by the larger and more powerful ASCAP, and for a time ASCAP ignored BMI as posing no threat.

As rock 'n' roll caught on and independent labels such as Sun, Atlantic, and Chess began to claim large parts of the pop market, ASCAP reacted vehemently. They helped spread the idea that rock 'n' roll was vacuous, and they tried to contain it with court cases. Sinatra's and others' comments may not have been spontaneous. Unable to contain the rock 'n' roll tsunami, Burton Lane, the president of ASCAP, sent a letter to the House Subcommittee on Legislative Oversight asserting that BMI's purpose was "to suppress genuine talent and to foist mediocre music upon the public." This letter triggered the payola investigation.

Payola was to be the major offensive of the anti-rockers. They knew the power that disc jockeys had over the public's musical preferences, especially those of teenagers. If they could just convince the American public that disc jockeys' choices were based on greed, on questionable if not illegal payments to play certain records, rock 'n' roll would become a tarnished brand. Combined with the pressure that many politicians were feeling from adults about music for various reasons—race, leer-ics, inciting dangerous behavior—an investigation into the music business, especially rock 'n' roll, seemed a sure way to garner publicity. After all, the voting population at the time was not teenagers; the voting age was twenty-one.

The House Subcommittee, chaired by Oren Harris, Democrat

of Arkansas, had just completed their investigation into the bribery and rigging of television quiz shows. When on November 7, 1959, they announced they would expand their investigation into payola in the music world, the country was reeling from the quiz show scandal, and payola thus became part of the larger issue of corruption within the media industry. Lane had charged that "commercial bribery had become a prime factor in determining what music is played on many broadcast programs and what music records the public is surreptitiously induced to buy." It also charged that the polls were rigged and that manufacturers paid teenagers to buy records at certain stores to promote sales.

Many DJs were targeted in the investigation, but Alan Freed and Dick Clark were the big fish they hoped to reel in. Freed was already reeling; his program on WNEW-TV had been canceled, and he had been fired from ABC for refusing to sign a statement that he had never taken payola. Frank S. Hogan, New York district attorney, also began an investigation, and was forced to subpoena Freed after he refused to keep an appointment to discuss the matter. Freed further refused to sign a waiver of immunity for his testimony to the grand jury about payola in the music business.

Freed and Clark were the last two DJs to testify before the House Committee. Freed was relatively open, explaining how payola worked in the music business, although he denied being complicit. Clark managed to deflect accusations, principally by claiming that payola implied a contract between the DJs and a record company, and that he had signed none. Although almost everyone dismissed this definition as a legal ploy, Clark managed to emerge relatively unscathed, while Freed remained the poster boy for the practice. On May 20, 1960, DA Hogan arrested five DJs, a program director, and two record librarians on payola charges. The *New York Times* headline, "Alan Freed and 7 Others Arrested in Payola Here," left no doubt who symbolized the practice.

Peter C. Tripp, disc jockey at WMGM, was the first to be tried. He put up a strong defense, but was found guilty, fined $500, and given thirty-five concurrent six-month jail sentences, which were suspended. With various delays Freed's trial and sentencing dragged on over a year. Sensing the outcome, Freed reached a plea bargain: a $500 fine, reduced to $300, and a suspended six-month sentence. During the interim, Freed had been offered a job at station KDAY in Los Angeles. A dispute with KDAY in which they forbade him to promote rock 'n' roll shows caused him to move to WQAM in Miami, Florida, a position that lasted two months. He returned to Los Angeles and worked briefly at KNOB, but his health was deteriorating, exacerbated by alcoholism. He died on January 20, 1965, 43 years old.

The different fates of Alan Freed and Dick Clark in the payola scandal exemplify the changing rock 'n' roll scene in the late 1950s. Freed represented the earlier, scrappy, wilder R&B side of rock 'n' roll, Clark the new toned-down version that sought to be as squeaky-clean as the TV image Clark tried to portray. For by 1959 the anti-rock backlash had taken its toll. Most of the major figures of the mid-decade were no longer active, for a variety of reasons. Elvis had been drafted into the army, Little Richard was about to forsake the stage for the pulpit, Chuck Berry had been arrested for violating the Mann Act and would soon begin a prison sentence, and Jerry Lee Lewis had already lost his rock 'n' roll status over his third marriage scandal.

One other singer, Buddy Holly, had established himself in late 1957 and seemed to be the next megastar. His band, the Crickets, had a clear rock 'n' roll sound, but there was little R&B in Holly's singing, and his image was different—a very proper-looking tall young man in a suit and horn-rimmed glasses, who sang softly with a nasal twitter. In some ways, however, he was less a part of the '50s than a precursor of what was to come. His style, including his appearance, vocal quality, and instrumentation, which focused on guitars, was a major influence on the Beatles. His career, however, ended abruptly when he was killed in a plane crash on February 3, 1959, along with two other singers, Ritchie Valens and the Big Bopper (J. P. Richardson Jr.). Holly was twenty-two.

By the end of the 1950s rock 'n' roll had become the province of a number of young, cute, white, nonthreatening singers, many named Bobby—Bobby Vinton, Bobby Rydell, Bobby Darin—as well as Paul Anka and Fabian. Fabian was one of the first manufactured singers. Even he admitted he couldn't sing, but he looked the part. All of these singers appealed almost entirely to teenagers, and seemed to be created for the *Dick Clark Show*, which promoted a handsome, wholesome type of entertainer just sexy enough for the toned-down time. Clark's show responded uncannily to what the late 1950s thought it wanted in its youth. That may have been the reason ABC supported him fully through the payola scandal while cutting Alan Freed loose.

As rock 'n' roll devolved into what Mitch Miller and others had predicted—music for young teenagers—older youth were latching onto a new trend led by three cool-looking college types from California, Dave Guard, Bob Shane, and Nick Reynolds, who formed the Kingston Trio. Soon the folk music boom would eclipse all other popular music forms, leading to new stars, such as Bob Dylan, Joan Baez, and Peter, Paul and Mary. The folk revival included a number of Black singers—Josh White, Harry Belafonte, Odetta—and many folk singers aligned themselves with the anti-Vietnam and the Civil Rights movement. Rock continued to evolve in the 1960s with major breakthroughs such as Motown and Chubby Checker's "Twist," but with the possible exception of Motown, the folk scene dominated until 1964. In that year a new rock sound appeared, this time from Great Britain, and a new chapter in the rock story began. The first and possibly most explosive phase of the revolution was long over, but had left an indelible imprint on the United States and the world.

CHAPTER 13

Anonymity and Its Ways: Classical Music in a Postwar World

There were several twentieth-century beginnings: in science, Heisenberg's Uncertainty Principle, the quantum, even relativity; in art, cubism, Dada, and surrealism; in literature, novels of Marcel Proust, Joseph Conrad, and Gertrude Stein. With science upending the Newtonian certainty of the universe, artists of many stripes turned inside to dismantle the self. For Proust and Conrad the self remained, yet hidden and fugitive, behind a reality that was reduced to "multiple and varied sensations," a fleeting effervescence whose grasp is uncertain and constantly changing. German writers such as Hermann Hesse continued this theme: the self did not disappear but disintegrated, fragmenting into pieces that could be arranged and rearranged. Wylie Sypher summarized Hesse, "Our personality is an illusion." Simon de Beauvoir voiced what Western culture had done to the female self: "He is the Subject, he is the Absolute—she is the Other." That is, she is identified as what she is not, the absence of the masculine self, leaving her a vessel with little or no agency.

Painting followed the same course, rejecting Renaissance conventions centered on humans or human vision. In 1907 Pablo Picasso and Georges Braque began to break down those conventions, by stressing the flatness of a canvas, depicting fragments of a scene derived from many points of view simultaneously. The subject disappeared in an agglomeration of patterns and overlapping shapes. Men and women portrayed were no longer individuals but abstract suggestions of human figures. Gertrude Stein clearly understood the mechanism at work when she called Picasso's *Three Musicians* a "still life." Any sense of self had been lost in the geometry.

Earlier, Friedrich Nietzsche had anticipated this development, although he understood it as a consequence of music: "Music alone allows us to understand the delight felt at the annihilation of the individual." Nietzsche remained in the throes of Romanticism, for he saw the loss of self as the intoxication felt when one is overpowered by music, specifically Wagner's. For Nietzsche it was the self against Wagner, and Wagner usually won.

In rejecting Romanticism, these early twentieth-century artists sought to dismantle, then erase, the Romantic, heroic self. What they began reached a climax at the end of the Second World War. Europe was exhausted, and many parts of it were decimated; Germany lay in ruins. Psychologically much of Western Europe was in shock. Heinrich Böll's short story "Pale Anna" featured an unnamed young German man consumed with ennui: "It wasn't until spring 1950 that I came back from the war, and I found there was nobody I knew left in town. I rented a room in the town, lay there on the bed, smoked and waited, and didn't know what I was waiting for. I didn't want to work. . . . There I dozed and vegetated, stubbed the cigarettes out against the wall, and so all over the wall by my bed there were black marks."

Artists and intellectuals reacted in multiple ways. Some wanted to start anew. This meant ridding the present of all vestiges of the past. Pierre Boulez, who was twenty years old in 1945, was particularly outspoken: "It is not enough to deface the *Mona Lisa* because that does not kill the *Mona Lisa*. All the art of the past must be destroyed." He explained, "The dilemma of music is the dilemma of our civilization. We have to fight the past to survive."

Boulez attended seminars led by Olivier Messiaen in 1944, which elicited Messiaen's observation that Boulez was "in revolt against everything." In 1945 Boulez studied composition with Rene Leibowitz, a disciple of Schoenberg, and adopted serialism. In 1952 he turned against Schoenberg and implicitly against Leibowitz. In his article "Schoenberg Is Dead," he described Schoenberg's twelve-tone music as a "catastrophe," and "a direction as wrong as any in the history of music." That this article came just one year after Schoenberg's death only sharpened the bite of his condemnation. At the time many composers saw dodecaphony, which the twelve-tone system was often called, as the wave of the future. This included many American composers who had benefited from Schoenberg's residency in Southern California since his immigration to the United States in 1933. Boulez never calmed down about Schoenberg or Leibowitz: he later commented, "The Leibowitz cult was repulsive to me . . . and Leibowitz was a joke. He was serviceable at the beginning, but I began to resent him when I saw how narrow and stupid he was."

In spite of his rebellious streak, Boulez knew that railing against the establishment was not sufficient; he must create something. The result was total or integral serialism, which meant extending the serial technique that Schoenberg applied to pitch to other parameters of music: rhythm, dynamics, texture. Ironically, Boulez's response was to expand Schoenberg's approach after condemning it.

Schoenberg's method involved creating a row or series of all twelve tones within the octave, which would form the governing structure underlying the piece. At its most basic, no note could be repeated until all the other eleven had been sounded. This guaranteed that no pitch would have priority, and consequently there would be no sense of a tonal center. The concept allowed considerable manipulation, however: the row could be played retrograde (backwards), inverted (turned upside down), or both; it could be moved to different pitch levels as long as the intervals stayed the same; and it could be broken into partial groupings. In practice, liberties could also be taken so the rules need not be followed precisely. Schoenberg and his pupil and colleague Alban Berg especially felt that the technique should allow some personal expression.

Yet by serializing the many different parameters of the piece, personal expression could be eliminated, which was the second and more pervasive reaction to World War II. Boulez was clear about what he sought: "Our problem was to make a new musical language, seeking out what was good from the past, and rejecting what was bad. . . . *What we were doing by total serialization was to annihilate the will of the composer in favor of a predetermining system.*" It was a means for achieving anonymity. Boulez also had ideas about the effect of a composition: "I think that is exactly what a work of art should do to you; it should in the end make you feel lost, and you should know you are lost, and that is the important thing."

Boulez's first piece based on his ideas of integral serialism was *Livre pour quatuor*, written in 1949. He was dissatisfied with it and a second work, *Polyphony X*, written in 1951, later withdrawing both from circulation. The first composition that Boulez felt fully represented his thinking was *Structures I*, written in 1952. This is considered a "milestone in the evolution of integral serialism," and cemented Boulez's reputation as an international leader of the post–World War II avant-garde.

Yet, apparently unknown to Boulez, an American composer had arrived at integral serialism even earlier. Milton Babbitt had a convoluted career leading to that point. From a wealthy family in Jackson, Mississippi, he began violin at four and later switched to clarinet; he enrolled in the University of Pennsylvania in 1931, to study mathematics, but two years later transferred to New York University to study music, where he was introduced to the music of Schoenberg. Following matriculation he remained in New York to study composition with Roger Sessions. In 1938 Sessions, who had begun teaching at Princeton, invited Babbitt to join the composition faculty, and in 1942 he was awarded an MFA. When World War II broke out, Babbitt was called to Washington, DC, to work on a project so secret that he insisted he could not reveal its nature even sixty years later. After two years in DC he was sent back to Princeton, only to teach mathematics, which was needed for the war effort.

Following the armistice, Babbitt, in collaboration with the librettist Richard Koch, wrote a Broadway musical, *Fabulous Voyage*, based on Homer's *Odyssey*. It was never produced, and Babbitt turned back to serial composition.

During the war Babbitt had completed a dense theoretical, mathematical work, "The Function of Set Structure in the Twelve-Tone System." He submitted it as his dissertation to the Princeton Music Department in 1946, but it was rejected. The department had only begun offering the PhD in historical musicology, and the thesis did not fit that mold. It was eventually accepted in 1992, and Babbitt received his Princeton PhD, even though he had been the William Shubael Conant Professor of Music there for twenty-seven years. The thesis did provide material for several theoretical works he produced in the interim decades.

In his theoretical writings of the 1950s and '60s Babbitt introduced terms such as "source set," "combinatoriality," "aggregate," "arrays," "secondary set," "derived set," "layers," "partitions," and "time points," many of which were taken from his rejected PhD thesis. Most of these concepts are derived from mathematics, and it is no coincidence that Boulez and Babbitt pioneered integral serialism, for both were also mathematicians. From the time of ancient Greece, music and mathematics have frequently been conjoined, but seldom in such an overt and direct way as in integral serialism.

"I never choose a note unless I know why it is there," Babbitt once said. And for Babbitt that often meant having several reasons, as a single note could occupy multiple positions in his complex array of intertwined sets. Babbitt thus saw integral serialism as a rational process, governed by head rather than heart, by intellect rather than emotion. His underlying compositional purpose, however, was quite different from Boulez's. Boulez sought anonymity. Babbitt never stated that such was behind his creativity, but in one article he did pull back the mathematical curtain enough to expose his motivation.

Babbitt's most famous, or infamous, article, "Who Cares If You Listen?," was published in *High Fidelity* magazine in 1958. Aside from the inflammatory title, which was not Babbitt's, it reveals many layers of insight not only about Babbitt and classical music of the time, but about 1950s society itself. Babbitt's original title was "The Composer as Specialist," but *High Fidelity*'s rebranding of the article not only helped sell the issue and make the article a classic, but in the end may have created a title more appropriate than Babbitt's original intended one.

In the article Babbitt views the current condition of composers as the final flowering of a half-century of "revolution in musical thought." The "universe of common practice" no longer exists, and the post–World War II composer must confront a musical geography of many divergent practices, a situation Babbitt characterizes as the "fall from musical innocence." Babbitt considers the new language as more "efficient," a term as telling as any about Babbitt's concepts of music. Sounding close to ideas about information theory, which was current in the 1950s and '60s, Babbitt states that the new music has less "redundancy," and then explains its potential as "a five-dimensional musical space determined by pitch-class, register, dynamics, duration, and timbre." He explains how the succession of five-dimensional events creates the structure of the work. Essentially this describes how integral serialism works.

Babbitt also discusses the implications of this new music relative to the public. He compares the situation in music to that of science and mathematics. The average layman can no longer expect to understand the latest developments in theoretical physics or mathematics, so why should he (Babbitt, like most writers of his time, defaults to the male pronoun) expect to do so in music? Babbitt is particularly disdainful of the concertgoer who responds to a piece with the comment "I didn't like it," and compares that to the absurdity of the layman who responds similarly to a lecture on "Pointwise Periodic Homeomorphisms."

Babbitt was already laying the groundwork for his most important argument: new music is science. He continually uses the word "research," rather than the more common term for composition, "creation." In the meantime, confronted with a public that does not understand, not does not like, the new music as Babbitt sees it, he suggests "that the composer would do himself and his music an immediate and eventual service by total, resolute, and voluntary withdrawal from this pubic world to one of private performance electronic media, with its very real possibility of complete elimination of the public and social aspects of musical composition."

This of course raises the question, what is the purpose of music? Is it to communicate? In this article Babbitt suggests that communication be limited to a very small group of like-minded musicians. Babbitt's own writings—those not for mass magazines—back up his point. Not only are they highly mathematical, but the very act of beginning an article with a sentence of 149 words, as he did with "Contemporary Music Composition and Music Theory as Contemporary Intellectual History," is a message in itself. Babbitt then suggests a solution: the university.

The university was the nexus of research and scientific advancement in the mid-twentieth century, and Babbitt's compositions served the same purpose to advance the field. It was a solution for its time. The days of the wealthy patron (usually a woman) personally supporting composers were over. With the Iron Curtain descending after World War II, the Soviet Union exploding its atomic bomb and launching Sputnik, the first satellite, American society feared greatly the Soviet threat. They turned to academia to neutralize the danger. The government responded by pouring millions of dollars into university research, in essence anointing the university as the savior of democracy. Support was not limited to the sciences; languages, linguistics, history, and the arts also benefited. Congress considered the arts another weapon to spread American values worldwide.

Congress undoubtedly did not have integral serialism in mind in reference to the arts, but Babbitt realized that the more he aligned his work with science, the better its acceptance into academia. Music was already entrenched in several institutions, but serialism promised the chance for more prestige because of its strong mathematical bent. Led by Babbitt, serialism made great strides, although the extent of its impact has been debated. There is no question, however, that many of the more important composers who matured in the post–World War II years were served a heavy dose of serialism, whether they wanted it or not. While a preponderance of composers continued to write in tonal or extended tonal idioms, a serial cloud hung over the aspiring composer determined to make a mark. Serialism was the hot new thing, and in their zeal serialists painted traditional composers as remnants of the past. Charles Wuorinen dismissed tonal composers as "backward-looking," and while acknowledging tonality as viable for popular and commercial music, he proclaimed that "it is no longer employed by serious composers of the mainstream."

Younger composers of the fifties, sixties, and seventies felt the pressure: Jacob Druckman, Michael Beckerman, and William Mayer voiced similar thoughts, only changing the metaphor: Druckman, "Not being a serialist on the East Coast in the sixties was like not being a Catholic in Rome in the thirteenth century"; Beckerman, "Trying to write tonal music at a place like Columbia University in the 1960s and '70s was like being a dissident in Prague during the same period"; Mayer, "One was shunned as the last teen-age virgin." George Rochberg extended the religious metaphor, noting how serialists sold it "as the only true faith. As such they have proclaimed an orthodox cultural church, with its hierarchy, gospels, beliefs and anathemas. After the end of World War II it very quickly captured and dominated American academic circles, which it monstrously and bluntly politicized."

In spite of serialists' belief in their approach as revolutionary, Babbitt, as serialism's acknowledged guru, was in the end a Romantic holdout. He clung to the nineteenth-century notion of progress: that music must continue to evolve in order to live. He viewed contemporary classical music in sacralized terms, with his phrase, the "fall from musical innocence," as if he and his contemporary composers had bitten a forbidden apple. His solution was pure Romanticism: retreat to the ivory tower, fully supported by the twentieth-century tower's landlord and patron, the university. The retreat not only symbolized the consequences of a fall from innocence, but rang as the twentieth-century version of the Faustian bargain: aligning your musical inspiration and compositional life to meet the principal pursuit of the research institution of the 1950s—the god of science.

Only a few composers adopted integral serialism, and Babbitt himself did not stick with it strictly. Yet the same anti-expressionism that both Babbitt and Boulez felt spread among many other American composers, and it soon became a badge of honor. Lukas Foss, who founded his Improvisation Chamber

Ensemble in 1957, referred to "the trend for anonymity which is built into current musical expression"; with the improvisation ensemble, "my group was undoubtedly the first and last to actually take the extreme step and discard our author's vanity. Steve Reich wanted to create " 'music that was completely impersonal,' by 'impersonal means.' "

Some composers approached depersonalization in completely different ways. It would be hard to find a composer and a person who appears more opposite Babbitt than John Cage, the leader of a compositional approach that on the surface eschews everything Babbitt stood for. Cage's thinking from the 1950s was rooted in his introduction to Buddhism in the late 1940s, through the lectures on Buddhism by Daisetz Teitaro Suzuki at Columbia University. Zen provided Cage with a new perspective on music as well as life. Artistically, three related injunctions from Suzuki's teaching guided Cage: relinquishing control, allowing the ego to dissolve, and living in the moment, with its corollary, abandoning the search for causality. This is admittedly a severe simplification of a difficult-to-fathom compositional philosophy, but its manifestations are easily demonstrable in Cage's subsequent approach to music. The approach was not without contradictions, but contradiction itself was part of Zen; Cage, confronted with a contradiction, dismissed it: "I'm not afraid of contradictions."

Cage applied Zen to sound itself. One of his most quoted lines, delivered in 1955: "A sound does not view itself as thought, as ought, as needing another sound for elucidation, as etc.; it has no time for any consideration." In a mock dialogue in the same article, the questioner asks,

> "Then what is the purpose of this 'experimental' music?"
>
> "No purposes. Just sounds."

To realize the music he sought, Cage adopted "chance" methods to determine what would happen. He used various techniques, but settled particularly on the *I Ching*, or *Book of Changes*, an ancient Chinese text. It consists of sixty-four hexagrams on 8 × 8 matrices. Each unit in the matrix consists of six horizontal bars, some solid, some broken in the middle. Coin flips determine the hexagram: heads equals a solid line, tails a broken line. The hexagrams are divided into moving and stable ones, depending on the variety within the flips. Accompanying the matrices are various questions and answers based on the outcome of the flips. The user is expected to begin with a question, and then various patterns will suggest an answer. Cage was less interested in this oracular aspect than the ensuing patterns as compositional determinants. In his Piano Concerto, 1957–58, he created a large chart that encompassed a number of parameters; in *Music of Changes* he used the *I Ching* to determine the piece itself: he had charts for tempi, durations, superpositions, sounds, and dynamics. Cage further developed elaborate instructions on how each chart was to be interpreted.

This particular technique was in the broadest sense an approach that Cage had used for some time, minus the coin flips. From the 1930s Cage had composed numerous percussion pieces as well as compositions using the prepared piano, a technique that involved inserting objects such as nails, screws, and spoons into or on the piano strings to create unusual percussive effects. The prepared piano in essence became a new type of percussion instrument. These pieces were based on various mathematical methods for determining durations.

Cage's percussion approach arose partly out of necessity—he had a job providing music for dancers at the Cornish School in Seattle—and partly out of his own musical limitations. Cage had grown up on the West Coast, in Los Angeles, and had studied piano, but originally had no interest in music professionally. After graduating high school he determined to be a writer or a painter, and spent eighteen months in Europe, dabbling in architecture, painting, and poetry as well as music. Near the end of his stay he made his first serious attempt at composition, writing short pieces based on a "complex mathematical system." Unfortunately, neither the pieces nor the system survived.

After he returned home, Cage's desire to become a composer gradually came into focus. He spent a few years doing various odd jobs and also making connections. He studied briefly with Henry Cowell, until Cowell recommended he study with Arnold Schoenberg, who had recently immigrated to Los Angeles. Cage considered him his guru, admitting, "I literally worshipped him," "like a God." Precisely when, where, and how long Cage studied with Schoenberg is not clear, but the most important outcome was Cage's realization of what he could not do. Cage often told the story: both he and Schoenberg recognized that Cage had no sense of harmony. Schoenberg told Cage that consequently he would run into a wall that would not yield. Cage responded, "In that case I will devote my life to beating my head against that wall."

Cage meanwhile had become interested in sounds, whether traditionally musical ones or not, and had some opportunities accompanying dancers and composing music for their performances. This led to his first big break in music, his appointment as composer-accompanist at the Cornish School. There, on April 28, 1940, Syvilla Fort, the first Black student at the Cornish School, was scheduled to give a dance recital, introducing a new piece, *Bacchanale*. She asked Cage to write music for it. Her dance was well suited for the percussion ensemble that Cage had founded, but the hall in which it was to be performed had no room for any instruments other than a grand piano. Cage began to experiment with placing various objects on the strings and eventually settled on bolts, nuts, and screws, whose threads could be inserted between two closely aligned strings, thus keeping them in place. The concert proved a success, and for Cage it

A prepared piano for a John Cage composition. Cage indicated precisely what he wanted where on the piano strings.

launched more than ten years of composing and experimenting with the possibilities. Throughout the 1940s his most important compositions were percussion works and the *Sonatas and Interludes for Prepared Piano.*

In 1941 Cage moved to Chicago, followed by a move to New York City. Matters looked promising at first. In Chicago he received an opportunity to compose music for a CBS radio drama by Kenneth Patchen, *The City Wears a Slouch Hat,* which aired May 31, 1942. In New York his ensemble gave a widely publicized concert at the Museum of Modern Art, about which *Life* magazine ran a feature article. Cage's situation quickly deteriorated, however: opportunities evaporated and commissions did not materialize. Cage went through several years of poverty and uncertainty, while his personal life was also in flux. Cage had married Xenia Andreyevna Kashevaroff in 1935, but he began to realize his attraction to the dancer Merce Cunningham was more than friendship. He and Xenia were divorced in 1945 and Cage and Cunningham formed an artistic and personal relationship that lasted the rest of Cage's life, and resulted in many fruitful collaborations.

Cage's life improved dramatically in the late 1940s. In early 1949 he received a grant from the National Institute for the Arts and Letters, which allowed him to travel to France. While there he received notice that he had also been awarded a Guggenheim Fellowship; at least for a brief period, Cage had no financial worries. Cage made the most of his time in France. He became interested in Erik Satie's music, and was quite excited when he discovered notebooks relating to Satie's *Furniture Music*, as they included sets of numbers that resembled Cage's own calculations. Some thirty years before, Satie had arrived at the same process as Cage's for creating his rhythmic structures, or so Cage thought. His excitement was short-lived, however. When he showed his find to Darius Milhaud, who had known Satie well, Milhaud replied, "Oh no, those numbers referred to shopping lists."

More important, Cage developed a close friendship with Pierre Boulez. At the time Boulez was not well known; his integral serial works were still to come, as were his most rebellious essays. Yet Virgil Thomson had heard of Boulez and suggested to Cage that he contact him. In typical Cage fashion, he gathered a number of his scores and knocked on Boulez's door. They realized they had much in common in spite of cultural, personal, musical, and age differences. Boulez was thirteen years younger, and a fine pianist with an exceptional ear and an angry, controlling personality; further, as he would later prove, he believed in the importance of institutions. Cage was a less proficient pianist, and by his own admission had a sunny disposition and no ear for harmony—in fact "I have no talent for music"—and he wanted no involvement with institutions.

While Cage was in Paris, Boulez introduced him to many French composers and other intellectuals, arranged a performance of Cage's *Sonatas and Interludes*, and gave a lecture prior to the performance. Cage maintained a close friendship with Boulez even after he returned to the United States. He worked to have Boulez's music introduced, and made two separate attempts to arrange a concert tour for Boulez. They exchanged lengthy letters discussing their philosophical and technical approaches to composition, and for a time seemed to be kindred spirits in their musical ideas. That friendship deteriorated quickly, however, when Boulez discovered that while Cage used the same type of mathematical matrices as Boulez for compositional determinants, Cage's numbers were the result of coin flips.

Thanks in large part to Suzuki's lectures and Cage's subsequent acceptance of Buddhism, around 1950 Cage began to pursue indeterminacy more deeply. He also became interested in *musique concrète,* a process pioneered by Pierre Schaeffer, whom Cage had met in Paris. Schaeffer had grown up interested in music but became an electrical engineer. He worked mostly at radio stations, which had collections of phonograph records that imitated everyday sounds—trains, cars, glass breaking, any effect a radio program might need. After World War II ended Schaeffer began to use *musique concrète,* everyday sounds, to create musical compositions. Later Schaeffer would use the tape recorder to capture sounds of the city and life, but in 1946 he used phonograph records from radio station archives. His first *musique concrète* composition was *Etudes de bruits* (Studies in Noise), three pieces each focusing on a specific set of sounds. The sounds were constructed to maintain some traditional musical qualities: the first, for instance, featured the sound of trains, with the rhythmic chugging and clacking of wheels, and the interjection of sounds such as the steam whistle.

Cage had previously used sounds from nontraditional objects in his percussion music, such as brake drums, beer bottles, and flower pots, but his first effort to incorporate such sounds non-percussively into his work was *Imaginary Landscape No. 4,* for twelve radios and twenty-four players. Twelve radios were placed onstage; half the players were to turn the tuning knob, the other half the volume control. Instructions were precise, although the precision, when and how the knobs were turned, was determined by *I Ching*. The premier at the McMillin Theater at Columbia University on May 2, 1951, was not entirely successful because instructions called for low volumes; in addition, the piece was programmed for the end of a long concert, and by then many of the stations had gone off the air. The audience sat puzzled by the activity of whirling knobs with very little sound emanating.

Cage wanted to experiment further with *musique concrète*, but not having access to a radio station, he needed a tape recorder, which in 1951 was a new type of technology, at least to the Western Hemisphere. It had just begun to impact some types of music in the United States, but in 1951 it was a still a rare and expensive piece of equipment, clearly out of Cage's reach. Soon, however, two serendipitous events gave Cage not only use of a professional machine but a weekly stipend to help alleviate his poverty. While on a lecture tour in 1948 he had met a young student at Black Mountain College, Paul Williams, who became an architect and who later inherited considerable wealth. Intrigued by Cage's work, Williams funded a "Project for Magnetic Tape," which included not only a stipend for the musicians but resources to finance taping.

By this time Cage had become friends with Morton Feldman and the pianist David Tudor, with whom he was to work closely for years. He had also gathered a group of younger artists around him, composer Earle Brown and his wife, dancer Carolyn Brown, and Christian Wolff, who had introduced him to the *I Ching*.

Most important, Cage met Louis and Bebe Barron, a couple whose work with electronic composition was both pioneering and groundbreaking. Ironically, they have not received the historical recognition they deserve. They established the first electronic studio in the United States in 1949, predating similar efforts by well-known composers such as Otto Luening and Vladimir Ussachevsky, who along with Milton Babbitt later founded the Columbia-Princeton Electronic Music Center ten years later. The Barrons experimented with magnetic tape manipulation while Pierre Schaeffer was still using turntables. They supplied music and sound effects for many avant-garde films and dance and theater productions, including some on Broadway and in Hollywood.

Although their work is acknowledged in electronic music circles, it seems to have been ignored in the music history canon, probably for several reasons: they had no institutional connection to provide an imprimatur of credibility, nor personal contact with theorists and musicologists, those who create the canon; they wrote no theoretical or descriptive tracts themselves; and they were most famously associated with Hollywood, but for only one film. While they were active, musicology largely ignored Hollywood film composition, except when it involved composers known for other activity. Later when the study of film music became a desired topic, the Barrons seemed only a sudden flash that disappeared. We now know that their being dropped by Hollywood had nothing to do with the quality of their work.

The Barrons were both born in Minnesota, although Bebe, née Charlotte May Wind, grew up in Fargo, North Dakota, before returning to the University of Minnesota. She graduated with a degree in Spanish in 1946, and a master's in political science in 1947. She had spent time in Mexico in 1945–46, and before going had been introduced to Louis, as he had just returned from there. Louis had studied music at both the University of Minnesota and University of Chicago, and in the early 1940s he was in Mexico working on a play that never came to fruition. He was also interested in electronics and, according to one source, had a ham radio license. This knowledge was to prove invaluable later.

After graduation, Bebe moved to New York City, and Louis

soon followed; he worked for the Gallup Organization and she, as a researcher with *Life* magazine. She also studied composition briefly with Wallingford Riegger and Henry Cowell. After Louis had been "pursuing me hotly," for about two years she decided, "I guess I better get married, who knows when I'll have another offer." They married in Minnesota on December 7, 1947, and almost immediately moved to Monterey, California. Given a wire recorder as a wedding present, they began to experiment with it, but quickly realized that it was not adequate for musical work. It did allow them to record voices, and soon they began to record authors reading their own work—Anaïs Nin, with whom they developed a close relationship, Henry Miller, Tennessee Williams, and Aldous Huxley. Their project to sell authors' recordings was not an economic success, so they moved back to New York. Because of a family connection, they had been able to buy a Stancil-Hoffman tape recorder in California, possibly the first tape recorder manufactured in this country. With it they set up a studio in Greenwich Village in 1949. Louis's cousin worked for 3M, and through that connection they were able to acquire magnetic tape, a product not readily available at the time.

Upon reading Norbert Weiner's book *Cybernetics*, published in 1948, their work took a new direction. Although Weiner's work has been almost forgotten, its impact on both the physical sciences and engineering as well as on the social sciences was substantial. The subtitle of the book referred to cybernetics as "Control and Communication in the Animal and the Machine." Beyond that, a precise definition is difficult to establish. In a letter to Norbert Weiner in the 1940s, Claude Shannon, whose work founded the field of information theory, suggested, "Use the word 'cybernetics,' Norbert, because nobody knows what it means." Generally it refers to the study of a topic, be it people, animals, or machines, as systems or processes, employing communication, feedback, control, recursiveness, and information. Weiner was a mathematician, and not surprisingly, most of his book consists of mathematical arguments. He included diagrams of the overall components of feedback and oscillation, but not necessarily related to electronic machines, and certainly no specific electronic schematics for the Barrons to build from. Nonetheless they saw Weiner's general ideas as applicable to electronic circuits, especially oscillators. Electronic oscillators are circuits that would create various types of sounds, the building block of later synthesizers. Since nothing like that existed then, Louis had to conceive and build them himself, using vacuum tubes. To the Barrons, these circuits acquired a life of their own.

Because the oscillators were new and experimental, the Barrons were never sure what they would produce: "We had very little idea what was going to emerge from these circuits, what it was going to sound like." They had a tape recorder set up to capture whatever sounds the oscillator made, which was necessary, as the oscillators often worked only once. Bebe described the situation:

> Each circuit we built had lifespans of their own, and I can't stress that enough—that was always amazing to me, and once they died we never could revive them. We always were innocents with the sense of wonder and awe of the beauty coming from the circuits. I mean we would just sit back and let them take over. We didn't want to control them at all. We were in a very receptive state like that of a child working with our eyes and minds open, paying attention to each circuit, and we were simply amazed at what great things came out of those circuits.

In some ways Barron's remarks suggest a Cageian aesthetic: do not try to control; be fascinated with the sounds that emerge; be receptive to the nature of each sound. Do not try to manipulate. Yet when Bebe's overall process is examined, it is not like Cage's at all.

Louis saw their work somewhat differently from Bebe. Although Louis realized that each circuit had its own life, he felt a need to exert some control: "They need prodding." When a circuit rebelled against its instructions, he said, "We have to knock it around electronically." Although it sounds ruthless, Louis understood what was necessary electronically, and he was willing to destroy his creations to get the greatest sonic possibility out of them: "'In order to create electronic life *you have to be free to abuse the circuit.*' That said, he pushed his oscillators to their limits, often overloading and destroying them in his quest to discover outrageous new sounds before the circuits ultimately expired."

In this context, abuse, rebellion, and obedience are not easily distinguished. They really were experimenting, and Bebe, possibly guided by gendered codes, felt comfortable with allowing them free rein, whereas Louis, possibly also guided by gendered expectations but also electronic expertise, realized a need to assert some form of electronic control even though he could not predict the outcome. He did have knobs to turn, adding some voltage here or resistance (electronic resistance, that is, ohms) or capacitance there, some of which was necessary to bring an inert circuit to life. Yet the most interesting aspect of their comments was their attribution of life to the machinery: they saw the circuits not simply as a jumble of wires and electronic components, but as living entities. Consistent with Weiner's concept of cybernetics as a system applicable to both animals and machines, they were once contacted by biologists. Bebe Barron remembered, "A group of four or five scientists came up from the Salk Institute [in La Jolla, California] to visit us. They were studying the secret of life, or the origins of life. . . . They were so intrigued by this, they spent a whole day talking to us about the life cycles of our circuits."

The Barrons' approach to oscillators differed dramatically from what Stockhausen in Cologne, Schaeffer in Paris, and Luening and Ussachevsky in New York later attempted. Each of these composers sought to create sound generators that could be precisely controlled and whose results were predictable, much like later synthesizers. The generators were simply tools, a way to realize a sound or group of sounds just as the composer envisioned. Their function was reproduction. The Barrons, in contrast, sought to create oscillators whose behavior was unpredictable. To the Barrons, the circuits had a will of their own. According to Louis, "These circuits are as if a living thing were crying out, expressing itself. There's an organic type of behavior going on."

The Barrons not only saw the circuits as organic, but the entire process including the final result as spiritual. Even though the circuits seemed alive with their unpredictability, the Barrons recognized that their work was guided by intuition and feeling, that "it only works if there is a sort of spiritual involvement with what's going on." At the physical level they were dealing with inanimate objects, tubes, wires, capacitors, resistors; but in a broader sense they were dealing with pure energy, voltage, feedback, electrons interacting. As such, it was elemental stuff of the universe.

Bebe and Louis divided the work based on their strengths. Louis was to build the many circuits. After they had captured them on tape, Bebe would identify those with the most potential. It was not easy to discern possibilities from the original unaltered, often harsh sound, but Bebe had a special skill for that. They would then both work putting together the final product, using many editing procedures later common with electronic composition or *musique concrète*, such as slowing or speeding up the tape, reversing it, cutting and splicing, and combining tracks. The work was, as Bebe explained, really all one process: "After a while, Louis and I got so that we didn't even have to talk about what we were doing—like playing in a string quartet. We just knew exactly where we were going, and what we wanted to do."

The final result was a carefully planned and controlled composition, differing only from traditional Western music in the source and nature of the sounds. It was, however, unusual in that the piece could not be captured by traditional notation. Even Cage was writing in standard Western notation at this time. It was only later that abandoning notation for either a graphic depiction, verbal description, tape, or a digital file as the fundamental source of the piece would become common. This also created problems with copyright, which at that time demanded a written score.

Even though they worked seamlessly together, it was not without personal costs. Bebe explained that each "knew their strong points, but we both wanted to be boss. It was very difficult because we each wanted to have the final say." She believed that was what ended their marriage in 1970, although it did not end their collaboration.

When the Barrons returned to New York in 1949 Anaïs Nin had recommended that they visit the newly founded Artists Club in Greenwich Village. Known among artistic circles as The Club, it was a hangout for many artists, poets, dancers, and musicians. Founded primarily by the abstract expressionists, it met in a rented loft on West Eighth Street, close to the Barrons' studio on the same street. Willem and Elaine de Kooning, Franz Kline, Robert Motherwell, Martha Graham, Frank O'Hara, John Ashbery, and many others frequented it. Lectures, readings, demonstrations of artists' works, and, of course, intense discussions were the principal fare. One day the Barrons decided to play one of their pieces—exactly what is unknown. While there is no record of the overall reaction to their music, it greatly interested two musicians who often came there, John Cage and David Tudor.

Serendipitously, the Barrons played their electronic piece just after Cage received his grant from Paul Williams. They all came to an arrangement, where he, Tudor, Feldman, and Brown would use the facilities and the Barrons would not only supply the equipment but record sounds for use on the tape. Williams's grant not only allowed Cage to focus on the project but also provide a stipend to the Barrons, helping to pay the rent and equipment costs.

Cage had put together a graphic score that was in essence a template, something like a pattern for an article of clothing. Tapes were to be cut in many small pieces, often at different angles, and then spliced together; the splicer simply laid the tape on the respective spot in the score and cut it to the proper configuration. Cage's source material called for six types of sounds, labeled A–F: A–city sounds, B–country sounds, C–electronic sounds, D–manually produced sounds, including those from musical instruments, E–wind sounds, including songs, and F–small sounds, inaudible without amplification. Each sound within each category could be divided into sub-sounds by characteristics or parameters of the sound such as frequency or loudness, and then used as it was or transformed in one or more parameters. Cage then used the *I Ching* to determine what sounds would be used and how they may or may not have been transformed.

The Barrons were commissioned to go out and record the sounds, not an easy job since early tape recorders were hardly portable. Somehow they managed, and altogether created a catalogue of approximately 600 sounds. Cage spent hours flipping coins and, using quadrille paper, drawing the score. With each second consisting of fifteen inches, as tape recorder speed then was fifteen inches per second, the score, which contained two systems of eight-track tape, could contain 20 inches of tape, resulting in a score of 192 pages. The laborious job of assembling the tape, which involved Cage, Tudor, and Brown mainly, took nine months of detailed cutting and splicing. The final result was *Williams Mix*, a four-plus-minute piece.

Williams Mix is a kaleidoscope of sounds, some recognizable, most not. Few last more than one second; some resemble the distortion caused by an overloaded microphone, others have a short pulsing quality, and a few have a discernible pitch, including those that are electronic. There are brief moments of silence. The more clearly delineated electronic sounds and an occasional human voice stand out against the overall jumble of what earlier in the century had been called noise. The very randomness, the great variety and the chaotic quality of many sounds, with the occasional punctuations of the familiar, are what engages the listener and makes the piece successful. For 1952 it was an unprecedented composition, but it still holds up today as one of the more intriguing experiments in electronic music. Cage opined that it probably never would be duplicated, because of the sheer labor of creating the tape with all its precise cutting. Computers and digital processes have changed that, however, with several interpretations appearing. The most ambitious so far has been *Williams Mix Extended*, where the work has been expanded to 32 minutes and draws upon 2,000 sound samples, with an abstract video derived from the sounds.

Although the Barrons were heavily involved in *Williams Mix*, and though Cage's grant was a godsend to them as it paid the studio's rent for a year, Bebe and Cage did not have a great affinity for each other's compositions. Cage thought the Barrons' work was too musical and orchestral. According to Bebe, *Williams Mix* "sounded like mush."

In spite of their aesthetic differences, Bebe at least (Louis was no longer alive to be interviewed, having died in 1989) held Cage in high regard as a person. She found him "wonderful to work with." Partly because of Cage, their studio also became a center for electronic musical activity. He brought Boulez there, and other musicians visited, although when is not clear. Lou Harrison was there early, Stockhausen at one time came, Harry Partch "was around all the time," and Edgard Varèse "really hung out there." Varèse was working on *Déserts* and had no equipment. *Déserts* and his well-known *Poème électronique* were composed well after many of the Barrons' most important pieces were created.

Prior to Cage the Barrons had already established a reputation for electronic compositions. Their first complete piece was *Heavenly Menagerie* in 1950. Little is known about it, as it has not survived. Although the Barrons kept a copy of all of their work, much of it was destroyed in Louis's studio in San Francisco during the 1989 earthquake. The earliest surviving work is music for the film *The Bells of Atlantis,* composed in 1952. The film was conceived and produced by Ian Hugo, Anaïs Nin's husband. In it Nin's voice recites material from her book *The House of Incest.* "I remember my first birth in water," she begins. Water becomes a metaphor for the "lost continent of ourselves," as the poet Marianne Moore described it. The drama is interior, psychological, and only near the end does it become more concrete.

The abstract undulations of the film matched by the rhythmic pulse generated by the Barrons' oscillators create an illusion of a shimmering watery world in which the viewer swims prior to the appearance of Nin's voice, which brings definition to this murky universe of indeterminate beings and some form of ur-life. Gradually, as Nin describes her birth in the water, her human form appears: first her full body in a hammock, then upright with arms lifted, all against the background of a shipwreck. As arms and legs protrude behind a square pillar—"A monster brought me up to the surface"—Nin rises from the water—"I arise, I always arise after the crucifixion, and I am in terror of my ascension"—the sounds become more intense as longer electronic tones correspondingly ascend in pitch. Overall the sounds create a mysterious underwater world, neither fully corporeal nor fully phantasmagoric.

By far the most successful of the Barrons' work and the one for which they are most remembered is their electronic score for the sci-fi film *Forbidden Planet.* Produced by MGM in 1956, *Forbidden Planet* had a breakthrough plot, with a strong psychological component as well as the gadgets and special effects that have come to define the genre. The film has been considered the *Star Wars* of the 1950s. It was the first high-budget science fiction film; MGM, one of the reigning studios of the time, was determined to go beyond the "giant bug"–type low-budget black-and-white sci-fi films that populated grade-B movie houses. The full resources of the studio were put behind it, to the extent they were even willing to borrow personnel from Disney when specialists were needed.

The plot itself, set in the twenty-third century, is a loose adaptation of Shakespeare's *Tempest*. A spaceship that can move faster than the speed of light is sent out to discover what happened to an expedition to the planet Altair IV twenty years earlier. Commander of the spaceship John J. Adams and the crew discover that all the humans have died except two, a Dr. Edward Morbius and his beautiful daughter Altaira. Morbius has discovered an extensive underground nuclear power system from an earlier civilization that no longer exists. He has also found a "plastic educator," a force field that can double one's intelligence. Morbius has used it on himself, and with his new-found abilities he has created Robby the Robot. Robby is capable of doing anything, from feats of great strength to sewing a dress for Altaira. Robby is a lovable entity, and clearly the predecessor to R2-D2. (He was famous in his own right, and he made appearances in several other films and some television series.)

Commander Adams and Altaira fall in love, much to Morbius's disapproval. Hampering both the lovers' affair and Adams's efforts to bring Morbius, Altaira, and the power station back is an invisible monster, seen only in the final scene in a harrowing outline of twisting light. When the earlier civilization created the plastic educator, they never worked out certain problems, and the monster was Morbius's id, released by the educator. After many twists and considerable destruction, Adams and Altaira confront Morbius, which causes the invisible monster to materialize. Morbius instructs Robby to kill it, but Robby has been programmed not to harm any human, and he knows that the monster is Morbius, himself. In fiery self-destruction Robby's circuits collapse. Morbius then disavows his id, but it costs him his life. Adams, Altair and the crew escape as the planet explodes from a chain reaction of its power system.

Nuclear power, extraterrestrial travel, robots, Freudian psychology, even plastics, *Forbidden Planet* touched many of the issues that excited the 1950s mind. It is in one sense a witness to the 1950s technological revolution. In another sense it goes beyond that toward new understandings of the nature of the mind and especially the unconscious. In that it aligns with *Bells of Atlantis* in exploring the deeper and darker side of humans. Freudian theory was prominent at this time, and the monster as a product of Morbius's id is directly out of Freud.

The Barrons' involvement with the film occurred through a not-entirely-chance meeting in New York with Dore Schary, head of film production at MGM. They asked if he would be willing to hear some of their electronic music. Schary politely responded that they should come by the studio when they were in California. Much to Schary's surprise, they soon arrived with tapes and films. The timing could not have been more fortuitous, as MGM's sci-fi film was in early stages of production, and here were music and sounds Schary had never heard before. It fit perfectly this unprecedented adventure. Soon a contract was worked out giving the Barrons free rein to use their best judgment. As James Wierzbicki observed, "The officially sanctioned best judgment of a pair of neophyte film composers resulted in a very unusual approach to a task that by the mid-1950s had become quite formulaic."

For several months they worked day and night. Particularly powerful was the music for the monster, Morbius's id. Because the monster is heard rather than seen until the climactic final sequence, it was defined by the Barrons' music. Ben Burtt, the sound designer for *Star Wars*, remembered, "Certainly the strongest part of the movie for me is the sounds of the Id monster. . . . Your imagination is fueled by the sound of that picture." Alan Dean Foster, science fiction writer and ghost writer for *Star Wars*, agrees, "Man, it was chilling."

The first sound of the Id monster is a continuous high pitch quivering between E-flat and E. Below that is a thumping sound, a clear but irregular pulse. Beneath these two sounds is a hum, wavering in the area of a B. The music for the death of Morbius and consequently the death of the Id monster was eerily close to the actual event in their studio, for the music was the climax and subsequent death of the Barrons' oscillator itself.

The success of *Forbidden Planet* did not lead to further Hollywood work for the Barrons, however. Here they ran into both the Musicians' Union and Hollywood's tendency to consume its own. The union objected that these sounds did not come from any known instrument at the time, and hence could not be considered music. Synthesizers were still much in the future. To placate them, Schary officially described their work as "electronic tonalities." The film was nominated for an Academy Award for "sound effects." That *The Ten Commandments* won the award disturbed the Barrons less than the absence of their names on the nomination; Wesley Miller as head of sound effects for MGM received the credit. They sued. The suit went nowhere in court, but because of it the Barrons were blacklisted from the Hollywood film industry. They continued to work on many other projects, however, with both avant-garde artists and Madison Avenue. Their "electronic tonalities" were used in a number of plays, some on Broadway, including Gore Vidal's *Visit to a Small Planet* and an adaptation of Aristophanes's *Lysistrata* called *The Happiest Girl in the World*. They also supplied sounds for commercials and industrial films for Ford, IBM, General Dynamics, and the Western Electric Company. They moved to California in 1962, and even though each remarried they did continue to work together until Louis's death in 1989.

After *Williams Mix*, Cage turned away from tape to something new. That something new soon appeared, in the woods of the Catskills. Maverick Concert Hall is a wooden barn-like structure located on what originally had been a 105-acre farm in the Catskills near Woodstock, New York. On August 29, 1952, the weather was unsettled. Poughkeepsie, the closest weather station, reported winds from 7 to 14 mph, and "fog, rain/drizzle."

Pianist David Tudor had programmed a concert of piano works by Cage, Christian Wolff, Morton Feldman, Earle Brown, Pierre Boulez, and Henry Cowell. Near the end of the program he came out, sat down at the piano, closed the keyboard lid, then remained motionless. Sounds of the wind sifted through the barn. After thirty seconds he opened and closed the piano lid, and sat—this time for two minutes and thirty-two seconds. It began to rain, softly, clear patters on the unblocked wooden roof. When Tudor opened and closed the piano lid a third time and sat for one minute and forty seconds, the audience began to get restless. Murmurs and shuffling filled the room.

It was a musically sophisticated assemblage; they knew what to expect from the program, but, what was this? Earle Brown remembers, "There was a lot of discussion, a hell of a lot of uproar. . . . It infuriated most of the audience." Peter Yates summarized, "The audience had come to be shocked, but not dismayed." The ending came when a local artist stood up and cried, "Good people of Woodstock, let's drive these people out of town." Whether Tudor was able to perform the last piece on the program, Henry Cowell's *The Banshee*, is not known.

Few that night suspected that with *4'33"* they were witnessing the premiere of what John McClure in 1969 would call "the pivotal composition of this century." In 1913 Stravinsky brought the musical world crashing into the twentieth-century with the pounding of *Le sacre du printemps*. Now Cage, quietly in less than five minutes, neutralized all the dissonance, all the atonalism, all the primitivistic rhythmic intricacies by gently suggesting, here is another way.

For at least four years several threads were spinning in Cage's life until they all conjoined to weave what Cage called "my most important piece." In 1948 Cage spoke of composing a silent piece and selling it to Muzak. Whether this had any deeper meaning than his annoyance with the ubiquity of canned music is unclear, but it brought the idea of silence more prominently into his compositional consideration.

By 1950 Cage's basic compositional philosophy was set. His intention was non-intention: sound was to be heard as sound, let it be, and his job was to get out of the way. To Cage any sound was acceptable, "even the dominant seventh chord if it happens to make an appearance." In his 1955 mock dialogue, Cage not only rejected purpose but also any real need for a composer:

> "Then what is the purpose of this 'experimental' music?"
> "No purposes. Just sounds."
> "But seriously, if this is what music is, I could write it as well as you."
> "Have I said anything that would lead you to think I thought you were stupid?"

Two more strands of the thread Cage was weaving needed to fall in place. The first was when he saw Robert Rauschenberg's *White Paintings*, shown in 1951. They are a series of five paintings, each with a different number of panels, one, two, three, four, and seven. All are painted a monochrome white with no other markings. They are intentionally non-intentional. Cage later acknowledged that the paintings gave him the courage to proceed with *4'33"*. The other thread necessary for Cage's weave of silence was his experience in an anechoic chamber at Harvard University. An anechoic chamber is a room designed so that no external sounds or echoes are heard; all are absorbed, usually by various types of baffles throughout the room. Cage went into the chamber expecting silence, but heard two sounds, a low-pitched one and a high-pitched one. On exiting the engineer told him the low-pitched sound was his blood running through his body, the high-pitched one his nervous system in operation. From that Cage knew silence did not exist "as long as we have ears to hear," and no matter what he created it would not be a silent composition.

Deprived of the reality of silence, Cage had to reconsider the concept of silence. The sound/silence dichotomy then became a dualistic sound distinction: there were sounds intended—sounds a composer purposefully creates—and sounds unintended—those that exist in the environment. And not only environmental sounds, but, as long as we are alive, sounds within us, if we will just listen. Cage's goal became to persuade listeners to tune into the world around and within them. Possessing an inventiveness few others equaled, for the rest of his life Cage created conditions to encourage that to happen.

The composition *4'33"* shows a side of Cage attuned to the twenty-first century. The message of *4'33"* is to listen to the environment; it speaks to us. That this message is only becoming broadly understood more than half a century later says how little we were listening then. That Rachel Carson's *Silent Spring* did not appear for another ten years after *4'33"* speaks to 1950s deafness. Europe and Japan were too busy recovering; America was too busy enjoying the postwar boom that war recovery allowed; the immediate threat was not environmental catastrophe but nuclear annihilation. Cage's quietness and reflectiveness, his art of stillness may have come from the East, but it was a message whose urgency has grown as our planet has aged, not always for the better.

With the core of his philosophy that the composer should remove his ego, not transmit any of his own feelings, what role is left for the composer? For Cage, once *4'33"* was done, many of his other works would in essence be variations on a theme. The goal became to create a template that the performers, or even the audience, could fill as they wished. This took many forms, and stands as possibly the strongest testament to the fecundity of Cage's imagination. Most directly he expanded *4'33"* to *0'0"* in 1962, the instructions indicating, "In a situation provided with maximum amplification (no feedback), perform a disciplined action." The new work was a "solo to be performed in any way by anyone," and even the time limitations that *4'33"* set were to be abandoned. Cage had made his definitive statement in 1952, and it would be hard to surpass that.

Another side to Cage's work was a mesmerizing choreography of action as performers maneuvered around the stage, pieces in which the visual dimension is essential. *Water Music* was written for a pianist who also uses a "radio, whistles, water containers, a deck of cards, a wooden stick, and objects for preparing a piano." The score consists of precise directions on how the objects are to be handled, with timing indicated down to one-thousandth of a second. Typical instructions include "Keyboard lid shut," "Gradually change radio to 125," "Duck whistle gradually into water." Other similar pieces followed, including *Water Walk,* which was performed live on national television on Gary Moore's *I've Got a Secret,* in 1960. Here the water consists of a partially filled bathtub and many other props. Asked about the title by Gary Moore, Cage explained, "Because there is water and I walk."

Cage created a number of pieces that were the antithesis of silence or environmental sounds, works that realized, in David Revill's words, "his enthusiasm for chaotic abundance." *Atlas*

Eclipticalis, composed for the New York Philharmonic, created a general din that the audience found at best bewildering. One of Cage's grandest works was *HPSCHD,* an event—it is hard to call it a piece—created in conjunction with the electronic music pioneer Lejaren Hiller at the University of Illinois in 1969. Its origin lay in requests that Cage write something for harpsichord, an idea he resisted because the instrument reminded him of a sewing machine. The final result was a massive array of sound, created as usual by Cage's coin flips, now gone digital. The computer sounds far eclipsed the twelve tones per octave, eventually generating 885,000 different pitches. Several pianists and harpsichordists were asked to perform from the traditional classical repertoire, the exact choice left to random. In addition, slides and movies were projected onto a 340-foot circular screen and several eleven-by-forty-foot rectangular ones. All in all, "seven pre-amplifiers were used, 208 computer-generated tapes, fifty-two slide projectors, eight movie projectors, 6,400 slides, and forty movies." The concert, in a large hall, went from 7:30 to midnight, with two tutti climaxes planned, one at 8:30, the other at 11:30.

How do we reconcile such monster works with Cage's Buddhist leanings, his dedication to non-intention, and his demonstrated love of quiet sounds if not true silence? Cage himself gave us an explanation. Addressing the convention of the Music Teachers National Association in Chicago in 1958 on "Experimental Music," Cage stated: "Where do we go from here? Towards theatre." Almost all of Cage's music was theater. Even in smaller works such as *Water Music,* or even *4'33",* the visual element was critical. When Cage allowed LP recordings to be made, giving only sound, the critics were ruthless: "twenty minutes and twenty seconds of protracted needle scratch is about as hallucinatory and attractive as scabies."

With the visual, the sounds take on another meaning, and

the event becomes Cage's theater. In an interview with Richard Kostelanetz, Cage later expanded on that point:

> *Would you consider this—now, here—a theatrical situation?*
>
> Certainly. There are things to hear and things to see, and that's what theater is.
>
> . . .
>
> *Would you say, then, that all life is theater, that all theater is life?*
>
> It could be such, if we change our minds.
>
> . . .
>
> *Could you remember what was in your mind when you did that [the Black Mountain piece, Theater Piece No.1], generally considered the first happening?*
>
> It was the making of theater—to bring all these things together that people could hear and see.
>
> . . .
>
> *Why didn't you develop anything in this area yourself?*
>
> I have been doing nothing else since.
>
> *So all your work since has been "theater" in your mind?*
>
> Surely.

For Cage, life itself was theater. This creates an immediate paradox; for years Cage had sought to extinguish his person in his compositions. Chance was the vehicle; he did not choose, the *I Ching* chose. Cage more than any other composer seemed to fulfill an overarching aspiration contained in the postwar world, for anonymity. Boulez, Babbitt, and Cage as well as many other artists and intellectuals sought it, each in their own way. Is it possible, however, to create without the ego, even when creation becomes mechanistic, as integral serialism was, or random, as Cage's coin flips were? There was a moment when each composer's music was difficult to distinguish, when Cage and

Boulez were both pursuing matrices and Babbitt was developing his own ultimately similar parameters. Each went his own way, however, and idiosyncrasies came more to the surface. Babbitt had his spikey, jazz-like rhythms, Boulez his dense, rapid, virtuosic gestures, and either a majestic or pompous sound depending on one's view. Cage expanded beyond both traditional and electronic sounds and paradoxically into silence and circus, or, to use Barbara Novak's phrase, into "the still small voice and grand opera." How could the bombast of *HPSCHD* or *Atlas Eclipticalis* occupy the same world as *4'33"*? No Western composer ever preached the (Buddhist) tenet of non-intention more than Cage; no composer ever sought to disappear the ego more than Cage. Yet not even Cage could succeed. Bebe Barron described it precisely: "He had devoted a great deal of his life trying to lose his identity. He didn't want people to say 'there's a Cage piece' when they heard it, but he never could achieve that. No matter what he did, it always sounded like Cage."

To many Westerners Buddhism itself is fraught with contradictions, and provides an easy way to explain Cage's grand paradoxes. Yet the answer to the riddle of the paradox, although not the solution, may be closer to home. It goes back to the most American of poets, Walt Whitman:

> I contradict myself?
> Very well then, I contradict myself,
> (I am large, I contain multitudes.)

As men of the American West, as staunch individuals breaking society's norms, as two highly creative American minds, Cage and Whitman suggest, yes, paradox is part of our world, to be neither shunned nor resisted.

Epilogue

Even the most casual listener today is acutely aware that musical revolutions did not end in the 1950s. Synthesizers, compact discs, the Internet, computers themselves, have affected the entire musical ecosystem, from creation to performance to distribution, to the listener's own choice of platform. The rock revolution has continued, split into many branches—hard rock, indie rock, electronicore, progressive metalcore, to name only a few. Further revolutions in musical genres have emerged, the most significant being rap or hip-hop. The visual dimension has become more important, whether it be the looks and dress of stars such as Lady Gaga and Beyoncé, the hats of country music, or the provocative outfits of the Bond Quartet. Many popular concerts feature elaborate light shows, with both lasers and video, and often pyrotechnics. The visual element at times overwhelms the aural. Classical music has moved to stress the visual also, both in new compositions in which the composer has created scene as well as sound, and in older ones where a visual element is added to works of the standard repertoire. Even the most staid of classical organizations, the symphony orchestra, has moved in that direction. The Houston Symphony Orchestra's most successful program of the past fifteen years has been

Gustav Holst's *The Planets*, with images from NASA of the planets projected onto a giant screen behind the orchestra as it plays.

Genre barriers are coming down. Classical composers consider rock as well as Bach to be part of their heritage, and draw from both in their compositions. Leonard Bernstein included a rock band and a blues band as well as the standard symphonic lineup in his *Mass*. That the Kronos Quartet performed Jimi Hendrix's "Purple Haze" no longer seems radical. Symphony orchestras now regularly program popular music and often feature pop and folk artists on their programs. Many popular songs incorporate classical music, either as a general influence or directly through sampling. Nas's "I Can" draws on Beethoven's "Für Elise," and Robin Thicke's "When I Get You Alone" on Walter Murphy's "A Fifth of Beethoven," which itself is derived from Beethoven's Fifth Symphony. The term "crossover" has become so common as to call into question its continuing need as a descriptor.

The Internet has also brought music from the entire world into the soundscape of the United States. Global artists such as Björk from Iceland, Bad Bunny from Puerto Rico, or Jungkook from South Korea have become established stars on the American popular music scene, and many American singers draw on global influences in their own music.

The digital revolution has also allowed voices previously silenced to be heard. This has changed our entire social landscape as much as anything. Internet sites, social media, and other electronic platforms have made possible a new kind of democracy, and have also made possible cultural manipulation with the potential to doom democracy. As I write, the jury is still out, and probably will be for some time.

In spite of all these developments, some things haven't changed. Black artists are accepted today in both classical and popular music, but the United States still exists in a time of racial strife and unrest. Black musicians can now stay in the hotels where they perform, but racial hostility continues. In some cases it has gotten worse.

This book has made no attempt to cover such recent issues, mainly because each would require a volume unto itself. In this book I have sought to demonstrate that cultural revolutions usually follow a pattern: following complexity theory discussed in Chapter 2, periods of stasis, when evolutionary change is inhibited, necessitate a leap to a new metaphorical landscape. This pattern is particularly apparent in the three decades that have framed this book, the 1840s, the 1920s, and the 1950s, and what shaped music in those decades is what has shaped American society at the same time. Music has been both a mirror and a motivator on the nationwide stage.

The 1840s saw the birth of the notion of art music in America and the first uniquely American popular music, the minstrel show. Both were dependent on new technology: the steamship made Atlantic travel quicker, safer, and more predictable, the railroad made touring feasible, and the telegraph greatly enhanced scheduling. Thanks to all three technologies, European virtuosi flooded the country, astounding Americans with unprecedented musical possibilities. Along with newly formed symphony orchestras, they transcended previous attitudes toward music. At the same time, the minstrel show, in its sudden popularity and its very premise, spoke directly to the most vexing issue of the still young nation, race. It aroused feelings on both sides of the racial divide. Yet in spite of the Civil War and the legal end of slavery, minstrelsy remained with us, and remains with us today, a caricature that continues to reflect a dark underside to remind a nation that some problems have not been solved.

That many stage performers, some as popular as Eddie Cantor and Al Jolson, continued to wear blackface into the 1930s speaks of the continuing effect of minstrelsy. Occurring when anti-Semitism was at its peak raises the question, were these two

Jewish stars using a mask behind a mask as a mask to further hide behind? Other twentieth-century examples of minstrelsy's legacy were the *Amos 'n' Andy* show on radio and later television; the minstrel stereotypes in advertising, particularly Aunt Jemima and Uncle Ben; films, most notably *Gone with the Wind;* and performers, such as Grace Slick, donning blackface on television as late as 1968.

While the minstrel show still claims much historical attention today, another European import of the 1840s is often overlooked: the polka. It was the first of many two-step dances that defined the optimistic, militaristic, "manifest destiny" spirit of the time. It replaced the waltz, seen as old world, and eventually led through Sousa's marches into ragtime, and ultimately jazz.

In the 1920s the United States shook off some of the last remnants of European cultural hegemony and Victorian outlook and found its voice in what has been called the most American of music, jazz. New sounds that were derived more from Africa than Europe heralded America's new global emancipation, even though social emancipation for many remained aspirational. Of all decades, the 1920s blended race and technology to create the most far-ranging changes in American musical culture, from creation to performance to audience, which was no longer limited to the soundscape of the event. The phonograph and radio changed drastically how music could be captured, preserved, and disseminated; they represent the most radical technological developments since the invention of music notation. Even in classical music, radical ultramodern composers found a way to break from the constraints of a musical establishment whose impact had been symbolized by the fate of arguably America's outstanding composer, Charles Ives. For three decades Ives had supported his family with a career in insurance, while creating a vast body of works that the musical world at the time ignored. Ultramodern composers drew on one of the oldest principles of the universe itself, self-organization, to create a society that, by bypassing the concert establishment, allowed their voices to bring America past the musical stasis that had existed since the nineteenth century.

Racism as well as gender discrimination remained strong in classical music of the 1920s. A few Black performers and composers were able to break through the biases, most notably Florence Price, Margaret Bonds, and William Grant Still, although all achieved their greatest success after 1930. All had to struggle with the attitudes of the time: Bonds had to endure intense racism while at Northwestern University in the late 1920s, Price had to claim a Latino heritage to be admitted into the New England Conservatory as a student, and Still, working for both W. C. Handy and Harry Pace in the 1920s, had to negotiate the schism between W. E. B. Du Bois's theory that "Black uplift" should be led by a small elite percentage of Blacks toward assimilation, and Handy's belief that spirituals, work songs, and blues form Black cultural identity. That is, should upper class or working class represent the essence of Black society? Du Bois was a leader in the Harlem Renaissance, and his ideas had a powerful impact on Black thought in the 1920s.

In popular music, the 1950s portended a more fully diverse society, at least culturally, as Black musicians were able to stare down the threat of cultural appropriation to have their voices succeed against white covers. In many ways what happened in popular music was a continuation of what had begun in the 1920s but had been sidetracked by the Depression and the Second World War. Rock 'n' roll emerged, largely an outgrowth of 1920s blues by way of rhythm and blues. Driven especially by white teenage demand, this new music proved to be more than a fad, as it spawned many variants for over half a century. Classical music saw new types and new possibilities also, especially with new technology that heralded both new compositional approaches and new ways of consumption. Full symphonies and operas could now be held in one hand, thanks to the LP and tape recorders, which also allowed recording sessions to be edited with a precision hitherto impossible.

Little has been written here about one revolution that has significantly changed American society, the feminist waves. That is because the feminist revolution occurred in stages, but not primarily in the decades discussed. In the 1840s women's role in music was seriously curtailed, and except for appearances onstage and a few instrumental performers, women were as invisible in the public musical sphere as in the workplace. In the 1920s, women were readily accepted as singers, if still not so readily as instrumentalists, and most important, women had just won the right to vote. As Victorian mores began to recede, the young modern woman found more freedom than she previously had. She was defined, however, by the flapper role that both emancipated and constricted her. The role was more a social than an encompassing one. She could wear outfits that no Victorian woman would countenance, she could drink, even smoke; but she was still expected to marry and settle into a family where her rights were highly circumscribed. Nor had the workplace changed much. A few vocations—teaching, secretarial work, nursing, and telephone operator—were acceptable, but little else. The world of business and the professions remained overwhelmingly male.

The 1950s saw a burgeoning new wave of feminism beginning to form, but it had to wait until the next decade to burst into the open. Traditional home and family expectations still dominated women's lives. Opportunities that had opened up during World War II closed soon after the GIs came home. Some professions, such as law and medicine, were pried open, but the door was ajar only a crack. In 1950 women comprised 6 percent of the medical profession and 3.5 percent of the law profession. Neither statistic changed much during the decade. When Supreme Court Justice Sandra Day O'Connor, who graduated near the top of her class at Stanford Law School in 1952, first sought a job, she was offered a position as a legal secretary. Ruth Bader Ginsburg, who graduated at the top of her class at Harvard Law School in 1959, was rejected by every firm she applied to.

Whether the cultural and political world of the 1950s was a throwback to earlier times or a decade of smoldering tinder waiting to be ignited continues to be debated. Musically at least, it was no step backward, as it brought new genres that have remained for decades. The '50s did begin to show the way forward in the acceptance of Black musicians, and in that sense music did more than reflect conditions. Music was an active voice, giving expression to what could no longer be suppressed. As much as any time, it portended a world that would be radically different. Yet as much as many times, that world proved to be fleeting.

The exact meaning of the hopes, dreams, unrest, and anxiety sounded in 1950s music may never be entirely disentangled, but what the 1950s, as well as the 1840s and 1920s, has taught us is that change, sudden change after times of stasis, is not only common, in art and in life, but more the norm than smooth linear development. As such it may be that history unfolds more by revolution than evolution.

ACKNOWLEDGMENTS

Writing a book may be a lonely undertaking, but no one writes a book alone. There are many people who have contributed in many ways to make this one happen. I want to thank a number of friends and colleagues who have read parts of the manuscript and have made comments or suggestions, or have allowed themselves to be peppered with questions: Steven Lewis, Tammy Kernodle, James Wierzbicki, Sandra Graham, James Mohr, Dale Cockrell, Dean Root, Barry Mazor, and two former students who are now my colleagues, Nate Ruechel and Haley Nutt. Some comments have been quite critical, for which I am thankful, and I know that those remarks have unquestionably made for a better finished product. I especially want to thank Laura Gayle Green, director of the Allen Music Library at Florida State University, for her personal help and for making the library a valuable asset to musical scholarship.

Parts of this book were tested and improved in graduate seminars here at Florida State University, one on the 1920s, and one on the 1950s. In these seminars I have learned as much from the students as I hope they have from me. Thank you Caroline Bishop, Nate Ruechel, Holly Riley, Haley Nutt, Miranda Penley, Elizabeth Uchimura, Rachel Bani, Rory Creigh, Hannah Denecke, and Emily Eubanks.

I want to thank three people in particular at Norton. In a conversation with Maribeth Payne, at the time music editor and vice president, I mentioned what was then a vague idea that might have possibilities. She encouraged me to develop what became the kernel for this book. After her retirement Chris Freitag took over as music editor. He has been extremely helpful in guiding me through the many stages of the creation and refinement of a manuscript; his many suggestions have done much to bring focus and readability to it. Norton assigned my manuscript to Jodi Beder, the best copyeditor that I have had. She has saved me from many pitfalls and errors, and had excellent suggestions for how to improve the messy bundle I handed to her.

Finally, none of this could have happened without the support of my family. My daughters Peggi and Tracy have been a source of pleasure and inspiration, and this book is enriched by the many valuable insights I gleaned from our stimulating conversations. And most of all, I want to thank my wife, Denise Von Glahn, for all that she has been, for her emotional support as well as her intellectual insights and support. Our discussions have been thought-provoking and challenging, and her presence goes far beyond that. I can't imagine accomplishing something like this were she not here.

NOTES

Introduction: A Personal Statement

xii **"The establishment, in some significant degree":** Renwick McLean and Jennifer Schuessler, "Bernard Bailyn, Who Transformed the Field of American History, Is Dead," *New York Times,* August 8, 2020; advertisement for *The 1619 Project, New York Times Book Review,* April 16, 2023.

Chapter 1: Three Pillars and the Nature of Revolution

3 **"the view from the academy":** Isaac Kramnick, "Reflections on Revolution: Definition and Explanation in Recent Scholarship," *History and Theory* 11, no. 1 (1972): 26.

6 **"the study of how complex systems manifest":** Neil Theise, *Notes on Complexity: A Scientific Theory of Connection, Consciousness, and Being* (New York: Spiegel & Grau, 2023), 4.

7 **"the beginning of a scientific revolution":** Theise, *Notes on Complexity,* 8; italics original.

7 **complexity theory:** For a general introduction to the field, see James Gleick, *Chaos: Making a New Science* (New York: Penguin, 1988); on its use in evolutionary biology, see Stuart Kauffman, *The Origins of Order: Self-Organization and Selection in Evolution* (New York: Oxford University Press, 1993).

7 **American musical historical writing:** Jean Ferris, *America's Musical Landscape* (Madison, WI: Brown and Benchmark, 1990); Richard Crawford, *The American Musical Landscape* (Berkeley: University of California Press, 1993).

8 **"that are too methodical and timid":** Stuart Kauffman, *At Home in the Universe: The Search for Laws of Self-Organization and Complexity* (New York: Oxford University Press, 1995), 27. This book is written for the layman. Kauffman discusses many of the same concepts in more technical detail in *The Origins of Order: Self-Organization and Selection in Evolution* (New York: Oxford University Press, 1993).

8 **emergence:** John Holland, *Emergence: From Chaos to Order* (Reading, MA: Helix Books, Addison Wesley, 1998); Steven Johnson, *Emergence: The Connected Lives of Ants, Brains, Cities, and Software* (New York: Simon and Schuster, 2001).

8 **butterfly effect:** In a paper given at the New York Academy of Sciences in 1963, Lorenz commented, "One meteorologist remarked that if the theory were correct, one flap of a seagull's wings would be enough to alter the course of the weather forever." In 1972 the seagull had evolved into the butterfly. At a December 1972 meeting of the American Association for the Advancement of Science in Washington, DC, he gave a paper entitled "Predictability: Does the Flap of a Butterfly's Wings in Brazil set off a Tornado in Texas?" Many other writers have substituted other geographic locales since then, but the idea is the same.

Chapter 2: Minstrelsy: An American Musical Contribution and America's Curse

14 **Irish immigrated to the United States:** Patrick J. Blessing, "Irish," in *Harvard Encyclopedia of American Ethnic Groups*, ed. Stephan Thernstrom (Cambridge, MA: Harvard University Press, 1980), 528.

14 **British policy toward the Irish and later crop failures:** See Tim Pat Coogan, *The Famine Plot: England's Role in Ireland's Greatest Tragedy* (New York: Palgrave Macmillan, 2012); Mark G. McGowan, "The Famine Plot Revisited: A Reassessment of the Great Irish Famine as Genocide," *Genocide Studies International* 11, no. 1 (Spring 2017): 87–104.

15 **fate of indentured servants:** Noel Ignatiev, *How the Irish Became White* (New York: Routledge, 1995); Bryan Giemza, "Turned Inside Out: Black, White, and Irish in the South," *Southern Cultures* 18, no. 1 (Spring 2012): 34–57.

16 **"low-browed," "savage":** Steve Garner, *Racism in the Irish Experience* (London: Pluto Press, 2004), 133.

16 **Thomas Dartmouth Rice:** W. T. Lhamon Jr., *Jump Jim Crow: Lost Plays, Lyrics, and Street Prose of the First Atlantic Popular Culture* (Cambridge, MA: Harvard University Press, 2003), 33–34.

17 **Picayune Butler:** W. T. Lhamon Jr., *Raising Cain: Blackface Performance from Jim Crow to Hip Hop* (Cambridge, MA: Harvard University Press, 1998), 181.

17 **"Corn Meal":** Lhamon, *Raising Cain*, 181; Lhamon, *Jump Jim Crow*, 36, 38.

18 **"I neeld to de buzzard":** Rice's and the Sea Island verse are taken from Lhamon, *Raising Cain*, 181–82.

18 **"The two most popular characters":** *Boston Post*, July 26, 1838, quoted in Dale Cockrell, *Demons of Disorder* (Cambridge, UK: Cam-

bridge University Press, 1997), 66. Queen Victoria had been crowned only the year before. She was eighteen years old at the time.

19 **tambourine and bones:** The musical instrument known as bones was a pair of animal bones, clicked together like a castanet.

20 **"a tall scrambling-looking man":** Lhamon, *Jump Jim Crow,* 32.

20 **"Douvernay . . . Taglioni":** Pauline Douvernay was a French ballerina also popular in England; Marie Taglioni was a prima ballerina in England and Russia.

20 **"all the velocity":** "Jim Crow," *Spirit of the Times: A Chronicle of the Turf, Agriculture, Field Sports, Literature and the Stage* 7, no. 13 (May 13, 1837): 99.

20 **"tumultuous":** Cockrell, *Demons of Disorder,* 65.

21 **"When their mouths were not filled":** *New York Mirror,* December 29, 1832. Quoted in Richard Butsch, *The Making of American Audiences: From Stages to Television, 1750–1970* (Cambridge, UK: Cambridge University Press, 2000), 50; JoAnne O'Connell, "Understanding Stephen Collins Foster: His World and Music" (PhD diss., University of Pittsburgh, 2007), 279.

21 **"In the scene with Lady Anne":** *Spirit of the Times: A Chronicle of the Turf, Agriculture, Field Sports, Literature and the Stage,* December 1, 1832. Quoted in Cockrell, *Demons of Disorder,* 31–32.

22 **"In London, Jim Crow is even more popular":** *New York Herald,* August 27, 1837. Quoted in Cockrell, *Demons of Disorder,* 65–66.

23 **T. D. Rice had . . . no European counterpart:** Some of the antecedents mentioned by various scholars are charivari mumming plays, carnival rituals, inversion rituals, the John Canoe ritual, and other various tricksters and clown derivatives.

24 **"That talent consisted in [Rice's] great fidelity":** Lhamon, *Raising Cain,* 169.

25 **"Life in Kentucky," . . . Jim Crow in New Orleans":** Lhamon, *Jump Jim Crow,* 41–42.

25 **replaced Shakespeare's "muscular free verse":** Lhamon, *Jump Jim Crow,* 73.

28 **"The Rose Tree":** Stephen Winick, "Turkey in the Straw," Library of Congress Online, https://blogs.loc.gov/folklife/2014/05/turkey-in-the-straw/, May 14, 2014.

32 **They assumed it would be a one-time event:** Cockrell, *Demons of Disorder,* 149–50; Hans Nathan, *Dan Emmett and the Rise of Early Minstrelsy* (Norman: University of Oklahoma Press, 1962), 117–18. Cockrell has found evidence that the four may have performed together earlier.

32 **"First Night of the . . . melodious Ethiopian band":** Nathan, *Dan Emmett,* 118. Although now obsolete, the term "Ethiopian" as a reference to a dark-skinned person had been in use since at least the seventeenth century.

32 **"the only representatives of the Negro":** Nathan, *Dan Emmett,* 136.

33 **he allegedly wrote:** "Authorship of 'Dixie' and 'The Old Folks at Home,'" *Mount Vernon Republican-News* (OH), March 26, 1908, reprint from *New York World,* March 15, 1908. Republished in Howard L. Sacks and Judith Rose Sacks, *Way Up North in Dixie: A Black Family's Claim to the Confederate Anthem* (Urbana: University of Illinois Press, 2003), 183–84.

34 **claim was made in 1904:** This claim was made by J. McD in a letter to the *Baltimore Sun.* It is quoted by Charles Burleigh Galbreath in *Daniel Decatur Emmett: Author of "Dixie"* (Columbus, OH: Fred J. Heer, 1904), p. 31. Galbreath does not give a date, but quotes his response, which is dated July 23, 1904, so a 1904 date of the original letter may be assumed.

36 **not a Japanese folk song:** William W. Austin, *"Susanna," "Jeanie," and "The Old Folks at Home"* (Urbana: University of Illinois Press, 1987).

38 **one hundred dollars from Peters:** Robert Peebles Nevin, "Stephen C. Foster and Negro Minstrelsy," *Atlantic Monthly,* November 1867.

38 **bulgine is the steam engine:** Ken Emerson, *Doo-dah! Stephen Foster and the Rise of American Popular Culture* (New York: Simon & Schuster, 1997), 127–32.

39 **"a recognition, which runs through":** Emerson, *Doo-dah!,* 133–34.

39 **"such pieces as are likely":** Firth, Pond & Co., letter to Stephen Foster, September 12, 1849. Quoted in John Tasker Howard, "Stephen Foster and His Publishers," *The Musical Quarterly* 20, no. 1 (January 1934): 79–80.

40 **bookbinder . . . earned approximately $730:** Information taken from "Prices and Wages by Decade: 1800–1809," University of Missouri Libraries, https://libraryguides.missouri.edu/pricesandwages/1800-1809 (accessed September 21, 2020).

42 **"they were the most cheerful":** Katrina Dyonne Thompson, *Ring Shout, Wheel About: The Racial Politics of Music and Dance in North American Slavery* (Urbana: University of Illinois Press, 2014), quotation, 138, description of coffle, 138–48.

43 **"might injure my reputation":** Quoted in O'Connell, "Understanding Stephen Collins Foster," 274.

43 **"rather than blaming the problems":** O'Connell, "Understanding Stephen Collins Foster," 285.

44 **a fall or suicide?:** The most detailed discussion of the accounts and sources of Foster's death is in O'Connell, "Understanding Stephen Collins Foster," 478–97.

45 **"Blacksound":** Matthew D. Morrison, "Race, Blacksound and the

(Re)Making of Musicological Discourse," *Journal of the American Musicological Society* 72, no. 3 (2019): 823.

Chapter 3: Polkamania and Polk

47 **William Sidney Mount documented:** See, for instance, William Sidney Mount's *Dance of the Haymakers*; Aileen Jacobson, "19th-Century Themes, Some Resonant Today," *New York Times*, March 23, 2012.

49 **The polka originally was a Czech dance:** An early report of the origins of the polka comes from Albert Czerwinski, *Geschichte der Tanzkunst bei den cultivirten Völkern von den ersten Anfängen bis auf die gegenwärtige Zeit* (Leipzig: J. J. Weber, 1862), 158–59; the most detailed account comes from Čeněk Zíbrt, *Jak se kdy v Čechách tancovalo* [How People Used to Dance] (Prague: Knihtiskárna F. Šimáček nakl., 1895), 336. Zibrt interviewed several witnesses from the time; that their memory is of events that happened more than sixty years prior is problematic.

49 **polka spread to other European capitals:** "History of the Polka," *Music: A Monthly Magazine*, 9 (1896), 308.

49 **"Whooror for our side":** "The Polka," *Sun* (Baltimore), July 19, 1844; "The Polka Dance," *Boston Evening Transcript*, July 13, 1844; "The Polka Dance!," *Macon Weekly Telegraph* (GA); "The Polka Dance," *New Hampshire Gazette*, June 18, 1844; "The Polka," *Times-Picayune* (New Orleans), July 25, 1844.

50 **"The '*Polk-a*' is destined":** *Macon Weekly Telegraph* (GA), June 18, 1844.

50 **"the ladies are enquiring":** "The Polka," *Sun* (Baltimore), July 19, 1844.

50 **polka was first danced in America:** Joseph Marks, quoted in Ralph G. Giordano, *Social Dancing in America: A History and Reference* (Westport, CT: Greenwood Press, 2007), 1: 168.

50 **"They have introduced the Polka":** *Times-Picayune* (New Orleans), July 4, 1844.

51 **"the real, sure enough polka"**: "La Polka," *Times-Picayune* (New Orleans), March 5, 1845.

51 **Charles later wrote several dance instruction books:** Charles Durang, *Durang's Terpsichore or Ball Room Guide* (New York: Turner & Fisher, 1848), includes the polka. Some of his other books were *The Ball-Room Bijou, and Art of Dancing* (Philadelphia: Fisher, 1850); *The Dancer's Own Book, and Ball-Room Companion* (New York: Turner & Fisher, 1854); and *The Fashionable Dancer's Casket, or, The Ball-Room Instructor* (Philadelphia: Fisher, 1856).

52 **his nephew T. George:** Allen Dodworth, *Dancing and Its Relations to Education and Social Life: With a New Method of Instruction* (New York:

Harper & Bros., 1853); Allen Dodworth, *Dodworth's Brass Band School* (New York: H. B. Dodworth, 1853); Allen Dodworth, *Allen Dodworth's Quadrille Dancer, for Dancing As It Is in New York* (New York: Nesbitt, 1859).

52 **resulting in a duel:** "Close of Fashionable Season at Saratoga and Newport," *New York Herald*, September 10, 1848.

52 **"an elegant and accomplished man":** "New Developments of the Polka," *New York Herald*, September 10, 1848.

52 **"set the fashionable world agog":** "Captain Korponay," *Times-Picayune* (New Orleans), February 18, 1853.

52 **"the polka was first introduced . . . the celebrated Korponay":** "New Developments of the Polka," *New York Herald*, September 10, 1848.

52 ***"The Polka.*—A teacher":** "The Polka," *Times-Picayune* (New Orleans), June 8, 1844.

54 **"is about to make quite a revolution":** "A New Move in the Poetry of Motion," *New York Herald*, October 29, 1844.

54 **"under his [Korponay's] judicious":** "Mons. Korponay and Dancing," *New York Herald*, July 1, 1844.

54 **they arrived as a family:** They apparently had one son who did not come with them. An obituary notice appeared in 1863 for Corporal Stephen De Korponay, born 1841, the eldest son of Gabriel and Mary De Korponay. *Public Ledger* (Philadelphia, PA), June 21, 1865.

54 **dancer Pauline Desjardins:** In the first volume of Giordano's *Social Dancing in America: A History and Reference*, the author refers to Pauline Desjardins as Korponay's partner. Giordano, *Social Dancing in America*, 168.

54 **"exceedingly well received":** *New York Herald*, November 2, 1844; *Times-Picayune* (New Orleans), November 24, 1844.

55 **"to enjoy his titles, wealth and honors":** Fashionable Intelligence," *New York Herald*, November 2, 1844.

56 **appointed an agent for the British Recruiting Service:** "Col. De Korponay in a New Phase," *Times-Picayune* (New Orleans), July 8, 1855; "Sickness at Utica, New York," *Sun* (Baltimore) July 20, 1855.

56 **translation business . . . was appointed interpreter:** Advertisement, *The Press* (Philadelphia), December 23, 1857.

56 **command of John W. Geary:** *New York Herald*, October 18, 1861.

57 **"no lady ought to dance the Polka":** Auguste Vitu and Paul Farnese, *Physiologie de la Polka d'apres Cellarius* [Physiology of the Polka: According to Cellarius] (Paris: A. Le Gallois, 1844).

57 **"disgusting and indecent":** Quoted by the *Maine Cultivator and Hallowell Gazette*, September 30, 1848.

57 **"nothing but a reel":** "Polka," *Barre Gazette* (MA), July 5, 1844.

57 **"The gallop and polka step":** "The Waltz, Gallopade, and Polka," *Southern Patriot* (Charleston), February 27, 1845.

58 **"'Polka' for the first time":** Vera Brodsky Lawrence, ed., *Strong on Music: The New York Music Scene in the Days of George Templeton Strong*, vol. 1, *Resonances, 1836–1849* (New York: Oxford University Press, 1987), 324.
58 **"Wish I had the man":** Lawrence, *Strong on Music*, 506.
58 **"The Polka Dance":** "The Polka Dance," *New Hampshire Gazette*, June 18, 1844.
58 **"The Polkamania, it is said":** *Weekly Houston Telegraph*, January 1, 1845.
59 **"will have to *dance the Polka*":** Quoted in "Dancing the Polka," *Morning News* (New London, CT), October 26,1846.
59 **"De Polka Daunce":** "Poetry," *Weekly Herald* (New York), August 24, 1844.
62 **"one of the most popular of the round dances":** *Beadle's Dime Ball-Room Companion and Guide to Dancing* (New York: Beadle, 1868), 29.
62 **"What father would like to catch":** "City Affairs," *North American* (Philadelphia, published as *North American and United States Gazette*), December 5, 1861; "A Lay Sermon on Dancing," *San Francisco Bulletin*, March 1, 1862.
62 **"plain Waltz, now almost excluded":** Edward Ferrero, *The Art of Dancing, Historically Illustrated* (New York: The Author, 1859), 72.
62 **"a large concourse of jumping jacks":** "Go as You Please," *Times-Picayune* (New Orleans), January 4, 1880, 10.
63 **"the ladies, several thousand":** "The Boston Jubilee. Exciting Events of the Second Day," *San Francisco Bulletin*, July 1, 1872, 1.
63 **"the spirit of '76":** "The Perils of the Polka by a Pupil of Korponay," *American Republican and Baltimore Daily Clipper* (MD) June 10, 1845.
63 **"age of progress":** Ferrero, *The Art of Dancing*, 148.
64 **"are indeed deeply imbued":** William Lines Hubbard, "Popular Music," in *History of American Music*, ed. William Lines Hubbard (New York: Irving Square, 1908), 91.
64 **"the polka without the hop":** Dodworth, *Dancing and its Relations to Education and Social Life*, 149.
64 **"manifest destiny":** John L. O'Sullivan, "Annexation," *The United States Magazine and Democratic Review* 17 (July–August 1845): 5–10.

Chapter 4: Classical Music Arrives

65 **"his bald pate bobbed from side to side":** John Hill Hewitt, "Fiasco in the White House: When Anthony Philip Heinrich Played for President John Tyler," reprinted online at *Bluegrass Special*.
66 **church music, at the apex:** Michael Broyles, *"Music of the Highest Class": Elitism and Populism in Antebellum Boston* (New Haven: Yale University Press, 1993), 271–72.

67 **Bowdoin Street Church:** Mason originally served six-month stints in several churches before settling into the Bowdoin Street Church under Lyman Beecher, one of the most influential New England preachers.

70 **"The art is infinite":** Theodore Hach, "Our Criticisms," *Musical Magazine,* October 1840, 366.

70 **"A music periodical, however much needed":** Theodore Hach, "Music in Boston," *Musical Magazine,* April 1842, 415.

71 **"The taste of the public":** Samuel Atkins Eliot, "Third Annual Report of the Boston Academy of Music," *North American Review,* July 1836, 53–85.

71 **"a great revolution in the musical character":** Samuel Atkins Eliot, "Annual Reports of the Boston Academy of Music, from 1833 to 1840," *North American Review,* April 1841, 320–38. This article has a retrospective quality as Eliot looks back upon the earlier reports.

72 **"The European artist imagines":** R. Allen Lott, *From Paris to Peoria: How European Piano Virtuosos Brought Classical Music to the American Heartland* (Oxford: Oxford University Press, 2003), 3–4.

72 **By 1840 the rail system had expanded:** "Maps Showing the Progressive Development of U.S. Railroads—1830 to 1950," from the pamphlet, "American Railroads: Their Growth and Development," The Association of American Railroads, January 1951; "Railroad Map, 1840," *American Rail: A Survey.*

73 **"the arduous task of playing alone":** Theodore Hach, *Musical Magazine,* March 1840, 111–12.

74 **Dolores Nevares de Gony**: Gony is sometimes spelled as Goni. I have taken these names from concert programs or reviews in contemporary journals, such as *The Musical Cabinet.*

74 **"as near perfection of his instrument":** Quoted in Vera Brodsky Lawrence, ed., *Strong on Music: The New York Music Scene in the Days of George Templeton Strong,* vol. 1, *Resonances, 1836–1850* (New York: Oxford University Press, 1988), 118.

75 **"New York now possesses":** "Vieux Temps; Ole Bull; Artot; Hurman; Europe; New York," *Daily Evening Transcript* (Boston), November 27, 1843; "Music," *Sun* (Baltimore), December 14, 1843.

75 **"superior to any man":** The *Tribune* quotations found in "Music," *Sun* (Baltimore), December 14, 1843.

76 **many narratives, some true, some false:** The extent and depth of these stories is most evident in *Watson's Art Journal,* which published seven separate articles about Bull in 1867–68.

76 **unsuitable for productive farming:** Einar Haugen and Camilla Cai, *Ole Bull: Norway's Romantic Musician and Cosmopolitan Patriot* (Madison: University of Wisconsin Press, 1993), 115–30.

77 **"individualism of the age" . . . "orchestra of genius:"** John S.

Dwight, "Music in Boston during the Past Winter," *Harbinger*, June 28, 1845, 155–59.

77 **"The most glorious sensation":** John S. Dwight, letter to Lydia Maria Child, October 1844. Quoted in George Willis Cooke, *John Sullivan Dwight, Brook-Farmer, Editor, and Critic of Music*: A Biography (Boston: Small, Maynard, 1898), 80–82.

78 **"The deep impression the man made":** Leonora Cranch Scott, *The Life and Letters of Christopher Pierce Cranch* (Boston: Houghton Mifflin, 1917), 90–91.

78 **"Into his [Beethoven's] hands he drew":** Robert N. Hudspeth, ed., *The Letters of Margaret Fuller*, vol. 2, *1839–1841* (Ithaca, NY: Cornell University Press, 1983), 225.

78 **"For, be it remembered":** John S. Dwight, "Music as a Means of Culture," *Atlantic Monthly*, September 1870, 322.

80 **members of the administrative board were musicians:** Howard Shanet believes that the New York Philharmonic's constitution was modeled largely on the 1813 London Philharmonic. Howard Shanet, *Philharmonic: A History of New York's Orchestra* (New York: Doubleday, 1975), 84.

80 **three concerts in its inaugural season:** *New York Philharmonic Leon Levy Digital Archives*, http://archives.nyphil.org (accessed September 23, 2020).

81 **"Beethoven's Symphonies arranged as duets":** "The Musical Pathfinder," *The Pathfinder* 1, no. 11 (May 6, 1843). Quoted in Shanet, *Philharmonic*, 94–95.

82 **"in order to further" . . . "equal rights, equal duties":** H. L. Albrecht, *Skizzen aus dem Leben der Music-Gesellschaft Germania* (Philadelphia, 1869). Quoted in H. Earle Johnson, "The Germania Musical Society," *Musical Quarterly* 39, no. 1 (January 1953): 75.

82 **"Seldom have we witnessed":** *New York Herald*, October 10, 1848. Quoted in Johnson, "The Germania Musical Society," 79.

83 **performed thirty-nine times:** Johnson, "The Germania Musical Society," 85.

83 **"The 'Germania Concerts' became our standard of excellence":** "Musical," *Evening Transcript* (Boston), January 28, 1854.

83 **"the rage for concerts" . . . "newer and handsomer":** C., "Music and Its Votaries in Boston," *Evening Transcript* (Boston), February 25, 1854.

84 **"Vieux Temps is decidedly handsome":** "Vieux Temps' First Concert in New York," *Daily Evening Transcript* (Boston), December 13, 1843.

84 **"the magical effect of the sounds":** Johnson, "The Germania Musical Society," 85.

84 **"no less than fourteen of [the Germanians]":** "Local Affairs," *Public Ledger* (Philadelphia), September 2, 1854.

Chapter 5: The Twentieth Century: Music Technology Collapses Time and Space

89 **two inventions broke the strictures:** Piano rolls could come close to reproducing a piano performance, but even the more sophisticated ones such as the Welte-Mignon or the Ampico could not capture all the nuances of a performance, let alone the actual sounds.

90 **invention of notation:** Western notation did not happen overnight, but only through a long period of evolution. The final result, modern music notation, is considerably more precise than what had existed in ancient Europe.

91 **"daguerreotyping the voice":** Patrick Feaster, "Daguerreotyping the Voice: Léon Scott's Phonautographic Aspirations," in *Parole #1: The Body of the Voice,* ed. Annette Stahmer (Cologne: Salov Verlag, 2009), 18–23. The phrase originally appeared in "Letters from New York," *Southern Literary Messenger* 15 (March 1849): 187, from which Feaster took it.

91 **"Can it be hoped":** Feaster, "Daguerreotyping the Voice," 4–5.

92 **realize the sound of some of Scott's recordings:** Feaster, "Daguerreotyping the Voice."

93 **"cost me many sore fingers":** Patrick Feaster, "Speech Acoustics and the Keyboard Telephone: Rethinking Edison's Discovery of the Phonograph Principle," *ARSC Journal* 38, no. 1 (Spring 2007): 24.

95 **"long after the speaker was dead":** Edward Johnson, "To the Editor of the Scientific American," *Scientific American*, October–December 1877, 616.

95 **"Phonograph or Speaking Machine":** Patent no. 200,521. See Feaster, "Speech Acoustics and the Keyboard Telephone."

95 **no definitive answer:** See Emma Jacobs, "Roundtable, Edison vs. Scott: The Complicated Story behind the Invention of Sound Recording," *Lapham's Quarterly,* May 31, 2017; Feaster, "Speech Acoustics and the Keyboard Telephone"; Merrill Fabry, "What Was the First Sound Ever Recorded by a Machine?" *Time,* May 1, 2018.

95 **Edison Speaking Phonography Company:** The five investors were Charles A. Cheever, Gardiner G. Hubbard, U. H. Painter, G. L. Bradley, and Hilborne L. Roosevelt. The Memorandum of Agreement is at the Edison Papers at Rutgers University, "Incorporation Record, Edison Speaking Phonograph Co, 1879," Edison Papers Digital Edition.

96 **"the phonograph . . . devoted to music"**: Thomas A. Edison, "The Phonograph and Its Future," *The North American Review,* May–June, 1878, 533.

96 **machine needed more work:** The tinfoil was good for only about four reproductions before sound deteriorated. And sound itself was not very good: it was often hard to distinguish words, especially sibilant vowels such as s and sh, as well as other letters such as d and t.

One unimpressed listener commented "it is a burlesque or parody of the human voice. Roland Gelatt, *The Fabulous Phonograph* (Philadelphia: Lippincott, 1955), 31.

96 **the "graphophone":** Jacobs, "Roundtable, Edison vs. Scott."

97 **installed throughout the country:** Mark Athitakis, "Riff Raff: Jukebox Hero and Gordon Dorsey," *San Francisco Weekly*, December 1, 1999.

97 **stiff anti-pornographic laws:** Jody Rosen, "There Once Was a Record of Smut . . . ," *New York Times*, July 8, 2007.

97 **"The 'coin-in-the-slot' device":** Gelatt, *The Fabulous Phonograph*, 45.

98 **Emile Berliner:** Most of the discussion of Berliner's career and the invention of the gramophone is taken from "Victor Record Pressing," *Victor Talking Machine Co.*, https://www.victorrecords.com/18971904 (accessed May 17, 2020); "The Gramophone: Early Sound Recording Devices," Library of Congress Collection, https://www.loc.gov/collections/emile-berliner/articles-and-essays/gramophone/ (accessed May 17, 2020); "Emile Berliner and the Birth of the Recording Industry," Library of Congress Collection, https://www.loc.gov/collections/emile-berliner/about-this-collection/ (accessed May 17, 2020); Gelatt, *The Fabulous Phonograph*, 83–99, 130–32.

100 **device discovered in Persia:** "Baghdad Battery," https://corrosion-doctors.org/Batteries/Baghdad-Battery.htm (accessed October 9, 2020).

101 **"unlocked the secret":** Gleason L. Archer, *History of Radio to 1926* (New York: The American Historical Society, 1938), 54.

101 **"to the Longara":** "The Birth of Pioneering Electrical Engineer Guglielmo Marconi," *The Telegraph*, April 28, 2017.

105 **"This may not mean much":** Quoted in Archer, *History of Radio to 1926*, 92.

106 **as far away as Florida:** Archer, *History of Radio to 1926*, 215.

107 **"they might place an order":** "First American Radio Charts Show Nation Is Now Blanketed by Wireless News and Music," *Popular Science Monthly*, March 1922, 72; *Radio Broadcast*, May 1922, Quoted in Archer, *History of Radio to 1926*, 241.

108 **"broadcast programs of merit":** Archer, *History of Radio to 1926*, 266.

108 **"Our first customer":** Archer, *History of Radio to 1926*, 276.

109 **United States . . . strictly commercial enterprise**: Orrin Elmer Dunlap, *The Story of Radio* (New York: The Dial Press, 1935), 295–302.

109 **NBC had two networks**: NBC added a third West Coast Network in 1927 in order to cover California and Oregon. It simply drew upon material produced by the two other networks, serving more as a subsidiary than an independent network.

110 **American Broadcasting Company:** Harold L. Erickson, "Ameri-

can Broadcasting Company," *Encyclopaedia Britannica*, February 21, 2019.

110 **Columbia Broadcasting System:** Arthur Judson, "How CBS Got Its Start," *American Heritage* 6, no. 5 (August 1955).

Chapter 6: The Jazz Age

112 **"The word [jazz] has been used":** Quoted in Joshua Berrett, *Louis Armstrong and Paul Whiteman: Two Kings of Jazz* (New Haven: Yale University Press, 2004), 41.

112 **"That music, it wasn't spirituals":** Sidney Bechet, *Treat It Gentle: An Autobiography* (London: Cassel, 1960). Quoted in Robert Walser, *Keeping Time: Readings in Jazz History* (Oxford: Oxford University Press, 2015), 2.

113 **Lulu White's Mahogany Hall:** Edward J. Bellocq's photographs of Storyville include several of the interiors of Mahogany Hall.

114 **traditional but erroneous jazz narrative:** for the traditional interpretation, see Jeff Taylor, "The Early Origins of Jazz," in *The Oxford Companion to Jazz*, ed. Bill Kirchner (New York: Oxford University Press, 2000), 47. For a revised take, see Jerah Johnson, "Jim Crow Laws of the 1890s and the Origins of New Orleans Jazz: Correction of an Error," *Popular Music*, 19, no. 2 (April 2000): 243–51.

115 **New Orleans guitarist Danny Barker**: Steven Lewis, "'Untamed Music': Early Jazz in Vaudeville" (senior honors thesis, Florida State University, 2012), 8. The term "cat," which meant someone hip or cool, was often used by musicians.

116 **"Down Home Rag":** Mark Berresford, *That's Got 'Em: The Life and Music of Wilbur C. Sweatman* (Jackson: University of Mississippi Press, 2010), 51–52.

117 **December 1, 1916:** *Discography of American Historical Recordings*, s.v. "Edison matrix 5186. That funny jas band from Dixieland / Collins and Harlan," https://adp.library.ucsb.edu/index.php/matrix/detail/2152468/5186-That_funny_jas_band_from_Dixieland.

118 **end of May 1917:** John Edward Hasse, "The First Jazz Recording Was Made by a Group of White Guys?" *Smithsonian Magazine*, February 24, 2017.

118 **ODJB topping one million:** Hasse O. Brunn, *The Story of the Original Dixieland Jazz Band* (Baton Rouge: Louisiana State University Press, 1960).

118 **"Stein's Dixie Jass Band":** Brunn, *The Story of the Original Dixieland Jazz Band*, 30.

119 **"that party really started":** Walter J. Kingsley, "Jazz Has Remarkable History as a Fad," *The Sun* (New York), February 9, 1919, Special Feature Magazine.

121 **Sweatman appeared onstage**: Eubie Blake thought, incorrectly,

that he was the first African American perfomer who did not blacken his face. Berresford, *That's Got 'Em!*, 69.

121 **"Wilbur Sweatman, clarionetist, . . . is in a class"**: Berresford, *That's Got 'Em!*, 81.

122 **Reisenweber's was so popular:** Brunn, *The Story of the Original Dixieland Jazz Band*, 53–54.

122 **"At that time, everybody from New Orleans":** Nat Shapiro and Nat Hentoff, eds., *Talkin' to Ya: The Story of Jazz Told by the Men Who Made It* (1955; repr., New York: Dover Publications, 1966), 78–79.

123 **Pekin Inn, . . . Café di Champion:** William Howland Kenney, *Chicago Jazz: A Cultural History, 1904–1930* (Oxford: Oxford University Press, 1993), 9–11.

124 **the term "speakeasy":** Robert Cross, "Prohibition Begins," *Chicago Tribune*, December 19, 2007.

125 **bring in top-line vaudeville acts:** "Aurall Dancing Academy Opens," *Chicago Defender*, September 26, 1915.

125 **"shooting affairs":** "Mayor William E. Dever Has Revoked All the Permits or Licences Held by Former Alderman Al Tearney," *Broad Ax* (Chicago), May 26, 1923.

125 **"Dreamland is one place":** "A Beauty Spot," *Chicago Defender*, November 13, 1920.

126 **"Down Hearted Blues":** "Lovie Austin," *The Syncopated Times*.

126 **as a solo pianist:** Tammy Kernodle, *Soul on Soul: The Life and Music of Mary Lou Williams* (Boston: Northeastern University Press, 2004), 27–62.

126 **Sweet Emma Barrett:** "Emma Barrett Is Dead at 85," *New York Times*, January 30, 1983.

126 **Billie Pierce:** "A Feminist Perspective on New Orleans Jazz Women," A NOJNHP Research Study by Sherrie Tucker, University of Kansas, 337–48.

126 **Dolly Jones**: Jonas Westover, "Jones, Dolly," *Grove Music Online*.

127 **Oliver had taken over the band**: Gene H. Anderson, "The Genesis of King Oliver's Creole Jazz Band," *American Music* 12, no. 3 (Fall 1994): 290.

127 **"Joe Oliver is my idol":** Terry Teachout, *Pops: A Life of Louis Armstrong* (Boston: Houghton Mifflin Harcourt, 2009), 62.

128 **Armstrong knew he was second cornet:** Laurence Bergreen, *Louis Armstrong: An Extravagant Life* (New York: Broadway Books, 1997), 203.

128 **"Boy, let me have":** From Bill Crow, *Jazz Anecdotes* (New York: Oxford University Press, 1990), 208. Even though most jazz players played the cornet, it was often referred to as a trumpet.

128 **several different labels:** Labels such as Gennett, OKeh, Paramount, and Columbia, among others, produced Oliver's recordings.

131 **"When you go up North":** Bergreen, *Louis Armstrong*, 173–74.

133 **"two high-grade Dance Orchestras":** Teachout, *Pops,* 81.
133 **Harry Pace formed Black Swan Records:** Michael Pollak, "Answers to Questions about New York," *New York Times,* July 29, 2011.
134 **the "Paul Whiteman of the race":** Hugues Panassié, *The Real Jazz* (New York: Smith & Durrell, 1942), 170.
134 **"It hit me hard":** "Paul Whiteman, 'the Jazz King' of the Jazz Age, Is Dead at 77; Made Jazz Respectable," *New York Times,* December 30, 1967.
134 **"My whole body began to sit up and take notice":** Don Rayno, *Paul Whiteman: Pioneer in American Music,* vol. 1, *1890–1930* (Lanham, MD: Scarecrow Press, 2003), 19.
135 **Even Armstrong was impressed:** Teachout, *Pops,* 68.
137 **supposedly willing to offer Armstrong $100:** Bergreen, *Louis Armstrong,* 235.
137 **Whiteman paid a minimum of $175:** Rayno, *Paul Whiteman,* 60.
137 **Henderson sought and recorded:** David Suisman, "Co-Workers in the Kingdom of Culture: Black Swan Records and the Political Economy of African American Music," *Journal of American History,* 90, no. 4 (March 2004): 1304–7.
137 **the spiritual, or "sorrow song":** W. E. B. Du Bois, *The Souls of Black Folk* (1903; repr., New York: Dover Publications, 1994), 251.
138 **"thinkers, strivers, doers":** Nathan Irvin Huggins, *Harlem Renaissance* (Oxford: Oxford University Press, 1971), 3.
138 **Ellington . . . modeled his band on Henderson's:** Duke Ellington, *Music Is My Mistress* (1973; repr., New York: Da Capo, 1976), 419. Quoted in Jeffrey Magee, "Before Louis: When Fletcher Henderson was the 'Paul Whiteman of the Race,'" *American Music* 18, no. 4 (Winter 2000): 392.
138 **"the elite level of jobs":** Thomas J. Hennessey, *From Jazz to Swing* (Detroit: Wayne State University Press, 1994), 242, 249–50. Quoted in Magee, "Before Louis," 402.
139 **"It was good money":** Jeffrey Magee, *The Uncrowned King of Swing: Fletcher Henderson and Big Band Jazz* (New York: Oxford University Press, 2005), 233.
140 ***Marrying Mary*:** *Evening News* (San Jose, CA), December 23, 1920.
140 **"latest revues, post-futurist art, [and] symphonic jazz":** Caroline E. MacGill, "Prospecting for Intelligence," *North American Review* 215, no. 804 (November 1922): 682.
140 **"opera houses" in Iowa:** George D. Glenn and Richard L. Poole, *The Opera Houses of Iowa* (Ames: Iowa State University Press, 1993), 6.
140 **"The soft jazz rhythms of the present day":** Paul Whiteman and Marry Margaret McBride, *Popular Culture in America, 1800–1925* (1926; repr., New York: Arno Press, 1974), 278.
140 **symphony stood at the apex of a musical pyramid:** That is,

among instrumental music. In the case of vocal music, opera held this position.

141 **"It seems to us that this music":** Henry O. Osgood, *So This Is Jazz* (Boston: Little, Brown and Company, 1926), 148.

141 **"the conservative, reactionary elements of music":** Osgood, *So This Is Jazz*, 146.

142 **"'Great is Rhythm!'":** Osgood, *So This Is Jazz*, 147.

142 **"a gorgeous piece of impudence":** Olin Downes, "Music: A Concert of Jazz," *New York Times*, February 13, 1924.

143 **"The World's Greatest Trumpet Player":** Bergreen, *Louis Armstrong*, 260.

143 **"redefining jazz":** Brian Harker, *Louis Armstrong's Hot Five and Hot Seven Recordings* (Oxford: Oxford University Press, 2011), 4.

144 **"I became so popular":** Robert Goffin, *Horn of Plenty: The Story of Louis Armstrong* (New York: Allen, Towne & Heath, 1947). Quoted by Bergreen, *Louis Armstrong*, 265.

145 **Armstrong's African roots**: Thomas Brothers, *Louis Armstrong: Master of Modernism* (New York: W. W. Norton, 2014), 6.

Chapter 7: Blues, Hillbilly, and Crooners

150 **"the mule":** Samuel B. Charters, *The Country Blues* (1959; repr., Boston: Da Capo Press, 1975), 835.

150 **"Now we have the pleasure":** "Making Records," *Chicago Defender*, March 13, 1920. Quoted in Daphne Duval Harrison, *Black Pearls: Blues Queens of the 1920s* (New Brunswick, NJ: Rutgers University Press, 1988), 46.

151 **"'an old bawdy song'":** As remembered by the pianist, Willie "The Lion" Smith (no relation to Mamie); in Ed Komora, "'Crazy Blues'—Mamie Smith, 1920," Library of Congress document, https://www.loc.gov/static/programs/national-recording-preservation-board/documents/CrazyBlues.pdf.

151 **75,000 recordings had been shipped to Harlem:** Samuel Charters and Leonard Kunstadt, *Jazz: A History of the New York Scene* (New York: Doubleday,1981), 85–86.

151 **lateral grooves:** In many early recordings the needle cut the grooves vertically, creating a hill-and-dale effect. It also limited dynamic range and caused the needle to jump out of the groove. Berliner's disc recordings cut the grooves sideways, which proved to be superior.

152 **"When you were hungry":** Tim Brooks, *Blacks and the Birth of the Recording Industry, 1890–1919* (Urbana: University of Illinois Press, 2004), 25.

152 **"the 'Laughing Song' by Geo. W. Johnson":** Brooks, *Blacks and the Birth of the Recording Industry*, 41.

154 **"The typical blues song":** "Mamie Booked," *Chicago Defender,* February 26, 1921.

155 **cut at least fifty sides:** *Discography of American Historical Recordings,* s.v. "Smith, Mamie," https://adp.library.ucsb.edu/names/109988 (accessed January 8, 2020).

155 **cape of ostrich plumes:** Charters, *The Country Blues,* 89.

155 **Born . . . in 1882:** The one official document, her death certificate, lists Ma Rainey's birth as November 20, 1882. Her gravestone lists 1886, as does the federal census of 1910. Both dates came from the family, and this census record is particularly suspect, as it also lists William Rainey as 25 years old, even though he was born in 1873. While most sources give Ella Allen Pridgett, Rainey's mother, as born in 1873, one census record lists her birth as 1865, another as 1867. Thus the earlier birthday of Gertrude is not out of line with the official record.

156 **first singer to incorporate blues**: Robert Palmer, *Deep Blues: A Musical and Cultural History of the Mississippi Delta* (New York: Penguin, 1981), 44; Harrison, *Black Pearl,* 34.

156 **acquired the title "Madame"**: *Chicago Defender,* February 9, 1924.

156 **William died:** Interview with Thomas Dorsey, her pianist and bandleader, cited in Sandra R. Lieb, *Mother of the Blues: A Study of Ma Rainey* (Amherst: University of Massachusetts Press, 1981), 201.

157 **"Madame 'Ma' Rainey":** *Chicago Defender,* February 2, 1924.

157 **"With her thick straightened hair":** Lieb, *Mother of the Blues,* 36.

158 **"one of the hottest shows"**: Bob Hays, "Ma Rainey's Review," *Chicago Defender,* February 13, 1926, p. 6.

158 **brother Andrew . . . guitar player and protector:** The Smith household consisted of Viola and her four younger siblings, Tennie, Lulu, Andrew, and Bessie, of whom Bessie was the youngest. Two older siblings, Clarence and Bud, were on their own by then. The most detailed discussion of Bessie's life in Chattanooga is Michelle R. Scott, *Blues Empress in Black Chattanooga: Bessie Smith and the Emerging Urban South* (Urbana: University of Illinois Press, 2008).

158 **Smith . . . member of the chorus:** Scott, *Blues Empress in Black Chattanooga,* 114.

159 **Rainey and Bessie were together again:** Chris Albertson, *Bessie: Revised and Expanded Edition* (New Haven: Yale University Press, 2003), 1–2.

159 **Wayne Burton and Bessie Smith:** Scott, *Blues Empress in Black Chattanooga,* 168.

160 **"Her voice is profoundly" . . . "Bessie has got it":** Lynn Abbott and Doug Seroff, *The Original Blues: The Emergence of the Blues in African American Vaudeville* (Jackson: University Press of Mississippi, 2017), 175.

160 **both singers soon left Tolliver's show:** Abbott and Seroff, *The Original Blues,* 174.

161 **"the greatest of them all":** Nat Shapiro and Nat Hentoff, eds., *Talkin' to Ya: The Story of Jazz Told by the Men Who Made It* (1955; repr., New York: Dover Publications, 1966), 243.

161 **elaborate dresses, jewelry:** Albertson, *Bessie*, 72.

161 **"She dominated a stage":** Shapiro and Hentoff, *Talkin' to Ya*, 243.

161 **"The Greatest and Highest Paid Race Star":** Albertson, *Bessie*, 87.

161 **"Queen of the Blues":** Albertson, *Bessie*, 67.

161 **"Blues Empress":** "'Come Along Mandy' at the Grand; Bessie Smith & Co. at the Avenue; Gaines Bros. Pack the Monogram," *Chicago Defender*, May 10, 1924; "Bessie Calls," *Chicago Defender*, May 17, 1924.

162 **The *Preston News* reported:** "Entertain at Midnight Show," *Pittsburgh Courier*, February 16, 1924. Quoted in Abbott and Seroff, *The Original Blues*, 180.

162 **"knocked all the tin off":** Frank H. Crockett, "Bessie Hits 'Em," *Chicago Defender*, August 4, 1923. Quoted in Abbott and Seroff, *The Original Blues*, 180.

162 **"The public seems to want":** W. R. Arnold, "Bessie Smith & Co. Break Attendance Record in Alabama," *Pittsburgh Courier*, December 14, 1928.

163 **The critics were unaware:** J. Brooks Atkinson, "The Play: To Be Read into the Record," *New York Times*, May 5, 1929; Albertson, Bessie, 191.

164 **Art Laibly of Paramount Records:** Alan Govenar, "Blind Lemon Jefferson: The Myth and the Man," *Black Music Research Journal* 20, no. 1 (2000): 12.

166 **"He was very, very rhythmic":** Jas Obrecht, *Early Blues: The First Stars of Blues Guitar* (Minneapolis: University of Minnesota Press, 2015), 71.

166 **Blake was back:** The two songs were released on October 2, 1926. "Blind Blake—Early Morning Blues/West Coast Blues," *Discogs*.

166 **a sign of otherness**: Joseph Witek, "Blindness as a Rhetorical Trope in Musical Discourse," *Black Music Research Journal* 8, no. 2 (Autumn, 1988): 192–93.

170 **"Two old-fashioned dance numbers":** *Chicago Tribune*, May 30, 1923.

172 **"Telephone calls, telegrams and letters":** Wayne W. Daniel, "'Fiddlin' John Carson (ca. 1868–1949)," *New Georgia Encyclopedia*.

172 **"For the past hour we have been listening":** Bill C. Malone, *Country Music USA: A Fifty-Year History* (Austin: University of Texas Press, 1985), 68–75.

172 **"He's not the best player":** Claire Ratliff, "20 Things You Didn't Know about Uncle Dave Macon," June 7, 2018, *Bluegrass Today*; Michael D. Doubler, *Dixie Dewdrop: The Uncle Dave Macon Story* (Urbana: University of Illinois Press, 2018), 193.

172 **"Black hillbilly music":** David C. Morton with Charles C. Wolfe,

DeFord Bailey: A Black Star in Early Country Music (Knoxville: University of Tennessee Press, 1991), 17.

173 **Bailey . . . on Barn Dance:** Morton, *DeFord Bailey,* 46.

175 **"If you can't feed little DeFord":** Morton, *DeFord Bailey,* 116.

176 **"I stayed in my place":** Morton, *DeFord Bailey,* 111.

176 **"This is a great big world":** Morton, *DeFord Bailey,* 118.

177 **"for arranging the session":** Morton, *DeFord Bailey,* 52.

178 **"He responded with disbelief":** Malone, *Country Music USA,* 37.

178 **estimated 165 songs:** Daniel, "'Fiddlin' John Carson."

178 **"The Big Bang of Country Music":** Nolan Porterfield, *Country: The Music and the Musicians: From the Beginnings to the '90s* (Nashville: Country Music Foundation, 1988), 16.

179 **high as 75 million:** Porterfield, *Country,* 381, 424.

180 **"the most famous hillbilly star":** Malone, *Country Music USA,* 81, 83.

182 **"She sang blues so well"**: W. C. Handy, *Father of the Blues: An Autobiography* (New York: Da Capo Press, 1985), 200.

182 **Elizabeth Ofosuah Johnson has posited:** Elizabeth Ofosuah Johnson, "Yodeling Music Is Not European, This Is the True African Origin of the American Folk Genre," *Face2Face Africa,* August 9, 2018.

183 **"eeoho-eeoho-weeioho-i":** Bart Plantenga, *Yodel-Ay-Ee-Oooo: The Secret History of Yodeling around the World* (New York: Taylor & Francis, 2004), 23.

183 **"Laughing Yodel":** Plantenga, *Yodel-Ay-Ee-Oooo,* 27.

184 **"In fact she is one of the first lady yodelers":** Lynn Abbott and Doug Seroff, "America's Blue Yodel," *Musical Traditions* 11 (Late 1993.

184 **"America's Greatest Yodler":** Abbott and Seroff, "America's Blue Yodel."

184 **"Every day, in every way":** Émile Coué was a French psychologist who believed that through repetition one could train the subconscious. Repeating the phrase become a fad in the United States in the late 1920s.

188 **"a national figure"**: "What Is the Secret of Rudy Vallee's Success?" *Radio Review,* December 1929, 3.

188 **She turned and shot him dead:** "Rudy Vallee, Singing Idol, Dies at 84," *New York Times,* July 5, 1986, 8.

188 **"Feminine Hearts Caught":** "Rudy Vallee Makes His Screen Debut," *Philadelphia Inquirer,* December 26, 1929, p. 7.

188 **"the crooning blonde whose hypnotizing vocalizing"**: "The Jazzologist from Yale Is Star for Talkie," *Chicago Daily Tribune,* December 27, 1929.

189 **"wistful rather than wisecracking" . . . "a refreshing change":** "What Is the Secret of Rudy Vallee's Success?," 4.

190 **"the smothering provincialism":** Gary Giddins, *Bing Crosby: A Pocketful of Dreams—The Early Years, 1903–1940* (Boston: Little, Brown and Company, 2001), 110.

Chapter 8: The Ultramodern Revolution and Music Appreciation

193 **"Too many musical organizations are Bourbons":** R. Allen Lott, " 'New Music for New Ears': The International Composers' Guild," *Journal of the American Musicological Society* 36, No. 2 (Summer, 1983): 267.

197 **"If he [the composer] has a nice wife":** Stuart Feder, *Charles Ives, "My Father's Song": A Psychoanalytic Biography* (New Haven: Yale University Press, 1992), 65.

197 **built a home on 18.5 acres:** Allan Kozinn, "Ives's Study Resurrected, Inch by Inch," *New York Times,* March 5, 2014.

198 **"It is incomprehensible to me":** Jan Swafford, *Charles Ives: A Life with Music* (New York: W. W. Norton, 1996), 318, 334.

199 **"the *diabolus in musica*":** Paul Rosenfeld, "Ornstein," *The New Republic,* May 27, 1916, 83–85; Frederick Herman Martens, *Leo Ornstein: The Man, His Ideas, His Work* (New York: Breitkopf & Hartel, 1918), 24–25.

199 **"Ornstein, the youngest":** Waldo Frank, typescript for an article "Leo Ornstein and the Emancipated Music," to appear in *The Onlooker* (1915), in Ornstein Collection, Yale Music Library. Quoted in Vivian Perlis, "The Futurist Music of Leo Ornstein," *Notes* 31, no. 4 (June 1975): 741.

200 **"I would say that Op. 31":** Terence J. O'Grady and Leo Ornstein, "A Conversation with Leo Ornstein," *Perspectives of New Music* 23, no. 1 (Autumn–Winter 1984): 127; David Joel Metzer, "The Ascendancy of Musical Modernism in New York City, 1915–1929" (PhD diss., Yale University, 1993), 122.

200 **"The International Composers' Guild . . . is an attempt":** "From Composers' Guild," *New York Times,* February 12, 1922.

201 **"for the right of each" . . . "composers refuse to die":** *Musical America* 34, no. 13 (July 23, 1921): 1, 6. A reproduction of the leaflet is in Louise Varèse, *Varèse: A Looking-Glass Diary,* vol. 1, *1883–1928* (New York: W. W. Norton, 1972), 151–52.

201 **"These modern musical explorations":** "Composers' Guild Gives First Concert," *New York Times,* December 18, 1922.

202 **"succession of disagreeable and unmusical noises":** Richard Aldrich, "Music," *New York Times,* February 5, 1923.

202 **"It is no longer possible":** Lawrence Gilman, "New Works at the Season's First International Guild Concert," *New York Herald Tribune,* December 8, 1924.

202 **"This is Varèse's society":** Louise Varèse, *Varèse,* 165, 188, 190–91;

Claire R. Reis, unpublished transcript of a recorded interview with Vivian Perlis, Jan. 1976–Jan 1977, Oral History American Music, Yale University, 64–65.

203 **Joly was satirizing the French reign**: Maurice Joly, *Dialogue aux enfers entre Machiavel et Montesquieu* (Brussels: Impr. de A. Mertens et fils, 1864).

203 **"Jazz is not" . . . "Heil to Hitler":** Olivia Mattis, "Edgard Varèse and the Visual Arts" (PhD diss., Stanford University, 1992), 175–76.

203 **"I agree with Adolph":** Marilyn J. Ziffrin, *Carl Ruggles: Composer, Painter, and Storyteller* (Urbana: University of Illinois Press, 1992), 136.

205 **"I discovered very quickly":** Rita H. Mead, "The Amazing Mr. Cowell," *American Music* 1, no. 4 (1983): 63.

205 **"bi-coastal life":** Joel Sachs, *Henry Cowell: A Man Made of Music* (New York: Oxford University Press, 2012), 63.

206 **"like olives":** Leta E. Miller, *Music and Politics in San Francisco: From the 1906 Quake to the Second World War* (Berkeley: University of California Press, 2006), 184.

207 **half of the subscribers withdrew:** Rita H. Mead, "Cowell, Ives, and 'New Music,'" *Musical Quarterly* 66, no. 4 (October 1980): 540. Michael Hicks, using ledger records, counted 594 original subscribers. Hicks, *Henry Cowell Bohemian* (Urbana: University of Illinois Press, 2002), 122.

207 **extent of Ives's generosity:** Mead, "Cowell, Ives, and 'New Music,'" 558.

208 **"He is a prophet":** Minna Lederman, *The Life and Death of a Small Magazine (Modern Music, 1924–1946)* (Brooklyn: Institute for Studies in American Music, Brooklyn College of the City University of New York, 1983), 22–23.

208 **Copland, however, remained her favorite:** Léonie Rosenstiel, *Nadia Boulanger: A Life in Music* (New York: W. W. Norton, 1982), 160–61; Howard Pollack, *Aaron Copland: The Life and Work of an Uncommon Man* (New York: Henry Holt and Company, 1999), 50.

209 **"His gift is decidedly proficient":** Paul Rosenfeld, *An Hour with American Music* (Philadelphia: J. B. Lippincott, 1929), 133–34.

211 **the frontier closed in 1892:** At least according to Frederick Jackson Turner, "The Significance of the Frontier in American History" (American Historical Association, Chicago, 1893), reprinted in *The Frontier in American History* (New York: Henry Holt, 1920), 1–28.

212 **"I would prefer to see":** Michael Broyles, *Mavericks and Other Traditions in American Music* (New Haven: Yale University Press, 2004), 146–47.

213 **"intelligent hearers":** Charles W. Pearce, "On Listening to Music," *Proceedings of the Royal Music Association*, 19th session (1892–93), 62.

213 **"Both are on the same low level"**: Pearce, "On Listening to Music," 63.

213 **"whether the composer"**: Pearce, "On Listening to Music," 65–66.

213 **first music appreciation textbook:** Thomas Whitney Surette and Daniel Gregory Mason, *The Appreciation of Music* (New York: The H. W. Gray Co., 1907), 222.

214 **augmented by radio programs:** The best-known early radio programs were by Walter Damrosch in the United States and Donald Francis Tovey in Great Britain, and later, on television, Leonard Bernstein. For detailed discussion of the music appreciation movement with focus on its cultural milieu, see Julia J. Chybowski, "Developing American Taste: A Cultural History of the Early Twentieth-Century Music Appreciation Movement" (PhD diss., University of Madison–Wisconsin, 2008).

214 **""use music" . . . "ideal listener";** Aaron Copland, *What to Listen for in Music* (New York: McGraw-Hill, 1939, rev. 1957), 9–16.

215 **"the precepts of Copland's typology"**: The phrase is David Paul's; personal email from David Paul, University of California, Santa Barbara.

215 **A log of the first day:** Archer, *History of Radio to 1926,* 266. Before the FCC established frequency allocation, multiple stations in one area such as New York City developed an informal arrangement of time sharing so each could be heard. That accounts for short broadcasting times.

216 **bring opera to many homes:** Archer, *History of Radio to 1926,* 259–62, 270–71.

216 **"Such concerts have captured":** "General Harbord Tells of Radio Progress in 1924," *The Talking Machine World,* March 1925.

216 **regulation of this new industry:** For instance, in 1927 the Federal Radio Commission determined that to avoid airwave interference the number of stations operating in New York City needed to be reduced from 48 to 19. One of the criteria to determine the survivors was the "public service they perform." *New York Times,* May 13, 1927, 27.

217 **culmination of his radio activities:** Numerous articles about his activities were chronicled in the *New York Times;* see October 29, 1923; October 18, 1925; November 8, 1925; January 17, 1926; January 24, 1926; September 19, 1926; October 10, 1926; October 24, 1926; May 1, 1927; May 13, 1927.

217 **"The radio audience is heterogeneous":** *Radio Broadcast,* October 1922. Quoted in Archer, *History of Radio to 1926,* 272.

Chapter 9: After the War

221 **shortage of rubber:** The rubber shortage was so severe that the administration actually considered "requisitioning the tires on private passenger cars" ("Henderson Hints Possible Seizure of Tires in Use," *Evening Star* [Washington, DC], March 5, 1942).

222 **she quickly had the marriage annulled**: Steve Silverman, "Her First Husband Was Still Alive," https://uselessinformation.org/her-first-husband-was-still-alive/.

222 **"he will think I'm too young":** Sheila John Daly, "Just Be Own True Self to Returning GI," *Chicago Daily Tribune*, June 14, 1945, 24.

222 ***The Man in the Gray Flannel Suit:*** The novel by Sloan Wilson about a World War II veteran's return, marriage, and rise through the corporate structure (New York: Simon and Schuster, 1955).

223 **"A woman's place is in the home":** The quotations are the conclusions of Alice E. Courtney and Sarah Wernick Lockeretz's article, "A Woman's Place: An Analysis of the Roles Portrayed by Women in Magazine Advertisements," *Journal of Marketing Research* 8, no. 1 (February 1971): 94–95.

223 **Two songs capture the mood of the postwar years:** "The Gypsy" by the Ink Spots is generally considered the number one recording of 1946 because it was number one on the *Billboard* charts for eleven weeks, from May 25 to July 7, but "To Each His Own" had four different versions reach number one at different times and two more versions charted in the top ten: Eddy Howard and His Orchestra was number one from July 11 to August 24; Freddy Martin and His Orchestra was number one August 31 to September 7; The Ink Spots held the number one position for one week, September 21; Eddy Howard and His Orchestra returned for October 5 to October 12 with a slightly different release—the performance was the same but the record had a different B side. Tony Martin's version reached number four and the Modernaires with Paula Kelley peaked at number five.

223 **"the greatest celebration the nation has ever known":** "Yesterday's Big Story," Universal Newsreel, 1945, YouTube video.

224 **"Five Minutes More" . . . "Kiss of Fire":** "Five Minutes More" was written by Sammy Cahn (lyrics) and Jule Styne (music) in 1946. It was featured in the film *The Sweetheart of Sigma Chi*, and recorded by several singers. The most popular version was by Frank Sinatra, which reached number one for one week on the *Billboard* charts on September 28, 1946. It was the last Sinatra song to reach number one in the 1940s. "Kiss of Fire" was originally an Argentine tango, "El Choclo," written by Ángel Villoldo in 1903. Several English versions under the title "Kiss of Fire" appeared in 1952, the most successful by Georgia Gibbs.

225 **"I thought the goddamned building was going to cave in":** Nancy Sinatra, *Frank Sinatra: My Father* (New York: Pocket Books, 1986), 76. Nancy Sinatra, probably erroneously, attributes the Goodman quote to Jack Benny. See Earl Wilson, *Sinatra: An Unauthorized Biography* (New York: MacMillan, 1946), 39-40.

226 **Columbus Day Riot:** James F. Smith, "Bobby Sox and Blue Suede Shoes: Frank Sinatra and Elvis Presley as Teen Idols," in *Frank Sina-*

tra and Popular Culture, ed. Leonard Mustazza (Westport, CT: Praeger Publishers, 1998), 62.

226 **"If this undersized, pleasantly homely kid":** Inez Robb, "Inez Robb Wonders What Frank Sinatra Has That Other Crooners Don't Have," *Atlanta Constitution*, July 11, 1943.

226 **"The screaming and moaning":** Janice L. Booker, "Why the Bobby Soxers?" in *Frank Sinatra: History, Identity, and Italian American Culture*, ed. Stanislao G. Pugliese (New York: Palgrave Macmillan, 2004), 77.

227 **"It was the war years":** Nancy Sinatra, *Frank Sinatra*, 48.

227 **"Sinatra had only one basic subject, loneliness":** Pete Hamill, *Why Sinatra Matters* (New York: Little, Brown and Company, 1998), 69.

227 **"such childish pastimes":** "Sinatra Fans Grow Up, Just Wear Uniforms Now," *Atlanta Constitution*, July 14, 1946.

229 **"It's about time you Jews":** John Simkin, "Journey of Reconciliation," *Spartacus Educational*, September 1997.

229 **The other white man, Felmet**: "Felmet's Life, Beliefs Began in the Asheville Area," *Asheville Citizen-Times*, March 29, 1978, p. 23.

230 **"race" was a positive term:** William Barlow, "Cashing In: 1900–1939," in *Split Image: African Americans in the Mass Media*, ed. Jannette L. Dates and William Barlow (Washington, DC: Howard University Press, 1990), 38.

230 **"Rhythm and Blues":** Bruce Weber, "Jerry Wexler, a Behind-the-Scenes Force in Black Music, is Dead at 91," *New York Times*, August 15, 2008, A17.

231 **"Paper Doll":** *Discography of American Historical Recordings*, s.v. "Decca 18318 (10-in. double-faced)," https://adp.library.ucsb.edu/index.php/objects/detail/317475/Decca_18318.

231 **he formed a trio:** There is some disagreement exactly when Cole's trio was formed. See Leslie Gourse, *Unforgettable: The Life and Mystique of Nat King Cole* (New York: St. Martin's Press, 1991), 26.

231 **"Straighten Up and Fly Right":** The King Cole Trio, "Straighten Up and Fly Right," November 1943, Capitol Records 154, 78 rpm.

232 **"The Christmas Song":** The King Cole Trio, "The Christmas Song" (Chestnuts Roasting on an Open Fire), June 1946, Capitol Records 311, 78 rpm.

233 **their "hotcha" sound:** Marv Goldberg, *More Than Words Can Say: The Ink Spots and Their Music* (Lanham, MD: The Scarecrow Press, 1998), 20, gives two examples.

233 **Deek whispered them to him:** Goldberg, *More Than Words Can Say*, 50.

233 **added a piano accompaniment:** *Discography of American Historical Recordings*, s.v. "Decca2286 (10-in. double-faced)," October 12, 2020, https://adp.library.ucsb.edu/index.php/objects/detail/311236/Decca-2286.

234 **double-sided discs:** Steve Schoenherr, "Recording History

Technology," revised July 6, 2005, https://web.archive.org/web/20070329065002/http://history.sandiego.edu/gen/recording/notes.html#cylinder.

235 **Gernsbach's system was never practical:** Herbert Gernsbach, "Television and the Telephot," *Modern Electrics* 2, no. 9 (December 1909): 404.

236 **soon up and running:** Evan I. Schwartz, *The Last Lone Inventor: A Tale of Genius, Deceit, and the Birth of Television* (New York: HarperCollins, 2002), 16.

237 **finance his idea:** Donald G. Godfrey, *Philo T. Farnsworth: The Father of Television* (Salt Lake City: University of Utah Press, 2001), 22.

237 **moving image of cigarette smoke:** Godfrey, *Philo T. Farnsworth,* 33–34.

237 **250 lines per inch:** Farnsworth claimed that he could achieve 600 lines per inch by simple adjustments. Godfrey, *Philo T. Farnsworth,* 38–39.

237 **began to attract visitors:** Schwartz, *The Last Lone Inventor,* 151–52.

239 **"the conception of the idea":** David Stashower, *The Boy Genius and the Mogul: The Untold Story of Television* (New York: Broadway Books, 2002), 209–10.

239 **he owned television:** Stashower, *The Boy Genius and the Mogul,* 212–14.

240 **large cash sum plus royalties:** Stashower, *The Boy Genius and the Mogul,* 243–44.

240 **by 1941 NBC and CBS were broadcasting:** Mitchell Stephens, "History of Television," *Grolier Multimedia Encyclopedia,* 2000 ed.

240 **42 million households had TV:** Data taken from Tom Genova and Michael Bennett-Levy, "Television History—The First 75 Years," *TVhistory.TV.*

240 **"The companies, the publishers and the talent agencies":** *Billboard,* February 27, 1951.

241 **The tape recorder as a concept began:** Leslie Hutchinson, "The Development of the Tape Recorder," *Science and Its Times: Understanding the Social Significance of Scientific Discovery,* Encyclopedia.com.

242 **glued steel filings onto a strip:** David L. Morton, "The History of Magnetic Recording in the United States, 1888–1978" (PhD diss., Georgia Institute of Technology, 1995), 273.

243 **two Model 200a machines:** "Jack Mullin," History of Recording, *AMPEX Corporation,* https://www.historyofrecording.com/Jack_Mullin.html (accessed August 21, 2019).

Chapter 10: Johnnie Ray and the Rise of Rock 'n' Roll

246 **every middle-class family owned at least one car:** Other than people living in urban poverty, the principal exception was affluent people in large cities with excellent public transportation, such

as New York and Boston. Especially as suburbs expanded, a car became a necessity rather than a luxury.

246 **rite of passage:** The exact age and terms of driver's licenses or driving courses varied from state to state.

246 **a fourth the price of the car:** the Motorola radio designed by the Galvin brothers, the first commercial success, cost $130 in 1930, when a Ford Model A Deluxe Coupe cost $540. Justin Berkowitz, "The History of Car Radios," *Car and Driver,* October 25, 2010.

247 **"It's Too Soon to Know":** The Orioles, "It's Too Soon to Know," recorded August 21, 1945, Natural 5, 45 rpm.

248 **"The old inflexible Ink Spots style":** *Billboard,* January 24, 1948, and January 31, 1948.

248 ***Billboard's* "Top Record Artists":** Goldberg, *More Than Words Can Say,* 205.

249 **"Johnnie Ray has smashed":** *Billboard,* March 29, 1952; *Los Angeles Times,* November 24, 1952, A13; *Atlanta Constitution,* July 26, 1952; *The Atlanta Journal and the Atlanta Constitution,* July 27, 1952.

250 **Ray played in small towns:** Whiteside interview with Elma Ray, Johnnie's sister, on January 10, 1993. Quoted in Jonny Whiteside, *Cry: The Johnnie Ray Story* (New York: Barricade Books, 1994), 47–48.

251 **he always returned to the Flame:** Ray's experience at the Flame Showbar is described in detail by Whiteside, *Cry,* 50–56, who includes quotations from many people involved with the club, including Al Green, the floor manager of the club and later one of Ray's managers, and LaVern Baker, and an extensive interview with Ray himself, May 11, 1989. See also Ray's own account in Johnnie Ray, "Negros Taught Me to Sing," *Ebony,* March 1953, 52–58.

251 **"because as soon as the headliners finish":** Whiteside interview with Kessler in Sherman Oaks, California, August 30, 1992. Quoted in Whiteside, *Cry,* 59.

252 **"Cry":** Johnnie Ray and the Four Lads, "Cry," recorded November 9, 1951, OKeh 4-6840, 78 rpm.

252 **recorded on Cadillac by Ruth Casey:** Ruth Casey, "Cry," recorded 1951, Cadillac 103, 78 rpm.

253 **"If I could find a white man":** Some sources replace "billion" with "million." This version comes from Sun Records secretary Marion Keisker, who claimed Phillips said it "over and over." Peter Guralnick, *Feel Like Going Home: Portraits in Blues and Rock 'n' Roll* (1971; repr., Boston: Little, Brown and Company, 1999), 172.

253 **"Negroes Taught Me How":** Johnnie Ray, "Negroes Taught Me How to Sing," *Ebony,* March 1953, 48.

254 **"We used to laugh all the time":** Ruth Brown interviewed on BBC documentary, "Johnnie Ray." Ken Howard, *The South Bank Show,* season 25, episode 12, "Johnnie Ray," hosted by Melvyn Bragg, 1978.

254 **Maude Thomas**: E. B. Rea, "Pennsylvania Avenue," *Baltimore Afro-*

American, November 26, 1949, 21. Ruth Brown mentions hearing her in the Midwest, location not specified, and being impressed. Quoted in Chip Deffaa, *Blues Rhythms* (Boston: Da Capo Press, 1999), 24.

254 **Little Miss Cornshucks:** Robert Sylvester, "Million-Dollar Teardrop," *Saturday Evening Post*, June 26, 1952, 112.

254 **"she could sing the blues better":** Ahmet Ertegun, *"What'd I Say?": The Atlantic Story: Fifty Years of Music* (New York: Welcome Rain Publishers, 2001), 15.

254 **"Little Miss Cornshucks was the most important":** Barry Mazor, "Who Is This Woman? Little Miss Cornshucks," *No Depression*, May–June 2003, 82.

256 **"She'd arrive on stage barefoot":** Mazor, "Who Is This Woman?," 84.

256 **direct imitation of Cornshucks's:** Marv Goldberg, "Lavern Baker," *Marv Goldberg's R&B Notebooks*.

257 **"Try a Little Tenderness":** Little Miss Cornshucks, "Try a Little Tenderness," December 1951, Coral 65090, 78 rpm.

258 **"Cry" was indeed selling in the white market:** Whiteside, *Cry*, 95.

259 **"He pulled off one of the greatest stunts":** Earl Wilson, *New York Post*, as quoted by Whiteside, *Cry*, 114.

259 **"I didn't want Johnnie to be noted":** Miller interview in Whiteside, *Cry*, 102.

260 **"this piece of crap":** Johnnie Ray with Ray Conniff and His Orchestra and Chorus, "Just Walking in the Rain," 1956, Columbia Records 4-40729, 45 rpm; Whiteside, *Cry*, 222.

260 **Two operations later:** Cheryl Herr, "Roll-Over-Beethoven: Johnnie Ray in Context," *Popular Music* 28, no. 3 (October 2009): 336.

260 **never with the same abandon**: Tad Mann, *Johnnie Ray: Beyond the Marquee* (self-published, AuthorHouse, 2006), 53–56.

260 **Ray is either ignored or barely mentioned:** For assessments of Ray, see John Covach, *What's That Sound: An Introduction to Rock and Its History* (New York: W. W. Norton, 2006), 33; Charles Hamm, *Yesterdays: Popular Song in America* (New York: W. W. Norton, 1979), ignores Ray completely; Charles Gillet, *The Sound of the City: The Rise of Rock and Roll*, 2nd ed. (New York: Da Capo Press, 1996), 7, 118; Louis Neihbur, "Ray, Johnnie," *Grove Music Online*, January 20, 2016; Larry Starr and Christopher Waterman, *American Popular Music, from Minstrelsy to MTV*, 2nd ed. (New York: Oxford University Press, 2007), 183.

260 **"Johnnie did something that was completely different":** Mann, *Johnnie Ray*, 39; Whiteside interview with Bennett, September 1, 1992. Quoted in Whiteside, *Cry*, 68.

261 **"I look back now":** Whiteside interview with Miller, June 9, 1992. Quoted in Whiteside, *Cry*, 78; John S. Wilson, "Johnnie Ray Is Back at East Side Club," *New York Times*, May 22, 1981, C17.

261 **John Lennon playing harmonica:** Wilson, "Johnnie Ray Is Back

at East Side Club"; Mann, *Johnnie Ray,* 39; Walter Everett, *The Beatles as Musicians: The Quarry Men Through Rubber Soul* (Oxford: Oxford University Press, 2001), 16.

261 **"was the first singer whose voice and style"**: Robert Shelton, *No Direction Home: The Life and Music of Bob Dylan* (New York: Beech Tree Books), 37; interview with Bernard Kleinman, 1984, in *The Bob Dylan Companion: Four Decades of Commentary,* ed. Carl Benson (New York: Schirmer Books, 1998), 35–36. I want to thank Sumanth Gopinath for pointing out the quote from the Shelton book to me.

261 **"Johnny [*sic*] Ray knocked me out":** Elijah Ward, *How the Beatles Destroyed Rock 'n' Roll: An Alternative History of American Popular Music* (New York: Oxford University Press, 2009), 36.

261 **Ray and Presley became friends:** Bill Franklin interview, West Hollywood, California, November 18, 1990, quoted in Whiteside, *Cry,* 382; Ray interview, West Hollywood, May 11, 1989, quoted in Whiteside, *Cry,* 207.

262 **"The Johnnie Ray Story is a tear jerking tale":** Larry Walters, "Johnnie Ray, Their Darling Crybaby," *Chicago Daily Tribune,* March 16, 1952, C5A; Paul Jones, "Johnnie Ray to Weep Self into Town Friday," *The Atlanta Journal and The Atlanta Constitution,* July 20, 1952.

Chapter 11: The Summer of '55: Rock 'n' Roll's Turning Point

267 **"crushing mob of 25,000":** Quoted in John A. Jackson, *Big Beat Heat: Alan Freed and the Early Years of Rock & Roll* (New York: Schirmer Books, 1991), 2–3.

268 **"the jukebox guy":** Clint O'Connor, "DJ Legend Bill Randle Dead at 81," *Cleveland Plain Dealer,* July 10, 2004.

268 **"On the larger scale":** Jim Dawson and Steve Propes, *What Was the First Rock 'n' Roll Record?* (London: Faber & Faber, 1992), xv.

269 **"caught the ear of the nation":** "Bursting Old Barriers," *Billboard,* April 24, 1954, 13.

269 **"Teen-agers have spearheaded":** "Teen-Agers Demand Music with a Beat, Spur Rhythm-Blues," *Billboard,* April 24, 1954, 1.

270 **"could guess the No. 1 record seller":** Albin Zak, *I Don't Sound Like Nobody: Remaking Music in 1950s America* (Ann Arbor: University of Michigan Press, 2012), 127.

270 **"What I heard was an appealing dance vitality":** Zak, *I Don't Sound Like Nobody,* 127.

271 **R&B a niche genre:** "Editorial: Bursting All Barriers," and Joe Martin, "Spotlight on Rhythm and Blues," *Billboard,* August 24, 1954, 13.

273 **no mention of the song:** Bosley Crowther, "The Screen: Blackboard Jungle; Delinquency Shown in Powerful Film," *New York Times,* March 21, 1955.

274 **"That's my boy, 'Fats' Domino":** Rick Coleman, *Blue Monday: Fats Domino and the Lost Dawn of Rock 'n' Roll* (Boston: Da Capo Press, 2006), 28.

274 **Chudd signed him on the spot:** Coleman, *Blue Monday*, 50.

275 **"I consider ['The Fat Man'] a revolutionary record":** Dawson and Propes, *What Was the First Rock 'n' Roll Record?*, 65.

276 **"I picked this up from an Amos Milburn recording":** Coleman, *Blue Monday*, 63–64.

278 **"they were just terrible":** Marv Goldberg, "The Platters," *Marv Goldberg's R&B Notebooks*, 2008.

281 **it was "different":** Bruce Pegg, *Brown Eyed Handsome Man: The Life and Hard Times of Chuck Berry* (New York: Taylor and Francis, 2005), 38.

282 **"It was 'Wee Wee Hours'":** Paul H. Fryer, "'Brown-Eyed Handsome Man,' Chuck Berry and the Blues Tradition," *Phylon* 42, no. 1 (1981): 64.

282 **Chess put the presses in motion:** Pegg, *Brown Eyed Handsome Man*, 41.

283 **"The tune has a catchy rhythm and a solid, driving beat":** "Review Spotlight," *Billboard*, July 23, 1955, 89.

286 **14.8 million teenagers:** "Pop1 Child Population: Number Of Children (In Millions) Ages 0–17 in the United States by Age, and Projected 2020–2050," ChildStats.gov.

287 **"rhythm and blues music no longer is limited":** "American Music Becomes National Rather Than Regional," *Cash Box*, April 2, 1955, 76.

Chapter 12: Rock 'n' Roll: Culmination and Collapse

290 **"quasar of rock":** Charles White, *The Life and Times of Little Richard, the Quasar of Rock* (1984; repr., New York: Da Capo Press, 1994).

290 **"He was a showman!":** White, *The Life and Times of Little Richard*, 11.

291 **"was very unnatural":** White, *The Life and Times of Little Richard*, 9.

291 **Richard was hooked on show business:** White, *The Life and Times of Little Richard*, 17.

292 **this song didn't have a chance:** "Music on Networks Get Scissors," *Billboard*, June 9, 1956, 18.

293 **Little Richard was on his way:** White, *The Life and Times of Little Richard*, 55.

293 **"I'm just the same as ever":** Glen C. Altschuler, *All Shook Up: How Rock 'n' Roll Changed America* (New York: Oxford University Press, 2003), 60.

294 **"By wearing this makeup":** Brian Ward, *Just My Soul Responding: Rhythm and Blues, Black Consciousness and Race Relations* (Berkeley: University of California Press, 1998), 52–53.

294 **inspired by Little Richard:** White, *The Life and Times of Little Richard*, 225–29.

294 **"considered himself the King of Rock 'n' Roll:** Flashbak, "Little Richard—The greatest rock 'n' roll star in August 1972," YouTube video, 7:48, August 7, 2017.

295 **"the three of us formed":** Peter Guralnick, *Last Train to Memphis: The Rise of Elvis Presley* (Boston: Little, Brown and Company, 1994), 15.

296 **Memphis radio:** Guralnick, *Last Train to Memphis,* 38; "It Happened Here," KWEM Radio, http://www.kwemradio.com/History.html (accessed October 18, 2020).

296 **"Home of the Blues":** "About," *Beale Street.*

297 **Humes High School annual minstrel show:** Guralnick, *Last Train to Memphis,* 43.

297 **in 1952, Sun Records:** "Sun Records—706 Union Avenue Sessions," http://www.706unionavenue.nl/68811872 (accessed October 18, 2020).

298 **"What kind of singer are you?":** Guralnick, *Last Train to Memphis,* 63.

298 **nothing more happened:** Peter Guralnick has discussed the variants at length. Guralnick, *Last Train to Memphis,* 497–98.

298 **"He was so ingenuous":** Guralnick, *Last Train to Memphis,* 65.

299 **"What are you doing?":** Interview with Scotty Moore and Bill Black. Quoted in Guralnick, *Last Train to Memphis,* 95.

299 **"His style is both country and r. & b.":** "Review Spotlight On . . . ," *Billboard,* August 7, 1954, 39; August 14, 1954, 46; November 6, 1954, 50.

301 **Philbin exercised his option:** Roger Lee Hall, *The Bill Randle Chronicles: From Electric Elvis to The Shakers,* vol. 6, *Promotion of Electric Elvis* (Skyland, NC: PineTree Press, 2015).

301 **"A WINNAH!":** *Billboard,* March 3, 1956, 54.

301 **"sole and exclusive Advisor":** Guralnick, *Last Train to Memphis,* 258.

302 **all parties reached an agreement:** Guralnick, *Last Train to Memphis,* 224–29.

303 **"I had looked at everything":** Elizabeth Kaye, "Sam Phillips: The Rolling Stone Interview," *Rolling Stone,* February 13, 1986.

303 **"slapback echo":** "Sun Records Echo—How Did Sam Phillips Achieve It?" Steve Hoffman Music Forums.

304 **Phillips was busy:** Guralnick, *Last Train to Memphis,* 238, 247.

304 **"just his way" . . . "natural way of performing":** Guralnick, *Last Train to Memphis,* 110–11.

305 **like Chet Atkins:** Jimmy Guterman, *Rockin' My Life Away: Listening to Jerry Lee Lewis* (Nashville: Rutledge Hill, 1991).

305 **"Who is this cat?":** *Jerry Lee Lewis: I Am What I Am,* directed by Mark Hall (White Star, 1987), DVD (Kultur/White Star, 2004).

306 **"There's only been four of us":** Guterman, *Rockin' My Life Away.*

306 **too risqué:** Guterman, *Rockin' My Life Away,* online.

307 **"the most frankly lecherous breakdown":** Guterman, *Rockin' My Life Away.*

308 **"I don't know what happened":** Rick Bragg, *Jerry Lee Lewis: His Own Story* (New York: Harper, 2014), 51–52.

308 **first time he heard . . . rock 'n' roll:** Bragg, *Jerry Lee Lewis,* 88.
309 **"Jerry, Jerry":** "Jerry Lee Lewis & Sam Phillips—Religious Discussion (1957)," YouTube video, 4:02, posted by robin haugsnes, January 23, 2009.
309 **"While the South is hardly Christ-centered":** Guterman, *Rockin' My Life Away,* online.
310 **"Can you play rock music?":** Bragg, *Jerry Lee Lewis,* 229.
310 **"Salvation bears down on me":** Jim Jerome, "Fame, Tragedy and Fame Again: Jerry Lee Lewis Has Been through Great Balls of Fire, Otherwise Known as Hell," *People,* April 24, 1978; Simon Hattersone, "Interview," *The Guardian,* August 8, 2015.
310 **The British tabloids screamed:** Bragg, *Jerry Lee Lewis,* 273–74; "Jerry Lee Lewis Tour Off," *New York Times,* May 28, 1958, 36.
311 **"I never shunned a show":** Bragg, *Jerry Lee Louis,* 290–91.
311 **"I Like My Baby's Pudding":** Tony Collins, *Rock Mr. Blues: The Life and Music of Wynonie Harris* (Milford, NH: Big Nickel Publications, 1995), 112.
312 **"It reinforced the white stereotype":** John A. Jackson, *Big Beat Heat: Alan Freed and the Early Years of Rock & Roll* (New York: Schirmer Books, 1991), 7.
312 **stations could even lose their franchise:** "Editorial: Control the Dim-Wits," *Billboard,* September 24, 1954, 33.
313 **"Our teenagers are already":** "Miscellany: A Warning to the Music Business," *Variety,* February 23, 1955, 2.
313 **San Antonio Commission:** Linda Martin and Kerry Segrave, *Anti-Rock: The Opposition to Rock 'n' Roll* (Hamden, CT: Archon Books, 1988), 18–23.
314 **"How can I restrict it":** Joel Friedman, "Music on Networks Get Scissors," *Billboard,* June 9, 1956, 1; *Billboard,* "Censor Can't Dig 'Sally,'" March 17, 1956, 18.
314 **physically accosted by some of the crowd:** "MIT: March 10, 1956," *Motherlode.TV.*
314 **"the basic, heavy-beat music" . . . "level of the N****r":** Gérald Côté, "Asa Carter," YouTube video, 0:15, March 17, 2012. Also quoted in Michael T. Bertrand, *Race, Rock, and Elvis* (Urbana: University of Illinois Press, 2004), 163.
315 **references to jungle music:** "Chi Cardinal Nixes R&R," *Billboard,* March 16, 1957, 30; Martin and Segrave, *Anti-Rock,* 42; Barbara Moon, "What You Don't Need to Know about Rock 'n' Roll," *Maclean's,* July 7, 1956, 14; Altschuler, *All Shook Up,* 40.
315 **"juvenile stuff" . . . "anyone over fourteen"::** "Mitch Miller Speech at DJ Convention," *Cashbox,* March 22, 1958, 24; Martin and Segrave, *Anti-Rock,* 46–47.
316 **"to suppress genuine talent":** *Variety,* November 11, 1959, 1. Quoted in James Wierzbicki, *Music in the Age of Anxiety: American Music in the Fifties* (Urbana: University of Illinois Press, 2016), 41.

317 **polls were rigged:** Milton Bracker, "Hogan Studies Fraud in RV Ads; 'Payola' Denied by Disk Jockeys," *New York Times,* November 8, 1959, 48.

317 **Freed further refused to sign:** Richard F. Shepard, "Alan Freed Is Out in 'Payola' Study," *New York Times,* November 22, 1959.

317 **who symbolized the practice:** Jack Roth, "Alan Freed and 7 Others Arrested in Payola Here," *New York Times,* May 20, 1960.

Chapter 13: Anonymity and Its Ways: Classical Music in a Postwar World

320 **"Our personality in an illusion":** Wylie Sypher, *Loss of Self in Modern Literature and Art* (New York: Random House, 1962), 60–61.

320 "**He is the Subject, he is the Absolute**": Simon de Beauvoir, *The Second Sex,* translated and edited by H. M. Parshley (London: Jonathan Cape, 1956), 16.

321 **"It wasn't until spring 1950":** Heinrich Böll, "Pale Anna," trans. Christopher Middleton, in *German Short Stories,* ed. Richard Newnham (Baltimore: Penguin Books, 1964), 13.

322 **"It is not enough to deface the *Mona Lisa*":** Joan Peyser, *Boulez* (New York: Schirmer, 1976), 19.

322 **"Schoenberg Is Dead":** Pierre Boulez, "Schoenberg Is Dead," *The Score* 6 (February 1952): 18–22, reprinted in *Stocktakings from an Apprenticeship,* comp. Paule Thévenin, trans. Robert Piencikowski (Oxford: Clarendon Press, 1991), 209–14; quotations from Boulez, *Stocktakings,* 211.

322 **"The Leibowitz cult":** Joan Peyser, *Boulez* (New York: Schirmer Books, 1976), 39.

323 **"Our problem was to make a new musical language":** Boulez, *Washington Post,* May 30, 1971, E2, italics mine; Boulez, "The Composer and Creativity," *Journal of the Arnold Schoenberg Institute* 11, no. 2 (1988): 121.

323 **"milestone in the evolution of integral serialism":** Robert Morgan, *Twentieth-Century Music: A History of Musical Style in Modern Europe and America* (New York: W. W. Norton, 1991), 342.

324 **Babbitt introduced terms:** For the reader interested in Babbitt's ideas, see *The Collected Essays of Milton Babbitt,* ed. Stephen Peles (Princeton: Princeton University Press, 2003).

325 ***High Fidelity*'s rebranding of the article:** Milton Babbitt, "Who Cares If You Listen?" *High Fidelity,* February 1958, 38–40, 126–27.

326 **how integral serialism works:** Babbitt, *Who Cares,* 38–39.

326 **"Pointwise Periodic Homeomorphisms":** Babbitt, *Who Cares,* 40.

326 **"that the composer would do himself":** Babbitt, *Who Cares,* 126.

326 **sentence of 149 words:** Babbitt, "Contemporary Music Theory as Contemporary Intellectual History," in *Perspectives in Musicology: The Inaugural Lectures of the Ph.D. Program in Music at the City University of*

New York, ed. Barry S. Brook, Edward O. Downes, and Sherman van Solkema (New York: W. W. Norton, 1972), 151.

327 **tonal composers as "backward-looking":** K. Robert Schwarz, "In Contemporary Music, A House Still Divided," *New York Times*, August 3, 1997, 24.

328 **"Not being a serialist on the East Coast":** Kyle Gann, *American Music in the Twentieth Century* (New York: G. Schirmer, 1997), 220; Joseph Straus, "The Myth of Serial Tyranny," *The Musical Quarterly* 83, no. 3 (Fall 1999): 309; Schwarz, "In Contemporary Music," 24.

329 **"the trend for anonymity" . . . "'impersonal means'":** Cole Gagne and Tracy Caras, *Soundpieces: Interviews with American Composers* (Metuchen, NJ: Scarecrow Press, 1982), 198; Emily Wasserman, "An Interview with Composer Steve Reich," *Artforum International* 10 (May 1972): 48.

329 **"I'm not afraid of contradictions":** David Revill, *The Roaring Silence, John Cage: A Life* (New York: Arcade Publishing, 1991), 112.

329 **"'Then what is the purpose'":** John Cage, *Silence* (Middletown, CT: Wesleyan University Press, 1961), 14.

330 **Cage further developed elaborate instructions:** Cage, *Silence*, 57–59.

331 **neither the pieces nor the system survived:** Revill, *The Roaring Silence*, 37.

331 **"In that case I will devote":** Revill, *The Roaring Silence*, 48, 53.

332 ***Sonatas and Interludes for Prepared Piano*:** Revill, *The Roaring Silence*, 69–70. Revill points out that Cage had actually experimented some with the idea of preparing a piano in the preceding two years, so it wasn't exactly a sudden *eureka* moment.

333 **"Oh no, those numbers referred":** Revill, *The Roaring Silence*, 99.

333 **"I have no talent":** The full quote is "But I don't have absolute pitch. I can't keep a tune. In fact I have no talent for music." John Cage, *A Year from Monday: New Lectures and Writings* (1963; repr., Middletown, CT: Wesleyan University Press, 1967), 118.

334 **result of coin flips:** These letters have been published in *The Boulez-Cage Correspondence*, ed. Jean-Jacque Nattiez, trans. Robert Samuels (Cambridge, UK: Cambridge University Press, 1993), 6–16, *passim*.

336 **acknowledged in electronic music circles:** See Elizabeth Hinkle-Turner, *Women Composers and Music Technology in the United States: Crossing the Line* (Burlington, VT: Ashgate, 2006), 15–16.

336 **knowledge was to prove invaluable later:** Ted Greenwald, "The Self-Destructing Modules behind Revolutionary Soundtrack of *Forbidden Planet*," originally printed in *Keyboard Magazine*, February 1986, 54–65, reproduced online in *Effectrode*. I have been unable to verify his amateur radio license.

337 **"pursuing me hotly":** Bebe Barron, "Bebe Barron Interview on

the Sounds of Forbidden Planet," interview with KFAI radio's Jerry Modjeski, recorded in 2000.

337 **Stancil-Hoffman tape recorder:** Thom B. Holmes, *Electronic and Experimental Music: Technology, Music, and Culture* (New York: Routledge, 2016), 111.

337 **"Use the word 'cybernetics'":** "Foundations, the Subject of Cybernetics: Defining 'Cybernetics,'" *American Society for Cybernetics.*

338 **"We had very little idea":** Barron, "Bebe Barron Interview on the Sounds of Forbidden Planet."

338 **"Each circuit we built":** "Bebe Barron," interviewed by Eric Chasalow, filmed by Barbara Cassidy, 1997, copyright 1997 Video Archive of Electroacoustic, https://youtube/Zg_5Eb8coTU.

339 **"We have to knock it around electronically":** Philip K. Scheuer, "Wail of Tortured Electrons Proves Eerie Film Score," *Los Angeles Times*, February 26, 1956, D2.

339 **"In order to create electronic life":** Phil Taylor, "Louis Barron: Pioneer of Tube Audio Effects," Effectrode.com (accessed May 18, 2019).

339 **"A group of four or five scientists":** Greenwald, "The Self-Destructing Modules." For those technically oriented, Rubén Hinojosa Chapel, writing in *Computer Music Modeling and Retrieval: International Symposium CMMR 2003*, provides a technical description of the Barrons' circuits. He also commented, "this acoustic behavior . . . confers personal characteristics to a particular considered system."

340 **"These circuits are as if a living thing":** Greenwald, "The Self-Destructing Modules."

340 **"it only works":** Louis, quoted in Greenwald, "The Self-Destructing Modules."

340 **"After a while, Louis and I":** Greenwald, "The Self-Destructing Modules."

342 **Cage then used the *I Ching*:** Richard Kostelanetz, *Conversing with Cage* (New York: Limelight Editions, 1994), 162–64.

342 **a score of 192 pages:** Revill, *The Roaring Silence*, 145–46. Cage's claim in his conversation with Kostelanetz that the score was 500 pages is questionable, or he may not have been referring to the final version.

343 ***Williams Mix Extended*:** Composed by Werner Dafeldecker and Valerio Tricoli, CD released June 6, 2014. They provide a detailed explanation of the piece at "Williams Mix Extended," http://www.dafeldecker.net/projects/pdf/WME+Video.pdf.

343 **"sounded like mush":** Chasalow, "Bebe Barron 1997."

343 **Varèse was working on *Déserts*:** Chasalow, "Bebe Barron 1997."

343 **"I remember my first birth":** Hugo lecture, http://anaisninblog.skybluepress.com/tag/bells-of-atlantis/, June 23, 2019.

346 **"The officially sanctioned best judgment":** James Wierzbicki, *Louis and Bebe Barron's Forbidden Planet: A Film Score Guide* (Lanham, MD: Scarecrow Press, 2005), 8.

347 **Certainly the strongest" . . . "Man, it was chilling":** Exactly how long the Barrons worked on the film is not clear, as Bebe has indicated different lengths at different times. The quotations in the paragraph are taken from interviews on Not B-ROLL, "Forbidden Planet (1956) Amazing! Exploring the far reaches of Forbidden Planet (Behind the Scenes)," YouTube video, 26:35, July 3, 2020.

347 **wavering in the area of a B:** These pitches are transcribed from an Internet reproduction of the scene, and consequently the precise pitches cannot be guaranteed. For a more detailed description of the music, see Wierzbicki, *Louis and Bebe Barron's Forbidden Planet*, 78–79.

347 **death of the Barrons' oscillator itself:** Jane Brockman, "The First Electronic Filmscore-Forbidden Planet: A Conversation with Bebe Barron," Effectrode.com.

347 **They also supplied sounds:** Wierzbicki, *Louis and Bebe Barron's Forbidden Planet*, 12–13.

348 **until Louis's death in 1989:** Barron, "Bebe Barron Interview on Sounds of Forbidden Planet."

348 **"There was a lot" . . . "out of town":** Revill, *The Roaring Silence*, 165–66.

349 **"the pivotal composition of this century":** Revill, *The Roaring Silence*, 166.

349 **"my most important piece":** Revill, *The Roaring Silence*, 166–67.

349 **selling it to Muzak:** David Nicholls, *John Cage* (Urbana: University of Illinois Press, 2007), 58.

349 **"'Then what is the purpose'":** John Cage, "Experimental Music: Doctrine," in *Silence* (Middletown, CT.: Wesleyan University Press, 1961), 17.

351 **"In a situation provided" . . . "in any way by anyone":** Revill, *The Roaring Silence*, 361.

351 **"enthusiasm for chaotic abundance":** Revill, *The Roaring Silence*, 229.

352 **"seven pre-amplifiers were used":** Revill, *The Roaring Silence*, 229.

352 **"Where do we go from here?":** John Cage, "Experimental Music," in *Silence*, 12.

352 **"twenty minutes and twenty seconds":** Oliver Daniel, "Loops and Reels," *Saturday Review*, April 12, 1969, 63.

353 ***"Would you consider this":*** Richard Kostelanetz, *John Cage: Documentary Monographs in Modern Art*, ed. Paul Cummings (New York: Praeger Publications, 1970), 22–23.

354 **"the still small voice and grand opera":** Barbara Novak, *Nature and Culture: American Landscape and Painting, 1825–1875* (New York: Oxford University Press, 1995), 18–29.

354 **"He had devoted a great deal of his life":** Chasalow, "Bebe Barron 1997."

Epilogue

358 **performers . . . donning blackface:** Many other actors appeared with blackened faces, but for reasons other than imitating a minstrel stereotype—Frank Sinatra, for instance, in *Oceans 11,* as part of a robbery gang who wishes to remain inconspicuous in the dark. For more about the continuing legacy of minstrelsy, see Yuval Taylor and Jake Austen, *Darkest America: Black Minstrelsy from Slavery to Hip-Hop* (New York: W. W. Norton, 2012).

360 **women comprised . . . law profession**: Statistic on medical profession from Jeff Nilsson and Maude Radford Warren, "The Fight for Women Doctors," *The Saturday Evening Post,* January 14, 2016. Statistic on legal profession from Gordon Hylton, "Adam's Rib as an Historical Document: The Plight of Women Lawyers in the 1940s," Marquette University Faculty Blog, June 4, 2013.

ILLUSTRATION CREDITS

page 23	New-York Historical Society
page 31	Library of Congress, Prints and Photographic Division, LC-USZ62-109816; [Fig. 2b] Library of Congress, Prints and Photographic Division, LC-DIG-pga-06320
page 37	Foster Hall Collection, Center for American Music, University of Pittsburgh Library System
page 53	Library of Congress, Prints and Photographic Division, LC-DIG-ppmsca-34158
page 60	Shutterstock
page 92	National Park Service
page 94	Library of Congress, Prints and Photographs Division, LC-DIG-cwpbh-04044.
page 195	Alfred Stieglitz Collection, The Art Institute of Chicago
page 255	Publicity photo
page 332	Courtesy Inara Ferreira

INDEX

Page numbers in *italics* refer to illustrations.